Newnes Amateur Radio Computing Handbook

by the same author

The Chaos Cookbook

Newnes Short Wave Listening Handbook

Newnes Amateur Radio Computing Handbook

Joe Pritchard, G1UQW

NEWNES

Newnes
An imprint of Butterworth-Heinemann Ltd
Linacre House, Jordan Hill, Oxford OX2 8DP

PART OF REED INTERNATIONAL BOOKS

OXFORD LONDON BOSTON
MUNICH NEW DELHI SINGAPORE SYDNEY
TOKYO TORONTO WELLINGTON

First published 1990
Reprinted 1991

British Library Cataloguing in Publication Data
Pritchard, Joe
Newnes amateur radio computing handbook
1. Computer systems
I. Title
004

ISBN 0 7506 0453 0

Printed and bound in Great Britain by
Biddles Ltd, Guildford and King's Lynn

Contents

Preface

When I acquired an interest in radio at the age of 10, I little dreamt that 18 years later I would spend as much time 'listening' to signals by reading text off a computer display as I did by donning my headphones! The advent of the microprocessor, the 'chip', bought about the widespread availability of small computers which soon found their way into the hands of radio amateurs and short wave listeners (SWLs). It was not long before old modes of communication, such as morse and even voice, were being joined by new, computer based, methods of communication. In addition, older modes of machine to machine communication, such as Radio Teletype (RTTY) were now being performed by silent computers rather than large, oily, clanking Teletype machines!

And it did not stop there – computers are used as circuit design tools, to replace test equipment, act as filing clerks and even control receivers and transmitters! Listeners use them to decode signals from amateur radio satellites, meteorological information and even use the computer to try to predict which frequencies to use for the best results. The limits on computer use for the radio hobbyist are purely those set by his or her imagination.

In this book, I hope to show how computers can be used by radio amateurs or short wave listeners in a wide variety of ways. It would be impossible to start from scratch in such a book, so I have assumed that the reader has a knowledge of the basics of radio and simple electronics and a little knowledge of programming their home computer in either BASIC or machine code. However, Chapters 1 and 2 provide a quick refresher course in radio and computing basics. In addition, the appendices list a variety of books which will be useful. If you are a computer buff, as a start I would say have a look at *Newnes Short Wave Listening Handbook* which describes the basic techniques of short wave radio listening. If you are already a listener, but want more information on computers, look at the manual that came with the machine and then look for books of the 'Getting the most from your . . . ' type in your local book shop.

This book is not aimed at any specific computer, but where program listings are given I have tried to detail the listings for the BBC Microcomputer (including the Electron and Master), the Amstrad 6128/464 series and GWBASIC on the IBM PC and clones. However, the general techniques mentioned will give owners of other machines inspiration, and in many cases the programs listed will work on other machines with few changes.

I hope that this book will encourage you to play around with the computer in your SWL activities; it will provide the solutions to many problems you may encounter, and hopefully inspire you with new ideas. Thanks must go to my publishers for commissioning the work, and to my clients who have been most understanding with regard to slipped deadlines during the final stages of the preparation of the book, and to the Systems Department of the South Yorkshire Passenger Transport Executive for allowing me to 'laser print' the listings. Finally, this book is dedicated to my parents and my wife, Nicky, who have done the hard work of putting up with aerials, boxes of electronic equipment and odd noises at all hours of the day and night for 18 years. Thanks, folks!

Joe Pritchard, G1UQW

ONE

Basic radio principles

Radio communication requires two things: a transmitter to generate the radio signals and a receiving system of some type to allow the intelligence carried on the radio signals to be understood. We need not be too worried about how the signals are generated at the radio transmitter, but a little knowledge of what a radio wave is will be useful.

The radio wave

A radio wave is a form of energy known as *electromagnetic radiation*, a category that includes light, X-rays and the microwaves that cook the Sunday roast. Electromagnetic radiation travels at a phenomenal speed – 300 000 000 metres per second – and consists of two parts: a magnetic field and an electric field, which are both at right angles to the direction of travel of the wave. Figure 1.1 shows this and some of the basic characteristics of an electromagnetic wave. The only thing that differentiates light, for example, from a radio wave is the *wavelength* of the radiation, as shown in Figure 1.1. The wavelength is the 'fingerprint' of electromagnetic radiation, but when describing radio waves we are more likely to describe the signal in terms of the number of cycles that occur in one second. This is called the *frequency* of the radio wave and is measured in *hertz*. However, because a radio signal has frequencies of thousands or even millions of hertz (Hz), the abbreviations kilo (k) for thousands and mega (M) for millions are used.

Switching between frequency and wavelength is quite straight forward:

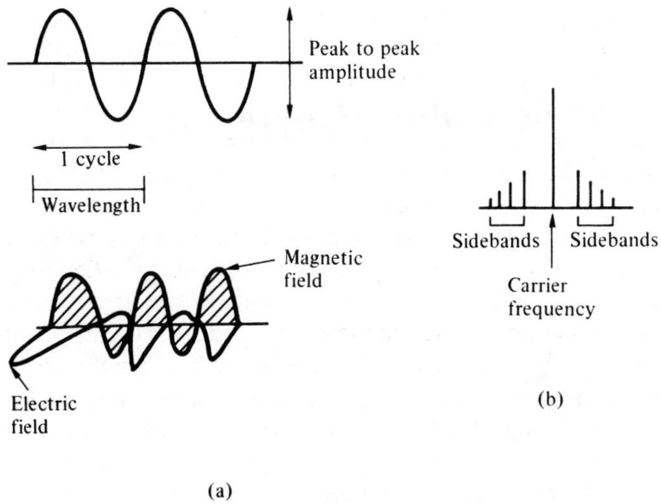

Figure 1.1

frequency = 300 000 000 / wavelength
wavelength = 300 000 000 / frequency

We can thus describe a radio signal in terms of its wavelength or frequency – a signal on 200m wavelength will have a frequency of 1500 kHz (1 500 000 Hz). Radio signals are categorised by their frequency in the following manner:

0 to 3 kHz	–	extra low frequency	ELF
3 to 30 kHz	–	very low frequency	VLF
30 to 300 kHz	–	low frequency	LF
300 to 3000 kHz	–	medium frequency	MF
3 MHz to 30 MHz	–	high frequency	HF
30 to 300 MHz	–	very high frequency	VHF
300 to 3000 MHz	–	ultra high frequency	UHF

Modulation

In order for useful information to be carried by a radio wave, the basic radio wave, often called the *carrier*, has to be processed so that some characteristic of it changes in some way to indicate whether information is being carried or not. Putting information on to a radio wave is called *modulation*. The simplest methods of modulating a signal are to change either the frequency of the signal or its amplitude, or to turn simply the radio wave on and off. For example, the music carried on Radio 1 on 1089 kHz in the UK is placed on the carrier signal by varying the amplitude of the carrier wave – this is called *amplitude modulation*. The same information carried on stereo VHF, however, is placed on the radio signal by slightly varying the frequency of the signal – this is called *frequency modulation*. Morse code transmission, as used by radio amateurs and shipping, in its simplest form is done by simply turning the radio wave on and off. This is called *continuous wave* modulation.

Any modulated radio wave no longer consists of just a single frequency, as does an unmodulated signal. As well as the carrier wave, a modulated radio wave also has *sidebands*, as shown in Figure 1.1b. The total amount of 'space' taken up by a modulated radio wave, the *bandwidth* of the signal, varies depending upon the type of modulation used and the amount of information actually put on the radio wave. The practical upshot of this is that, for a given range of frequencies you can only fit so many information-carrying radio signals, because if you were to allow the information-carrying sidebands of different signals to overlap then interference would result. As the range of frequencies suitable for radio communication is fairly limited, radio spectrum users tend to use modulation techniques that require the minimum bandwidth to get the job done. Let us complete this survey of modulation with a quick review of the different techniques available.

Continuous wave (CW)

The carrier wave is modulated by simply turning the transmitter on and off. Known as A1A modulation, and modulation is done using morse code. Typical bandwidth is only a few hundred Hz, and A1A signals are very good at cutting through interference.

Amplitude modulation (AM)

The amplitude of the carrier wave is varied in sympathy with, for example, an electrical signal representing music, voice or one of the more complex modulation methods such as radio teletype (see Chapter 10). It is known as A3E modulation, is cheap to produce, and can be resolved on even the simplest radio receivers. Transmissions on long wave and medium wave, such as Radio 4 on 198 kHz and Radio 1 on 1089 kHz, use A3E modulation.

Single sideband (SSB)

If you are trying to get a radio signal as far as possible with as little power as possible, then A3E is not much good; A1A is much better, but cannot be used to carry voice signals. Single sideband is more efficient than A3E, although it still involves varying the amplitude of the radio wave in sympathy with the signal with which you want to modulate the carrier wave, and can be used to carry voice signals and is designated J3E. It is also less susceptible to interference than A3E and occupies less bandwidth. The reason for the better performance of J3E signals is in the way that the power in the radio signal is distributed. For A3E signals, half the power is in the carrier wave and half is in the sidebands. Each sideband carries the same information, and so one of these sidebands is redundant. In addition, the carrier does not actually contain useful information at all. SSB signals are like A3E signals but with one sideband and the carrier removed; all the power in the radio signal is now concentrated in the remaining sideband, which gives the signal more 'punch'. There are two types of SSB transmission, depending upon which of the two sidebands is transmitted; USB, or upper sideband, is where the sideband higher in frequency than the carrier frequency is transmitted and LSB, or lower sideband, is where the other sideband is used. The disadvantage of SSB signals is that special receivers are required to hear the signals. SSB is, however, widely used by radio amateurs, aircraft and shipping.

Frequency modulation (FM)

Frequency modulation, known as F3E, is another means of modulation that allows voice or music transmission. The carrier wave is modulated by varying its frequency in sympathy with the modulating signal. There are two forms of FM, narrow band FM, where the frequency only varies by ± 3 to 5 kHz, and wide band FM, where the frequency of the carrier is varied by several tens of kilohertz. NBFM is used by amateurs, and WBFM is used on the VHF broadcast bands for the high quality FM broadcasts that we can receive between 88 and 108 MHz.

Transmission modes

Apart from voice, music and morse code there are a vast array of other types of information that can be carried on a radio wave, such as facsimile pictures or textual information. All of these types of information, however, can be placed on a radio wave using variations on the types of modulation listed above. The differing ways in which information is carried by radio are known as transmission modes, and as well as differing in the type of information carried, such as whether it is voice or pictures or text, and the type of modulation used, they differ in terms of whether a transmission mode is *analogue* or *digital.*

Analogue modes

An analogue transmission mode is one in which the parameter of the radio wave that is used for modulation varies smoothly between certain limits. For example, using A3E modulation to carry music is an analogue transmission mode, as is facsimile transmission of pictures.

Digital modes

A digital transmission mode is one where the parameter of the radio wave that is used for modulation has only a set number of possible values. For example, morse code sent using A1A is the simplest digital mode, having just two states – the presence or absence of a radio wave. Similarly, text can be sent over the air using F3E and two separate tones, and each letter is sent as a collection of tones (Chapter 10). Because only two tones are involved, this is a digital transmission mode.

At the receiving end

The modulated radio wave is transmitted into space through an aerial, and arrives at the receiving aerial where at the minimum a radio receiver is required to resolve the information carried by the radio waves. For voice or morse signals, a receiver capable of resolving the modulation used will be required, but for certain modes, a computer or some other specialist equipment, such as a facsimile machine or a teleprinter, will be required in addition to the receiver to present the information carried by the radio wave into a form that can be understood by us mere humans!

If we first consider the radio receiver, it must perform the following functions:

Tuning a specific signal

A radio receiver must be able to pick just one signal out of the many thousands that may arrive at the radio receiver. The receiver can be tuned in a variety of ways, such as by a mechanical tuning control or through a keypad, a bit like a pocket calculator. We shall look into tuning methods later in this chapter. A receiver must be able to select one signal, even if another signal is on another frequency close by. The ability to select between two stations that are so close together in frequency is known as the *selectivity* of the receiver, and the better the selectivity is, the better job the receiver is likely to do at differentiating between signals.

Amplify radio signals

Radio signals, when they arrive at the receiving aerial, are extremely weak and must be amplified, or made larger, before we can do anything useful with them. A receiver that can convert weak radio signals into a form which we can understand is said to be a *sensitive* receiver, and the sensitivity of a receiver is a measure of how well the receiver can cope with weak radio signals; the better the sensitivity, the weaker the signal arriving at the receiver can be and still be resolved.

Resolve signals

The receiver must convert the electrical signals produced in the receiver by the radio wave into understandable sound signals, via the loudspeaker of the radio set, or into electrical signals that can be converted by a computer or other ancillary equipment into pictures or text. The ability of a receiving system to convert signals into a form that is readable by human beings is the ability of the system to resolve signals. The resolving ability of a receiving system is dependant upon all aspects of the system, from the receiving aerial through to the computer software used when digital transmission modes are being employed.

Stability

In addition, any receiver must stay tuned to the desired frequency. This is called the stability of a receiver, and for morse reception, SSB reception and reception of signals such as facsimile or teletype good stability is essential.

For voice, music and morse signals all that will be required is a radio receiver and a pair of ears! However, for other transmission modes additional equipment will be required. This can be in the form of:

Teleprinters

The old mechanical teleprinter machines take in teletype signals and convert them into text on paper. In a transmitting system, text can be typed in and converted in to a form capable of being transmitted over the air. Further discussion of Teletype (known as RTTY) will be found in Chapter 10.

Facsimile machines

These machines, similar to those found in many modern offices, are used to convert suitable radio signals into a picture image on paper (Chapter 12).

Terminal units

These occur in various types, and are designed to fit between the radio and a computer. Depending upon the complexity of the TU and the programs employed in the computer, a TU and computer can resolve virtually any transmission mode with the exception of voice/music signals (for which it is not needed!). Terminal units will be discussed later in the book in great detail.

TV monitors

Radio amateurs use a particular type of television transmission called slow scan television, and for this a suitable TU or a special SSTV monitor can be used (Chapter 12).

The radio receiver

It would be quite possible to write a whole book on the subject of radio receivers; indeed, in the Appendices of this book you will find several listed. The rest of this chapter will go into a little more detail about radio receivers that short wave listeners can use to resolve the various types of signal already discussed.

The receiving aerial

Any receiver requires an *aerial*; in some receivers this is built into the receiver, but other receivers require an external aerial of some sort. For serious short wave listening, an external aerial is almost essential, and there are a variety of aerials for the listener to try.

Long wire aerial

The simplest aerial for a short wave receiver is simply a length of copper wire connected to the input of the radio receiver. In general terms, the longer and higher the wire, the better the results will be (Figure 1.2). A long wire aerial can work on a wide range of frequencies.

Tuned dipole

A tuned dipole aerial is a special form of aerial that is particularly good at particular frequencies. Figure 1.2b shows how it is connected to the input of a suitable receiver. Although the dipole is good at specific frequencies, it is poor at other frequencies. A dipole is most sensitive at a wavelength that is about twice the physical length of the dipole, as shown, and the corresponding frequency is called the *resonant frequency* of the aerial.

Active aerials

An active aerial is basically a short piece of wire or a dipole aerial connected to an amplifier which boosts up the signal picked up by the wire or dipole.

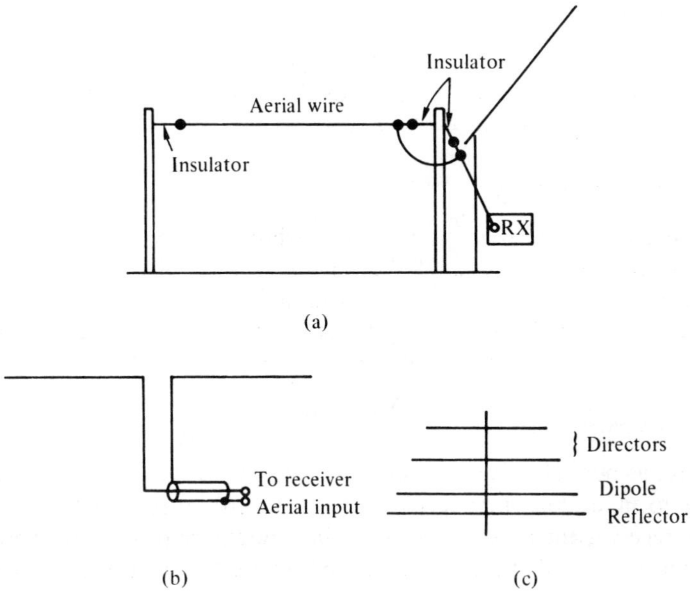

Figure 1.2

Aerial arrays

An aerial array is basically a dipole surrounded by other wires or metal rods, as shown in Figure 1.2c. These aerials are, like dipoles, good at particular frequencies and are also highly directional, in that they are much more sensitive to signals coming from one particular direction.

All aerials are directional, and although the type of aerial dictates the behaviour of the aerial to a great degree, the placing of the aerial with respect to other metal objects, houses, hills, trees, telephone wires or virtually anything else will affect the coverage of the aerial. In addition, an aerial can be either vertically or horizontally arranged; the difference is shown in Figure 1.3. The differences in behaviour are detailed in the various books listed in the appendix, but for our purposes suffice to say that a vertical aerial will give you all round reception, and the directional effects of a horizontal aerial are removed.

A radio wave, when it hits an aerial, causes a small electrical signal to be generated in the aerial. This signal is then amplified by the radio, but for maximum efficiency as much of the electrical

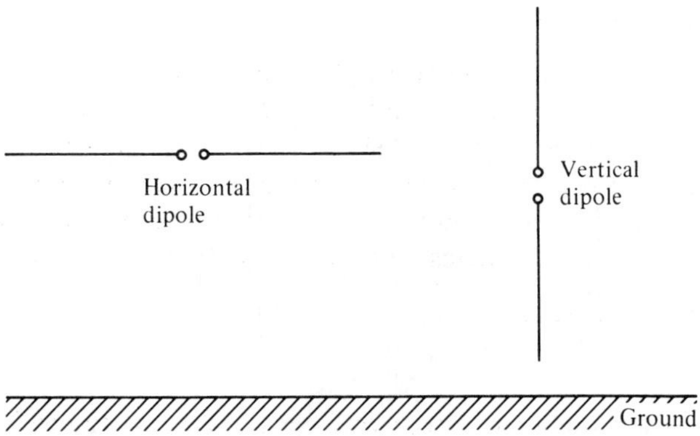

Figure 1.3

signal as possible must be transferred into the radio's circuits. For this to take place, an electrical parameter of both the aerial and the receiver input, called *impedance*, should be as close to each other in value as possible. We do not need to go into great detail about impedance, but here is a quick review.

Receivers generally have one of two types of aerial input if they are capable of using an external aerial; one is a *low impedance input* and the other type is a *high impedance input*. A dipole, at the resonant frequency, exhibits a low impedance and for best results would be connected to a low impedance input on the receiver. Away from the resonant frequency of the dipole, the impedance of the aerial changes, and so the efficiency of transfer of signal from the aerial to the receiver will vary with frequency. A long wire aerial generally has a high impedance, but again this varies with the frequency of the signal being received. An active aerial is usually designed so that it offers a low impedance output at *any* frequency that is received, thus maximising signal transfer to a low impedance receiver input. For dipoles or long wire aerials to be useful over a wide range of frequencies, the aerial is often connected to the receiver via a circuit known as an *aerial tuning unit* or *aerial matching unit* which can be adjusted to allow the maximum signal to be transferred from the aerial to the receiver for any frequency.

The crystal set

There are several different types of radio receiver in use amongst short wave listeners. The simplest, and probably least used, is called the *crystal set*. Figure 1.4 shows a typical crystal set, and it is only useful for resolving AM voice or music signals. It requires no external power supply, and requires a good signal input from the aerial. However, it carries out the basic functions of a radio receiver;

Tuning

Tuning, when applied to a receiver, is the ability of the receiver to respond to just one signal out of the many thousands hitting the aerial. The tuning of a crystal set is rather unselective, however, and when the tuning control is at a particular setting it is likely that more than one station will be heard, if signal strength is good.

Detection

Detection is the process of extracting the information from a radio signal – it is basically the task of resolving the signal. The crystal set can resolve A3E signals, but that is all; it cannot resolve morse

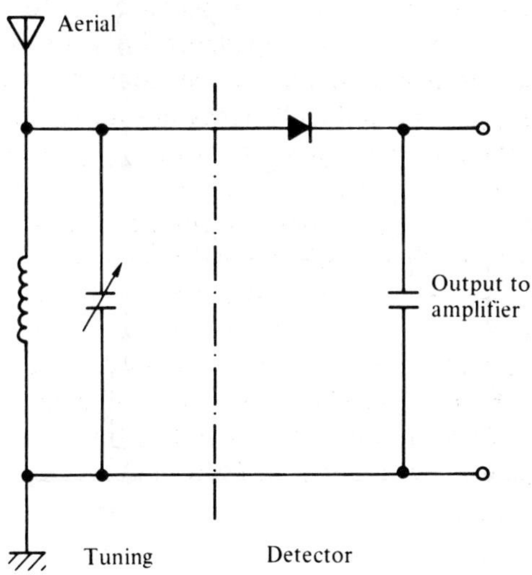

Figure 1.4

or SSB and is incapable of receiving any of the more complex modes such as RTTY.

A crystal set is unselective and rather insensitive. Any serious receiver must provide some means of amplifying the radio signal as well as resolving it. The simplest receiver to offer this is called the *regenerative* receiver.

The regenerative receiver

The regenerative receiver is the simplest type of receiver to offer reasonable selectivity, sensitivity and the ability to resolve morse and single sideband signals. The stability of regenerative receivers is often a little poor, and so they are not really suitable for reception of RTTY or similar modes. Figure 1.5 shows a simple regenerative receiver; it consists of an amplifier to boost the signal tuned by the tuned circuit, and part of the amplified signal is fed back to the input of the RF amplifier such that the signals fed back to the input add to the signals coming from the aerial, thus increasing the amplification given by the circuit. Indeed, this

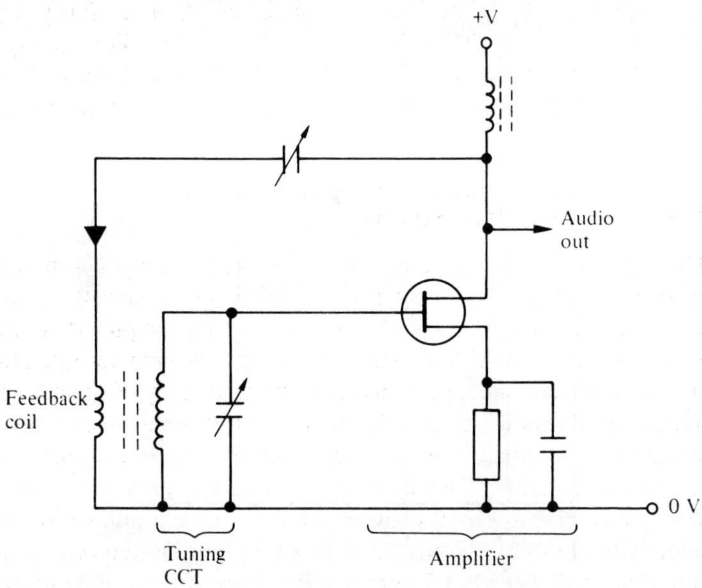

Figure 1.5

positive feedback must be controlled as otherwise the circuit would start producing radio signals itself at the frequency to which the tuned circuit is tuned!

By adjusting the circuit so that it is just short of producing its own signals (in technical terms, the set is adjusted to be on the *threshold of oscillation*) the sensitivity and selectivity are very good indeed, and excellent results with A3E signals are experienced. To resolve SSB or CW signals, the set is adjusted so that it is just oscillating – in this mode CW signals are heard as tones and SSB signals can be resolved into readable speech.

An audio amplifier is often included in these receivers to allow loudspeaker reception of signals. The signal from the aerial is amplified by the RF amplifier at the frequency of the desired signal; the audio signal is then boosted to a level to drive headphones or a loudspeaker. Because the RF signal is amplified at the frequency of transmission, regenerative receivers are called *straight* receivers. This has the advantage of simplifying the circuitry, but has the disadvantage of making the performance of the set in terms of stability, sensitivity and selectivity rather dependent upon frequency. In general terms, a straight receiver will perform better at lower frequencies than at fairly high frequencies, where instability is quite common. For example, careful construction is required to avoid the tuning of the set being disturbed by the presence of the user's hand on the tuning control!

The superheterodyne receiver

The superheterodyne receiver, or superhet, is the most commonly used type of radio receiver, combining good selectivity and sensitivity. Its basic theory of operation is very simple. It is fairly easy to produce amplifiers which will give very high amplification at a certain frequency, provided that the frequency of operation is fixed; this allows the circuit designer to optimise his or her design around that frequency. What a superhet receiver does, then, is to convert all incoming signals to one frequency, called the *intermediate frequency* and then provide the receiver's amplification and selectivity at this IF. Figure 1.6 shows a block diagram of a simple superhet, and Figure 1.7 shows some typical basic circuits that make up each 'block'.

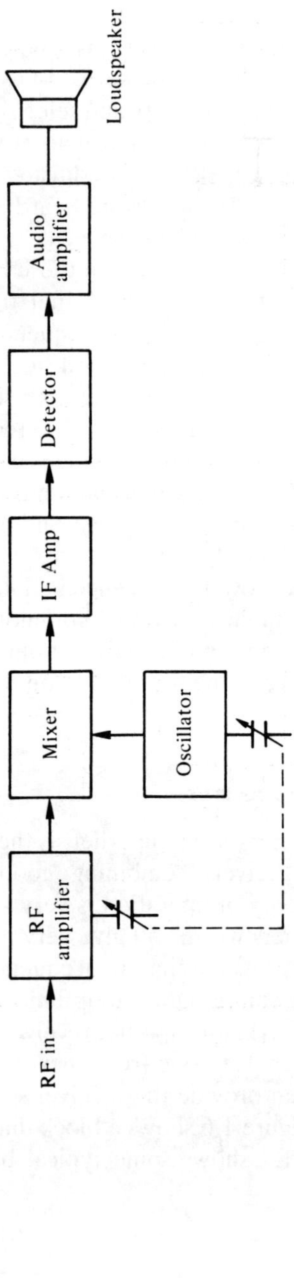
RF in
RF amplifier
Mixer
Oscillator
IF Amp
Detector
Audio amplifier
Loudspeaker

Figure 1.6

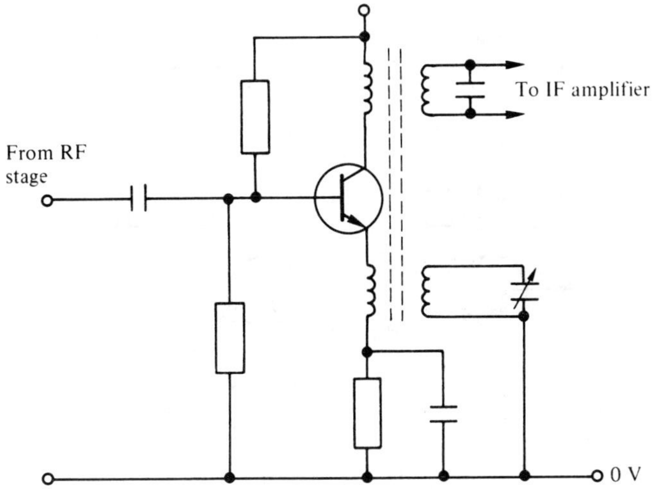

Oscillator/mixer combined

(a)

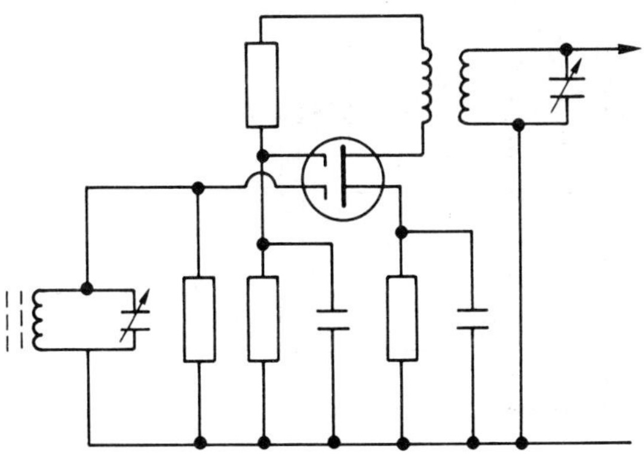

RF input stage

(b)

Figure 1.7 *continued*

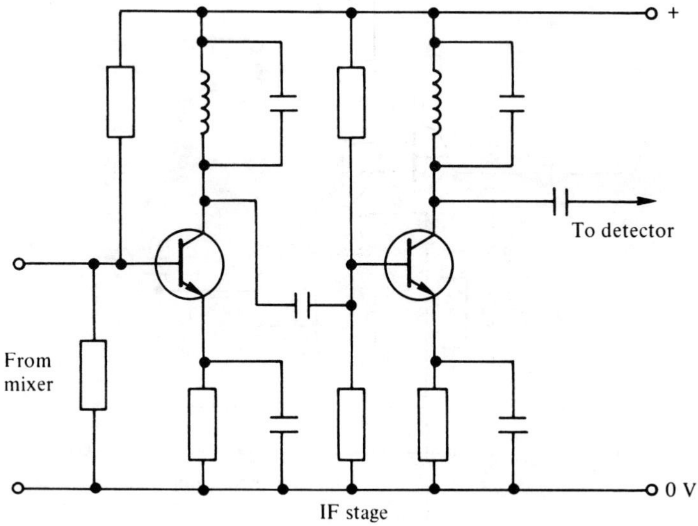

(c)

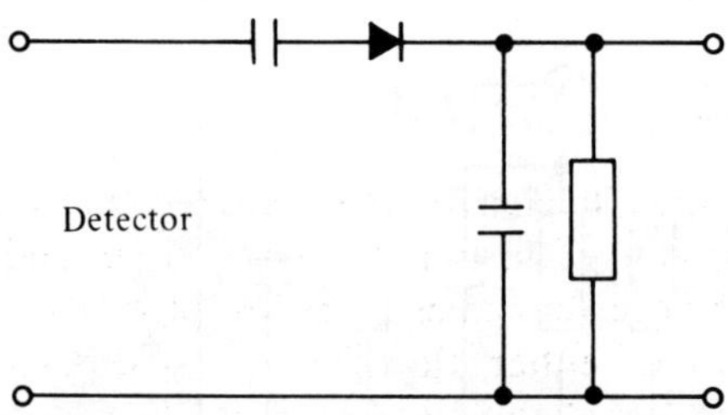

(d)

Figure 1.7 – *continued*

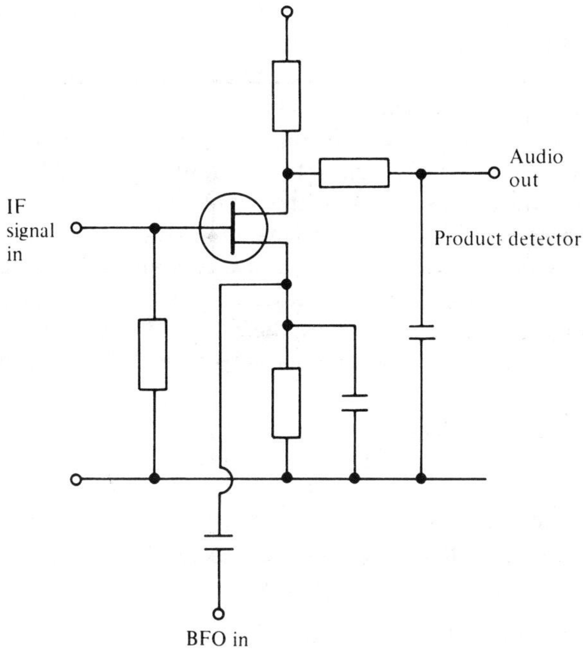

(e)

Figure 1.7 – *continued*

The RF amplifier

This serves to boost up signals arriving at the receiver aerial, and also tunes a signal in. This tuning is very broad, and none of the selectivity of the receiver comes from this stage. The tuning of this stage is connected, either electrically or mechanically, to the tuning of the local oscillator stage, so that when the tuning of one is adjusted the tuning of the other changes.

The local oscillator

This provides a fairly strong signal separated from the signal that we want to receive by the IF of the receiver. If we had a set with an IF of 1000 kHz, and we wanted to receive a signal on 6000 kHz, the local oscillator (LO) would produce a signal at either 5000 kHz or 7000 kHz, as each of these frequencies will produce the desired IF. Whether the local oscillator produces a signal above or below the desired signal is a matter of choice for the designer; let us say 7000 kHz. When the LO is tuned to this frequency, the RF amplifier tuning will be tuned to the desired 6000 kHz. A good superhet will always maintain this separation between RF amplifier tuning and LO tuning, and the ability to keep this as close to the IF as possible is called the *tracking* ability of the receiver. Clearly, a receiver with poor tracking will have only moderate performance at the points where the tuning of the two parts of the circuit are separated by an amount even slightly different to 1000 kHz.

The mixer

This circuit takes the LO signal and the desired signal, as two inputs, and mixes them to produce a variety of output frequencies:

local oscillator frequency	7000 kHz
signal frequency	6000 kHz
LO + signal frequency	13 000 kHz
LO − signal frequency	1000 kHz

There are other frequencies as well, but these are the main ones, and the mixer is designed to isolate the IF frequency (LO – signal frequency) and pass it on to the IF amplifier stage of the receiver.

The IF amplifier

At the heart of the superhet is the IF amplifier. This circuit provides virtually all of the sensitivity and selectivity of the receiver. It is fairly easy to build a circuit which is very selective and provides a considerable amount of amplification, provided that the circuit is working at a fairly low frequency. Typical receiver IFs are between 455 and 9000 kHz, but some receivers may have several IF stages, each with its own local oscillator and mixer, to help prevent *images* (see below). Such a receiver is called a multiple conversion superheterodyne, and may have, for example, IFs of 45 MHz, 2MHz and 455 kHz. In such a receiver, the gain and selectivity would be spread throughout these three stages. A set that is highly selective is often said to have a narrow *bandwidth* to allow it to differentiate between neighbouring signals. Of course, the selection of bandwidth depends upon the type of signals being received; for example, if we built an IF amplifier with a very narrow bandwidth, it would be great for CW signals but we would not be able to resolve A3E or J3E signals. So, in good quality receivers it is often possible to vary the bandwidth by switching in filters as needed. Typically, a receiver might provide an effective bandwidth of 500 Hz for CW, 3 kHz for J3E and 6 kHz for A3E. If the receiver were capable of resolving F3E, then a bandwidth of up to 20 kHz might be required. For wideband FM reception, much wider bandwidths would be needed.

The detector stages

In order to resolve the signals amplified by the receiver IF stages, a detector circuit is needed. The techniques used vary depending upon the mode of transmission. For AM, a detector that works like a crystal set is used, as shown in Figure 1.7. This is no use for A1A or J3E transmissions, though, for this detector requires a carrier wave as well as the information imposed on it. The simplest way around this is to re-insert a carrier wave just before the detector. An oscillator, called a *beat frequency oscillator* or a *carrier insertion oscillator* tunes ± 3 kHz or so around the frequency of the last IF stage in the receiver, and mimics the missing carrier wave. The A1A signals will be resolved as a series of tones, and the J3E signals will be a rather 'Dalek like' voice, unless the tuning of the BFO is spot on. For USB signals the BFO needs to be set a little below the IF while for LSB signals it should be set a little above the IF. An alternative form of detector suitable for detection of A1A and J3E is called the *product detector* and is shown in Figure 1.7.

The detected signal is then passed on to the audio stages of the receiver, but the level of the signal at this stage is often used to control the gain of the IF stages of the receiver. The larger the signal is, the less gain is supplied by the IF stages. This is called *automatic gain control (AGC)* and in most good quality receivers can be disabled, allowing the user of the receiver to set the IF gain to whatever is required.

The audio stages

The final stages of the receiver are concerned with processing the resolved signal into a form that we can listen to or output to a terminal unit, computer or other decoding device. By this point in the receiver, the signals are all in the audio range and the frequencies present depend upon the bandwidth selected in the IF stages. The receiver may provide outputs for tape recorders or other audio processing at this stage, so that the listener can by-pass the audio stages of the receiver if so desired. The audio stages will include volume and possibly tone controls, and will usually provide headphone output as well as loudspeaker output.

Superhet problems

Superheterodyne receivers have a few problems. The first is that of image reception. Here, a station can be tuned in on a frequency where it is not actually transmitting. This is best explained by example; imagine a receiver with an IF of 470 kHz tuned to a station on 14 300 kHz. The local oscillator will often be running above the signal frequency, and so will be operating on 14 770 kHz. A few minutes thought, however, will indicate that a strong signal 470 kHz *above* the local oscillator signal will also give an IF of 470 kHz. So, a signal on 15 240 kHz will also be heard as well as the real signal on 14 300 kHz. This problem is best solved by improving the selectivity of the stages before the mixer, to reduce the unwanted signal getting to the mixer, and by using a very high IF.

Birdies are 'tweets' that are heard as you tune the receiver. This is due to the local oscillator putting out signals at more than one frequency, which interact in the receiver to cause whistles and, in some cases, image reception.

Cross modulation occurs where the mixer is overloaded by very strong signals. Again, this problem manifests itself as stations which are not really there and untunable signals and 'mush' in the loudspeaker. This is best cured by reducing the signal that reaches the mixer.

In some modern superheterodynes, the local oscillator is a digital circuit called a frequency synthesizer; more details about this will be given later, but suffice to say at this stage that this approach allows a variety of features to be added to receivers, such as memories to hold frequencies and modes, and computer control of the receiver.

Converters

Many short wave radio listeners have a considerable investment in terms of cash in a good quality receiver on which to hear broadcasts. However, they may wish to receive signals on frequencies that their receiver does not cover. A typical example is that someone with a set covering 100 kHz to 30 MHz may wish to listen to VHF signals from radio amateurs on 144 MHz. Rather than buying a new receiver, a device called a *converter* can be purchased or built.

A converter is simply a superheterodyne receiver without the IF amplifier, detector or audio stages. A block diagram and a simple circuit diagram are shown in Figure 1.8. As can be seen, the converter consists of an RF amplifier, local oscillator, and mixer. The output signal may be tuned in on a receiver, which then acts as IF, detector and audio stages of this 'composite' receiver.

Converters come in two basic types. In the first, the RF input stage and local oscillator are tunable, and the output to the receiver is fixed in frequency. In use, the receiver is tuned to the IF of the converter and then stations are tuned in by tuning the converter. In the second type, the converter RF amplifier and local oscillator are untunable, and the receiver is tuned to select a particular frequency from the many that will be present at the converter output.

Both designs have pros and cons; the former allows a wider range of tuning and reduces interference from stations working

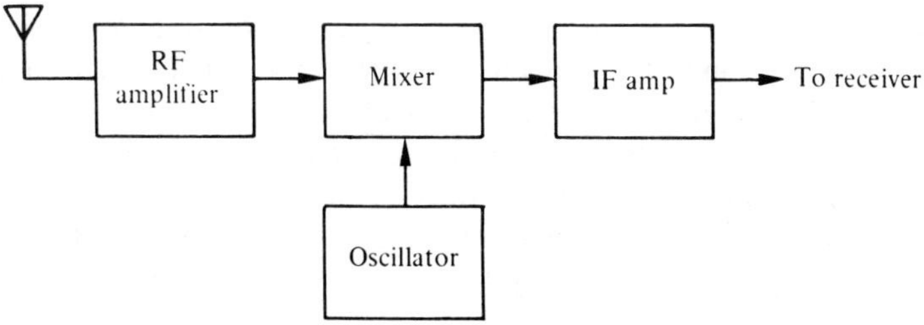

Figure 1.8

around the IF of the converter; you simply alter the IF a little. The latter offers easy construction, and allows the use of the receiver tuning scale, but as the receiver is tuned, stations operating on the frequencies to which the receiver is tuned may be heard as well as stations on the input frequency of the converter.

Direct conversion receivers

These are popular sets amongst listeners who specialize in listening to amateur radio stations. They are effectively superhet receivers with an IF of between zero and a few kHz; in other words, within the audio frequency range. This signal is then amplified and fed to headphones or a loudspeaker. These receivers are very simple to build, but are really only suitable for reception of SSB and CW signals.

Propagation

Nothing to do with seeds in the greenhouse; propagation refers to the ways and means by which a radio signal gets from the transmitting aerial to the receiving aerial.

Reception of radio signals from a long way away relies upon the fact that frequencies of more than a few hundred kHz will be bent by a layer in the upper atmosphere known as the *ionosphere*. This layer is about 40 miles above our heads, and consists of ionised gases and free electrons, and these bend radio waves back to earth in a way dependent upon the frequency of the signal and the amount of ions.

In order of height above our heads, we have the lowest layer, the D layer, then the E layer and finally the F layer. In daylight hours, these layers are all present; indeed, the F layer splits into two, F1 and F2 in daylight. At night, the ionisation falls, dependent as it is upon radiation from the sun, and we are left with the E layer and a single F layer.

A transmitted radio wave can be seen as two signals; a ground wave which travels along the surface of the earth, and a sky wave which goes off into the ionosphere to be absorbed or reflected back to earth, perhaps many thousands of miles away from the transmitter site.

The D layer

The D layer is an absorptive layer; it never bends radio signals back to earth. Signals below about 7–8 MHz are absorbed, and so in daylight signals received below this frequency range are heard purely by virtue of the ground wave signal. Signals above this frequency pass through and go on to the E and F layers. Solar storms, great disturbances on the surface of the sun, can cause the D layer to absorb all signals right up to 15 or 20 MHz.

The E layer

This layer is responsible for long distance reception of radio signals between a few hundred kHz and 10 MHz or so. At night, once the D layer vanishes, the E layer can reflect signals below 7 MHz, giving a single earth ionosphere – earth 'skip' of a few thousand miles. Around dusk, the ground wave coverage area and reflected signals from the E layer may overlap, giving fading and distortion of signals.

The F layer

The F Layer. The two F layers reflect signals up to about 30 or so MHz, and have skip distances of about 1500 km for the F1 layer and 3000 km for the F2 layer.

Propagation is an enormous subject area, and we shall be returning to it later in this book. For the time being, though, that is all I want to say about the subject.

TWO

Basic computer principles

In this chapter, I shall briefly examine the basic principles of the personal computer. In general terms, a computer is simply an electronic device capable of carrying out a pre-determined sequence of instructions to perform a particular task. Any computer system thus requires, as a minimum, a *memory* to hold the instruction sequence, a *processor* to carry out the appropriate instructions and some sort of *input / output system* to accept information and instructions from a user and to give the results to the user.

The microprocessor

The microprocessor is at the heart of any personal computer, and is often called the *central processing unit*, or CPU. The CPU is the 'brains' of the computer, executing the instructions stored in the computer memory. The CPU is often described as a 'fast idiot'; it can perform very simple tasks, such as adding two numbers together, very quickly and all the complex tasks performed by a computer are made possible by the CPU being able to execute very simple operations very quickly. There are a variety of different types of CPU, but they all operate on the same basic principles. The first is that numbers and instructions processed by the CPU are in the form of binary numbers, collections of '1's and '0's. A '1' is represented by a 5V electrical signal and a '0' by 0V. Binary is simply base-two arithmetic, and is used in electronic computers because it corresponds to the two states possible in simple electronic circuits – ON ('1') and OFF('0').
The first few binary numbers are as follows:

Binary	**Decimal**	**Binary**	**Decimal**
0000	0	0110	6
0001	1	0111	7
0010	2	1000	8
0011	3	1001	9
0100	4	1010	10
0101	5	1011	11

The right-most column of the binary numbers represents '1's, the next is '2's, then '4's, then '8's and so on, each column going up in powers of two. This is analogous to the way we count in tens, but using powers of two instead of powers of 10. A single binary digit, a '1' or a '0', is called a *bit*, and we form bits into groups; 4 bits are called a *nibble*, 8 bits a *byte*, 16 bits a *word*. A special notation was formulated to allow us to more easily write down the numbers coded for by binary numbers. This is called *hexadecimal* notation, and is simply base 16 arithmetic. The binary numbers 10 to 15 are represented by the letters A to F. This technique allows us to write down an 8-bit byte in two hexadecimal digits, by splitting the 8 bits into two groups of 4. A little practice soon allows you to work in hexadecimal very easily, and it gives the advantage of being able to see what binary pattern the number represents. Chapter 3, by the way, includes a base conversion program for you to experiment with.

$$11110001 = 1111\ 0001 = \mathrm{F1}$$

The right hand bit of any binary number is called the *least significant bit* and the left hand bit the *most significant bit*. Similarly, if we look at a 16-bit word as being made of two bytes, the left byte is the most significant byte and the right byte is the least significant byte.

Although humans can handle information in a variety of ways, everything that a computer deals with has to be represented in some sort of numeric fashion. There are two basic types of information stored in a computer. The first is a computer *program*, that is, the sequence of instructions needed to make a computer do anything useful. The second is *data*, information that the computer processes while executing its program. The CPU has no way of telling whether a particular number is an instruction or a piece of data, and it is the responsibility of the programmer to ensure that the CPU only ever tries to process real instructions and not someone's date of birth!

Anyway, back to the CPU; what does it consist of? Well, each type of CPU has a different internal structure – architecture – but the basic principles are the same in each case. In this chapter, we shall use the popular Z80 CPU, found in Amstrad CPC464, 6128 and Sinclair Spectrum and Plus 2 machines as a typical processor chip. Figure 2.1 shows a diagram of the architecture of this chip. All CPUs contain *registers*, which are places where numbers can be temporarily stored while the CPU acts upon them. The main register in any CPU is the *accumulator*, which is where many of the arithmetic operations are stored. In the Z80 chip, the A register is the accumulator. This is an 8-bit register, capable of holding 8-bit numbers. The B,C,D,E,H and L registers are also 8 bit registers, but can be easily teamed up to form 16-bit registers if the programmer wishes. When used like this, the HL register can be treated like a 16 bit accumulator. The F register is the *flag* register, and rather than holding a number each bit represents whether some event has occurred while the CPU has been processing data. For example, if the answer to a particular arithmetic operation is zero, a bit in the F register, known as the zero flag, is set to '1'. The programmer can check these flags and thus allow the program

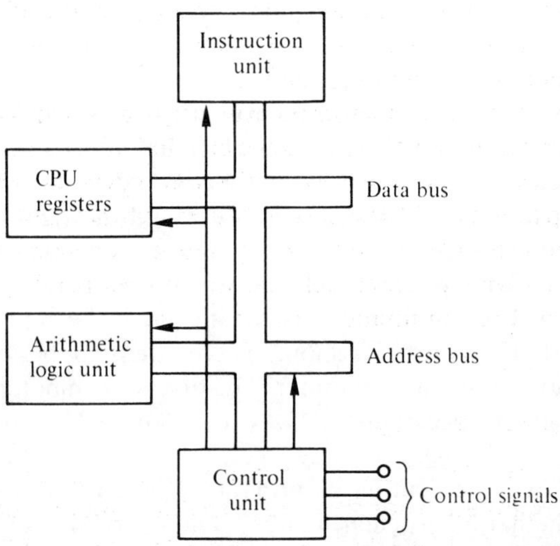

Figure 2.1

to perform in different ways depending upon the state of these flags.

The *stack pointer* is a special 16-bit register used to reference an area of memory in the computer called a stack. A stack is simply an area of temporary data storage.

Program counter

The program counter is a 16-bit register that points to the place in memory where the next instruction is to be found.

The control unit

The control unit is the coordinator of the CPU's activities. It is responsible for reading an instruction, in the form of one or more bytes, from memory and acting upon it.

The ALU

The arithmetic and logic unit is the 'calculator' of the CPU, responsible for the various arithmetic, logical and comparison operations that the CPU can perform. The ALU is a very simple device; it can only perform addition, subtraction and various types of bit manipulation tasks. In addition, it can only work on 8 or 16-bit numbers, which are integers. Floating point arithmetic, or arithmetic using larger numbers than 8 or 16 bits, must be programmed for by the programmer.

The Z80 and 6502 microprocessor chips are said to be 8 bit chips, in that data travels around the chip in 8 bit chunks across an internal data highway called a *bus*. Other chips are 16 or even 32-bit chips because of the way in which data is transferred, and these are much faster than the 8 bit chips in carrying out various operations. Some microprocessors, as well as handling addition and subtraction, can do multiplication as well!

The computer memory

The computer is useless without its memory. The memory is the place where programs or data are stored for future access by the CPU. There are two types of memory present in a computer, *ROM* and *RAM*.

ROM

Read only memory, stores data which will be used frequently by the computer, such as the programs which tell the CPU what to do when the machine is turned on. The data stored in ROM is permanent, and is not destroyed when power is removed. The amount of ROM in machines varies; the IBM PCs and similar machines have very little ROM in comparison to the total amount of memory they have available, and need extra programs to do anything useful. Smaller machines have a considerable amount of ROM, which often includes interpreters for the BASIC computer language, an *operating system*, simple text editing programs, and so on – enough, in fact, to write your own programs with no further ado.

RAM

Well, if we write our own programs, where do we store them? We have already said that ROM is unchangeable. All computers have *random access memory* as well as ROM. RAM contents are easily altered, but the memory loses whatever it contains when the power to the computer is removed. RAM is thus used as the 'scratchpad' memory of a computer, and any RAM contents that we wish to save must be stored on tape or magnetic disc.

The size of a number that a single box in RAM or ROM can hold depends upon the CPU. Memory locations associated with 8-bit processors can hold 8 bit numbers, and memory attached to 16-bit processors is arranged so as to store 16-bit words. How does the CPU actually access memory? Any CPU has a series of electrical connections from it called the *address bus*; these wires are connected to the memory chips and the CPU puts a pattern of '1' and '0' signals on to the address bus to determine which memory location is accessed. A further line, called a *control line* determines whether the memory location selected is to be read from or written to, and a further collection of electrical connections, called the *data bus* carries the number stored in the memory location to or from the CPU. The amount of memory that can be accessed by the CPU is thus determined by the number of address lines. The Z80 and 6502 CPUs can access a total of 65 536 memory locations at any one time, but other processors can access up to a few million memory locations. The capacity of a computer's memory is usually quoted in kilobytes or megabytes (K or M) where 'K' is 1024 locations and M is about a million memory locations. Once a byte is recovered from memory, it is processed by the CPU control unit.

Computer software

Computer programs are often called software, and for our purposes we can split software down into three groups; *operating systems*, *languages* and *applications*.

Operating systems

Operating systems are programs which instruct the computer how to do very simple tasks, such as read the keyboard, transfer information to and from disc or tape, display information on the computer's display device or print things on a printer. Operating systems or OSs, as they are known, are written in *machine language*, which is the language understood by the CPU. Machine language programs are very fast and efficient, and are stored in memory as a series of numbers representing instructions such as 'add the number in register A to the number in register B and put the answer in A'. They are also difficult to write, and so machine language programming is only carried out where all the speed possible is required or when direct control of some part of the computer hardware is required.

Languages

Languages are programs which allow us to write other programs! Most computers come with a language called BASIC, which allows us to write programs which look a little like English rather than a series of odd-looking codes, which is what a machine code program looks like. The text making up a BASIC program is examined by part of BASIC called the *interpreter* which causes the CPU to execute pre-written sequences of machine language instructions to do the job required, calling upon the machine operating system facilities as and when required. Pieces of text which constitute a sequence of instructions for the computer to execute in this way are often called *source code*, and any errors in the source code that the BASIC interpreter cannot make sense of are known as *syntax errors*.

There are many other types of error, many specific to particular languages or even machines, but basically we can split the errors into two groups; syntax errors and *run time* errors. The latter errors occur once the program has started running, and can include such things as the language trying to divide a number by zero, running out of memory or logic errors, errors made by the programmer in actually deciding which operations need be carried out to perform a particular task. The problem with interpreters is that they have to interpret the source code every time the program is run. This makes interpreted programs fairly slow. A solution is to write your programs in machine code (or in *assembler language* where the sequences of numbers have been replaced by simple instructions which are easier for people to get to grips with) or in a *compiled* language. A compiler takes source code just once and converts it into machine code. This can then run very quickly on the computer as it no longer has to be interpreted, and most languages available on machines such as the IBM PC clones are compiled. BASIC is not the only computer language around; others include Pascal, C, Lisp and Forth. The first two are general purpose languages, the last two being specifically suited for artificial intelligence and control applications, respectively. In this book, however, we shall be sticking to BASIC and machine code for the most part.

Finally we come to *applications*. These are programs written in a language to do a specific job, such as word processing, the accounts, decoding morse code and so on. Applications are usually written in machine language/assembler or a compiled language, but there is nothing to stop us using BASIC. Some applications programs are very sophisticated, even to the point of containing within themselves a language of their own!

The rest of the hardware

The CPU and memory would be pretty useless on their own, as we would not be able to see what the results of programs were or even to tell the CPU to actually execute a program! Any computer system will thus also include the following items of electronic equipment. Figure 2.2 shows how these things fit together in a 'typical' small computer.

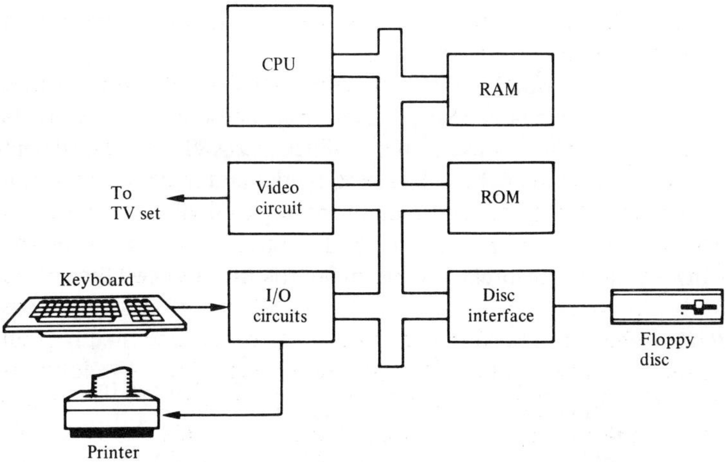

Figure 2.2

Visual display unit

This is often called a VDU, or 'monitor', and allows us to see what the computer is up to. Simple computers use a television set for this role, but more complex ones require the better quality of a specially made unit. The computer will incorporate sufficient electronics to convert the number used to represent the letter 'A', for example, into a pattern of dots on the VDU screen that we recognise as a letter A. Computer operating systems and languages also include means of drawing lines on the display, plotting individual points on the display and making use of what colours are available. Languages often add more complex graphing facilities, such as the ability to draw circles. The 'video memory' shown in Figure 2.2 is an area of RAM in the computer which the display electronics uses to form the picture which is to be displayed. Bits and bytes in memory are set to 1 or 0 depending on what is to be shown on the screen, and the memory is scanned many times each second to send data to the video processing part of the system, which then creates the signals required by the VDU from the RAM contents.

Keyboards

In order for us to enter any data into a computer, a keyboard of some type is provided which the OS examines several times a second to see if any keys are pressed. Most of these keyboards are similar to those found on electronic typewriters, although a few extra keys are usually added. A few experiments have been tried to simplify and make cheaper keyboards. These have included the *membrane keyboard* used on the Sinclair ZX80 and ZX81 computers, where the keyboard was totally flat and the 'switches' were actually made of a plastic membrane with metal on one side. It worked, but was a bit uncomfortable to use for long periods, and so the majority of present-day keyboards use real switches.

Bulk storage devices

Here we solve the vexing question of what we do with the data stored in RAM when we wish to turn the computer off or use the RAM for another program. Well, we simply store it on a more permanent storage medium. For most computers, this is some sort of magnetic medium, the simplest of which is cassette tape. RAM contents are taken by the operating system and converted into a series of audio tones, at a rate of, say, 1200 bits of data per second (1200 *baud* in the jargon), and sent to a normal domestic cassette recorder via sockets on the computer. The data can then be recovered from the tape when required at a later date. Very few computers still use cassette tape, mainly because it is slow and not as reliable as we would like it to be. Instead, magnetic *floppy discs* are used (Figure 2.3) which store the data as patterns of magnet-

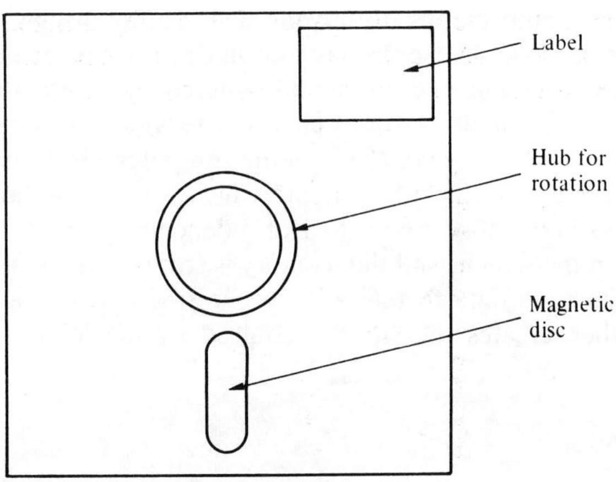

Figure 2.3

ism on the disc surface. Discs are faster, more reliable, and well worth having! Discs store data in different ways on different computers, and depending upon the computer and the disc we can expect to store anywhere between 100 K or 1.4 M of data on a single floppy disc. Larger discs, called *hard discs* are available for some computers, but whereas we can simply change floppy discs when we need a new program, hard discs are built in to the computer. However, they are big – anywhere between 20 and 115 Mb at the time of writing! Hard discs are also faster in use than floppy discs.

Printers

All computers have the means by which a printer can be connected to get a permanent record of data displayed on the screen or stored in RAM. The most popular type of printer in common use today is the *dot matrix* printer, where characters on a page are made up of a series of very closely spaced dots which, in a well designed printer, can give the appearance of continuity (Figure 2.4). As well as printing letters and digits, a dot matrix printer can, under control of a program running on the computer, print pictures or graphs. This makes it very versatile. The second type of printer to consider is the *daisy wheel* printer, where letters and other characters are printed on paper in a similar way to how an electronic typewriter does the job. A piece of plastic carrying a raised impression of the letter is hit against the printer ribbon and so makes a character on the paper. The quality is high, but they are not as flexible as dot matrix printers; they cannot draw graphical images or any character not on the print wheel fitted to

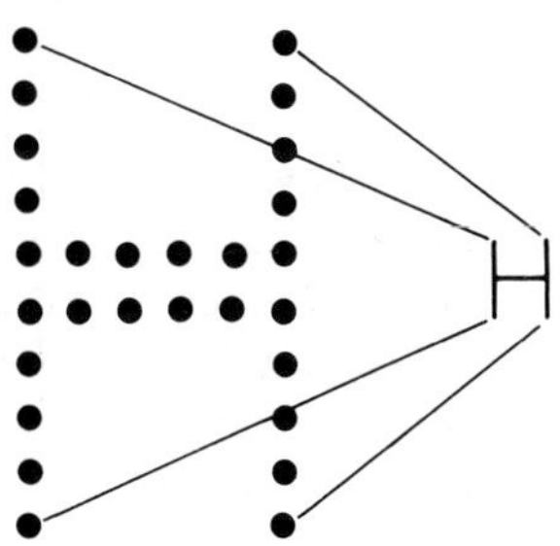

Figure 2.4

the printer. *Laser printers* give us the best of both worlds, being capable of a high quality of print out and also being very versatile. They are also rather expensive.

Other hardware and interfacing

It is possible to add a variety of other pieces of hardware to the basic computer system, and we shall come across many of these devices later on in this book. The science of adding bits of electronic equipment to computers is called *interfacing* and is worth a book in its own right. Interfacing involves both the electronics required to do the job and the software to allow the computer to make use of the newly added device. Interfacing allows us to expand the capabilities of the computer without having to start from scratch all over again and buy a new computer.

You might ask, why bother? Well, the computer can be programmed to do simple tasks very quickly, and most control systems are very simple, usually requiring the detection of a particular event taking place and then switching an electrical circuit on or off accordingly. For example, using a computer to read morse code would require that the computer be able to detect whether the morse key is open or closed. A program can then turn the openings and closings of the morse key into text and display it on the screen, but an interface will be required to convert the closing and opening of the morse key into 5V and 0V signals that the computer can deal with. Likewise, we could use the computer to control a morse code practice oscillator, turning it on and off to send letters in morse for practice purposes. Here, we would need an interface to turn the '1's and '0's that the computer usually deals with into electrical signals capable of operating the oscillator.

To connect any device up to a computer, the computer must make some of its CPU signals available to the outside world in some form. The simplest way for the computer manufacturer to do this is to run the address and data buses, and the important control signals, to a socket of some type on the case of the computer. This is often called an *expansion bus* and gives the interfacer great versatility in what can be added. It also causes lots of problems, as we cannot just attach, say, a morse key to a bit of the data bus and expect the CPU to read morse, even if the computer has appropriate software loaded in. What is most likely to happen is that as soon as the morse key is pressed, the CPU will 'crash', assuming you do not actually damage the CPU! No, for using the expansion bus of a computer, or any method of interfacing involving direct connection to the lines of the CPU, we have to be a bit smarter. In general terms, the steps are as follows:

1 ***Address the device***
   Any device to be added to the computer must be given an address at which the computer can transfer data to or from it. In many computers, this address will be a memory location, but some computers have a separate set of addresses called I/O addresses which can be used instead. This address cannot already be occupied by another device or byte of memory, as otherwise a clash will occur which will most likely crash the CPU. Once the address is chosen, an electronic *address decoder* can be built out of simple circuits called logic gates to provide an electrical signal whenever that address is accessed by the CPU.
2 ***Provide read/write decoding***
   A device added to the computer may be required to provide data to the CPU or accept data from the CPU. For example, an interface circuit to read signals from a morse key would need to transfer signals to the CPU from the morse key. This is called a read operation, and so the CPU control line that is responsible for indicating whether an access of a particular memory or I/O location is a read or write would indicate a 'read' operation by assuming a 5V or 0V signal, depending upon the particular CPU. In this particular example, the read signal and the decoded address signal would be used to *enable* the interface circuit when the CPU tried reading it, thus putting the signal from the morse key on to the data bus for the CPU to read. Similarly, if the interface circuit was designed to have data sent to it from the CPU, the CPU would generate a 'write' signal, set up the address required on the address bus then put the data to be written to the interface on the data bus for the interface to accept.
3 ***Three state devices***
   We have already seen that computers work on two electrical signals – 5V or 0V, '1' or '0'. However, when a device is connected to the data bus of the CPU the CPU must ignore it

until that particular device is addressed by the CPU for a read or write operation. Otherwise, all the devices connected to the data bus, including all the RAM and ROM in the computer, would be trying to put data on the data bus at once. Not a clever state of affairs! For this reason, any device connected to a data bus of the computer must have the ability to effectively hide itself from the CPU until required – this is where the three-state device comes in useful. This is a chip that can assume one of *three* states rather than the usual two; 5V, 0V or an intermediate 'float' state in which the CPU is oblivious to the presence of the device on the data bus. The float state is the normal state for such a device, until it is addressed for read or write operations.

Logic gates and address decoders

The address decoder circuit we briefly mentioned previously is crucial in interfacing, but it is very simple to create. It makes use of a series of chips called *logic gates* which provide an output signal that depends upon the state of the input signals to the chip.

AND gates

An AND gate gives a '1' output only when all of its inputs are set to '1'. This can be described in a table called a *truth table*, and such a table for a two input AND gate would be:

Input A	Input B	Output C
0	0	0
1	0	0
0	1	0
1	1	1

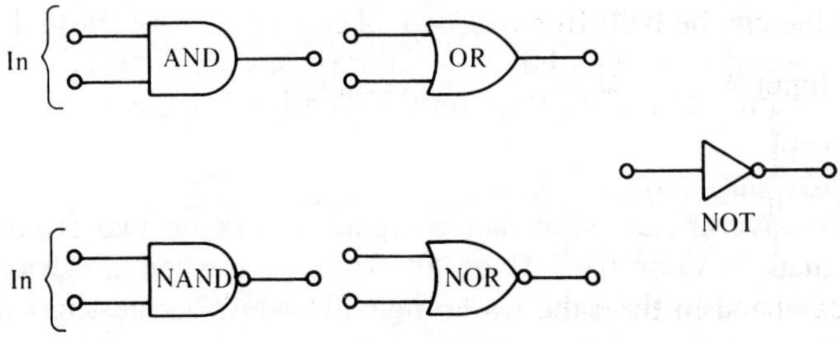

Figure 2.5

Figure 2.5 shows the symbol used for an AND gate in electrical circuits.

OR gates

An OR gate will give a '1' output if any of its inputs are '1'. A truth table for a two input OR gate is:

Input A	Input B	Output C
0	0	0
1	0	1
0	1	1
1	1	1

NOT gate

A NOT gate is a single input device, which gives an output opposite to the input:

Input	Output
0	1
1	0

These are the basic units of digital logic, as this branch of electronics is called, but there are other gates which are made up of these simple units.

NAND gate

This is probably the most widely used logic gate in electronic circuits, and has the interesting property that any other logical function can be built from NAND gates!

Input A	Input B	Output C
0	0	1
1	0	1
0	1	1
1	1	0

As can be seen from the truth table, a NAND gate is simply an AND gate followed by a NOT gate.

NOR gates

A NOR gate is made up of an OR gate followed by a NOT gate, and has a truth table of:

Input A	Input B	Output C
0	0	1
1	0	0
0	1	0
1	0	0

Exclusive OR

This gives a '1' output when the two inputs are different:

Input A	Input B	Output C
0	0	0
1	0	1
0	1	1
1	1	0

These gates can be combined to form many other functions, and gates are also available in chip form that have, for example, eight inputs rather than just the two we have discussed above. The same principles still apply, however.

A practical example

Later in this book we shall take a closer look at this aspect of interfacing, but for now let us see how we might use logic gates to set up address decoding for a simple device to pass signals from a morse key to the CPU. First of all, let us assume that we are using a CPU that has 16 address lines, and that a control line called read/write goes to '0' whenever the CPU wants to read data. The circuit to which the morse key is attached can be ignored for this example, suffice to say that whenever a '0' is present on the input marked 'device select' the current state of the morse key will be output to the output marked 'data' (Figure 2.6). The address at which the CPU is to read the morse key is address 65000.

We can start by working out what pattern of '1's and '0's will be present on the address bus when the CPU puts address 65000 on to its address bus. You can use the program in Chapter 3 to do this,

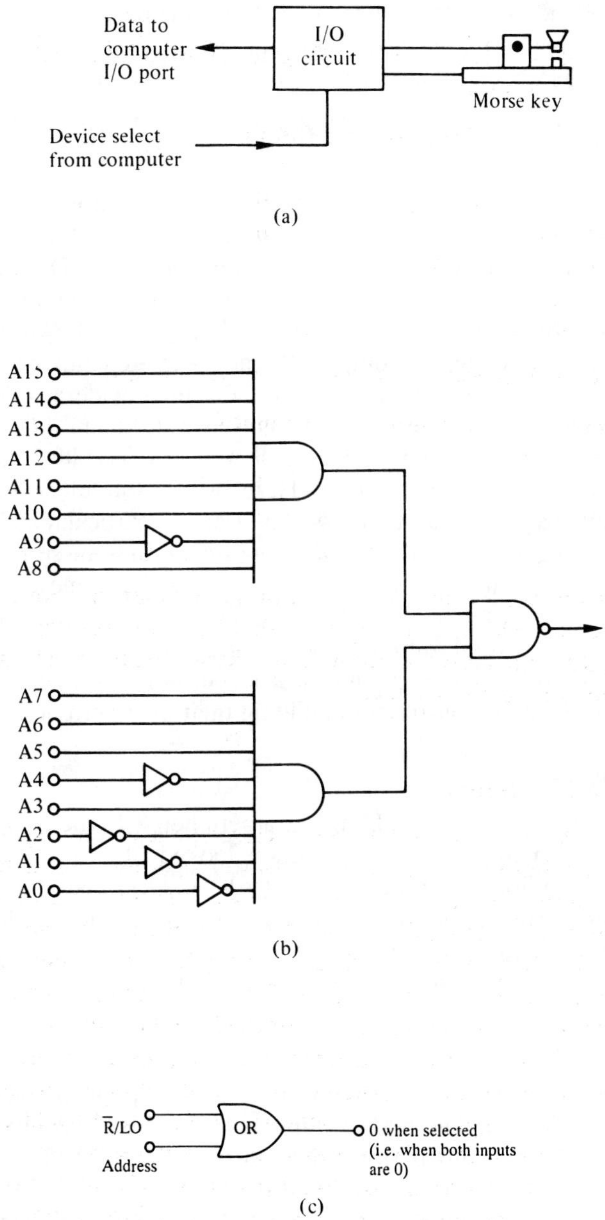
Data to
computer
I/O port
I/O
circuit
Morse key
Device select
from computer
(a)
A15
A14
A13
A12
A11
A10
A9
A8
A7
A6
A5
A4
A3
A2
A1
A0
(b)
R̄/LO
Address
OR
0 when selected
(i.e. when both inputs
are 0)
(c)

Figure 2.6

but the 16 address lines will carry the following pattern of '1's and '0's. By convention, the most significant bit on a 16-bit address bus is called A15 and the least significant bit is called A0.

A15	A14	A13	A12	A11	A10	A9	A8	A7	A6	A5	A4	A3	A2	A1	A0
1	1	1	1	1	1	0	1	1	1	1	0	1	0	0	0

Let us start by combining these so that we get a '0' output when the address lines carry the pattern of bits shown above. Figure 2.6b shows how we might get this, using two 8-input AND gates, a 2-input NAND gate and some NOT gates. This circuit will only give a 0 output when the input address lines are as shown; in all other cases it will give a 1 output. We now need to combine this 0 signal with the read signal from the CPU to provide a 0 device select signal for the interface. This is shown in Figure 2.6c. This process is carried out whenever a new device is added to the expansion bus of the computer. Here, where the added device (also called a *peripheral*) is accessed only at one particular address, the decoding is said to be *full address decoding*. In some situations, we may save chips by only decoding a few address lines. This is cheaper and easier but has the effect that a peripheral may be accessed at several different addresses. This is called *partial address decoding* and is popular in cheaper home computers and amongst amateur constructors building their own peripherals.

User ports

User ports are means of adding extra peripherals to the computer where the manufacturer has already looked after the address decoding and provided the three-state devices to isolate the CPU from the peripheral until the address of the port is accessed. The BBC Microcomputer, for example, has a couple of these interfaces, specifically designed to make interfacing easier.

Standard buses

Some methods of connection have become very popular and have become standard. The best example is the 'PC Bus' which is the method of connecting peripheral circuitry to IBM PCs. These are similar to expansion buses, but are used in several different computers and so allow circuits designed for use in one computer to be used in another machine, provided both computers use the same bus standard. Some manufacturers have adopted a standard interface bus between different machines that they make. An example of this is Acorn computers with their BBC Microcomputer range.

The Centronics standard

The Centronics interface is a means of connecting printers to computers, and most computers have a suitable socket to add printers with this type of interface. Centronics is a *parallel* interface, in which all the data bits that constitute a byte of data being sent to the printer are sent simultaneously. Centronics is an output only interface, in which data is transferred from the computer to the printer. The standard also includes 'handshaking' signals, whereby the printer can tell the computer 'hold on, do not send anything else, I am busy' or 'OK, fire away!'. Computers and printers using the full version of this standard can also detect whether a printer has run out of paper or not!

RS232 Serial standard

Parallel interfaces are useful, but are limited in the distances over which they can operate. If there is more than a few metres between computer and printer, for example, the Centronics standard becomes unreliable. A different standard of data transfer exists in which data is sent *serially*, that is, one bit after another rather than simultaneously. This allows fewer wires in a cable, and makes two way data transfer much easier, as well as allowing communication between pieces of equipment over a wide distance. The standard means of serial data communication is something called RS232, which defines voltage levels to be used, what different signal lines in the cable between the different devices do, maximum speed of data transfer and so on. Data is transferred as a string of '1's and '0's, but as well as the data bits there are other bits transferred on most systems to act as error checking or control signals. On standard RS232 systems, + 12V is used to represent a '1' and − 12V is used to represent a '0', and in this system special devices are required to convert these signal levels to the 5 and 0V normally used in computers. A more recent version of this standard uses 5V and 0V for '1' and '0', and is called RS423 and is used in the BBC Microcomputer machines. By using RS232 we can also connect computers to devices called modems, which allows computers to communicate via the telephone system. For radio amateurs, RS232 or RS423 is important as it is via this interface that we can use packet radio terminals or data decoders (Chapter 13–14).

In comparison with parallel interfaces, serial interfaces are harder to build and program but have become fairly standardized over the years and are to be found on most computers, whereas the only widely found parallel interface is the output only Centronics port. RS232 is a two way data transfer system, and looks very much like it is here to stay.

That concludes this section on computer basics; if you need further information, try some of the books listed in the appendices. In Appendix 1, you will also find a short resume of the BASIC computer language, which may be useful if you are a bit out of practice before going on to the next chapter, where we start examining the use of computers in amateur radio and short wave listening.

THREE

Software for electronic design

In this chapter I shall be examining the use we can put the computer to in an area which is best described as 'number crunching' – helping us out with the calculations involved in designing and building electronic equipment. There will be plenty of listings to type in, so get your typing fingers ready!

Arithmetic and general purpose routines

Let us start with a couple of simple programs in the realm of general arithmetic. The first, in Listing 3.1, is a simple routine for carrying out conversions between binary, decimal and hexadecimal numbers. This listing also gives me the chance to explain the standard I shall be using in this book.

```
10 REM Any base to decimal number conversion
20 REM Joe Pritchard
30 :
40 GOSUB 1000 : REM Get input information
50 GOSUB 2000 : REM do the conversion
60 GOSUB 3000 : REM print the results
70 END
80 :
1000 REM Get the input information into a string, as we might
1010 REM be dealing with hexadecimal numbers
1020 INPUT "Input the number to be converted ",A$
1030 INPUT "Base of number input            ",BASE
1040 RETURN
1050 :
2000 REM Now carry out the conversion to base 10
2010 :
2014 POSITION = 0
2016 VALUE=0
2020 FOR I=LEN(A$) TO 1 STEP -1
2021 B$=MID$(A$,I,1):POSVAL = 0
2022 IF B$="A" THEN POSVAL = 10
2023 IF B$="C" THEN POSVAL = 12
2024 IF B$="D" THEN POSVAL = 13
```

```
2025 IF B$="E" THEN POSVAL = 14
2026 IF B$="F" THEN POSVAL = 15
2027 IF B$="B" THEN POSVAL = 11
2028 IF POSVAL = 0 THEN POSVAL = VAL(MID$(B$,I,1))
2030 VALUE=VALUE+POSVAL*(BASE^POSITION)
2040 POSITION=POSITION+1
2050 NEXT I
2060 RETURN
2070 :
3000 PRINT "Converted value is ";VALUE
3010 RETURN
```

Listing 3.1 Base conversion

This program is written in GW-BASIC, but uses no special commands from that language. It is easy to convert to any other dialect of BASIC; indeed, for the BBC and Amstrad 6128 machines you can simply type the program in as it stands with no changes.

In all program listings, I have used a fairly modular approach to split the program into subroutines (or PROCedures), each of these sub units performing a well defined task. The body of the program consists of the first block of program lines, and will usually be a set of subroutine calls, with possibly a looping construct such as REPEAT . . . UNTIL, GOTO or FOR . . . NEXT to allow repetitive runs of the program. The subroutine definitions will then follow in the listing, and these will be REMmed for ease of conversion to other languages or machines.

As to variable names, I use meaningful names in most cases, and things like I, J or K usually indicate a counting variable. Variable names followed by the '%' sign indicate integer variables, and those followed by the '$' symbol are string variables. Specific instructions for converting programs to other BASIC dialects will be given with each program, rather than listing all programs three or four times. However, for reference purposes Appendix 2 details major differences between GWBASIC, Amstrad BASIC and BBC BASIC.

In use, Listing 3.1 is quite simple. Enter the number to be converted, the base of the number inputted and the value of the number in decimal will be printed. The subroutines used are easily taken and used in other programs, as described in the REM statements.

Listing 3.2 does the reverse of this job, and this is listed as a BBC BASIC program as well as a GWBASIC program to illustrate the conversion process. Amstrad BASIC users can enter the GWBASIC version.

```
10 REM Decimal to Base n converter program
20 REM written in GWBASIC
30 :
40 GOSUB 1000 : REM get input information
50 GOSUB 2000 : REM carry out conversion
60 GOSUB 2120 : REM print the answer
70 END
80 :
1000 REM Subroutine to get inputs
1010 INPUT "Positive Decimal Integer to be converted: ";DECNUM
1020 INPUT "Convert to base: ";BASE
1030 RETURN
1040 :
2000 REM Now carry out the conversion of the number to a base, and
2010 REM put the result into a string variable. We need to allow for
2020 REM hexadecimal digits A-E
2030 :
2040 NUM$=""
2050 QUOT = INT(DECNUM / BASE)
2060 REMAINDER = ((DECNUM/BASE)-QUOT)*BASE
2070 DECNUM = QUOT
2071 NUM$=CHR$(55+REMAINDER)+NUM$
2078 GOTO 2090
2080 NUM$=RIGHT$(STR$(REMAINDER),1)+NUM$
2090 IF QUOT<>0 THEN GOTO 2050
2100 RETURN
2110 :
2120 REM print out routine
2130 PRINT NUM$
2140 RETURN
```

Listing 3.2 Decimal to base ‘n’ conversion (GWBASIC)

I have not used any special features of either BASIC here, but as you can see the BBC BASIC version which follows is easier to read and understand.

```
    10 REM Decimal to Base n converter program
    20 REM written in BBC BASIC
    30 :
    40 PROCinputnumbers            : REM get input information
    50 PROCconvert(decnum,base)    : REM carry out conversion
    60 PROCprintout(num$)          : REM print the answer
    70 END
    80 :
    1000 DEF PROCinputnumbers
    1010 INPUT "Positive Decimal Integer to be converted:
";decnum
    1020 INPUT "Convert to base: ";base
    1030 ENDPROC
    1040 :
    1990 DEFPROCconvert(t_decnum,t_base)
    2000 REM Now carry out the conversion of the number to a
base, and
    2010 REM put the result into a string variable. We need to
allow for
    2020 REM hexadecimal digits A-E
```

```
2030 :
2040 num$=" "
2050 QUOT = INT(t_decnum / t_base)
2060 REMAINDER = ((t_decnum/t_base)-QUOT)*t_base
2070 t_decnum = QUOT
2071 IF REMAINDER < 10 THEN GOTO 2080
2072 num$=CHR$(55+REMAINDER)+num$
2078 GOTO 2090
2080 num$=RIGHT$(STR$(REMAINDER),1)+num$
2090 IF QUOT<>0 THEN GOTO 2050
2100 ENDPROC
2110 :
2115 DEFPROCprintout(t_num$)
2120 REM print out routine
2130 PRINT t_num$
2140 ENDPROC
```

Listing 3.3 Decimal to base 'n' conversion (BBC BASIC)

Some BASIC dialects have functions to convert decimal to hexadecimal, binary or octal (base 8) but these routines are general purpose ones which will run on any machine and with any number base.

Time calculations

Listing 3.4 shows some subroutines for doing calculations with times – this can be quite useful when working out durations of QSOs, etc. Again, these subroutines have been written to run on as many machines as possible. If your particular computer supports user defined functions, there is nothing to stop you writing the subroutines as functions.

```
10 REM time conversion subroutines
20 REM Joe Pritchard
30 :
40 GOSUB 1000 : REM get time as 99:99 format
50 GOSUB 2000 : REM convert times to deciam, calculate differenece
60 GOSUB 3000 : REM print out times
65 END
70 :
1000 REM Get two times as strings and put in tim1$ and tim2$
1010 REM times need entering in 24 hour format - currently no
1020 REM validation of these times
1030 :
1040 INPUT "Input earliest time as XX:XX ",TIM1$
1050 INPUT "Input second time as XX:XX   ",TIM2$
1060 RETURN
1070 :
2000 REM Accepts two strings, tim1$ and tim2$. Converts to 'decimal
2010 REM times' and calculates difference. Then converts difference
2020 REM back into the hours and minutes format.
2030 :
2040 TEMPTIM$=TIM1$
2050 GOSUB 2100 : REM convert to decimal time
2060 TIME1=TEMPTIME
```

```
2070 :
2080 TEMPTIM$=TIM2$
2081 GOSUB 2100 : REM convert second time to decimal time
2082 TIME2=TEMPTIME
2083 :
2084 TEMPTIME = TIME2-TIME1
2085 GOSUB 2200 : REM return time in temp_time as hours, minutes
2086 RETURN
2088 :
2100 REM convert time in temp_tim$ to a decimal time to be
2105 REM returned in the variable temp_time
2110 :
2120 IF LEN(TEMPTIM$)<>5 THEN TEMPTIME=0: RETURN
2121 :
2122 REM first check length - if it's not 5 then return 0
2123 :
2124
TEMPTIME=VAL(LEFT$(TEMPTIM$,2))+((VAL(RIGHT$(TEMPTIM$,2))/60))
2125 RETURN
2199 :
2200 REM accepts a time in temp_time and returns an hours and minutes
2202 REM string in tem_tim$.  String always 5 characters long
2203 :
2204 THOUR$="0"+STR$(INT(TEMPTIME))
2210 I=(TEMPTIME-INT(TEMPTIME))*60:I=INT(I+.5)
2211 TMIN$=RIGHT$(STR$(I),2)
2220 TEMPTIM$=RIGHT$(THOUR$,2)+":"+RIGHT$(TMIN$,2)
2230 RETURN
3000 REM Accept tim1$, tim2$ and temp_tim$ and prints them out
3010 :
3020 PRINT "First time was  "+TIM1$
3030 PRINT "Second time was "+TIM2$
3040 PRINT "Difference is   "+TEMPTIM$
3050 RETURN
```

Listing 3.4 Time interval calculation

Input routines

BASIC supports the INPUT statement as a means of entering data into programs. This works well in many circumstances, but sometimes, especially if the program is to be used by others, it is useful to limit the characters typed into the keyboard somewhat, such as to allow the user to type in only numbers for numeric inputs. Listing 3.5 details some input routines which you might like to consider for use in some of your programs. Listing 3.5 is in GWBASIC, with suitable comments as to any conversion required for BBC BASIC or Amstrad BASIC.

```
6000 REM Input Subroutines in GWBASIC with conversion notes for
6010 REM BBC and Amstrad 464/6128 BASIC
6020 :
6030 REM General Purpose String Input Routine.  Accepts the
6040 REM following parameters:
6050 REM            content$   -   string holding legal characters
6060 REM            x          -   x position on screen of the input
```

```
6070 REM          y          -   y position on screen of input
6080 REM          l          -   length of input string
6090 :
6100 REM returns the string 'in$' containing the string that was entered
6110 REM string entry terminated by pressing RETURN key
6120 :
6130 IN$=""
6140 CH$=INKEY$: IF CH$="" THEN GOTO 6140
6145 :
6146 REM For BBC BASIC we can use ch$=GET$ instead of lines 6130 and 6140
6147 REM For Amstrad and PCs we need to loop around
6148 :
6150 DELETEFL=0 : REM flag is 1 if delete / backspace key is pressed
6160 :
6200 IF INSTR(CONTENT$,CH$) = 0 THEN GOTO 6140
6202 :
6203 REM first string is searched for occurrences of second string
6204 :
6210 CH=ASC(CH$) : REM now work with ASCII code for a while
6220 :
6230 REM now check for the two important control keys - chr$(13) from
6235 REM RETURN key and whatever code is generated by the delete or
6236 REM back space key.  On Amstrad and PCs using GWBASIC, use backspace
6240 REM but on BBC BASIC use chr$(127) as generated by delete key.
6250 :
6260 IF CH=8 AND IN$="" THEN GOTO 6140
6262 :
6263 REM if trying to delete from an empty string, go back
6264 :
6270 IF CH=8 THEN DELETEFL=1
6272 :
6273 REM if the delete code detected, set delete flag
6275 :
6280 IF CH=13 AND IN$="" THEN GOTO 6140
6290 IF CH=13 THEN RETURN
6295 :
6296 REM If string is not empty, return if RETURN key pressed with the
6297 REM inputted string in IN$
6298 :
6300 :
6310 IF DELETEFL=0 THEN IN$=IN$+CH$ : IN$=LEFT$(IN$,L)
6320 IF DELETEFL=1 THEN IN$=LEFT$(IN$,LEN(IN$)-1):LOCATE Y,X:PRINT IN$+" "
6322 :
6323 REM LOCATE is supported by GW BASIC and Amstrad BASIC but for the
6234 REM Amstrad BASIC version the syntax is LOCATE x,y.  The BBC BASIC
6235 REM language doesn't support locate, but uses PRINTTAB(x,y) instead
6236 REM of LOCATE.
6237 :
6330 LOCATE Y,X : PRINT IN$
6340 GOTO 6140
6350 :
6360 REM Yes/No subroutine.  Returns a 'Y' in in$ for Yes and 'N' in in$
6370 REM for No.
6380 CH$=INKEY$ : IF CH$="" THEN GOTO 6380 : REM see above.
6390 IF INSTR("YyNn",CH$)=0 THEN GOTO 6380
6400 IF INSTR("YyNn",CH$)<3 THEN IN$="Y" ELSE IN$="N"
6410 RETURN
6420 :
6430 REM case conversion routine.  takes two variables:
6440 REM        upcase    -      0 convert input string to lower case
6450 REM                         1 convert input string to upper case
6460 REM        in$       -      string to be converted
6470 REM in$ is returned converted.
6480 :
6490 CH$=""
6500 IF UPCASE=0 THEN GOTO 6560
6510 FOR I=1 TO LEN(IN$)
6520 IF MID$(IN$,I,1)>="a" AND MID$(IN$,I,1)<="z" THEN
```

```
CH$=CH$+CHR$(ASC(MID$(IN$,I,1))-32) ELSE CH$=CH$+MID$(IN$,I,1)
6530 NEXT
6540 IN$=CH$
6550 RETURN
6560 FOR I=1 TO LEN(IN$)
6570 IF MID$(IN$,I,1)>="A" AND MID$(IN$,I,1)<="Z" THEN
CH$=CH$+CHR$(ASC(MID$(IN$,I,1))+32) ELSE CH$=CH$+MID$(IN$,I,1)
6580 NEXT
6590 IN$=CH$
6600 RETURN
6610 :
6620 REM remove trailing spaces from in$.  Returns string in in$
6630 :
6640 FOR I=LEN(IN$) TO 1 STEP-1
6650 IF MID$(IN$,I,1)<>" " THEN IN$=LEFT$(IN$,I) : I=1
6660 NEXT I
6670 RETURN
6680 :
6690 REM remove leading spaces from in$. Returns string in in$
6700 :
6710 FOR I=1 TO LEN(IN$)
6720 IF MID$(IN$,I,1)<>" " THEN IN$=MID$(IN$,I,LEN(IN$)): I=300
6730 NEXT
6740 RETURN
6750 :
6760 REM check format of a string.  pic$ holds the format of the string
6770 REM and  in$ holds the input string to be checked.  The variable
6780 REM ok is returned set to 0 if the string is not of the correct
6790 REM format and 1 if the string is of correct format.
6800 :
6810 REM pic$ can contain folowing characters:
6820 REM
6830 REM     !   -   Position must contain upper case letter
6840 REM     #   -   Position may contain any character
6850 REM     9   -   Position must contain a digit in range 0-9
6860 :
6870 IF LEN(PIC$)<>LEN(IN$) THEN OK=0 : RETURN
6880 :
6890 REM if length not same, return 0.
6900 :
6910 OK=1
6920 FOR I=1 TO LEN(PIC$)
6930 P$=MID$(PIC$,I,1)
6940 I$=MID$(IN$,I,1)
6950 :
6960 REM P$ holds a picture character, I$ an input character
6970 :
6980 IF P$="!" THEN GOSUB 7050 : REM subroutine to handle "!"
6990 IF P$="#" THEN GOSUB 7090 : REM subroutine to handle "#"
7000 IF P$="9" THEN GOSUB 7130 : REM subroutine to handle "9"
7010 IF OK=0 THEN I=300
7020 NEXT I
7030 RETURN
7040 :
7050 REM check character if pic$ element is "!"
7060 IF I$>="A" OR I$<="Z" THEN OK=1 ELSE OK=0
7070 RETURN
7080 :
7090 REM check for any character
7100 OK=1
7110 RETURN
7120 :
7130 REM check for a digit or '.'
7140 IF INSTR("0123456789.-",I$)=0 THEN OK=0 ELSE OK=1
7150 RETURN
```

Listing 3.5 Input limiting subroutines

These subroutines can be used in any of your own programs where some control over input is required. In use, simply initialize the variables required by the subroutine before calling it. For example, to initialise the input routine for digit input only, we would use a sequence of code like:

```
100 content$="0123456789"   : REM digits only
110 x=10                    : REM x position of input 10
120 y=10                    : REM y position of input 10
130 l= 4                    : REM input number 4 digits or less
140 GOSUB 6100              : REM do it, return string in in$
```

The string can now be converted into a number by using the VAL function. The 'format' routine at line 6760 is of use when validating character strings of set format, like a callsign – for example, a format string of '!9!!!' would cover the GnAAA type amateur radio callsigns.

Simple electrical calculations

Some calculations commonly used in electronics and radio are not really worth doing on a computer, because it is easier to do them using a pocket calculator. However, I shall document the formulae to use so that you can include these calculations in any programs you write. Where the calculations benefit immediately from the use of a computer program, I have written routines to demonstrate the equations in use. Some applications, like the circuit analysis programs, can only be done with a computer program so there you will find full listings.

Ohm's law

Voltage, current and resistance are linked by the relationship:

$$V = IR$$

and from this we can get three relationships, listed below in a form acceptable to most BASIC interpreters. The equations refer to Figure 3.1.

Voltage calculation

$$V = I \ldots R$$

where R is the resistance in ohms, I the current in amps.

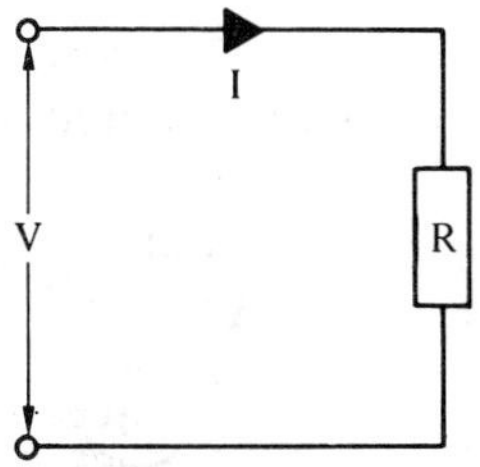

Figure 3.1

Current calculation

$$I = V / R$$

where V is the voltage in volts, R the resistance in ohms.

Resistance calculation

$$R = V / I$$

where V is the voltage in volts, R the resistance in ohms.

Power calculations
Power can be expressed in two ways:

$$P = V * I$$

where P is the power in watts, V the voltage in volts and I the current in amps, or:

$$P = I * I * R$$

where I is the current in amps and R the resistance in ohms.

RMS/peak voltage conversions

Figure 3.2 shows a typical sinusoidal voltage. Of course, the voltage varies with time and so any voltage measurement must take this into account. The instantaneous voltage is the voltage at a precise moment in time, but we usually quote the *peak voltage* and the *RMS voltage*. The peak voltage is shown in Figure 3.2. The value of a DC voltage that would give the same heating effect when applied across a resistance is called the RMS voltage; it is a sort of average voltage. The equations are:

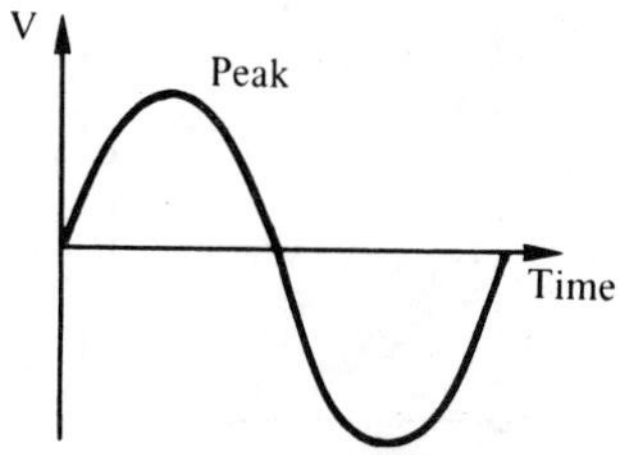

Figure 3.2

RMS voltage

$$V = VP / 1.414$$

where V is the RMS voltage in volts and VP the peak voltage in volts.

Peak voltage

$$VP = 1.414 * V$$

where V is the RMS voltage and VP the peak voltage in volts.

There are many other equations of this type that you could easily convert into functions or subroutines on your microcomputer, but I shall now go on to examine slightly more complex calculations.

Parallel and serial connection of components

A common problem in electronics is the calculation of an effective value of resistance, capacitance or inductance when several components of different values are placed in series or parallel. Listing 3.6 shows a simple series/parallel calculator.

```
10 REM Parallel and Serial Component Calculator
20 REM Joe Pritchard 1989
30 :
40 REM declare an array for the component values
50 DIM VALS(20)
60 :
70 CLS
80 INPUT "Type of component: ",C$
90 INPUT "Parallel or Series:    ",P$
100 :
110 REM R is resistor, L is Inductance or C is capacitance
120 :
125 GOSUB 3000 : REM get input values
130 IF P$="P" THEN GOSUB 1000
```

```
140 IF P$="S" THEN GOSUB 2000
150 PRINT TOTVAL : REM print total value out
160 END
170 :
200 REM Series Connection for R and L, Parallel Connection for C
210 TOTVAL = 0
220 COUNT = 1
230 TOTVAL = TOTVAL + VALS(COUNT)
240 COUNT = COUNT + 1
250 IF VALS(COUNT) <> 0 THEN GOTO 230
260 RETURN
270 :
300 REM Parallel Connection for R and L, Series Connection for C
310 TOTVAL = 0
320 COUNT = 1
330 TOTVAL = TOTVAL + 1/VALS(COUNT)
340 COUNT = COUNT + 1
350 IF VALS(COUNT) <> 0 THEN GOTO 330
360 TOTVAL = 1/TOTVAL
370 RETURN
400 :
1000 REM Parallel Connection Routine
1001 IF C$="C" THEN GOSUB 200
1002 IF C$="R" THEN GOSUB 300
1010 IF C$="L" THEN GOSUB 300
1020 RETURN
1030 :
2000 REM Series Connection Routine
2010 IF C$="C" THEN GOSUB 300
2020 IF C$="R" THEN GOSUB 200
2030 IF C$="L" THEN GOSUB 200
2040 RETURN
2050 :
3000 REM Input Routine
3010 COUNT = 1
3020 INPUT "Component Value (0 to finish): ",VALS(COUNT)
3025 IF VALS(COUNT)=0 THEN RETURN
3030 COUNT = COUNT+1
3040 GOTO 3020
```

Listing 3.6 Series/parallel calculator

The program is simple in use; enter whether you want to calculate the connection for resistors, capacitors or inductors and then whether the connection is series or parallel. Then simply enter the component values, finishing with a 0 entry. The total value of the components will then be displayed.

Generating tables of data

So far, we have used the computer as a glorified pocket calculator; let us now take a brief look at two applications using a little more power before going on to more complex circuit calculations. Listing 3.7 shows how we might produce a conversion table of frequency to wavelength; I shall leave it to you to write a program to do wavelength to frequency. We can generate these tables of data very easily with computers, as repetitive calculations, like we are doing here, are the forte of the microcomputer.

```
10 REM Generate a Frequency / Wavelength Conversion Table for a user
20 REM defined frequency range.
30 :
40 INPUT "Start Frequency:   ",F1
50 INPUT "Finish Frequency:  ",F2
60 INPUT "Step Size:         ",FSTEP
70 :
80 FOR I=F1 TO F2 STEP FSTEP
90 PRINT I,3E+08/I
100 NEXT
110 END
```

Listing 3.7 Frequency/wavelength conversion

Mixing products

A common problem with superheterodyne sets is the presence of spurious signals which are generated by mixing of strong signals in the receiver front ends. These signals might be from genuine transmitters, or they might be harmonics of oscillator circuits within the receiver. Listing 3.8 generates a table of first order mixing products for two frequencies, going up to the twentieth harmonic of each input signal; it does not calculate the products of two mixer products mixing together, but I have found this program to be quite useful.

```
10 REM Mixer Products from two oscillator frequencies
20 REM up to the 20th Harmonic.
21 :
22 REM dimension arrays for frequencies
23 DIM FIRST(20),SECOND(20)
24 :
30 :
40 INPUT "Enter 1st frequency:  ",F1
50 INPUT "Enter 2nd frequency:  ",F2
60 INPUT "Up to which harmonic? ",HARMONIC
70 :
80 REM now set up the harmonic frequencies in the two arrays
90 :
100 FOR I=1 TO HARMONIC
110 FIRST(I)=F1*I
120 SECOND(I)=F2*I
130 NEXT
140 :
150 REM now go through all the possible combinations of first order
160 REM mixing products. If you want a hard-copy print out of the
170 REM listing, then use VDU 2 and VDU 3 to turn the printer on and
180 REM off for BBC BASIC, PRINT#8 for the Amstrad 6128/464 machines
190 REM and LPRINT for IBM PCs.
200 :
210 FOR I=1 TO HARMONIC
220   FOR J=1 TO HARMONIC
230     PRINT FIRST(I)+SECOND(J),I,J,"Additive"
```

```
240    PRINT FIRST(I)-SECOND(J),I,J,"F1 - F2"
250    PRINT SECOND(I)-FIRST(J),I,J,"F2 - F1"
260   NEXT J
270 NEXT I
280 :
290 END
```

Listing 3.8 mixing products

To use the program, simply enter the two frequencies of interest and the maximum harmonic that you wish to consider. A table will then be generated.

Reactance, impedance and tuned circuits

The design of tuned circuits and other circuits involving reactances and impedances is a common requirement for amateur radio. The main equations that we need to consider in this area are as follows:

Capacitative reactance

$$Xc = 1 / (6.28*F*C)$$

where Xc is the reactance, F the frequency of interest and C is the capacitance, in farads.

Inductive reactance

$$Xl = 6.28*F*L$$

where F is the frequency, Xl is the inductive reactance and L is the inductance in henries.

A circuit containing reactance and resistance is said to possess the property of *impedance* and will offer a frequency dependant opposition to the flow of an alternating current. There will be a *phase shift* applied to the signal, as shown in Figure 3.3, and the output signal level will depend upon the input signal level and its frequency. Later on in this chapter, I shall list a program that can analyse the behaviour of simple circuits containing resistance, capacitance and impedance, but at the moment I shall consider just the practicalities of tuned circuit design.

Tuned circuits

$$F = 1 /(6.28*SQR(L*C))$$

where F is the resonant frequency (Figure 3.4), L is the inductance and C is the capacitance. Let us see what we can do with this

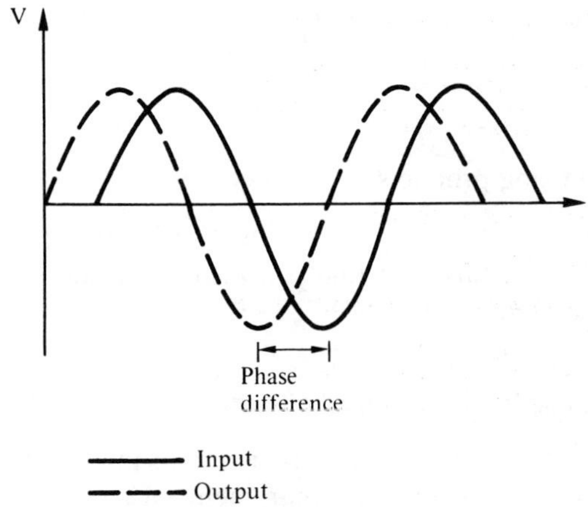

Figure 3.3

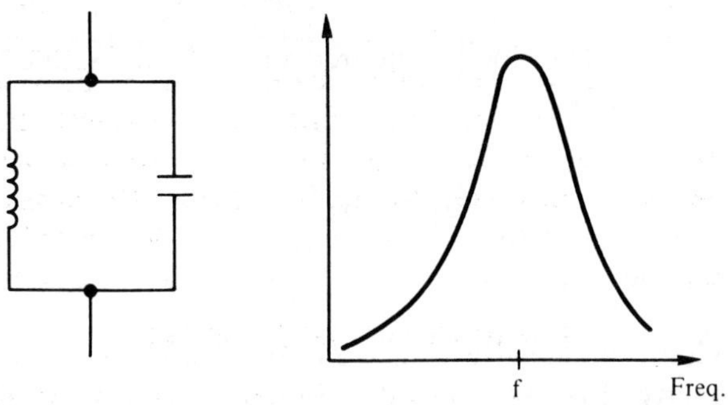

Figure 3.4

equation. Listing 3.9 shows a program that can be modified to give a graphical output, though I shall leave that for you to do. Enter an inductance, and a capacitor range – put the same capacitance in if you have just got one value of capacitance in which you are interested. The program will then print out frequencies that this combination will cover, and from this table we can judge whether the particular combination of capacitor and coil is suitable for our needs.

```
100 REM Tuned Circuit Calculator - Joe Pritchard
110 :
120 INPUT "Inductance value in uH             ",L
130 INPUT "Lowest value of capacitance (pF)  ",CLOW
140 INPUT "Highest value of capacitance (pF) ",CHIGH
150 INPUT "Capacitance Step Size (pF)        ",CSTEP
160 :
170 L=L/1000000!
180 PREVFREQ = 0
190 FOR I=CLOW TO CHIGH STEP CSTEP
200 C=I/1E+12
210 PRINT USING "######.###";I;
220 PRINT " pF        ";
230 PRINT USING "########";(1/(6.28*SQR(L*C)))/1000;
240 PRINT " kHz";
250 IF PREVFREQ <> 0 THEN PRINT USING
"#######";PREVFREQ-((1/(6.28*SQR(L*C)))/1000)
255 IF PREVFREQ=0 THEN PRINT
260 PREVFREQ = (1/(6.28*SQR(L*C)))/1000
270 NEXT I
```

Listing 3.9 Tuned circuit calculator

Shortly we shall examine similar programs for calculating the frequency of operation for Hartley and Colpitts oscillators. One thing that this program demonstrates is the distinct non-linearity of tuned circuits! Oncc an inductance is chosen, we then can either buy one of the appropriate value or wind our own. Provided that air cored, single layer coils are wound, we can calculate the turns required to create a particular inductance. Multiple layers or ferrite or brass cores make life more difficult. The design equations listed in the *ARRL Handbook* for a simple, single layer, air cored coil are:

$$L = d*d*n*n \; / \; (18*d + 40*w)$$

where L is the inductance in μH, d is the diameter of the winding, w the winding length and n the number of turns. Both length and diameter are in inches. Rearranging this to be more useful – i.e. to give us the number of turns needed for a particular inductance given a set length and radius, we have:

$$n = SQR(L*(18*d+40*w)) \; / \; d$$

These equations can easily be included in a computer program for it to calculate. These calculations are approximate, and at higher frequencies will give errors. However, given that the tuned circuits using these inductors will be using variable capacitance tuning, this will negate any errors in the calculation.

Simple network design

Once we start combining components together, we end up with simple *networks* of components, and the design techniques of the most useful networks are simply plugging numbers into a suitable equation – the perfect job for a computer! For the more complex networks, more advanced techniques are used to predict the behaviour of the circuit, as we shall later see when we discuss circuit analysis techniques. However, for the moment let us look at some simple network design.

Resistor networks

The potential divider

The potential divider is the simplest circuit network, consisting in its basic form of two resistors arranged as shown in Figure 3.5a. If the load resistor is large compared to the value of R2, then the output voltage can be calculated by:

Vout = Vin * R2 / (R1 + R2)

where Vin and Vout are the input and output voltages and R1 and R2 the resistor values in ohms, kilohms or megohms. If the load resistance starts approaching the value of R2 we need to take its value into account; the load resistance becomes a resistor in parallel with R2 and so its effect can be calculated. The program for the potential divider calculations is to be found in Listing 3.10, along with subroutines for the other networks shown in Figure 3.5.

Minimum loss matching

Figure 3.5b shows a minimum loss network, designed to couple two different impedances together with the minimum of loss. The design calculations used in the program are:

Loss = SQR(Zin/Zout)+SQR((Zin/Zout)−1) as a ratio
R1 = Zin * SQR(1−(Zout/Zin))
R2 = Zout / (SQR(1−(Zout/Zin)))

where Loss is the minimum loss expected as a ratio of Vin/Vout, R1 and R2 the resistor values in ohms and Zin and Zout the impedances in ohms.

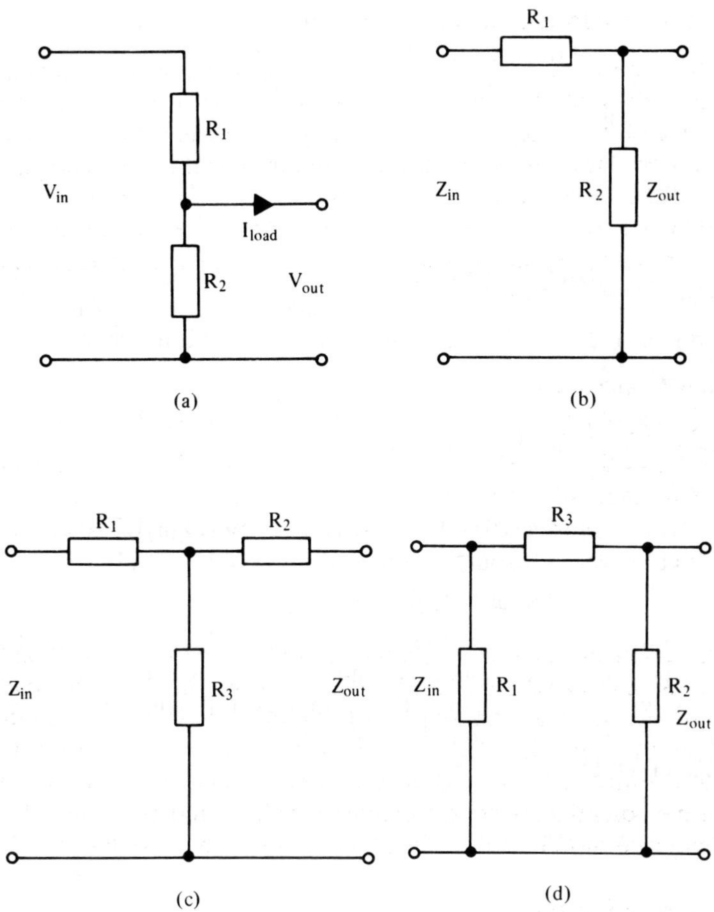

Figure 3.5

The 'T' attenuator

From minimising losses to inserting them! A common requirement in amateur radio or electronics is to reduce a signal by a known amount. This process is done by a circuit called an attenuator, and in its simplest form the potential divider could be seen as that. However, the potential divider gives us no control over the impedances that the input and output voltages see, and this is rather important in most work, as we shall introduce further, unintentional losses if we do not consider the input and output impedances of the attenuator. The 'T' attenuator circuit, shown in Figure 3.5c, gives one solution to this problem. The design equations are:

R3 = (2/(ratio−1)) * SQR(ratio*Zin*Zout)
R1 = Zin*(ratio+1)/(ratio−1) − R3
R2 = Zout*(ratio+1)/(ratio−1) − R3

where R1, R2 and R3 are the resistor values in ohms and Zin and Zout are the impedances in ohms. Ratio is the ratio of Vin/Vout, and so is the amount by which the input signal is attenuated.

The PI attenuator

This is another attenuator, so called because of its likeness to the Greek letter PI (π). Figure 3.5d shows the circuit and the equations are:

R3 = 1 / (2/(ratio−1) * SQR(ratio/(Zout*Zin)))
R2 = 1 / ((1/Zout)*((ratio+1)/(ratio−1)) − 1/R3)
R1 = 1 / ((1/Zin)*((ratio+1)/(ratio−1)) − 1/R3)

Listing 3.10 will allow these calculations to be carried out. The only point to note about this listing is that BBC Microcomputer users will need to change the 'print resistor' and 'print ratio' subroutines as indicated because the Beeb does not support PRINT USING.

```
10 REM Resistive Network Calculator Program
20 REM Joe Pritchard
30 :
40 CLS
41 PRINT : PRINT
50 PRINT "1 - Potential Divider Calculation"
60 PRINT "2 - Minimum Loss Matching"
70 PRINT "3 - T Attenuator Design"
80 PRINT "4 - PI Attenuator Design"
85 PRINT "5 - Quit
90 INPUT "Which Option:   ",CHOICE
100 :
110 REM The above menu is very rudimentary but will run on any of the
120 REM machines. Next, decide which subroutine to call
130 :
140 IF CHOICE = 1 THEN GOSUB 1000
150 IF CHOICE = 2 THEN GOSUB 1210
160 IF CHOICE = 3 THEN GOSUB 3000
170 IF CHOICE = 4 THEN GOSUB 4000
171 INPUT "Press RETURN to continue",A$
175 IF CHOICE <> 5 THEN GOTO 40 : REM loop around
180 :
200 END
210 :
```

```
220 REM Print out a resistance in ohms. a$=text and X is the value
225 :
226 REM If using BBC BASIC, then replace line 240 with
227 :
228 REM 240 @%=&0002010A : print X; : @%=10
229 :
230 PRINT A$;
240 PRINT USING "#######.#";X;
250 PRINT " ohms"
260 RETURN
270 :
300 REM print out a ratio
301 :
302 REM If using BBC BASIC, then replace line 310 with:
303 :
304 REM 310 @% = 131850 : print X : @%=10
305 :
310 PRINT USING "#.###";X
320 RETURN
330 :
1000 REM Potential divider calculation
1010 :
1020 CLS
1030 INPUT "Value of R1:        ",R1
1040 INPUT "Value of R2:        ",R2
1050 INPUT "Load resistance:    ",RL
1060 :
1070 REM first of all, work out total resistance of Rl in parallel with
1080 REM R2
1090 :
1100 R2 = R2*RL / (R2+RL)
1110 :
1120 REM now work out the ratio of Vout to Vin and display the result
1130 :
1140 PRINT "Ratio of Vout to Vin will be:  ";
1150 X = R2/(R2+R1) : GOSUB 300
1160 :
1170 REM ratio will never be greater than 1 - otherwise we've rewritten the
1180 REM laws of physics!
1190 RETURN
1200 :
1210 REM Minimum Loss Matching Resistive Network.
1220 :
1230 CLS
1240 INPUT "Input Impedance:   ",ZIN
1250 INPUT "Output Impedance:  ",ZOUT
1260 LOSS = SQR(ZIN/ZOUT) + SQR((ZIN/ZOUT)-1)
1270 R1 = ZIN * SQR(1-(ZOUT/ZIN))
1280 R2 = ZOUT / (SQR(1-(ZOUT/ZIN)))
1290 PRINT "Minimum loss ratio of Vin/Vout will be:  ";
1300 X=LOSS : GOSUB 300 : REM Print a ratio out
1310 X=R1 : A$="R1 will be " : GOSUB 220 : REM print resistor R1
1320 X=R2 : A$="R2 will be " : GOSUB 220 : REM print resistor R2
1330 PRINT
1340 RETURN
1350 :
3000 REM T Attenuator Design
3010 :
3020 CLS
3025 PRINT "T Attenuator Design"
3030 INPUT "Loss Ratio (Vin / Vout) desired:  ",RATIO
3040 INPUT "Input Impedance:                  ",ZIN
3050 INPUT "Output Impedance:                 ",ZOUT
3060 R3 = (2/(RATIO-1))*SQR(RATIO*ZIN*ZOUT)
3070 R1 = (ZIN*(RATIO+1)/(RATIO-1))-R3
3080 R2 = (ZOUT*(RATIO+1)/(RATIO-1))-R3
3090 PRINT
```

```
3100 A$="R1 will be " : X=R1 : GOSUB 220
3110 A$="R2 will be " : X=R2 : GOSUB 220
3120 A$="R3 will be " : X=R3 : GOSUB 220
3130 PRINT
3140 RETURN
3150 :
4000 REM PI Attenuator Design
4010 :
4020 CLS
4025 PRINT "PI Attenuator Design"
4030 INPUT "Loss Ratio (Vin / Vout) desired:  ",RATIO
4040 INPUT "Input Impedance:                  ",ZIN
4050 INPUT "Output Impedance:                 ",ZOUT
4060 R3 = 1 / (2/(RATIO-1) * SQR(RATIO/(ZOUT*ZIN)))
4070 R2 = 1 / ((1/ZOUT)*((RATIO+1)/(RATIO-1))-1/R3)
4080 R1 = 1 / ((1/ZIN)*((RATIO+1)/(RATIO-1))-1/R3)
4090 PRINT
4100 A$="R1 will be " : X=R1 : GOSUB 220
4110 A$="R2 will be " : X=R2 : GOSUB 220
4120 A$="R3 will be " : X=R3 : GOSUB 220
4130 PRINT
4140 RETURN
```

Listing 3.10 Resistive network calculator

Passive filter design

Once we start combining resistor networks with components exhibiting reactance, we end up with networks that show frequency dependent behaviour. The *transfer function* of the network – effectively the ratio of output to input signal for our purposes – depends upon the frequency of the input signal, and so we can design circuits to let a particular band of frequencies through whilst seriously reducing the level of signals whose frequency is outside the desired band. Such a circuit is called a filter, and if it contains only resistance, capacitance and inductance it is called a passive filter. In this section I should like to look at the equations to design a few common passive filter types. Figure 3.6 shows three types of filter using resistance and capacitance. For the single stage high pass and low pass filters, the equations are identical; filters with a 'sharper' cut off point can be constructed by simpling connecting several of the single stage filters end to end but this will lead to considerable losses, even at the frequencies that you wish to pass through the filter! A better solution is to use an active filter as described later in this chapter. The equations for these two simple circuits are:

Vout / Vin = 1 / SQR(1+(6.28*F*R*C))
3DB POINT = 1 / (6.28 * R * C)

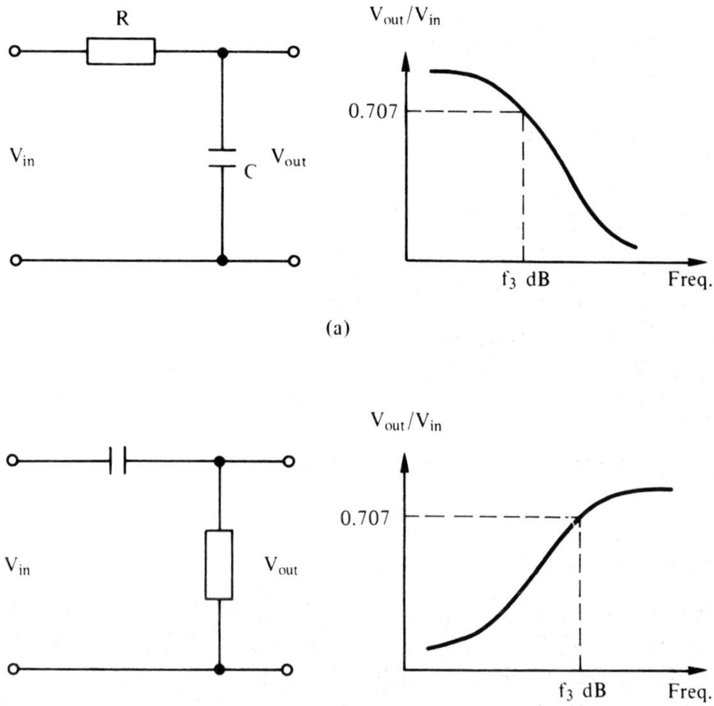

(b)

Figure 3.6

where Vout is the output voltage, Vin the input voltage, F the frequency of interest in hertz, R the resistance in ohms and C the capacitance in farads. The 3 dB point of a filter is the frequency at which Vout / Vin = 0.707. These equations can easily be written into a BASIC program. Note that the load resistance will have an effect on the frequency response of such simple circuits; you may care to investigate this effect with the circuit analysis program given later in this chapter. The simple RC notch filter removes signals of a particular frequency, given by:

$$F = 1/ (6.28*R1*C1)$$

where R1=R2=2*R3 and C1=C2=0.5*C3. Similar circuits can be constructed using inductors instead of resistors; indeed, the tuned circuit considered above is a perfect example of this type of filter.

Other filter arrangements can be found in many textbooks, and in many sources you will find tables of pre-calculated values to help you design your own filters.

Circuit analysis

With the circuit configurations that we have examined so far, we can approximately predict the behaviour of the circuit by simply plugging values in to a simple equation. For example, we could calculate the 3 dB point for the single stage filter given above, but we could not tell from the equations given what the output voltage would be, for example, a couple of milliseconds after a DC voltage had been applied to the input. Similarily, imagine a complex network like that shown in Figure 3.7 – we do not have a standard equation for it so we would have to derive one from first principles or build the circuit and test it. Well, we can get approximate answers for both these problems by the techniques of *circuit analysis* which is simply a means of building a mathematical model of a particular electronic circuit. Analysis can be carried out without computers, but the maths can be quite horrendous. Computers make it much easier, and programs have been written that allow the analysis of circuits containing anything from resistors to field effect transistors or logic chips! Such programs are rather beyond the scope of this book, but in this section I shall demonstrate the basic principles of two methods of analysing linear passive circuits using simple computer programs.

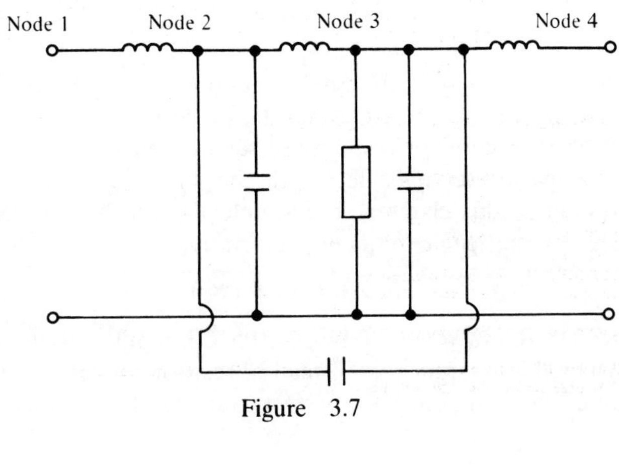

Figure 3.7

A network can be described in two ways. The first is in its frequency response – the way in which the circuit behaves with signals of different frequencies as inputs. This allows us to see the losses of the circuit at different frequencies and the phase shift introduced at different frequencies, and so will allow us to investigate the responses of filters. This is called *frequency domain* analysis. The second way a circuit can be analysed is in its response to a set level of input signal for a period of time after that input voltage was applied. For example, we might see what happens in the seconds following the application of a DC voltage to the input of a single-stage low-pass filter. This approach is often called *time domain* or *transient* analysis.

Transient analysis

Let us look at the way in which we might analyse the simple low pass filter in this way. There are a couple of ways in which we can do it. The first is to get a differential equation that describes the system, and then integrate that equation, either by formal mathematical analysis or numerically. For the circuit shown, an analytic solution for Vin=0 at time t=0 is:

$$Vout = Vin*(1-2.718-t/R*C))$$

At time t=0, a DC voltage is applied at Vin, say of 5V. Listing 3.11 prints a table of output voltage against time, and also calls a subroutine to draw a graph of these output voltages against time. Note the changes needed for BBC and Amstrad 6128 BASIC. Figure 3.8a shows the type of graph we can expect to get. Of course, this technique requires that we can derive equations for the circuit – not always easy for complex circuits.

```
10 REM Demonstration of transient response of RC circuit
20 REM draws graph in GWBASIC
30 :
40 REM initialise R, C and Time Step
50 :
60 INPUT "Resistor value:      ",R
70 INPUT "Capacitor value:     ",C
80 INPUT "Time Step:           ",T
90 INITTIME = 0  : REM initialise time to 0.
100 VIN = 5       : REM Voltage switched to 5V at time = 0
110 :
120 SCREEN 0      : REM graphics mode set
130 :
140 REM For BBC Micro replace line 120 with 120 MODE 4.  For the Amstrad
150 REM 6128 replace line 120 with 120 Mode 2
160 :
```

```
170 CLS
180 FOR I=0 TO 200: REM do 200 points
190 INITTIME = INITTIME + T : REM increment time by time step
200 VOUT = VIN*(1-2.718^(-INITTIME/(R*C))) : REM Calculate Vout
210 :
220 REM Now plot a point on the screen. For BBC Micro, replace line 280 with
230 REM the following    280 PLOT 69,I*6,50*Vout.
240 :
250 REM If you've got the Amstrad 6128, replace line 280 with the following:
260 REM 280 PLOT I*3,30*Vout
270 :
280 PSET(I*3,200-20*VOUT)
290 NEXT I
```

Listing 3.11 RC transient response

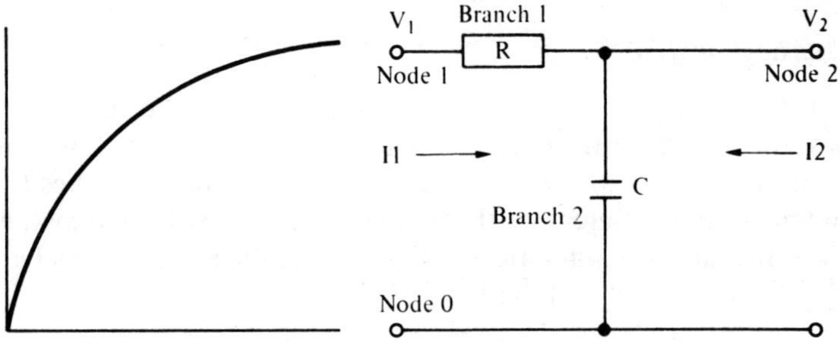

(a) (b)

Figure 3.8

A related technique is to treat the voltage present at the circuit as a 'step' voltage, so that it is at 0 at time 0, say 0.1V at 0.1 seconds, 0.2V at 0.2 seconds and so on, with no continuum of voltage between the steps. If the steps are small, then the analysis of the circuit will be fairly accurate. For each step, the voltage at individual points in the circuit can be calculated by some fairly straightforward equations. For example, the RC network shown in Figure 3.6 can be analysed in a stepwise manner by knowing Ohm's law and the formula for the voltage on a capacitor at a certain time:

$$Vc = Ic * T / C$$

The current flowing into this capacitor, Ic, will be given by Ic = Vin/R, where Vin is the input voltage and R is the resistance in ohms. T is the time in seconds, and C the capacitance in farads. Listing 3.12 produces a graph using this technique of analysis, which is effectively a form of numerical integration of the differential equations describing the system.

```
10 REM Demonstration of transient response of RC circuit
20 REM draws graph in GWBASIC
30 :
40 REM initialise R, C and Time Step
50 :
60 INPUT "Resistor value:     ",R
70 INPUT "Capacitor value:    ",C
80 INPUT "Time Step:          ",T
90 INITTIME = 0  : REM initialise time to 0.
100 VIN = 5      : REM Voltage switched to 5V at time = 0
110 :
120 SCREEN 2     : REM graphics mode set
130 :
140 REM For BBC Micro replace line 120 with 120 MODE 4.  For the Amstrad
150 REM 6128 replace line 120 with 120 Mode 2
160 :
170 CLS
180 FOR I=0 TO 200: REM do 200 points
190 INITTIME = INITTIME + T : REM increment time by time step
194 :
195 IC = (VIN-VOUT)/R
200 VOUT = VOUT+IC  * INITTIME / C : REM Calculate Vout
210 :
220 REM Now plot a point on the screen.  For BBC Micro, replace line 280 with
230 REM the following    280 PLOT 69,I*6,50*Vout.
240 :
250 REM If you've got the Amstrad 6128, replace line 280 with the following:
260 REM 280 PLOT I*3,30*Vout
270 :
280 PSET(I*3,200-20*VOUT)
290 NEXT I
```

Listing 3.12 RC transient response

To test these routines, enter R values of 1000, C of 0.001 and time increments of 0.01. A graph like that in Figure 3.8 should be seen on the screen. The second method can be expanded to multistage circuits by writing equations for each stage of the circuit, although this can get tedious. However, this analysis technique can be useful in detecting phenomena such as 'ringing' in networks, which could indicate potential instability in the circuit.

Frequency analysis

The second method of circuit analysis that can be carried out on a microcomputer is frequency domain analysis, where we look at the transfer characteristic of a network at different frequencies. The technique commonly used to do this is called *nodal analysis*. To see how this works, we must first look at a little theory. Consider a simple circuit, such as that shown in Figure 3.8b. In circuit analysis terminology, it has three *nodes* and two *branches*. A node is a point at which two components are connected, and a branch is made up of components connected between two nodes. One of these nodes, in this case node 0, is taken as a reference node for the circuit. For circuit analysis purposes, we look at the *admittance* of each node and branch in the network. Admittance is the reciprocal of impedance, and for resistors, capacitors and inductors the admittance is given by:

Radmittance = 1/R
Cadmittance = 6.28 * F * C
Ladmittance = 1/6.28 * F * L

where F is the frequency of interest, in Hz, R the resistance in ohms, C the capacitance in farads and L the inductance in henries.

Armed with these new parameters, we can describe a circuit such as this in terms of a matrix:

$$\begin{matrix} Y11 & Y12 \\ Y21 & Y22 \end{matrix} * \begin{matrix} V1 \\ V2 \end{matrix} = \begin{matrix} I1 \\ I2 \end{matrix}$$

where Y is a matrix of admittances, V voltages and I currents. I1 is the sum of all currents flowing into node 1 of the circuit, and V1 is the voltage at that node relative to node 0, which is the reference node. If I1 were negative, then a current would be flowing from that node rather than into it. The reference node never gets included in any of these matrices. Y11 is called the *self admittance* of node 1, and is arrived at by adding all the admittances that are connected to node 1. Y12 is the *coupling admittance* between nodes 1 and 2 and is given by minus the sum of all the admittances connecting nodes 1 and 2. The coupling admittance between nodes 2 and 1, given by Y21, will be the same as this. Any admittance connected between a node and the reference node will be entered as the self admittance of that node, with no coupling admittances.

A brief examination of the circuit will show that V1 is the input voltage and I1 the input current, and that V2 and I2 are the voltage and current at the output node. We can work out the input impedance of the circuit as:

Zinput = V1/I1

provided that a load has been connected between the output node and the reference node. When carrying out analysis of these *two port networks* as such a simple circuit is called, we can get around needing to know input voltages and currents by looking at the ratio of input and output voltages – V1 and V2 in our case. This is not the place for all the maths involved, but suffice to say that the ratio can be calculated by the equations:

```
Ztemp = Z2*ZL/(Z2 + ZL)
V2/V1 = Ztemp / (Z1 + Ztemp)
```

In addition,

Vout / Vin = Z2 / Z1

where Z2 and Z1 are the impedances offered by branches 2 and 1 of the circuit. We can calculate these impedances from the admittances already known, knowing that the admittances are the reciprocals of the impedances. The admittances that we would use for this calculation are the coupling admittance between nodes 1 and 2 and the self admittance of node 2. In algebraic terms, these admittances are admittances Y12 and Y22 and the voltage ratio can be obtained by:

Vout / Vin = Y21 / Y22

The only complication is that the impedances involved have to be treated as complex numbers, containing both real and imaginary parts. Any textbook on electronics will discuss this issue, but it means that the calculations must take both parts into account, and so when analysing circuits using computers we often have arrays of real and imaginary admittances and impedances. The ratio above must therefore be calculated by taking both the real and imaginary parts of the admittances into account, and to get the magnitude of a complex number – in this case the ratio, Vout / Vin, we need to evaluate it as:

```
ratio = SQR(realpart*realpart + imagpart*imagpart)
```

We now have an important characteristic of the circuit – the magnitude of the output voltage with respect to the input voltage at any frequency we choose. In addition, we can work out the phase difference by which the output voltage leads the output current. This is given by the arctangent of the angle represented by:

ABS(imagpart / realpart)

and will be in degrees.

So far, we have managed to do this analysis on a simple network – what about more complex ones? Well, the theory remains the same, in that we first have to create admittance matrices containing the real and imaginary parts of the admittances. However, the resultant matrix is then 'boiled down' to a matrix that is like that above – a 2*2 one representing a two port network. Rows and columns of the matrix, representing admittances, are removed and the effects of these admittances transferred to other rows and columns in the matrix. One method of doing this is by a technique called *pivotal condensation*, in which a particular row and column, say row 4 and column 4, is to be removed. This can be done by a fragment of BASIC such as:

```
FOR i=1 to 3
FOR j=1 to 3
  Y(i,j) = (Y(i,4) * Y(4,j) / Y(4,4)
NEXT j
NEXT i
FOR l=1 to 4
  Y(l,4)=0
  Y(4,l)=0
NEXT l
```

Thus we eventually end up with a matrix like that above containing the effective admittances offered by the circuit when all the admittances present have been taken into account and their effect on nodes 1 and 2 evaluated by this technique. There are other methods of removing rows and columns from a matrix, but this one is fairly simple. Anyway, enough of the theory; Listing 3.13 shows a simple program to analyse passive LCR networks. Examine the listing as you type it in and you will find plenty of comments to help explain what is happening.

```
10 REM Simple Circuit Analysis program
20 REM Joe Pritchard
25 :
30 GOSUB 1270 :                      REM initialise arrays
40 GOSUB 1390 :                      REM Get component data from user
50 GOSUB 2260 :                      REM Print out components for
                                     reference
60 :
70 GOSUB 2350 :                      REM Get frequency range
80 GOSUB 2430 :                      REM calculate and display transfer
                                     characteristics for
90           :                       REM for each frequency in the
                                     range
100 INPUT "Repeat for new frequency range?",A$
110 IF A$="Y" OR A$="y" THEN GOTO 70
120 END:
130 :
140 REM Now list the subroutines needed for the program
150 :
160 REM COMPLEX NUMBER MULTIPLICATION.
170 REM accepts two complex numbers as x1,y1 (real and imaginary parts
180 REM of first number) and x2,y2 (real and imaginary parts of second
190 REM number. Returns real part of product in REALPROD and imaginary
200 REM part of product in IMAGPROD
210 :
220 REALPROD = (X1*X2) - (Y1*Y2)
230 IMAGPROD = (X2*Y1) + (Y2*X1)
240 RETURN
250 :
260 REM COMPLEX NUMBER DIVISION.
270 REM accepts two complex numbers as x1,y1 and x2,y2. Returns the
280 REM real part of the quotient in realquot and the imaginary part in
290 REM IMAGQUOT
300 :
310 REALQUOT = ((X1*X2)+(Y1*Y2))/((X2*X2)+(Y2*Y2))
320 IMAGQUOT = ((Y1*X2)-(X1*Y2))/((X2*X2)+(Y2*Y2))
330 RETURN
340 :
350 REM CALCULATE PHASE OF OUTPUT
360 REM Takes the IMAGQUOT and REALQUOT variables and evaluates the
angle
380 :
390 AN=ATN(ABS(IMAGQUOT/REALQUOT))
432 :
433 REM Next line converts from radians into degrees, as I think better
434 REM In degrees....
435 :
440 PHASEDIFF = AN*57.32
450 RETURN
460 :
470 REM Accepts the three component value matrices and converts the componet
480 REM values in to admittances. These are then stored in REAL(), which is
490 REM storing real admittances and IMAG() which stores the imaginary parts
500 REM of the admittances.
510 :
520 REM First, create the real and imaginary admittance matrices
530 :
540 FOR I=1 TO MAXNODES   :          REM maxnodes is total number of
                                     circuit nodes
550 FOR J=1 TO MAXNODES
560 :
570 REM First of all, get the real admittance for this particular
580 REM component from the R() array by getting the value from R()
590 REM and storing it as an admittance in real()
600 :
610 REAL(I,J) = R(I,J) :             REM get conductance for inclusion
620                    :             REM in the admittance matrices.
```

```
630 :
631 REM Now work out the imaginary parts of the admittance which come from
632 REM the L and C components linking these nodes.  To evaluate the
633 REM admittance, simply calculate as per notes in text.  FREQ is the
634 REM frequency under test.
635 :
640 IMAG(I,J) = C(I,J)*FREQ*6.28 :          REM Now do it for the capacititive susceptance
650 :
660 IMAG(I,J) = IMAG(I,J) + L(I,J)/(6.28*FREQ) :REM Finally do it for the
670                                         :REM inductive susceptance
680 NEXT J
690 NEXT I
700 RETURN
710 :
720 REM PIVOTAL CONDENSATION - METHOD DESCRIBED IN TEXT
730 REM Now we've got all the component values converted in to admittances
740 REM and stored in the REAL and IMAG admittance matrices.  Now we come to
750 REM converting the the matrices into a two port network for the purposes
760 REM of analysis.
770 :
780 FOR K=(MAXNODES-1) TO 2 STEP -1
790 FOR I=1 TO MAXNODES
800 FOR J=1 TO MAXNODES
810 IF (I=K) OR (J=K) THEN GOTO 1040 :  REM if either same as k, don't bother
820 :
830 REM Now prepare to remove column k and row k of the matrix.
840 :
850 REM First of all, calculate Yik*Ykj.  This is a complex calculation so
860 REM we need to use the real and imaginary arrays for these nodes.
870 :
880 X1=REAL(I,K):Y1=IMAG(I,K):X2=REAL(K,J):Y2=IMAG(K,J)
890 GOSUB 160 :                         REM Complex Number Multiplication
900 :
910 REM Now take the product of the above and divide by Ykk.
920 :
930 X1=REALPROD:Y1=IMAGPROD:X2=REAL(K,K):Y2=IMAG(K,K)
940 GOSUB 260 :                         REM Complex Number Division
950 :
960 REM To finish off the condensation, subtract the real and imaginary parts
970 REM of the quotient from the last stage from the Yij node being processed
980 :
990 REAL(I,J)=REAL(I,J)-REALQUOT
1000 IMAG(I,J)=IMAG(I,J)-IMAGQUOT
1010 :
1020 REM Now simply repeat for all other i,j nodes.
1030 :
1040 NEXT J
1050 NEXT I
1060 :
1070 REM The admittances stored in row k and column k of the matrix have now
1080 REM been dealt with, so we can zero row k and column k
1090 :
1100 FOR I=1 TO MAXNODES
1110 REAL(I,K)=0 : IMAG(I,K)=0
1120 REAL(K,I)=0 : IMAG(K,I)=0
1130 NEXT I
1140 NEXT K :                           REM round again for the next row and column
1150 :
1160 REM Now set up two port network matrices.  The preceeding process will
1170 REM will have removed all rows and columns from the real and imaginary
1180 REM admittance matrices except for row and column 1 and row and column
1190 REM maxnodes.
```

```
1200 :
1210 TWOREAL(1,1) = REAL(1,1) : TWOREAL(1,2) = REAL(1,MAXNODES)
1220 TWOREAL(2,1) = REAL(MAXNODES,1) : TWOREAL(2,2) =
REAL(MAXNODES,MAXNODES)
1230 TWOIMAG(1,1) = IMAG(1,1) : TWOIMAG(1,2) = IMAG(1,MAXNODES)
1240 TWOIMAG(2,1) = IMAG(MAXNODES,1) : TWOIMAG(2,2) =
IMAG(MAXNODES,MAXNODES)
1250 RETURN
1260 :
1270 REM Initialise Array Variables
1280 :
1290 NODENUM = 10 :                     REM maximum number of nodes
1300 DIM R(NODENUM,NODENUM) :           REM Resistance Values
1310 DIM C(NODENUM,NODENUM) :           REM Capacitance Values
1320 DIM L(NODENUM,NODENUM) :           REM Inductance values
1330 DIM REAL(NODENUM,NODENUM) :        REM Read admittance values
1340 DIM IMAG(NODENUM,NODENUM) :        REM Imaginary admittance values
1350 DIM COMP$(40)
1360 DIM TWOIMAG(2,2), TWOREAL(2,2) :   REM Real and imaginary two port
                                        network
1370 RETURN :                           REM end of initialisation
1380 :
1390 REM GET COMPONENT DATA FROM USER
1400 REM this routine sets up the C, L and R arrays with values of components
1410 REM connected between nodes node1 and node2.  Component values are
1420 REM entered in ohms, farads and henrys.  Routine also sets up the
1430 REM maxnodes variable indicating the maximum number of nodes used.
1440 :
1450 REM first, set all arrays to zero
1460 :
1470 FOR I=1 TO NODENUM
1480 FOR J=1 TO NODENUM
1490 R(I,J) = 0
1500 C(I,J) = 0
1510 L(I,J) = 0
1520 NEXT J
1530 NEXT I
1540 :
1550 COMPCOUNT = 1
1560 INPUT "Number of Nodes         ",MAXNODES
1570 :
1580 INPUT "Component Type (R/L/C) or Q to finish",A$
1581 IF A$="Q" OR A$="q" THEN RETURN
1590 INPUT "First Node              ",N1
1600 INPUT "Second Node             ",N2
1610 INPUT "Value                   ",V
1620 :
1630 COMP$(COMPCOUNT) = "Between node "+STR$(N1)+" and "+STR$(N2)+"
"+A$+" of value " + STR$(V)
1640 :
1650 REM Now process each component type
1660 :
1670 IF A$="R" OR A$="r" THEN GOSUB 1750 :  REM Resistor
1680 IF A$="C" OR A$="c" THEN GOSUB 2140 :  REM Capacitor
1690 IF A$="L" OR A$="l" THEN GOSUB 1990 :  REM Inductance
1700 :
1710 COMPCOUNT=COMPCOUNT+1: GOTO 1570
1720 :
1730 RETURN :                           REM end of data input section
1740 :
1750 REM ENTER RESISTOR INTO COMPONENT ARRAYS
1760 :
1770 REM First, check the special case of one node being 0.  Node 0 is
1780 REM assumed by this program to be the ground connection.
1790 :
1800 IF N1=0 THEN R(N2,N2)=R(N2,N2)+1/V : RETURN
1810 IF N2=0 THEN R(N1,N1)=R(N1,N1)+1/V : RETURN
```

```
1820 :
1830 REM Add the admittance of the resistor to the none zero nodes
1840 :
1850 REM now the usual case, where neither node is node 0.  First of all
1860 REM subtract the new admittance value from any already existing
1870 REM between nodes n1 and n2.  Because the matrix is symmetrical we
1880 REM can put the same value in R(n1,n2) and R(n2,n1)
1890 :
1900 R(N1,N2) = R(N1,N2)-1/V : R(N2,N1) = R(N1,N2)
1910 :
1920 REM Now add then new admittance to the admittances already connected to
1930 REM the admittances at nodes n1 and n2.
1940 :
1950 R(N1,N1) = R(N1,N1)+1/V : R(N2,N2) = R(N2,N2)+1/V
1960 :
1970 RETURN
1980 :
1990 REM NOW ADD INDUCTANCE TO INDUCTANCE ADMITTANCE
MATRIX
2000 REM Inductance admittance is a negative value, so although the
2010 REM process is analogous to that described above for resistance, the
2020 REM signs in the arithmetical operations have been changed where
2030 REM appropiate.  Multiplication by 6.28*FREQ occurs at run time.
2040 :
2050 IF N1=0 THEN L(N2,N2)=L(N2,N2)-1/V : RETURN
2060 IF N2=0 THEN L(N1,N1)=L(N1,N1)-1/V : RETURN
2070 :
2080 L(N1,N2) = L(N1,N2)+1/V : L(N2,N1) = L(N1,N2)
2090 :
2100 L(N1,N1) = L(N1,N1)-1/V : L(N2,N2) = L(N2,N2)-1/V
2110 :
2120 RETURN
2130 :
2140 REM NOW ADD CAPACITANCE TO CAPACITANCE ADMITTANCE
MATRIX
2150 REM We can now revert to the arithmetic signs shown in the resistor case
2160 REM as capacititive admittance is a positive value
2165 REM Multiplication by 6.28*FREQ occurs at run time.
2170 :
2180 IF N1=0 THEN C(N2,N2)=C(N2,N2)+V : RETURN
2190 IF N2=0 THEN C(N1,N1)=C(N1,N1)+V : RETURN
2200 :
2210 C(N1,N2) = C(N1,N2)-V : C(N2,N1) = C(N1,N2)
2220 C(N1,N1) = C(N1,N1)+V : C(N2,N2) = C(N2,N2)+V
2230 :
2240 RETURN
2250 :
2260 REM PRINT OUT COMPONENT DATA
2270 REM Simply go through the nodes and print out the component
2280 REM values connected between different nodes
2290 :
2300 FOR I=1 TO COMPCOUNT
2310 PRINT COMP$(I)
2320 NEXT
2330 RETURN
2340 :
2350 REM NOW GET FREQUENCY RANGE AND STEP SIZE
2360 :
2370 INPUT "Start Frequency: (Hz)    ",F1
2380 INPUT "Stop Frequency:  (Hz)    ",F2
2390 INPUT "Step Size:       (Hz)    ",FSTEP
2391 INPUT "Ratio or dB:     (R/D)   ",D$
2400 :
2410 RETURN
2420 :
2430 REM CALCULATE TWO PORT NETWORK BEHAVIOUR AND DISPLAY
THE RESULTS
```

```
2440 REM works out ratio of output to input and displays it along with
2450 REM the frequency in use and the phase difference caused at this
2460 REM frequency.  The frequency is always in Hz.
2470 :
2480 FOR FREQ=F1 TO F2 STEP FSTEP :  REM step through the frequencies of
                                     interest
2490 :
2500 GOSUB 470 :                     REM put component admittances
                                     into matrices
2510 GOSUB 730 :                     REM Condense matrices down to 2
                                     port network
2520 :
2521 REM Now carry out evaluation of two port network as in text by calc-
2522 REM ulating the voltage ratio as a ratio of the input and output
2523 REM impedances of the two port network as described in the text.  We
2524 REM have to use complex number arithmetic here.
2525 :
2530
X1=TWOREAL(2,1):Y1=TWOIMAG(2,1):X2=TWOREAL(2,2):Y2=TWOIMAG(2,2)
2540 GOSUB 260 :                     REM Complex number division
2550 :
2560 REM Now calculate the ratio of out to in by summing real and imaginary
2565 REM parts of the quotient arrived at above - see text for details
2570 :
2580 RATIO = SQR(REALQUOT*REALQUOT+IMAGQUOT*IMAGQUOT)
2581 :
2582 REM Now convert into a dB figure if required:
2583 :
2584 IF D$="D" OR D$="d" THEN RATIO=20*LOG(RATIO)/LOG(10)
2585 REM log function in GWBASIC is natural logs, so convert
2586 REM to base 10.  BBC Micro users can use the LOG function:
2587 REM ratio = LOG(ratio) and Amstrad users can use ratio = LOG10(ratio)
2590 :
2600 REM Now calculate the phase difference
2610 GOSUB 350
2620 :
2621 REM BBC Micro users should replace the following line with something
2622 REM like PRINT FREQ,RATIO,PHASEDIFF.
2623 :
2630 PRINT USING "#######.####";FREQ,RATIO,PHASEDIFF
2640 :
2650 NEXT FREQ :                     REM get next frequency step.
2660 RETURN
```

Listing 3.13 Simple circuit analysis

The program is fairly simple to use. The first thing to do is to draw the circuit to be analysed, numbering each node. The program assumes that the 0V line will be node 0, and that the input will be to node 1 and the output voltage will be read from the highest numbered node. Components are typed in as a single letter followed by the nodes and the component value. Once all components have been entered, enter 'Q' as a component type, then enter the lowest frequency to be examined, the highest and the frequency step to be used. Finally, enter whether you want the losses introduced by the circuit to be expressed as a ratio of output to input voltage or in terms of dB loss. The program will then trundle off and do the sums! To help you test that you have entered the program correctly, try analysing the following circuit: (Figure 3.9). We have already seen how we can work out the rejection frequency for such a network, and a calculation reveals it to be about 15.9 Hz. Let us see if the analysis program comes up with the same figures. Enter the components in as:

C 1 2 0.5E−6
C 2 3 0.5E−6
R 1 3 20000
R 3 4 20000
C 3 0 1E−6
R 2 0 10000

Press RETURN after each entry, and when all the components have been entered enter 'Q' as a component.

Request a frequency range of 1 to 30 Hz with a step of 2, and ask for the ratio to be displayed in decibels. You should find that the loss at 15 and 17 Hz is as follows:

15	− 30.5	88'
17	− 29.7	88'

Try a few other circuits – they all need at least three nodes, and take care in the numbering of nodes to ensure that the input node is always to node 1 and the output node is always the highest numbered one. Try altering the values of components in Figure 3.9, for example, to see what effect there is – you may find something new!

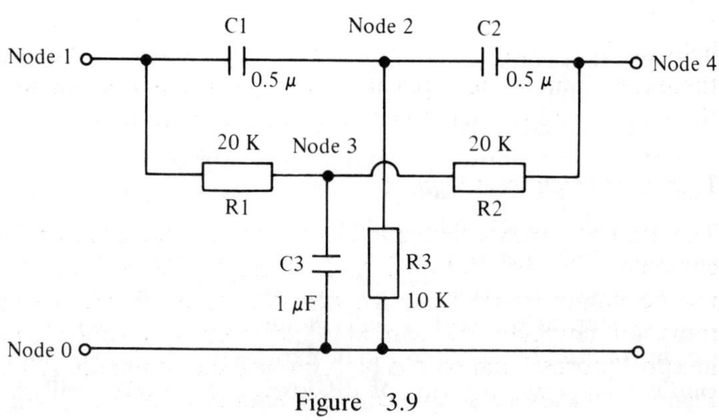

Figure 3.9

Suggested amendments

This program is the most complex we have come across so far, and I could have added several more facilities to it. Some that you may like to consider are:

1 Output to printer for all output data.
2 Draw a graph of the dB loss or ratio and phase difference against frequency.
3 Allow the program to save 'circuits', in the form of node lists, to disc or tape and also allow the program to re-load such circuits at a later date.
4 Allow the input node list to be put together using a word processor.
5 For IBM PC owners especially, allow output to go to a CSV file (see later in this book) so you could plot the output graphs on a spreadsheet graphics package.

As it stands, this program works only for LCR circuits. Any electronic device can be represented by an admittance matrix, although active devices require breaking down in to an *equivalent circuit* for inclusion in this sort of analysis. Such equivalent circuits may include current or voltage sources as well as R, C and L components. This is, however, beyond the scope of this book and so if you are interested I suggest that you read some of the books and articles suggested in the appendices.

Active circuit design

Again, this subject could fill a whole book in itself. In this section I shall briefly examine the ways in which we can use a computer to help us design certain common 'building block' circuits. Again, there is no limit to the applications that you can put the micro to in these areas and so I shall just scratch the surface here.

Transistor amplifier design

The transistor amplifier still has a role in the days of micro computers. In this section I shall examine how we can use the microcomputer to help design a single stage, common emitter transistor amplifier. Design of these circuits is very much an iterative process, and so it is better to use the computer as a tool. Figure 3.10 shows a simple common emitter amplifier. There are

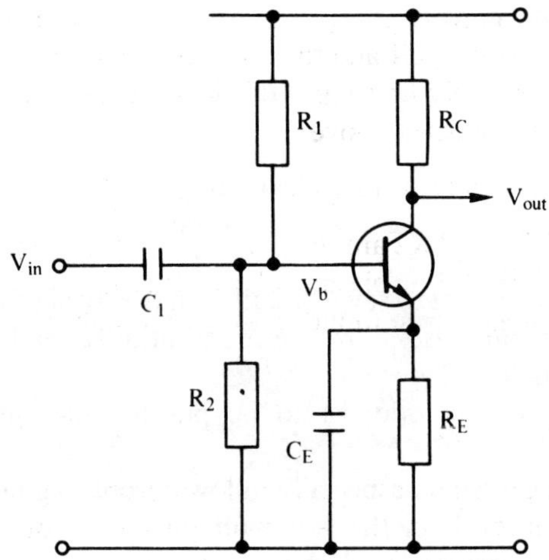

Figure 3.10

two aspects to the design of this circuit; the first is to bias the transistor in such a way that it will work in a stable fashion over a range of temperatures and transistor parameters and the second is to set the transistor up to provide the gain, input and output characteristics that are required. The following equations can all be entered into a BASIC program. The first equation describes the voltage gain of the circuit:

$$Vg = -Rc / Ret$$

where Ret is given by:

$$1 / Ret = 1/Re + 6.28 * F * C$$

where F is the frequency of operation and C the capacitance of the emitter bypass capacitor. In general, the capacitor is chosen so that its reactance is fairly low at the frequency of operation, thus increasing the gain at the desired frequency but maintaining DC characteristics. (see below). It is suggested that Re be set to 1k. The output impedance is given by:

$$Rout = Rc$$

The input resistance of the circuit in the absence of the capacitor C1 is given by:

$$1/Rinput = 1/R1 + 1/R2 + 1/(hfe*Re)$$

where hfe is the current gain parameter of the transistor. When we take C1 into account, C1 and the input resistance form a high pass filter, thus effectively limiting the low frequency response of the amplifier to frequencies above about:

Flow = 1 / (6.28 * Rinput * C1)

The values of R1 and R2 are thus selected with the input resistance in mind as well as the biasing of the transistor. The details of transistor biasing can be found in any text book.

Transistor parameters

A further application for computer programs in the design of transistor circuits is in the approximate design of transistor h-amplifiers using the commonly available h-parameters in specification sheets which are for common emitter circuits. The equations for four common amplifier design requirements are:

Common base

Voltage gain = (hfe * RL) / hie
Input resistance = hie / (1+hfe)
Output resistance = (1+hfe) / hoe
Current gain = − hfe / (1+hfe)

Common emitter

Voltage gain = (−hfe * RL) / hie
Input resistance = hie
Output resistance = 1 / hoe
Current gain = hfe

Common collector

Voltage gain = 1
Input resistance = hie + (1+hfe)*RL
Output resistance = (hie + RI) / (1 + hfe)

See Figure 3.11 for details of these circuit configurations. Multi-stage amplifiers can be viewed in a similar way by looking at each stage and the analysing the coupling components using a program like the circuit analysis program listed above.

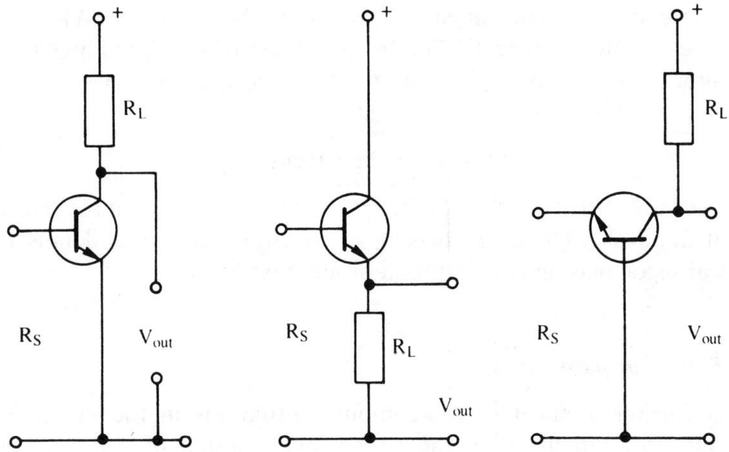

Figure 3.11

Oscillator circuits

Simple computer programs can make oscillator design easier as well. The following equations will give the frequency of oscillation for three common LC oscillator designs shown in Figure 3.12 and they can easily be turned into function calls.

FET oscillator

F = 1 / (6.28 * SQR(L*C))

Colpitts oscillator

F = 0.159 * SQR((C1 + C2) / (L * C1 * C2))

Hartley oscillator

F = 1 / 6.28 * SQR((L1+L2)*C1)

Power supply calculations

The next category of circuits that I want to briefly look at are those associated with power supply designs. Again, rather than producing a computer program listing I shall give some design equations for a couple of power supply topics. The first is a simple full wave rectifier circuit, as shown in Figure 3.13a.

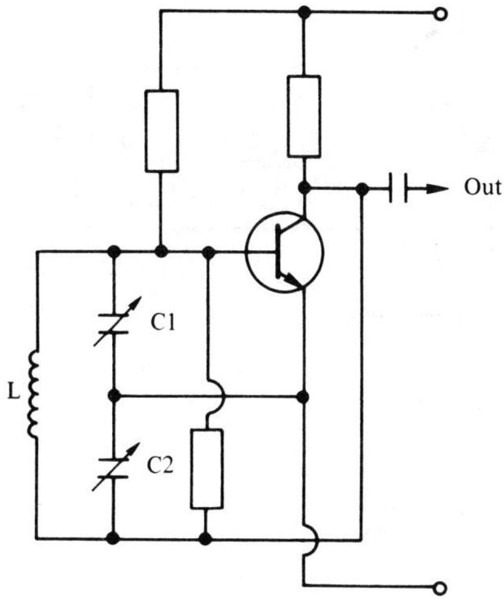

Colpitts

(a)

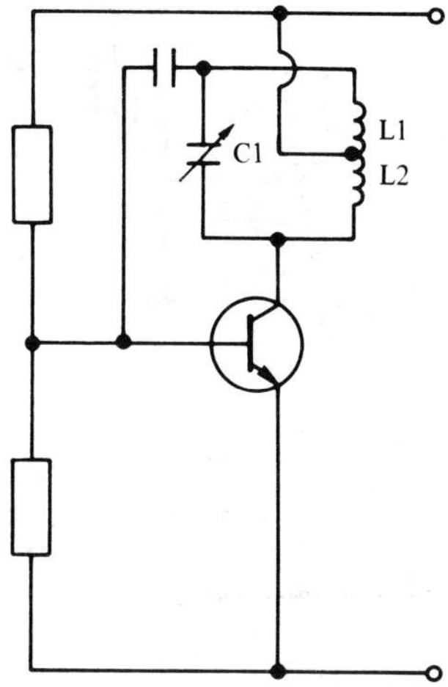

Hartley

(b)

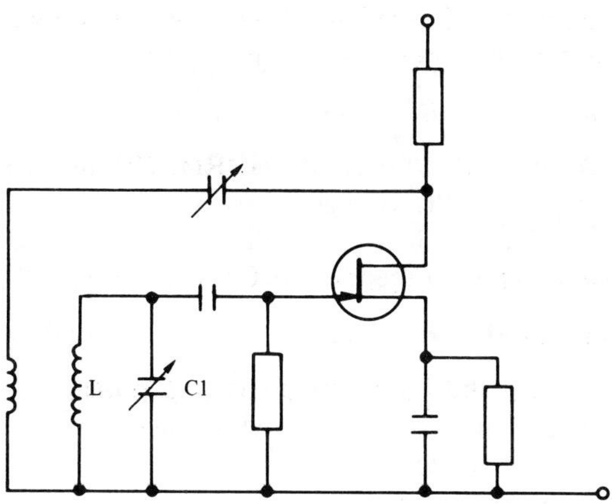

Reinartz

(c)

Figure 3.12

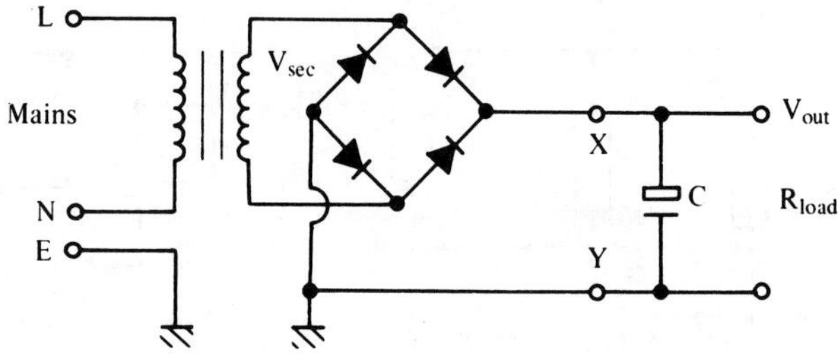

(a)

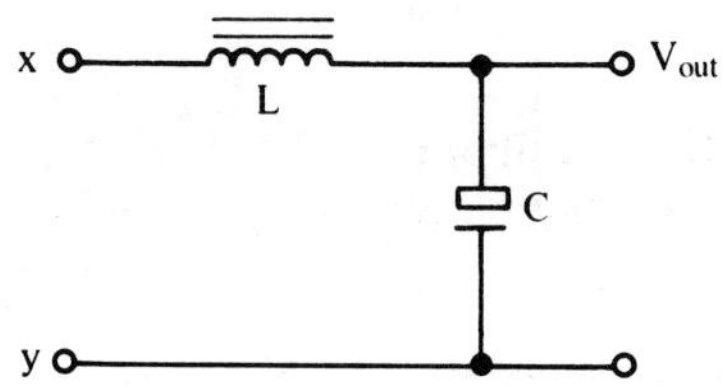

(b)

Figure 3.13

$$Vsec = (Vout + 1.4) / 1.41$$
$$C = Iload / Ripple$$

where Iload is the load current and Ripple is the desired ripple voltage and Vsec is the voltage rating of the transformer secondary. If we replace the capacitor with the inductance arrangement shown in Figure 3.13b then:

$$Vout = 0.9^*Vsec - I^*(Rchoke + Rsecond) - 1.4$$

where Rchoke is the DC resistance of the choke and Rsecond is the resistance of the secondary of the transformer plus the forward resistance of two diodes. Finally:

$$L = (Rsec + Rload) / (18.84 * F)$$

where F is the frequency of ripple on the rectified DC input to the choke. Figure 3.14 shows a simple zener diode stabiliser arrangement, and the equations for its design are:

$$Rs = (Vmin - Vout) / (1.1 * Iload)$$

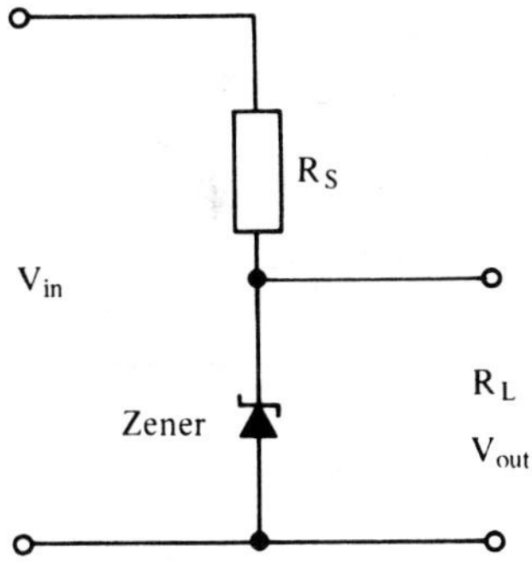

Figure 3.14

where Vmin is the minimum input voltage, Vout the zener voltage, which will set the output voltage, and Iload is the current drawn by the load.

PowerDis = (((Vmax − Vout)/Rs)−Iloadmin) * Vout

where Powerdis is the power dissipated by the diode, Vmax is the maximum input voltage to the stabiliser, and Iloadmin is the minimum load current to be drawn.

Operational amplifiers

Finally, you might like to write some programs for the design of simple operational amplifier circuits. The equations for the circuits shown in Figure 3.15 are as follows:

Inverting amplifier (Figure 3.15a)

Vout / Vin = −(R2 / R1)
R3 = (R1 + R2)/(R1 * R2)

Non-inverting amplifier (Figure 3.15b)

Vout / Vin = (R2 + R3) / R3
R1 = (R2 * R3) / (R2 + R3)

Differential amplifier (Figure 3.15c)

Vout = − (R3 / R1) * (Vin1 − Vin2)

where Rx = R1 = R2 and Ry = R3 = R4.

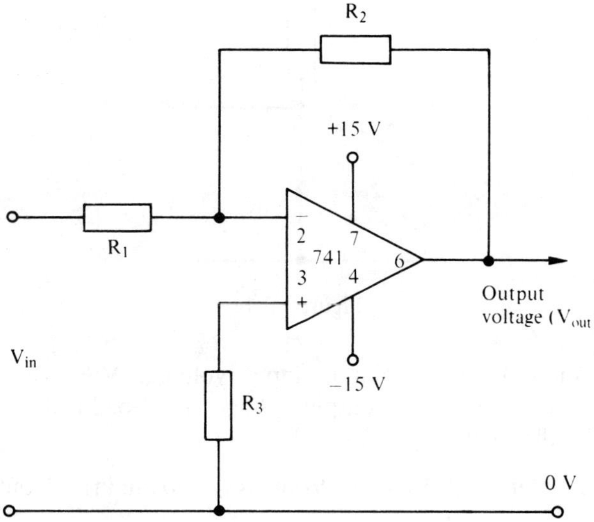

Inverting amplifier

(a)

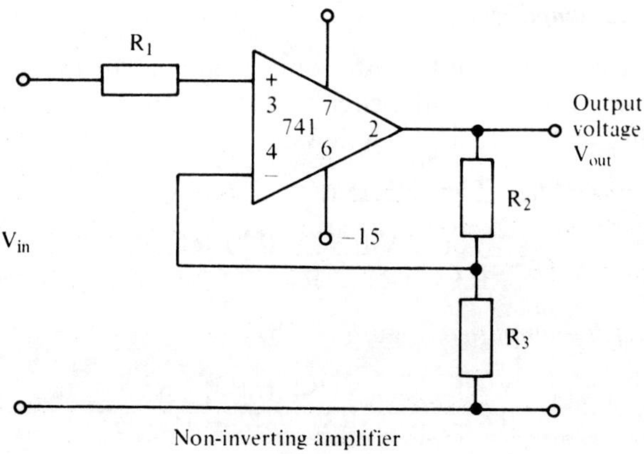

Non-inverting amplifier

(b)

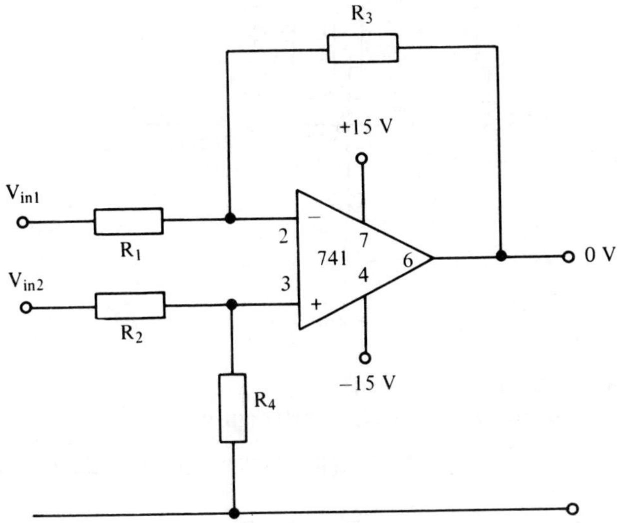

Differential amplifier

(c)

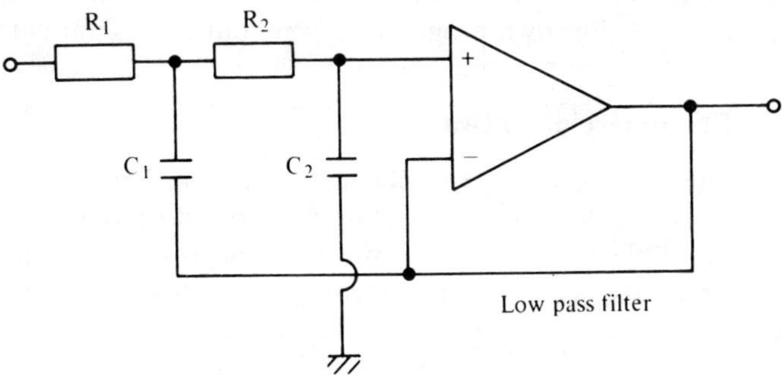

Low pass filter

(d)

Figure 3.15 *continued*

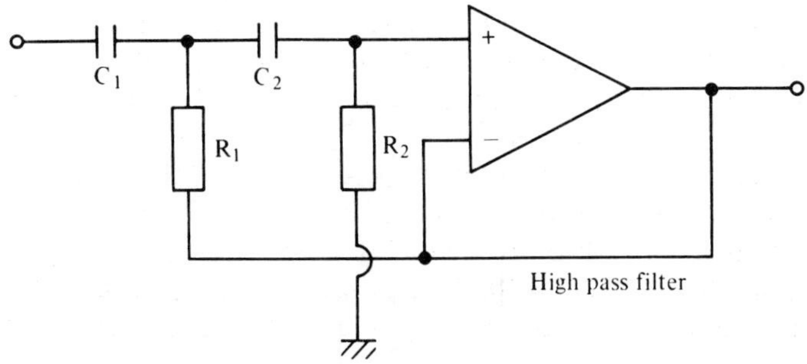

(e)

Figure 3.15 – *continued*

Low pass filter (Figure 3.15d)
Cut-off point of the low pass filter (Figure 3.15) is:

F = 1 / (6.28 * SQR(R1*R2) * SQR(C1*C2))

High pass filter (Figure 3.15e)
Cut-off point of the high pass filter (Figure 3.18) is:

F = 1 / (6.28 * SQR(R1*R2) * SQR(C1*C2))

That completes this survey of simple design techniques using microcomputers. Armed with the above equations and routines you can build your own programs to suit your own requirements.

Use of commercial software

Commercial packages are available to carry out circuit analysis techniques and these will be most useful if you do a lot of this sort of work. Other commercial software that you might like to consider are the spreadsheets and commercial statistics and numerical analysis packages. Packages that you might like to look at are:

Spreadsheets

Spreadsheet programs allow calculations to be done quickly and repeatedly by setting up equations in a computer program that simulates an accountant's spreadsheet. Many spreadsheets include statistical and scientific functions, and many of the formulae mentioned in this chapter could be set up and calculated in a spreadsheet. Many PC spreadsheets also offer the opportunity to draw graphs of data and to plot these graphs on a printer.

Popular PC spreadsheets are SuperCalc 3,4 and 5, Lotus 1–2–3 and the various low cost systems such as VP-Planner or PC-Calc. Any of these would be worth looking at if you intend doing a lot of calculation work. For BBC Micro users, the range is less; Intersheet and Viewsheet are the most common spreadsheets here.

Numerical or statistical packages

Software packages exist to do such things as solve differential equations and carry out other complex mathematical and statistical functions. These are either stand alone packages into which data is typed or are toolboxes which add facilities to existing languages or packages. Most of these packages are for the IBM PC, but several exist for the BBC Micro as well.

Circuit design and analysis

Complex circuit design software requires considerable amounts of memory and so the vast majority of packages that are available tend to be for the IBM PC or above machines, although at least one, produced by Pineapple, has been made available on the BBC Micro.

Details of suppliers of software will be given in the appendices.

FOUR

Software for aerial design and propagation

In this Chapter I want to examine the basic principles behind using computers for designing aerials and for helping to predict propagation conditions. It should be noted, however, that there is not a computer program written that can accurately predict what conditions will be like on a particular day – it is a bit like weather forecasting – we get it partially right part of the time! Similarly, some aerials, which should not work at all if you go by the rules, are good performers. It would appear, therefore, that in the field of aerials and propagation the rules are guidelines only.

Design of aerials

Let us start off with the simplest of all aerials – the dipole antenna. The half wave dipole has a total length in metres of approximately:

143/frequency in MHz

The reason why it is not precisely 150/frequency in MHz is due to 'end effects' which affect the electrical characteristics of the aerial at frequencies in the short wave regions of the spectrum. At VHF, these end effects can be ignored and we can go back to using 150/frequency in MHz. The aerial is then connected to a 75Ω coaxial feeder by cutting it at the centre and connecting one arm of the dipole to the feeder cable core and one arm to the feeder cable sheath. For a simple dipole like this, we can also calculate the approximate voltage that we will obtain at the centre of the dipole into the 75Ω feeder for a given signal strength at the receiving aerial or even for a given power at the transmitter (assuming the dipole is positioned such that it will receive maximum signal strength from the transmitter). The equations for this are as follows:

Knowing the signal strength at the aerial

$$\text{Centre EMF} = ((\text{field strength} \times (\text{wavelength}/3.14))/2$$

where the centre EMF is in volts, the field strength in V/m and the wavelength in metres.

Knowing the transmitted power

$$\text{PRD} = \frac{\text{TP} \times \text{gaint} \times 1.64 \times \text{wavelength} \times \text{wavelength}}{12.56 \times \text{distance} \times 12.56 \times \text{distance}}$$

where PRD is the power at the receiving dipole, TP the transmitter power, gaint the relative gain of the transmitting aerial, wavelength the wavelength of the signal in metres and distance the distance between the aerials. The received power can be converted into a voltage by:

$$\text{Centre EMF} = \text{SQRT}(\text{PRD} \times \text{impedance})$$

where impedance the aerial impedance – in this case, 75Ω. Note that these calculations are truly valid only for the simple cases where there are no ionospheric effects. Listing 4.1 shows a simple program incorporating these features.

```
10 REM Simple Dipole Aerial calculations
20 REM Joe Pritchard
30 :
40 GOSUB 1000 : REM print out options
50 IF OPT=1 THEN GOSUB 2000
60 IF OPT=2 THEN GOSUB 3000
70 IF OPT=3 THEN GOSUB 4000
80 GOTO 40
90 :
1000 REM print out the options
1010 CLS
1020 PRINT:PRINT:PRINT
1030 PRINT "1 - Calculate length of dipole"
1040 PRINT "2 - Voltage at centre of dipole (Field Strength Known)"
1050 PRINT "3 - Voltage at Centre of dipole (Received Power)"
1060 PRINT:PRINT
1070 INPUT "Please enter your choice: ",OPT
1080 RETURN
1090 :
2000 REM calculate length of dipole. Arbitrarily select 50MHz as the
2010 REM break point between HF and VHF signals
2020 CLS
2030 PRINT:PRINT:PRINT
2040 INPUT "What is the frequency, in MHz? ",F
```

```
2050 FACTOR=143
2060 :
2065 REM decide if factor can be set to 150 rather than 143
2066 :
2070 IF F>=5E+07 THEN FACTOR = 150
2075 :
2080 PRINT "Dipole Length is ";FACTOR/F;" metres"
2085 INPUT "Press RETURN to go on",A$
2090 RETURN
2100 :
3000 REM Voltage at centre of dipole when the field strength is known
3001 :
3006 CLS
3010 PRINT:PRINT:PRINT
3020 INPUT "Frequency of signal in Hertz ",F
3030 INPUT "Received Field Strength (V/m) ",S
3040 PRINT:PRINT "Voltage at dipole centre is: ";S*((3E+08/F)/3.1415)/2;" Volts"
3050 INPUT "Press RETURN to go on",A$
3060 RETURN
3070 :
4000 REM Calculation of centre voltage when transmitter details are known
4010 :
4020 CLS
4030 PRINT:PRINT:PRINT
4040 INPUT "Transmitter Power: ",TP
4050 INPUT "Transmitting Aerial Gain: ",TG
4060 INPUT "Distance in km: ",DIST
4070 INPUT "Frequency in Hz: ",F
4080 :
4090 DIST = DIST*1000 : REM distance now in metres
4100 W=3E+08/F : REM W IS WAVELENGTH OF SIGNAL
4110 RECP = (TP*TG*1.64*W*W)/(157.75*DIST*DIST)
4120 PRINT:PRINT
4130 PRINT "Received power is ";RECP;" Watts"
4140 PRINT "Centre Voltage is ";SQR(RECP*70);" Volts"
4150 PRINT
4160 INPUT "Press RETURN to go on",A$
4170 RETURN
```

Listing 4.1

The simple Yagi

The Yagi antenna is the simplest directional aerial that we can use and is also fairly easy to design using a program to calculate the length of the different elements and the separation of the elements. Listing 4.2 shows a program that designs a simple three element Yagi, as shown in Figure 4.1. On running the program, it will ask for various parameters and then print out the dimensions for the aerial.

```
10 REM Simple 3 element Yagi Calculations based on published
20 REM Algorithms. These can be found in most Amateur Radio
30 REM Text Books.
40 :
50 cls
60 Input "Type in Frequency in Hertz ",F
70 :
```

```
80 REM Now calculate the wavelength
90 :
100 W = 3E8 / F
110 print "Director is  ";0.95*W/2;" metres long"
120 print "Dipole is    ";w/2;" metres long"
130 print "Reflector is ";1.05*W/2;" metres long"
140 :
150 rem now calculate element separations
160 :
170 print "Director and Dipole are  ";0.1*W;" metres apart"
180 print "Reflector and Dipole are ";0.15*W;" metres apart"
190 end
```

Listing 4.2

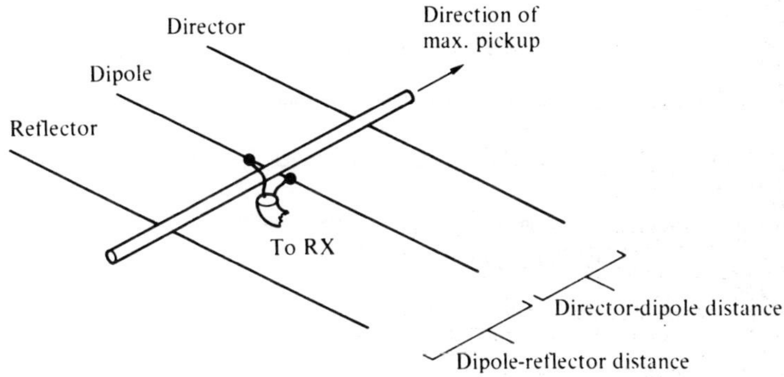

Figure 4.1

ERP calculations

One important calculation for transmitting amateurs is to calculate the effective radiated power (ERP) for their radio station. This is the RF power that gets squirted out from the aerial in a particular direction, and is dependent upon the directional gain of the aerial, the power output of the transmitter and any losses incurred in the feeder between the aerial and the radio transmitter. Listing 4.3 gives a program that calculates the approximate ERP for a transmitter – feeder – aerial system after prompting the operator for the various parameters. It assumes that the system is properly matched, i.e., the impedances of the transmitter, feeder and aerial are the same. Different aerials and feeder types can be added to the lists included in the program, and the loss and gain factors added to the DATA statements as documented in the REM statements.

Possible additions to this program could include a means of bringing in other loss making factors, such as impedance mismatches between the feeder and aerial, but that is rather beyond the scope of this book.

```
10 REM ERP Calculator. The gains for aerials are in dB and are best
20 REM theoretical figures. It is not likely that your aerials will
30 REM give this perfromance. Cable losses are in db per 1m lengths
40 :
50 CLS
60 :
70 REM first of all select the aerial type.
80 :
90 GOSUB 1000
100 :
110 REM then select the cable type and length.
120 :
130 GOSUB 2000
140 :
150 REM Now loop around until user enters a 0 transmitter output power.
160 :
170 PRINT:PRINT:PRINT
180 INPUT "Transmitter Output Power (0 to finish) ",TXPOWER
190 IF TXPOWER=0 THEN END
200 PRINT:PRINT
210 PRINT "Total System Directional Gain is ";GAIN+LOSS;" dB"
220 PRINT "ERP is  ";
230 PRINT (10^((GAIN-LOSS)/10))*TXPOWER;"  Watts"
240 PRINT "EIRP is ";
250 PRINT (10^((GAIN-LOSS+2)/10))*TXPOWER;"  Watts"
260 GOTO 170
270 :
1000 REM Enter an aerial type
1010 RESTORE 1800
1020 READ NUM
1030 :
1040 REM num is the number of entries in the table. Aerial gains are
1050 REM relative to a half-wave dipole, which has a gain in this case of
1060 REM 0dB. Gains quoted against an isotropic radiator will need 2dB
1070 REM taking off before inclusion in this table.
1080 :
1085 CLS
1090 FOR I=1 TO NUM
1100 READ A$,GAIN
1110 PRINT I;" - ";A$
1120 NEXT I
1130 RESTORE 1810
1140 PRINT:PRINT
1150 INPUT "Enter an aerial ",AERIAL
1160 FOR I=1 TO AERIAL
1170 READ A$,GAIN
1180 NEXT
1185 RETURN
1190 :
1200 REM 'gain' now holds the db gain of the selected aerial
1210 :
1800 DATA 5
1810 DATA "2 Element Yagi (Dipole and Director)",5
1820 DATA "3 Element Yagi ",7
1830 DATA "4 Element Yagi ",8
1840 DATA "HB9CV Aerial ",6
1850 DATA "Quarter Wave Whip ",-6
1900 :
```

```
2000 REM Enter a cable type, length and frequency of operation
2010 REM and return the cable losses in the variable loss
2020 :
2030 CLS
2040 RESTORE 2800
2050 READ NUM
2060 RESTORE 2810
2070 FOR I=1 TO NUM
2080 READ A$,LO1,LO10,LO100,LO1000
2090 PRINT I;" - ";A$
2100 NEXT I
2110 PRINT:PRINT:
2120 INPUT "Select Cable Type: ",CAB
2130 INPUT "Length of cable, in metres ",L
2140 INPUT "Closest Frequency (1,10,100,1000 MHz) ",F
2150 RESTORE 2810
2160 FOR I=1 TO CAB
2170 READ A$,LO1,LO10,LO100,LO1000
2180 NEXT I
2190 IF F=1 THEN LOSS=LO1*L
2200 IF F=10 THEN LOSS=LO10*L
2210 IF F=100 THEN LOSS=LO100*L
2220 IF F=1000 THEN LOSS=LO1000*L
2230 RETURN
2800 DATA 2
2810 DATA "RG58/U ",0.01,0.04,0.15,0.57
2820 DATA "RG59A/U",0.01,0.036,0.11,0.39
^Z
```

Listing 4.3

There are many other aerial types that are easily designed with the aid of simple computer programs – indeed, the calculations involved are usually so straight forward that a pocket calculator could be used to do the work rather than a computer. So, rather than look at these other aerial designs I shall move on to examine a slightly more complicated area that offers the potential for some experimentation as well as programming – propagation prediction.

Propagation prediction

In Chapter 1 we saw how radio waves travel around the world by virtue of the ionosphere, an ionised area of the upper atmosphere which has the ability to refract radio waves back to earth at distances several thousand kilometres from the transmitting station. There are several rules of thumb about propagation; for example, we can say at night the lower frequencies are better for long distance radio reception than the higher ones, and that in years with a high sunspot count the higher frequencies will give better results than in years with a low sunspot count. SWLs or amateurs with even a few months of listening or transmitting experience will soon start to establish patterns of propagation, and over the years listeners soon get a 'gut feeling' about what propagation will be like on a certain frequency at a certain time. Of course, oddities do occur, but in general there are trends of behaviour in propagation and, to a degree, computers can be used to give us some ideas as to what conditions will be like on certain frequencies at certain times of the day. In this section I shall demonstrate the various ways in which this can be done.

Methods of propagation prediction

There are two methods by which the propagation of radio signals over a particular path can be estimated. These are *analytic* approaches and *heuristic* approaches.

Analytic method

The analytic method of predicting propagation requires that a mathematical model of the ionosphere be set up, taking into account things like time of day, sunspot count and other factors likely to affect radio wave propagation. This model then accepts certain parameters from the user, like the location of both ends of the path, time and sunspot count and provides an output that gives the following parameters for the path at that time:

Highest probable frequency
The highest probable frequency (HPF) is the frequency that is likely to be the highest that will allow reliable communications between the two specified points.

Maximum usable frequency
The maximum usable frequency (MUF) is the highest frequency that can be used on this path without the radio signal shooting off into space. Amateurs frequently use MUF paths for DX working, but for commercial use the MUF is not much good as in reality the ionosphere will be sufficiently disturbed for a signal at the MUF to be bent back to earth only part of the time.

Lowest usable frequency
The lowest usable frequency (LUF) is the lowest frequency that is able to penetrate the E layer of the ionosphere without being absorbed.

```
10 REM MINIMUF - 3 program based on the listing published by Levine, Rose
20 REM and Martin in the IEE proceedings on Antennas and Propagation in
30 REM 1978. Program modified by Joe Pritchard, G1UQW
40 :
50 GOSUB 90 : REM get input data from user
60 GOSUB 510 : REM print out the table of MUFs
70 END
80 :
90 REM This subroutine inputs the lattitude and longitudes from the
100 REM user of the two stations involved, month and sunspot count
110 :
120 CLS
130 INPUT "Lattitude and Longitude of transmitter (N,E)",L1,W1
140 INPUT "Lattitude and Longitude of receiver (N,E)",L2,W2
150 INPUT "Month: (1-12) ",M0
160 INPUT "Sunspot Count ",S0
170 :
180 REM Algorithm uses angles in radians, so convert the lattitudes and
190 REM longitudes into radians. NOTE that lattitude is in range -90 to 90
200 REM and longitude is in range 0 to 360 East.
210 :
220 W1=360-W1 : W2=360-W2
230 L1 = L1*3.14/180 : W1 = W1*3.14 / 180
240 L2 = L2*3.14/180 : W2 = W2*3.14 / 180
250 :
260 REM now calculate the number of F2 'hops' there will be between the
270 REM transmitter and receiver. Firat thing to do is to calculate the
280 REM path length in terms of radians.
290 :
300 H1=SIN(L1)*SIN(L2)+COS(L1)*COS(L2)*COS(W2-W1)
310 G1=ATN(SQR(1-H1*H1)/H1)+1.571*(1-SGN(H1))
320 :
330 REM g1 now holds path length
340 :
350 H0=1.59*G1
360 IF H0<1 THEN H0=1
370 :
380 REM h0 now holds number of F2 hops that the signal makes
390 :
400 REM Now set up a few constants that are used in the algorithm to
410 REM set the way in which various factors, such as sunspot count,
420 REM have on the MUF
430 :
440 SSPOTFAC = 250
450 P0=8
460 TAU0=9.7
470 A0=6
480 A1=58
490 :
500 RETURN
510 REM Calculate the MUF for a series of times through the day
520 REM using inputted data. Calculate for once every 4 hours.
530 :
540 FOR RECTIME=0 TO 24 STEP 4
550 MUF=999 : REM set MUF to a silly value
560 :
570 REM first, get the first control point and calculate the MUF at that
580 REM that point
590 :
600 CONTROL=1-.5/H0
610 GOSUB 760 : REM do the minimuf calculation
620 IF TEMPF<MUF THEN MUF=TEMPF
630 :
640 REM Now calculate the MUF at the second control point
```

```
650 :
660 CONTROL=1-CONTROL
670 GOSUB 760 : REM do the minimuf calculation
680 IF TEMPF < MUF THEN MUF=TEMPF
690 :
700 REM now we can print the time, MUF and HPF
710 :
720 PRINT RECTIME;" hrs      MUF is ";TAB(22);INT(MUF);" MHz   HPF is ";INT(1.27*MUF)
730 :
740 NEXT RECTIME : REM go back for next time
750 :
760 REM MINIMUF routine.  This routine does the calculations.  It accepts
770 REM as parameters:
780 REM l1,w1 are lat. and long. of transmitter in rads
790 REM l2,w2 are lat. and long. of receiver in rads.
800 REM rectime is time in hours (0 to 24)
810 REM m0 is the month
820 REM h1 is path length in radlans
830 REM control is proportion of path length at which control point occurs
840 REM s0 is sunspot count
850 :
860 REM first, calculate latitude of the control point
870 :
880 L0=SIN(G1*(1-CONTROL))*SIN(L1)+SIN(CONTROL*G1)*SIN(L2)
890 L0=L0/SIN(G1)
900 L0=ATN(L0/SQR(1-L0*L0))
910 :
920 REM now calculate longitude of the control point
930 :
940 W0=COS(L1)*COS(W1)*SIN(G1*(1-CONTROL))
950 W0=W0+COS(L2)*COS(W2)*SIN(G1*CONTROL)
960 W0=W0/(COS(L0)*SIN(G1))
970 W3=.7855*(1-SGN(3.14-W1-W2))
980 W3=W3*(1+SGN(1.57-ABS(W1-W2)))
990 W0=ATN(SQR(1-W0*W0)/W0)+W3
1000 :
1010 H9=SIN(L1)*SIN(L0)+COS(L1)*COS(L0)*COS(W0-W1)
1020 H9=ABS(ATN(SQR(1-H9*H9)/H9))
1030 IF ABS(H9-G1*CONTROL)>=.01 THEN W0=6.28-W0
1040 :
1050 REM Now a series of calculations to work out noon at the point being
1060 REM being considered, sunrise and sunset times
1070 REM First equation puts local noon into 'noontime' for 15th day of
1080 REM month
1090 :
1100 TEMP1=.0172*(10+(M0-1)*30.4+15)
1110 TEMP2=.409*COS(TEMP1)
1120 NOONTIME=3.82*W0+12+.13*(SIN(TEMP1)+1.2*SIN(2*TEMP1))
1130 NOONTIME=NOONTIME MOD 24
1140 DURATION=0
1150 G0=0
1160 :
1170 REM Next line checks to see if there is actually any sunlight
1180 REM at this site at this time and place
1190 REM if there isn't, don't check day / night but just return
1200 :
1210 IF COS(L0+TEMP2)<=-.26 THEN GOSUB 1780: GOSUB 1890: RETURN
1220 :
1230 REM Now calculate the duration of sunlight at this place
1240 :
1250 DURATION=(-.26+SIN(TEMP2)*SIN(L0))/(COS(TEMP2)*COS(L0))
1260 DURATION=12-ATN(DURATION/SQR(ABS(1-DURATION*DURATION)))*7.6
1270 :
```

```
1280 REM now calculate the sunrise and sunset times for this place
1290 :
1300 SUNRISE=(NOONTIME-DURATION/2) MOD 24
1310 SUNSET=(NOONTIME+DURATION/2) MOD 24
1320 :
1330 REM Now calculate the relaxation time for this location, and force
1340 REM minimum value to avoid the risk of overflow errors from BASIC
1350 REM although extra precaustions are taken in the program
1360 :
1370 C0=ABS(COS(L0+TEMP2))
1380 RELAXTIME=TAU0*C0^P0
1390 IF RELAXTIME<.1 THEN RELAXTIME=.1
1400 :
1410 REM Now go and see what time of day we're using, and whether we
1420 REM need to use the calculations for day or night time
1430 :
1440 IF SUNSET<SUNRISE THEN GOTO 1470
1450 IF (RECTIME-SUNRISE)*(SUNSET-RECTIME)>0 THEN GOTO 1510
1460 GOTO 1690
1470 IF (RECTIME-SUNSET)*(SUNRISE-RECTIME)>0 THEN GOTO 1690
1480 :
1490 REM Next section of code calculates COSX - the cosine of the solar zenith angle
1491 REM for a specific point and time. This factor is proportional to
1492 REM the amount of solar radiation received at this point and is the
1493 REM factor used to estimate MUF. Adjustments are then made to include location,
1494 REM sunspots, etc.
1500 :
1510 T6=RECTIME+12*(1+SGN(SUNRISE-RECTIME))*SGN(ABS(SUNRISE-RECTIME))
1520 G9=3.14*(T6-SUNRISE)/DURATION
1530 G8=3.14*RELAXTIME/DURATION
1540 TPOWER=(SUNRISE-T6)/RELAXTIME
1541 :
1542 REM There are  two possible values for COSX that can be obtained; we
1543 REM the higher of the two. G0 will hold one, G3 the other.
1544 :
1550 IF ABS(TPOWER)>85 THEN TPOWER=85*SGN(TPOWER)
1560 G0=C0*(SIN(G9)+G8*(2.718^(TPOWER)-COS(G9)))
1570 G0=G0/(1+G8*G8)
1580 TPOWER=(-DURATION/RELAXTIME)
1590 IF ABS(TPOWER)>84 THEN TPOWER=SGN(TPOWER)*84
1600 G3=C0*(G8*(2.718^(TPOWER+1)))*  2.718^((DURATION-24)/2)/(1+G8*G8)
1602 :
1603 REM Now decide which of the two figures calculated is to be used for
1604 REM MUF calculations. The higher of the two is used.
1605 :
1610 IF G0<G3 THEN G0=G3
1615 :
1616  REM G0 holds the COSX value to be converted to a MUF
1620 :
1630 GOSUB 1780
1640 GOSUB 1890
1650 RETURN
1660 :
1670 REM Next piece of code calculates COSX at night time
1680 :
1690 T6=RECTIME+12*(1+SGN(SUNSET-RECTIME))*SGN(ABS(SUNSET-RECTIME))
1700 G8=3.14*RELAXTIME/DURATION
1710 TPOWER=(-DURATION/RELAXTIME)
1715 :
1716 REM next line avoids possible overflows
1717 :
1720 IF ABS(TPOWER)>84 THEN TPOWER=SGN(TPOWER)*84
1730 G0=C0*(G8*(2.718^(TPOWER+1)))*  2.718^((SUNSET-T6)/2)/(1+G8*G8)
```

```
1734 :
1735 REM G0 now holds COSX value to be converted into an MUF figure, so do it
1736 :
1740 GOSUB 1780
1750 GOSUB 1890
1760 RETURN
1770 :
1780 REM This subroutine sets the 'fudge' factor to bring the MUF calcuklated
1790 REM into line with reality!
1800 :
1810 MUFFUDGE=3.5
1820 IF 2.5*G1*CONTROL > 1.57 THEN RETURN
1830 MUFFUDGE=SIN(2.5*G1*CONTROL)
1840 MUFFUDGE=1+2.5*MUFFUDGE*(MUFFUDGE^1.5)
1850 RETURN
1860 :
1870 REM Next line introduces sunspots into the equation
1880 :
1890 G2=(1+S0/SSPOTFAC)*MUFFUDGE*SQR(A0+A1*SQR(G0))
1900 :
1910 REM This next factor introduces effects of thickening of the
1920 REM F2 layer that occurs under 'midnight sun' conditions
1925 REM and also adjusts the MUF to take geographical considerations
1926 REM into account
1930 :
1940 G2=G2*(1-.1*(2.718^((DURATION-24)/3)))
1950 :
1960 G2=G2*(1+(1-SGN(L1)*SGN(L2))*.1)
1970 G2=G2*(1-.1*(1+SGN(ABS(SIN(L0))-COS(L0))))
1971 :
1972 REM Returns a MUF value in TEMPF in MHz
1980 TEMPF=G2
1990 RETURN
```

Listing 4.4

Listing 4.4 is a version of a system called MINIMUF developed by Levine, Rose and Martin and published originally in *IEE Conference Publication 169; Antennas and Propagation*. This program does not calculate the LUF, but for those of you who are interested, the RSGB *Amateur Radio Software* does feature a version of MINIMUF that includes LUF calculations. To use the program, simply enter the parameters as requested and the program will evaluate the MUF and approximate the HPF for the time and path requested. You will note that certain parameters are commented upon in the program listing, for example, the trans-equatorial correction factor, as being estimates. Indeed, these are factors introduced to allow for certain effects noted in the real world but not modelled in the MINIMUF equations – for example, in this case the MUF on transequatorial paths is higher than would be expected from the calculations and so a factor is introduced to put this right. The control points referred to, by the way, are used in all methods of MUF calculation, not just MINIMUF. They are required because of the length of a single 'hop' from ground to F2 layer to ground. If the distance between stations is less than 4000 km, then we say that there is a control point at a point half way between the two stations and the MUF calculated is that for the single hop between station 1, the control point and station 2. If the stations are separated by more than 4000 km, then two control points are used, located 2000 km from each of the two stations. The MUF is then taken as the lowest of the two MUFs calculated for these two hops.

This approach gives a reasonable approximation to propagation, although there are differences between the results obtained and those obtained by experiments using special radar systems called ionospheric sounders. The big advantage of analytic systems like this is that we do not have to prime the system with any data from the real world, unlike prediction systems that use the heuristic approach.

Heuristic method

We have already mentioned that propagation prediction can be as much of an art as a science, with 'gut feelings' often giving reasonable indications of how propagation will be over a certain path at a particular time and season. It is possible to have a heuristic approach to propagation forecasting, based upon the fact that if we have a large quantity of data available, we can analyse this data, look for trends, and then use that data to predict future propagation. There is no analysis involved, and no complex mathematical model, but accurate results are only possible with a large database of past MUFs to work on. Alternatively, we could set up a series of rules for a simple expert system, along the lines of:

IF SunspotCount = High and Time > Noon
then MUF is likely to be high

Again, the more rules we have, the more accurate the predictions of the system would be. Such a set of rules can easily be coded in a BASIC program as a set of IF . . . THEN statements, the user typing in answers to prompts and then getting a result from the program based on these rules. This sort of program, though simple (if tedious) to write, will only reflect the goodness of the rule set fed into it.

Listing 4.5 shows a very simple system for giving ideas about what frequency band you should try listening on at a particular time of

```
10 REM Very simple rule based propagation predictor for the Europe
20 REM to North America path based on simple IF...THEN rules.
30 REM Joe Pritchrard, 1989
40 :
50 CLS
55 PRINT:PRINT
56 PRINT "Times of day are: Morning (includes dawn)   Afternoon (includes noon)"
57 PRINT "                  Evening (includes dusk)   Night"
58 PRINT
60 INPUT "Time of day (MAEN) ",T$
70 INPUT "Sunspots ([H]igh / [L]ow) ",S$
80 PRINT:PRINT
90 PRINT "Seasons are:  [A]utumn/Spring    [S]ummer    [W]inter"
100 PRINT
110 INPUT "Season (ASW) ",Y$
120 :
130 REM all data in so now apply the rules that we've defined
140 REM These rules could easily be refined to give better results
150 REM but they will serve to give you the main idea
160 :
170 REM First of all, set the band variables to "Unlikely"
180 :
190 BAND18$="Unlikely"
200 BAND38$=BAND18$
210 BAND7$=BAND18$
220 BAND14$=BAND18$
230 BAND21$=BAND18$
240 BAND28$=BAND18$
250 :
260 REM Now apply the rules to see where it is possible for a path
270 REM to exist between the US and Britain
280 :
290 IF Y$="W" AND T$="N" THEN BAND18$="Possible"
300 IF M$="W" AND (T$="N" OR T$="M") THEN BAND38$="Possible"
310 IF (T$="E" OR T$="M") THEN BAND7$="Possible"
320 IF S$="H" THEN IF (Y$<>"W" AND T$<>"N") THEN BAND14$="Possible"
330 IF S$="L" AND Y$="A" AND (T$="A" OR T$="E") THEN BAND14$="Possible"
340 IF S$="L" AND Y$="W" AND T$="A" THEN BAND14$="Possible"
350 IF S$="L" AND Y$="S" AND (T$="E" OR T$="N") THEN BAND14$="Possible"
360 IF S$="H" AND (T$="A" OR T$="E") THEN BAND21$="Possible"
370 IF S$="H" AND (T$="M" OR T$="A") THEN BAND21$="Possible"
380 :
390 REM Now print out the display of bands and possibilities
400 :
410 PRINT "1.8 MHz Band:       ";BAND18$
420 PRINT "3.8 MHz Band:       ";BAND38$
430 PRINT "7 MHz Band:         ";BAND7$
440 PRINT "14 MHz Band:        ";BAND14$
450 PRINT "21 MHz Band:        ";BAND21$
460 PRINT "28 MHz Band:        ";BAND28$
470 :
480 END
```

Listing 4.5

day for a signal from the United States in Europe. The rule set here is extremely simple, but could be extended. Expert systems like this that use a rule set are very easy to set up on commercially available expert system development software, but are basically making use of the experience of the person providing the knowledge base. A further disadvantage of a system like this is that, like the purely mathematical model detailed above, it cannot give us any indication of anomalous propagation that sometimes occurs, unless the circumstances under which it happens are fairly well understood. One way around this is to develop a system based on data as to what stations were heard on the bands at particular times of the day. For example, you could monitor beacon stations continuously, and record whether they were present or absent at a particular time. Over a period of time, this would allow you to develop a comprehensive 'knowledge base' from which it would be possible to make inferences about future propagation as follows.

1 for a particular month, frequency band – say a couple of MHz wide – and time range (say three hours) count the number of times that a beacon was listened for and the number of times it was heard. Say 50 per cent of the time you heard the beacon. As an example, we now have:

Sunspots	Month	Freq	Time	%	Part of World
180	June	14	0900	50	North America

The sunspot count can be gathered from various reference sources, and is also transmitted on the RSGB news bulletins.

2 this data can be stored in a computer readable form, either in a commercial database package, or arrays in a BASIC program. Obviously, the more months and sunspot counts for each frequency band and target area that we can get, the more accurate the predictions based on this information will be. Listing 4.6 is a simple BASIC program holding such data (the data is fictitious, by the way) and allowing simple predictions to be made based on the stored data.

```
10 REM Simple Inference program using stored data to make simple
20 REM predictions about whether a station will be heard or not
30 REM based on logged reception.
40 :
50 CLS
60 PRINT:PRINT:PRINT
70 PRINT " 1 - Get probability of given country being heard"
80 PRINT " 2 - Enter probability and print countries"
```

```
85 PRINT " 3 - Finish"
90 PRINT:PRINT
100 INPUT "Please enter your choice",OPT
110 :
120 REM You can enter morse options here, based upon the data stored
130 :
140 IF OPT=1 THEN GOSUB 1000
150 IF OPT=2 THEN GOSUB 2000
160 IF OPT<>3 THEN GOTO 50
170 :
180 REM end of calling program
190 :
1000 REM This subroutine evaluates the probability of a particular country
1010 REM being heard based upon the data entered by the user and the data
1020 REM stored in the DATA statements at line 10000. You could read these
1030 REM items into arrays if you wanted to.
1040 :
1050 CLS
1060 PRINT:PRINT:PRINT
1070 PRINT "Enter the data needed, use UPPER CASE"
1080 INPUT "Lowest Sunspot Count ",LSC
1090 INPUT "Highest Sunspot Count ",HSC
1100 :
1110 REM enter a range of sunspot counts so that we can 'bracket' the stored
1120 REM data - it's unlikeley that we'll get a 'spot on' figure.
1130 :
1140 INPUT "Month (1 to 12) ",MONTH
1150 INPUT "Frequency (integer MHz) ",FREQ
1160 INPUT "Start Time ",ST
1170 INPUT "Finish Time ",FT
1175 INPUT "Part of world ",WO$
1180 :
1190 REM Frequency should be entered as 14 for frequencies in range 13.5
1191 REM to 14.5 MHz, 15 for range 14.5 to 15.5 MHz and so on. Start and
1195 REM finish times used again to bracket the times that might be stored
1197 REM in the data base of logged data. Part of world must be typed in
1198 REM EXACTLY as it is stored in the data base.
1199 :
1200 RESTORE 10000
1210 :
1211 REM first of all, read the number of data entries into num
1212 :
1215 READ NUM
1216 RECCOUNT=0
1217 PERCENT=0
1219 :
1220 REM reccount will record number of records that agree with criteria
1230 REM that we've specified. percent will totalise the percentage in
1235 REM each record.
1236 :
1240 FOR I=1 TO NUM
1250 READ SSPOTS,DMONTH,DFREQ,DTIME,DPERCENT,DWORLD$
1260 IF DWORLD$<>WO$ THEN GOTO 1400
1270 IF SSPOTS<LSC AND SSPOTS>HSC THEN GOTO 1400
1280 IF DMONTH <> MONTH THEN GOTO 1400
1290 IF FREQ<>DFREQ THEN GOTO 1400
1300 IF DTIME<ST AND DTIME>FT THEN GOTO 1400
1305 :
1306 REM if we get here, then we've got a record that satisfies the
1307 REM criteria that are entered by the user, so do the additions.
1309 :
1310 RECCOUNT=RECCOUNT+1
1320 PERCENT=PERCENT+DPERCENT
1400 NEXT I
1410 :
1420 PRINT:PRINT
1430 PRINT "Total records meeting criteria: ";RECCOUNT
```

```
1440 PRINT "Average probability is:          ";PERCENT/RECCOUNT
1450 :
1460 INPUT "Press RETURN to go on",A$
1470 RETURN
2000 REM This subroutine lists parts of the world heard more than a given
2010 REM percent of the time for a set of input criteria.
2020 :
2050 CLS
2060 PRINT:PRINT:PRINT
2070 PRINT "Enter the data needed, use UPPER CASE"
2080 INPUT "Lowest Sunspot Count ",LSC
2090 INPUT "Highest Sunspot Count ",HSC
2100 :
2110 REM enter a range of sunspot counts so that we can 'bracket' the stored
2120 REM data - it's unlikeley that we'll get a 'spot on' figure.
2130 :
2140 INPUT "Month (1 to 12) ",MONTH
2150 INPUT "Frequency (integer MHz) ",FREQ
2160 INPUT "Start Time ",ST
2170 INPUT "Finish Time ",FT
2175 INPUT "Greater than percentage: ",PERCENT
2200 RESTORE 10000
2210 :
2211 REM first of all, read the number of data entries into num
2212 :
2215 READ NUM
2219 :
2220 REM reccount will record number of records that agree with criteria
2230 REM that we've specified.
2235 :
2240 FOR I=1 TO NUM
2250 READ SSPOTS,DMONTH,DFREQ,DTIME,DPERCENT,DWORLD$
2260 IF DPERCENT < PERCENT THEN GOTO 2400
2270 IF SSPOTS<LSC AND SSPOTS>HSC THEN GOTO 2400
2280 IF DMONTH <> MONTH THEN GOTO 2400
2290 IF FREQ<>DFREQ THEN GOTO 2400
2300 IF DTIME<ST AND DTIME>FT THEN GOTO 1400
2305 :
2306 REM if we get here, then we've got a record that satisfies the
2307 REM criteria that are entered by the user, so do the additions.
2309 :
2310 PRINT DWORLD$;" received ";DPERCENT;"% of the time"
2400 NEXT I
9900 :
9910 REM data is stored in order:
9920 REM sunspots,month,freq,time,percent,part of world
9930 :
10000 DATA 8 : REM Number of data records stored first
10010 DATA 100,3,14,0900,30,"NORTH AMERICA"
10020 DATA 80,3,14,1000,50,"NORTH AMERICA"
10030 DATA 110,3,15,0900,30,"NORTH AMERICA"
10040 DATA 100,3,4,2300,40,"NORTH AMERICA"
10050 DATA 120,3,4,0900,2,"NORTH AMERICA"
10060 DATA 110,3,4,2100,25,"NORTH AMERICA"
10070 DATA 150,3,21,1200,75,"NORTH AMERICA"
10080 DATA 120,3,21,1300,60,"NORTH AMERICA"
```

Listing 4.6

3 the data is used to make predictions by the user entering the sunspot count, time, month and part of world of interest. The program searches the stored data for records of any previous occasions on which this data has been recorded in the system. For example, sunspot counts of 180 in June with a path to North America at 0900. It will then evaluate average percentages for all the records it finds meeting this match, and display the percentages for each frequency band found. The program might also look for a range of sunspot counts, say 150 to 200, or even search the records for a month either side of the desired month to get a bigger selection of records to choose from. If you were to do this, the average might be a weighted average, with 'June' entries contributing more than 'May' or 'July' entries to the final percentage. The final percentage effectively gives us a probability of the part of the world being heard at that time.

Clearly, there are disadvantages with this technique. The main one is that you need to gather up a lot of information – your log could provide a lot of it – and process it into a form readable by the program above. However, a computer based listening log would allow you to directly transfer data from one file to another fairly easily. The more data you have, over a wide time range, the more accurate the resultant predictions will be, provided that the ionosphere continues to act in roughly the same way in the future as it has done in the past! The corollary of this is that the less data you have, the less accurate the predictions will be and there may well be gaps in the coverage of predictions.

One interesting advantage of this method is that with sufficiently large amounts of data the system will reflect the existence of anomalous propagation, as this will be reflected in the percentage of times a station from an area has been heard on a certain band at a certain time. A system similar to this, but more complex, is used for commercial propagation prediction, but these systems use vast amounts of data – much more than can be fitted into a simple home computer.

FIVE

Logkeeping and QSL software

One job that has to be done by all amateur radio operators and most SWLs is that of logging received stations. This is simply the task of recording date, time, frequency and a few details about stations heard or spoken to. Transmitting amateurs also record the power used, and frequently details of the signal strength and quality of the stations heard or transmitted to. A log can be anything, from an old exercise book to a full blown computer program that prints out recorded stations when required. In this chapter, I shall examine the basic principles behind putting a log onto computer, demonstrating this with a BASIC program and also outlining how commercial software packages can be used for log keeping. In addition, I shall explore the way in which computers can help us with QSL card production.

A listener's log

Let us start by looking at the data that we need to record on paper when an SWL is logging radio stations. In computer parlance, an item of data that is going to be stored in a computer file as part of a structured list in this way is called a field, and the collection of fields that make up a log entry for a radio station is called a record. The whole log can be called a simple database. Generally, the data stored is:

Date
This is the date on which the station was heard.

Time
This is the time at which the station was first heard, and is traditionally in GMT (or, as it is now known, UTC).

Frequency
This is the frequency on which the station was heard, usually quoted in kHz.

Station
This is simply the name or callsign of the station heard.

Comments
This piece of data is recorded occasionally, often as an aid to getting a QSL card from the station. I use the comments field in my system to record anything interesting about the station received, how signal quality varied, etc.

SINPO/RS
These are means of recording signal strength, interference, etc.

The data stored in the log of a transmitting station will be slightly different to this. To start with, there are two times recorded – the time of starting transmission to a particular station and the time at which the contact with that station was finished. In addition, an extra SINPO/RS field is common, so you can record the quality of your signals as heard by the other station. A field to record transmitted power is now a requirement in the UK Amateur Radio Licence, and you may also like to include a field to indicate whether you have sent a QSL card to this station. Further information that is commonly required, especially if you are into award hunting or contesting, is the locator square of the station heard or worked.

What the software must do

A logging program must, at the very least, offer the following facilities:

Add a new log entry to the list of recorded stations already on file.

Print a list of stations recorded in the file. Most people still prefer to look at paper lists rather than VDU screens!

If we were to produce a program that just did these two things, we would be missing out on a lot of the facilities that a computer can offer us. Computer logging programs will also, in general, offer the following facilities:

Sort the list

The program will allow you to sort the list of recorded stations into order based upon the contents of one of the fields of data. Usually, data will be entered into the file in date and time order, as stations are received in this way. However, you may wish to group together all the times you have received Radio Australia, and so the ability to sort on station name would be valuable here. Similarly, being able to sort the log into locator square order will make checking for duplicate squares in contests much, much easier.

Select records

Many programs will allow you to enter selection criteria before a list of stations is produced on paper. For example, you might be able to select only those log entries that occurred between the 1st and 3rd of January, 1989, inclusive, and then list the data in locator square order.

```
10 REM Listeners Log in GWBASIC by Joe Pritchard
20 REM October 1989
30 :
40 GOSUB 1000 :                     REM initialise arrays
50 GOSUB 2000 :                     REM display menu
60 IF OPT = 1 THEN GOSUB 3000 :     REM enter new data
70 IF OPT = 2 THEN GOSUB 3500 :     REM save data to disc
80 IF OPT = 3 THEN GOSUB 3700 :     REM load data from disc
90 IF OPT = 4 THEN GOSUB 4000 :     REM sort data into order
100 IF OPT = 5 THEN GOSUB 5000 :    REM print data
110 IF OPT <> 6 THEN GOTO 50
120 :
130 END :                           REM end of program
140 :
1000 REM initialise arrays and variables needed by rest of program
1010 :
1011 RECNUM = 50 :                  REM number of records to be
                                    stored.
1012 :
1020 DIM DAT$(RECNUM) :             REM dates held here in yy/mm/dd
                                    format for the
1030          :                     REM purposes of indexing on the
                                    date field if req.
1040 DIM TIM$(RECNUM) :             REM time in 'hhmm' format - 4
                                    digits.
1050 DIM FREQ(RECNUM) :             REM frequency held as a number
1060 DIM STA$(RECNUM) :             REM station name
1070 DIM CO$(RECNUM) :              REM comments
1080 DIM SI(RECNUM)  :              REM SINPO / RS held as a number
1082 DIM TEMP$(RECNUM):             REM temporary array for sorting
                                    strings
1084 DIM TEMP(RECNUM) :             REM temporary array for sorting
                                    numbers
1085 DIM INDEX(RECNUM):             REM index array
1090 :
1100 REM enough space here for 50 entries
1110 RETURN
1120 :
```

```
2000 REM this subroutine puts up a menu and returns an option in the
2010 REM variable 'opt'.
2020 CLS :                          REM Clear the screen
2030 PRINT:PRINT:PRINT:             REM move down screen a little
2040 :
2050 PRINT "1 - Enter a new log entry"
2060 PRINT "2 - Save data to disc"
2070 PRINT "3 - Load Data from disc"
2080 PRINT "4 - Sort data on a field"
2090 PRINT "5 - Print all data out"
2095 PRINT "6 - Finish with program"
2100 :
2110 PRINT:PRINT
2120 INPUT "Please make a choice  ",OPT
2130 RETURN
2990 :
3000 REM add a new record here
3010 NBLANK = 0 :                   REM nblank is array element
                                    holding next blank
3011            :                   REM record for filling in
3012 FOR I = 1 TO RECNUM
3013   IF DAT$(I)="" THEN NBLANK = I : I=RECNUM + 2
3014 NEXT I
3015 :
3016 REM now nblank points at first of unused records.
3017 IF NBLANK <> 0 THEN GOTO 3040
3018 CLS:PRINT "File is full"
3019 INPUT "Press RETURN to go on",A$
3020 RETURN
3030 :
3040 REM get here if there's space!
3050 CLS
3060 INPUT "Date (yy/mm/dd) ",DAT$(NBLANK)
3070 INPUT "Time (hhmm)     ",TIM$(NBLANK)
3080 INPUT "Frequency       ",FREQ(NBLANK)
3090 INPUT "Station Name    ",STA$(NBLANK)
3100 INPUT "Comments        ",CO$(NBLANK)
3110 INPUT "SINPO / RS      ",SI(NBLANK)
3120 PRINT:PRINT:
3130 INPUT "Enter another station? ",A$
3140 IF A$="N" OR A$="n" THEN RETURN
3150 NBLANK = NBLANK + 1
3160 IF NBLANK <> RECNUM THEN GOTO 3050
3170 PRINT "File is full"
3180 INPUT "Press RETURN to go on",A$
3190 RETURN
3400 :
3500 REM Save data to disc. This option must be used to save the data onto
3510 REM disc as otherwise the data will be lost when the computer
3520 REM is turned off.  The user is prompted for a file name, so that a
3530 REM variety of different logs can be stored on one disc.
3540 :
3545 CLS
3546 INPUT "Save a file to disc.  What is the name? ",NAM$
3547 :
3548 REM Now open the file for use.  Line 3550 does it in GWBASIC
3549 :
3550 OPEN "O",1,NAM$
3551 :
3552 REM for Amstrad BASIC, use OPENOUT nam$.  For BBC BASIC use the
3553 REM line Y%=OPENOUT(nam$)
3554 :
3555 FOR I=1 TO RECNUM
3560 :
3570 REM now write the data out to file.  The following line will work on
3571 REM GWBASIC.  For Amstrad BASIC use WRITE #9.
3572 :
```

```
3575 WRITE #1,DAT$(I),TIM$(I),FREQ(I),STA$(I),CO$(I),SI(I)
3580 :
3590 REM for BBC BASIC use PRINT #Y%,dat$(i),tim$(i),freq(i),sta$(i),co$(i),
3595 REM si(i)
3600 :
3605 NEXT I
3610 REM now close the file.  Use CLOSEOUT on Amstrad BASIC and
CLOSE#Y% on
3620 REM BBC machines.
3630 :
3640 CLOSE #1
3650 RETURN
3660 :
3700 REM read a file from disc.  This can be used to process stored files
3710 REM and add new data to existing logs.
3720 CLS
3730 INPUT "Load a file from disc.  What is the name? ",NAM$
3740 :
3750 REM Now open the file for use.  Line 3770 does it in GWBASIC
3760 :
3770 OPEN "I",1,NAM$
3775 :
3776 REM for Amstrad BASIC, use OPENIN nam$.  For BBC BASIC use the
3777 REM line Y%=OPENIN(nam$)
3780 :
3785 FOR I=1 TO RECNUM
3786 :
3787 REM now read the data from the file.  The following line will work on
3790 REM GWBASIC. For Amstrad BASIC use INPUT #9.
3800 :
3810 INPUT #1,DAT$(I),TIM$(I),FREQ(I),STA$(I),CO$(I),SI(I)
3820 :
3830 REM for BBC BASIC use INPUT #Y%,dat$(i),tim$(i),freq(i),sta$(i),co$(i),
3840 REM si(i)
3850 :
3855 NEXT I
3860 REM now close the file.  Use CLOSEIN on Amstrad BASIC and
CLOSE#Y% on
3870 REM BBC machines.
3880 :
3890 CLOSE #1
3891 RETURN
3900 :
4000 REM sort data into order depending upon the field chosen.
4010 :
4020 CLS
4030 PRINT:PRINT:PRINT
4040 PRINT "1 - Sort on Date"
4050 PRINT "2 - Sort on Time"
4060 PRINT "3 - Sort on Frequency"
4070 PRINT "4 - Sort on Station Name"
4080 PRINT:PRINT:PRINT
4090 INPUT "Choose a field to sort on ",SRT
4100 :
4105 PRINT:PRINT:
4106 PRINT "Please Wait"
4110 REM now copy contents of the chosen field into the appropiate
4120 REM temporary array, depending upon whether it's a string or a
4130 REM numeric array that we're sorting.  Set index up as well.
4140 :
4150 IF SRT <> 3 THEN GOTO 4200 :      REM lines 4160 to 4200 copy
                                        numeric
4160                           :        REM array information
4170 FOR I=1 TO RECNUM
4180    TEMP(I) = FREQ(I)
4190 NEXT I
4192 SRT = 1 :                          REM now srt set to 1 indicates numeric array
```

```
4195 GOTO 4300
4196 :
4200 REM here we copy contents of string arrays over.
4210 FOR I=1 TO RECNUM
4220    IF SRT = 1 THEN TEMP$(I) = DAT$(I)
4230    IF SRT = 2 THEN TEMP$(I) = TIM$(I)
4240    IF SRT = 4 THEN TEMP$(I) = STA$(I)
4250 NEXT I
4255 SRT = 2 :                          REM now srt = 2 indicates a string
                                        array
4260 :
4300 REM now back together to initalise index array
4310 FOR I=1 TO RECNUM
4320    INDEX(I) = I
4330 NEXT I
4340 :
4350 REM now sort the arrays depending upon whether a string array or
4360 REM a non string array has been selected
4370 :
4375 IF SRT = 2 THEN GOTO 4500 :        REM go to 4500 to sort strings
4380 FOR K=RECNUM TO 2 STEP -1
4390 FOR I=2 TO K
4400    IF TEMP(I) < TEMP(I-1) THEN
T=INDEX(I):INDEX(I)=INDEX(I-1):INDEX(I-1)=T
4401    IF TEMP(I) < TEMP(I-1) THEN
T=TEMP(I):TEMP(I)=TEMP(I-1):TEMP(I-1)=T
4410 NEXT I
4420 NEXT K
4430 :
4440 GOTO 4600: REM RETURN FROM ROUTINE
4450 :
4500 FOR K=RECNUM TO 2 STEP-1
4510 FOR I=2 TO K
4520    IF TEMP$(I) < TEMP$(I-1) THEN
T=INDEX(I):INDEX(I)=INDEX(I-1):INDEX(I-1)=T:FLAG = I-1
4525    IF TEMP$(I) < TEMP$(I-1) THEN
T$=TEMP$(I):TEMP$(I)=TEMP$(I-1):TEMP$(I-1)=T$
4530 NEXT I
4540 NEXT K
4550 :
4600 RETURN
4900 :
5000 REM print out data in order of index.  Does not print out any records
5010 REM with blank dates.  Data is sent to printer, and you will need to set
5011 REM in place your own paging routines, etc.
5020 :
5021 REM for BBC Computers, insert a VDU 2 command here to turn printer on
5022 :
5030 FOR I=1 TO RECNUM
5040 :
5045 J=INDEX(I)
5046 :
5047 REM line 5050 prints data for GWBASIC.  For Amstrad BASIC replace
LPRINT
5048 REM with PRINT #8.
5049 :
5050 IF DAT$(J)<>"" THEN LPRINT DAT$(J);"  ";TIM$(J);"  ";FREQ(J);"
";STA$(J);"  ";CO$(J);"  ";SI(J)
5060 NEXT I
5070 :
5080 REM for BBC Computers, insert a VDU 3 command here
5090 :
5100 RETURN
```

Listing 5.1

Listing 5.1 shows a simple listeners log written in GWBASIC. However, it is easy to convert into other dialects of BASIC and I have commented the listing where appropriate, especially in the saving and loading sections. The program offers the ability to add new log entries, list them, sort into different orders and also select on date. It is quite limited, but is easily expanded to add other facilities. Listing 5.2 shows a similar program modified for transmitting use by the addition of extra fields. Each field is stored as an array – you could store all the data in one array, but this would involve us in having to chop up the strings in the array to extract particular pieces of information. However, using different arrays is more expensive in terms of computer memory, and is also a little more complicated when we come to sort the file into order. Note that when sorting, I do not shuffle the arrays around; instead, I create an index array which has an integer as each element. This integer is the number of the log entry in the other arrays that corresponds to that position in the sorted file. This saves time and also memory. The sort technique used is not very fast, and can easily be improved upon. However, it does the job and as it is a subroutine can be replaced by a more efficient sort.

```
10 REM Transmitting Log in GWBASIC by Joe Pritchard
20 REM October 1989
30 :
40 GOSUB 1000 :                      REM initialise arrays
50 GOSUB 2000 :                      REM display menu
60 IF OPT = 1 THEN GOSUB 3000 :      REM enter new data
70 IF OPT = 2 THEN GOSUB 3500 :      REM save data to disc
80 IF OPT = 3 THEN GOSUB 3700 :      REM load data from disc
90 IF OPT = 4 THEN GOSUB 4000 :      REM sort data into order
100 IF OPT = 5 THEN GOSUB 5000 :     REM print data
110 IF OPT <> 6 THEN GOTO 50
120 :
130 END :                            REM end of program
140 :
1000 REM initialise arrays and variables needed by rest of program
1010 :
1011 RECNUM = 50 :                   REM number of records to be
                                     stored.
1012 :
1020 DIM DAT$(RECNUM) :              REM dates held here in yy/mm/dd
                                     format for the
1030            :                    REM purposes of indexing on the
                                     date field if req.
1040 DIM TIM$(RECNUM) :              REM start time in 'hhmm' format
                                     4 digits.
1045 DIM tif$(recnum) :              REM finish time of QSO in hhmm
                                     format
1050 DIM FREQ(RECNUM) :              REM frequency held as a number
1060 DIM STA$(RECNUM) :              REM station name
1065 DIM loca$(recnum):              REM locator held as a string
1070 DIM CO$(RECNUM)  :              REM comments
```

```
1075 DIM pow(recnum)  :            REM transmitter power
1076 DIM mo$(recnum)  :            REM transmitter mode used
1080 DIM SIS(RECNUM)  :            REM RST sent held as a number
1081 DIM SIR(recnum)  :            REM RST received held as a
                                   number
1082 DIM TEMP$(RECNUM):            REM temporary array for sorting
                                   strings
1084 DIM TEMP(RECNUM) :            REM temporary array for sorting
                                   numbers
1085 DIM INDEX(RECNUM):            REM index array
1090 :
1100 REM enough space here for 50 entries
1110 RETURN
1120 :
2000 REM this subroutine puts up a menu and returns an option in the
2010 REM variable 'opt'.
2020 CLS :                         REM Clear the screen
2030 PRINT:PRINT:PRINT:            REM move down screen a little
2040 :
2050 PRINT "1 - Enter a new log entry"
2060 PRINT "2 - Save data to disc"
2070 PRINT "3 - Load Data from disc"
2080 PRINT "4 - Sort data on a field"
2090 PRINT "5 - Print all data out"
2095 PRINT "6 - Finish with program"
2100 :
2110 PRINT:PRINT
2120 INPUT "Please make a choice  ",OPT
2130 RETURN
2990 :
3000 REM add a new record here
3010 NBLANK = 0 :                  REM nblank is array element
                                   holding next blank
3011          :                    REM record for filling in
3012 FOR I = 1 TO RECNUM
3013   IF DAT$(I)="" THEN NBLANK = I : I=RECNUM + 2
3014 NEXT I
3015 :
3016 REM now nblank points at first of unused records.
3017 IF NBLANK <> 0 THEN GOTO 3040
3018 CLS:PRINT "File is full"
3019 INPUT "Press RETURN to go on",A$
3020 RETURN
3030 :
3040 REM get here if there's space!
3050 CLS
3060 INPUT "Date (yy/mm/dd)              ",DAT$(NBLANK)
3070 INPUT "Time QSO started (hhmm)      ",TIM$(NBLANK)
3072 input "Time QSO finished (hhmm)     ",tif$(nblank)
3080 INPUT "Frequency                ",FREQ(NBLANK)
3090 INPUT "Station Contacted        ",STA$(NBLANK)
3093 input "Locator of Station     ",locA$(nblank)
3094 input "Transmission Mode      ",mo$(nblank)
3096 input "Transmitter Power      ",pow(nblank)
3100 INPUT "Comments                     ",CO$(NBLANK)
3110 INPUT "RST Sent to other station  ",SIS(NBLANK)
3120 INPUT "RST from other station     ",sir(nblank)
3125 PRINT:PRINT:
3130 INPUT "Enter another station? ",A$
3140 IF A$="N" OR A$="n" THEN RETURN
3150 NBLANK = NBLANK + 1
3160 IF NBLANK <> RECNUM THEN GOTO 3050
3170 PRINT "File is full"
3180 INPUT "Press RETURN to go on",A$
3190 RETURN
3400 :
3500 REM Save data to disc. This option must be used to save the data onto
```

```
3510 REM disc as otherwise the data will be lost when the computer
3520 REM is turned off. The user is prompted for a file name, so that a
3530 REM variety of different logs can be stored on one disc.
3540 :
3545 CLS
3546 INPUT "Save a file to disc. What is the name? ",NAM$
3547 :
3548 REM Now open the file for use. Line 3550 does it in GWBASIC
3549 :
3550 OPEN "O",1,NAM$
3551 :
3552 REM for Amstrad BASIC, use OPENOUT nam$. For BBC BASIC use the
3553 REM line Y%=OPENOUT(nam$)
3554 :
3555 FOR I=1 TO RECNUM
3560 :
3570 REM now write the data out to file. The following line will work on
3571 REM GWBASIC. For Amstrad BASIC use WRITE #9.
3572 :
3575 WRITE
#1,DAT$(I),TIM$(I),FREQ(I),STA$(I),CO$(I),SIr(I),sis(i),locA$(i),pow(i),mo$(i),tif$(i)
3580 :
3590 REM for BBC BASIC use PRINT #Y% instead of WRITE#1
3600 :
3605 NEXT I
3610 REM now close the file. Use CLOSEOUT on Amstrad BASIC and
CLOSE#Y% on
3620 REM BBC machines.
3630 :
3640 CLOSE #1
3650 RETURN
3660 :
3700 REM read a file from disc. This can be used to process stored files
3710 REM and add new data to existing logs.
3720 CLS
3730 INPUT "Load a file from disc. What is the name? ",NAM$
3740 :
3750 REM Now open the file for use. Line 3770 does it in GWBASIC
3760 :
3770 OPEN "I",1,NAM$
3775 :
3776 REM for Amstrad BASIC, use OPENIN nam$. For BBC BASIC use the
3777 REM line Y%=OPENIN(nam$)
3780 :
3785 FOR I=1 TO RECNUM
3786 :
3787 REM now read the data from the file. The following line will work on
3790 REM GWBASIC. For Amstrad BASIC use INPUT #9.
3800 :
3810 INPUT
#1,DAT$(I),TIM$(I),FREQ(I),STA$(I),CO$(I),SI(I),SIr(I),sis(i),locA$(i),pow(i),mo$(i),ti
f$(i)
3820 :
3830 REM for BBC BASIC use INPUT #Y% instead of INPUT #1
3840 REM si(i)
3850 :
3855 NEXT I
3860 REM now close the file. Use CLOSEIN on Amstrad BASIC and
CLOSE#Y% on
3870 REM BBC machines.
3880 :
3890 CLOSE #1
3891 RETURN
3900 :
4000 REM sort data into order depending upon the field chosen.
4010 :
4020 CLS
```

```
4030 PRINT:PRINT:PRINT
4040 PRINT "1 - Sort on Date"
4050 PRINT "2 - Sort on Start Time"
4060 PRINT "3 - Sort on Frequency"
4070 PRINT "4 - Sort on Station Name"
4071 print "5 - Sort on Locator"
4080 PRINT:PRINT:PRINT
4090 INPUT "Choose a field to sort on ",SRT
4100 :
4105 PRINT:PRINT:
4106 PRINT "Please Wait"
4110 REM now copy contents of the chosen field into the appropiate
4120 REM temporary array, depending upon whether it's a string or a
4130 REM numeric array that we're sorting.  Set index up as well.
4140 :
4150 IF SRT <> 3 THEN GOTO 4200 :        REM lines 4160 to 4200 copy
                                         numeric
4160                           :         REM array information
4170 FOR I=1 TO RECNUM
4180    TEMP(I) = FREQ(I)
4190 NEXT I
4192 SRT = 1 :                           REM now srt set to 1 indicates
                                         numeric array
4195 GOTO 4300
4196 :
4200 REM here we copy contents of string arrays over.
4210 FOR I=1 TO RECNUM
4220    IF SRT = 1 THEN TEMP$(I) = DAT$(I)
4230    IF SRT = 2 THEN TEMP$(I) = TIM$(I)
4240    IF SRT = 4 THEN TEMP$(I) = STA$(I)
4245    IF sRT = 5 then temp$(i) = locA$(i)
4250 NEXT I
4255 SRT = 2 :                           REM now srt = 2 indicates a string
                                         array
4260 :
4300 REM now back together to initalise index array
4310 FOR I=1 TO RECNUM
4320    INDEX(I) = I
4330 NEXT I
4340 :
4350 REM now sort the arrays depending upon whether a string array or
4360 REM a non string array has been selected
4370 :
4375 IF SRT = 2 THEN GOTO 4500 :         REM go to 4500 to sort strings
4380 FOR K=RECNUM TO 2 STEP -1
4390 FOR I=2 TO K
4400    IF TEMP(I) < TEMP(I-1) THEN
T=INDEX(I):INDEX(I)=INDEX(I-1):INDEX(I-1)=T
4401    IF TEMP(I) < TEMP(I-1) THEN
T=TEMP(I):TEMP(I)=TEMP(I-1):TEMP(I-1)=T
4410 NEXT I
4420 NEXT K
4430 :
4440 GOTO 4600: RETURN FROM ROUTINE
4450 :
4500 FOR K=RECNUM TO 2 STEP-1
4510 FOR I=2 TO K
4520    IF TEMP$(I) < TEMP$(I-1) THEN
T=INDEX(I):INDEX(I)=INDEX(I-1):INDEX(I-1)=T:FLAG = I-1
4525    IF TEMP$(I) < TEMP$(I-1) THEN
T$=TEMP$(I):TEMP$(I)=TEMP$(I-1):TEMP$(I-1)=T$
4530 NEXT I
4540 NEXT K
4550 :
4600 RETURN
4900 :
5000 REM print out data in order of index.  Does not print out any records
```

```
5010 REM with blank dates.  Data is sent to printer, and you will need to set
5011 REM in place your own paging routines, etc.
5020 :
5021 REM for BBC Computers, insert a VDU 2 command here to turn printer on
5022 :
5030 FOR I=1 TO RECNUM
5040 :
5045 J=INDEX(I)
5046 :
5047 REM line 5050 prints data for GWBASIC.  For Amstrad BASIC replace
LPRINT
5048 REM with PRINT #8.
5049 :
5050 IF DAT$(J)<>"" THEN LPRINT DAT$(J);"  ";TIM$(J);" to ";tif$(j);"
";FREQ(J);"  ";
5055 if dat$(j)<>"" then lprint STA$(J);"  ";pow(j);"  ";mo$(j);" · ";locA$(j)
5060 NEXT I
5070 :
5080 REM for BBC Computers, insert a VDU 3 command here
5090 :
5100 RETURN
```

Listing 5.2

Additional techniques

The programs listed above are easily altered to add more facilities, and you might like to consider the following:

1 editing an existing entry to correct an error.
2 the ability to delete a log entry.
3 extend the selection criteria so you can select from any field in the database.
4 extend the sorting facilities so you can sort on a composite sort key, such as date and station name or date and frequency.

Once you have got a computer logging system, there are a variety of uses to which it can be put, apart from simply providing lists of stations heard. These applications are possible with any system, though they will be easier with more complex systems that allow more involved sorting and selection.

Duplicate checking and contest logging

Logging in contests is slightly different, as a number indicating the contact or station heard also has to be recorded, along with any particular information required by the contest adjudicators. In addition, a contest logging system should store the data on disc as soon as it has been logged, in case of a power cut or other disaster, rather than waiting for the user to commit the data to tape or disc, as above. Furthermore, in most contests points are lost for undocumented duplicate contacts or stations heard. There are two ways around this:

1 at the logging stage, check the callsign/station name against those already on file, and alert the operator if a match is found so that the logging can be aborted.
2 at the listing stage, either do not print duplicates or print them with a '*' or something similar against the list entry to indicate a duplicate.

Use in propagation studies

Over a period of time, you can list stations heard between particular times on particular frequencies. This will allow you to see what parts of the world were received at your location at those times, and will thus allow you to make predictions as to what stations might be heard at these times and frequencies in future. Such data could be fed into the expert systems mentioned in Chapter 4 to provide the knowledge base.

Printing QSLs from such a log

We shall see later how you might print QSL cards based on the data in such a log file. If you are interested in getting QSL cards from a station, you can supplement your report with a list of previous occasions when the station has been heard on the frequency, with the signal strength, etc., noted at that time. This will give the station staff an idea of how their signals are getting through over a longer period of time than just the single logging that is normally received by them from listeners seeking a QSL card.

Compiling frequency lists

By listing the stations in frequency order, you can compile your own frequency list – quite useful if you are into weather station listening or listening for tropical band stations where data might be a bit scarce or out of date in other published sources. These personalized lists can save a lot of time when listening. For example, a few months ago I heard a station, quite faint, on a frequency which was listed as having a station in China as the only occupant. It transpired, after an announcement was heard, that the station I had heard was a European broadcaster who had recently changed frequency. By recording this, I knew that I would not get caught out again, spending half an hour listening for an announcement only to be sorely disappointed!

Using a commercial database package

In Chapter 7 I shall mention how some commercial programs not aimed at radio amateurs can be used in the shack. Here, I would like to mention just briefly a couple of commercial packages that can be used for logging purposes. The obvious packages to look at are database management systems (DBMS), although spreadsheets can also be used to make a simple log. As well as using BASIC to create a logging program, you can use one of available DBMS packages instead. The advantages of this are:

1 tasks such as indexing or sorting the data into order are much easier in these systems, and new sorts can often be put together without having to re-write large chunks of the software, as would be the case with the BASIC program above.
2 these packages often come with the means of generating printed reports containing precisely the data you want. Again, this saves us having to re-write the BASIC program.
3 because the BASIC program above loads the data into memory from tape or disc and stores it in arrays, we are ultimately limited by the memory of the computer. Most DBMS systems are limited only by the size of the disc drive of the computer, so if you have got a PC with a 20 M byte hard disc you can log quite a few stations before the system gets full!
4 because DBMS systems are designed for this work, rather than BASIC which is a 'jack of all trades' amongst computer languages, logging systems using DBMS systems are usually faster than BASIC programs doing the same job.

Of course, there are a couple of disadvantages as well. These are:

1 you get BASIC with your computer, but you will have to spend cash on a DBMS system. This can be anything from a few pounds on the simpler home computers for a simple database

system to several hundred pounds for top of the range packages on PCs. I offer a couple of suggestions below.

2 you need to learn how to use the DBMS. This may make it difficult for non-experts to use the program, unless you can write a user friendly version of the program using the DBMS. This is possible using the popular dBase II and dBase III systems (and their look alikes) on IBM PC clones but is less easy on other systems. Even then, you still have to learn a new computer language, even if it is going to be very useful!

3 unless the DBMS can generate stand-alone systems, which do not use any of the facilities of the DBMS package, you cannot give thc log to other people who have not got the DBMS system. This problem does not occur if you have written your own version in BASIC because you own the copyright and most computers do have BASIC!

DBMS systems to consider

On the BBC Microcomputer, I used Viewfile for a while, but eventually wrote a database system in BASIC which did the job with greater ease! I have found the BBC Micro to be very good for interfacing with hardware and BASIC programming but a bit limited in terms of commercially available serious software that can be used in the shack.

On the Amstrad 6128, I use a package called At Last which is a simple database management system. This allows me to define sorts, selection criteria and reporting formats fairly easily. You can also get dBase II on this machine to run under CP/M, but dBase II is not as easy to use unless you are willing to sit down and read the manuals!

On the IBM PC and clones, you will be spoilt for choice! There are many good public domain database systems, such as PC-File, which offer good facilities and are not too expensive. Alternatively, you can use any of the dBase III/IV clones which offer amazing facilities but take a bit of getting used to and leave a hole in the bank account. I wrote my existing logging system in a language called Clipper, which is a dBase compiler, purely because I have it available and it is the language I write in to earn my money!

In addition, there are several logging programs written by amateurs available from various software houses or via the public domain. I cannot give any firm information here, because I have not used any of them myself.

Computer produced QSL cards

The natural next step from keeping a log on a computer is to get the data in the logging program into a format suitable for inclusion on a QSL card. The obvious advantage here is that you do not have to transcribe large amounts of data from the log to QSL cards – you can get the computer to print the relevant data and all you have to do is sign the card, enter any extra comments that did not get into the log and that is that. The main technical problem is actually formatting the data for printing. There are three approaches that you can take, two of them suitable for virtually any computer and the third limited to systems with desk top publishing facilities available.

Printing on a card

In this technique the QSL card is pre-printed with the standard information and any picture, etc. required. There are several printing houses who specialise in this sort of thing, and the cards are usually quite inexpensive. A subroutine is then written to print the data from the log into the suitable gaps on the card. To do this requires that the printer can feed the card through without slipping, and this may cause problems with some printers, especially if the card is thick or glossy. All you have to do then is to keep feeding a card into the printer as required. This can give good results, but care is needed when writing the software and when feeding the card into the printer.

Printing a label

I do not like this method very much, but it has the advantage of being very easy to do and is great if you are having to produce hundreds of QSL cards – say after running a special event station. The details are printed on to a sticky label, and the label is then stuck on to the back of a preprinted QSL card. Labels are available on continuous stationery, so if you use this method you can set the computer going and then go and have lunch!

Printing a full card

If you have access to desk top publishing software, you can create a QSL card in the software, then import the data from your logging program into the card and print the card and data as a single entity on thin card in the printer. The software to do this, though, is really only available on IBM PCs and their clones, and is very expensive, but might be a method worth considering if you have access to such software.

I shall not go into the details of writing such a subroutine, as the 'guts' of it depend upon the layout of the card. However, you should write it so that you can select, say, on a 'QSL Sent' field as detailed above so that you can detect which log entries have not yet been QSLed. The subroutine can then set this field to 'Y' to indicate that a card has now been printed. In addition, if you sort the file into callsign order before printing you will have all the cards coming out in callsign order, ready to go to the QSL Bureau. If you are printing on a dot matrix printer, you may find it useful to send suitable control codes to the printer to put it into letter quality, bold or double strike mode for printing the details on the card, as this will be easier to read on the card than the standard single pass draft quality output, especially if the ribbon is getting on a bit.

There has been considerable debate about the merits of computer produced QSL cards; some operators do not like them, claiming that they are easier to forge than normal QSL cards. Personally, I write mine out by hand, but if I had a lot to do I might well use the label printing method – if I was really forced to!

Commercial software for card production

It is, of course, quite possible to use software to create a card and then fill in the details by hand, as with a standard printed QSL card. An example of such a card is shown in Figure 5.1. This was produced using PC Paint, a graphics package available on the IBM PC. Similar and better results are available using such packages as GEM Draw, Fleet Street Editor and similar graphics and DTP packages. There are also a wide variety of programs available for printing greetings cards, etc., and these are well worth a look at if

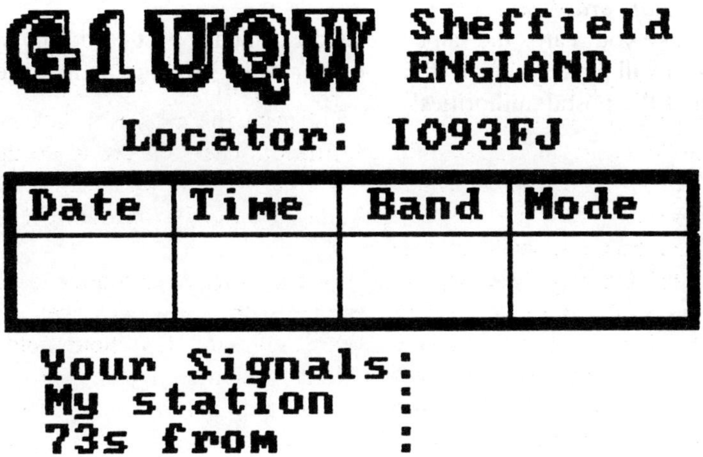

Figure 5.1

you want to try this technique out. Many of these packages include 'clip art' – graphics images that can be used 'off the shelf' – or there might be facilities to create your own graphics images or import them from other packages. There are just a couple of points to remember when creating a QSL card like this.

Style

It is tempting to use as many different print styles and sizes as there are in the package when you start out, but you should not succumb! Stick to one style, and just vary the size if needed. Also, avoid the fancy styles like Gothic – Frankenstein was not a radio amateur, and such styles are rather difficult to read.

Printing

A dot matrix printer will be required, or access to a laser printer. With a dot matrix printer good results are possible but if there are large areas of black on the card you will get through ribbons very quickly and the printer will get a bit hot in use! I find it easier to set up the system so that, say, three cards are printed on an A4 sheet of thin card which can then be cut to get the separate cards later.

Size of cards

Make your cards the same size as the standard post-card; this way you will make yourself more popular with QSL Bureau managers and the postal authorities!

SIX

Satellite and geographical software

One use for computers in the shack is the prosaic business of working out how to get from point A to point B; if you are using a directional aerial, it is vital to know where to point it to receive signals from a certain geographical location, and it often adds interest if you can calculate the distance between your receiver and a radio station being received. It is not as simple as reaching down the old school atlas, as you cannot take bearings from such a map and it is very difficult to get accurate measurements of distance from Mercator Projection maps. No, we need to remember that the world is roughly spherical when carrying out such calculations, and in this chapter I shall be examining some geographical calculations that are useful to SWLs and amateurs.

In addition, with the increasing numbers of amateurs and SWLs interested in satellite work via the many amateur radio satellites above our heads, I shall examine how we can calculate the approximate position of a satellite, and also briefly examine the decoding of satellite telemetry channels.

Distance and bearing calculations

For most applications, we can treat the earth as a sphere; this is not quite true, but is close enough for our purposes. If you are attempting to break any world distance records, though, you will need to use the more accurate equations for calculating bearings and distances which reflect the fact that the earth is, in fact, slightly flattened at the poles. However, the simple equations for bearing and distance are:

Cos(Distance) = Sin(Lat1) * Sin(Lat2) + Cos(Lat1) * Cos(Lat2) * Cos(Long1 – Long2)
Sin(Bearing) = Cos(Lat2) * Sin(Long1 – Long2) / Sin(Distance)

Although the distance is returned here in terms of an angle, this is easily converted into a distance in nautical miles. Listing 6.1 uses these equations to provide a simple bearing and distance calculator.

```
10 REM Calculation of Distances and Bearings between two locations
20 REM on Earth's surface
30 :
35 CLS
36 PRINT:PRINT:PRINT
37 PRINT "Enter Lattitude and Longitude as degrees,minutes"
38 PRINT "BOTH degrees and minutes need - sign if required"
40 INPUT "Home Lattitude (- if South, + if North) ",HLATD,HLATM
50 INPUT "Home Longitude (- if West, + if East)  ",HLONGD,HLONGM
60 :
70 PRINT
80 INPUT "Other Lattitude (- if South, + if North) ",OLATD,OLATM
90 INPUT "Other Longitude (- if West, + if East)  ",OLONGD,OLONGM
100 :
110 :
120 LAT1 = HLATD+(HLATM/60) : LAT1=LAT1*3.1415 / 180
130 LAT2 = OLATD+(OLATM/60) : LAT2=LAT2*3.1415 / 180
140 LONG1 = HLONGD+(HLONGM/60) : LONG1 = LONG1*3.1415 / 180
150 LONG2 = OLONGD+(OLONGM/60) : LONG2 = LONG2*3.1415 / 180
160 :
170 COSDIST = (SIN(LAT1) * SIN(LAT2))+ (COS(LAT1) * COS(LAT2) *
COS(LONG1-LONG2))
171 DIST = ATN(SQR(1-COSDIST*COSDIST)/COSDIST) : TEMPDIST = DIST
172 IF DIST < 0 THEN DIST=DIST+3.1415
174 DIST=DIST * 6367
190 PRINT "Distance is: ",DIST;" km"
200 SINBEAR = (COS(LAT2)*SIN(LONG1-LONG2)) / (SIN(TEMPDIST))
201 BEARING = ATN(SQR((SINBEAR)/(1-SINBEAR*SINBEAR)))
202 IF (SIN(LONG2-LONG1)*COS(LAT2)*COS(LAT1)) < 0 THEN
BEARING=-BEARING
203 IF (SIN(LAT2)-SIN(LAT1)*COS(TEMPDIST)) < 0 THEN
BEARING=3.1415-BEARING
204 IF BEARING < 0 THEN BEARING=BEARING+6.283
210 PRINT "Bearing is: ",BEARING*57.297
^Z
```

Listing 6.1

Locator to position conversions

Radio amateurs rarely give their location in terms of latitude and longitude; instead, they are much more likely to quote the ‘locator’ of their station. For example, my locator is IO93FJ, and I quote this over the air when I am in contact with distant stations.

This locator defines a square on the earth's surface of a size 5 minutes of longitude by 2.5 minutes of latitude. This system is called the *Maidenhead Locator System* (or IARU Locator System) and is made up as follows:

The first two letters indicate a square 10 degrees of longitude by 20 degrees of latitude, the first letter indicating the longitude and the second letter designating the latitude. The latitude starts with letter 'A' at 90°S (−90°, the south pole) and goes to 'R' at 90°N (+90°, the north pole). Similarly, the longitude letters start with 'A' at 180°W and work through to 'R' at 180°E. Thus the first two letters of my locator, IO, indicate that I am somewhere in a square between 0 and 20° longitude and 40 and 60°N latitude.

The second two characters are digits and they break the first large square down into 100 smaller pieces, on a 10 by 10 grid. The two digits here range from 0 to 9, the first digit being the east-west position in 2° steps from left to right and the second the north–south position in 1° steps from bottom to top. Thus, 00 indicates the bottom left hand corner of the square. Thus in my locator, 93 indicates that my station is in a square between 0 and 2°W longitude and 3 to 4°N latitude.

The final two letters of a Maidenhead Locator serve to reduce this 2 by 1 degree square down to a square 2.5 minutes of latitude by 5 minutes of longitude. Here, the letters reference a grid 24 by 24 squares, starting with AA in the bottom left of the square, and XX in the top right hand corner of the square.

Using this information, it is possible to put together a program that will convert from a latitude and longitude to a Maidenhead Locator, and also, from a locator to an *approximate* latitude and longitude, thus allowing us to get approximate distances and bearings between two locator squares. Listing 6.2 shows a BASIC program (GWBASIC) to do this. As usual, there are comments in the listing to enable conversion to other BASICs.

```
10 REM Maidenhead Locator Conversion program
20 REM :
22 CLS
23 PRINT:PRINT:PRINT
30 INPUT "Enter 1 for Locator to Lat/Long, 2 for Lat/Long to Locator",OPT
40 IF OPT = 1 THEN GOSUB 1000
50 IF OPT = 2 THEN GOSUB 2000
60 END
70 :
1000 REM Locator to Lattitude and Longitude
1010 INPUT "Locator square (e.g. IO93FJ): ",L$
```

```
1020 :
1030 REM now calculate the longitude
1040 :
1045 LA=-90
1050 A$=MID$(L$,2,1)
1060 FOR I=ASC("A") TO ASC("R")
1070 IF A$<>CHR$(I) THEN LA=LA+10
1080 IF A$=CHR$(I) THEN I=255
1090 NEXT
1100 A$=MID$(L$,4,1)
1110 FOR I=ASC("0") TO ASC("9")
1120 IF A$<>CHR$(I) THEN LA=LA+1
1130 IF A$=CHR$(I) THEN I=255
1140 NEXT
1150 A$=MID$(L$,6,1)
1160 FOR I=ASC("A") TO ASC("X")
1180 IF A$<>CHR$(I) THEN LA=LA+2.5/60
1190 IF A$=CHR$(I) THEN I=255
1200 NEXT
1210 LO=-180
1220 A$=MID$(L$,1,1)
1230 FOR I=ASC("A") TO ASC("R")
1240 IF A$<>CHR$(I) THEN LO=LO+20
1250 IF A$=CHR$(I) THEN I=255
1260 NEXT
1270 A$=MID$(L$,3,1)
1280 FOR I=ASC("0") TO ASC("9")
1290 IF A$<>CHR$(I) THEN LO=LO+2
1300 IF A$=CHR$(I) THEN I=255
1310 NEXT
1320 A$=MID$(L$,5,1)
1330 FOR I=ASC("A") TO ASC("X")
1340 IF A$<>CHR$(I) THEN LO=LO+5/60
1350 IF A$=CHR$(I) THEN I=255
1360 NEXT
1370 PRINT:PRINT
1380 PRINT "Lattitude is:      ",LA
1390 PRINT "Longitude is:      ",LO
1400 RETURN
1900 :
2000 REM Lat / Longitude to Maidenhead Locator
2010 CLS
2020 PRINT:PRINT:PRINT
2030 INPUT "Enter Lattitude,Longitude as 53.23,-34.2 ",LA,LO
2040 :
2050 LOCAT$=""
2055 TLO=-180
2060 FOR I=ASC("A") TO ASC("R")
2065 TLO = TLO + 20
2070 IF TLO > LO THEN A$=CHR$(I):I=255:TLO = TLO-20
2090 NEXT
2100 LOCAT$=LOCAT$+A$
2105 LO=LO-TLO
2106 TLA=-90
2110 FOR I=ASC("A") TO ASC("R")
2120 TLA=TLA+10
2125 IF TLA > LA THEN A$=CHR$(I):I=255:TLA = TLA-10
2140 NEXT
2142 LOCAT$=LOCAT$+A$
2144 LA=LA-TLA
2145 TLO=0
2150 FOR I=ASC("0") TO ASC("9")
2160 TLO=TLO+2
2170 IF TLO > LO THEN A$=CHR$(I):I=255:TLO=TLO-2
2180 NEXT
2190 LOCAT$=LOCAT$+A$
2200 LO=LO-TLO
```

```
2210 TLA=0
2220 FOR I=ASC("0") TO ASC("9")
2230 TLA=TLA+1
2240 IF TLA > LA THEN A$=CHR$(I):I=255:TLA=TLA-1
2250 NEXT
2260 LOCAT$=LOCAT$+A$
2270 LA=LA-TLA
2280 TLO=0
2290 FOR I=ASC("A") TO ASC("X")
2300 TLO=TLO+5/60
2310 IF TLO > LO THEN A$=CHR$(I):I=255
2320 NEXT
2330 LOCAT$=LOCAT$+A$
2350 TLA=0
2360 FOR I=ASC("A") TO ASC("X")
2370 TLA=TLA+2.5/60
2380 IF TLA > LA THEN A$=CHR$(I):I=255
2390 NEXT
2400 LOCAT$=LOCAT$+A$
2410 PRINT "Locator is: ",LOCAT$
2420 RETURN
```

Listing 6.2

Satellite tracking and reception

This topic is big enough for a book of it is own, so in this section I shall briefly examine the basic concepts of tracking a satellite and receiving data from satellites.

Satellites placed in earth orbit generally traverse one of three types of orbit. These are:

Circular orbit
In this orbit, the spacecraft describes a rough circle around the earth, always being roughly the same distance from the earth's surface. It is fairly easy to get a satellite into such an orbit, but the spacecraft is subject to drag and so the life of a satellite in such a circular orbit is not always that long!

Elliptical orbit
Here, the satellite travels in an ellipse around the earth, being closer to the earth for part of its travels than for other parts of the orbit. This type of orbit is more difficult to set up, but it is more stable, and more amateur radio satellites are using it.

Geostationary orbit
This is used by commercial satellites, such as TV transponders, and is such that the speed of orbit of the satellite is the same as the speed of rotation of the earth, thus allowing the satellite to stay at the same position relative to the earth's surface.

Early amateur radio satellites occupied circular orbits, but later ones have tended to go for elliptical ones. Details of calculations for elliptical orbits can be found in *Amateur Radio Software* from the RSGB, and Amsat-UK (see Appendices) can supply lists of orbit calculation software, more accurate than the simple calculators given here. Before looking at a calculator program for circular satellite orbits, it might be useful to go through some of the terminology that you will come across in other sources.

AOS and LOS
These stand for acquisition and loss of satellite, respectively. These are the times at which the satellite first becomes audible at your receiving station and when it is last heard. In a perfect world, which is what the times given represent, this is when the satellite comes over the horizon, but actual AOS occurs shortly after this due to local factors such as buildings, radio conditions, etc.

Apogee and perigee
These are the points of furthest and closest approach to the earth of a satellite, respectively. For a circular orbit, the distance between the earth and apogee and the earth and perigee will be the same but for elliptical orbits they will differ, often by very large amounts. The *argument of perigee* is the angle between a line from the centre of the earth to the perigee and a line from the centre of the earth to where the satellite crosses the equator at EQX.

Ascending and descending nodes
These are the points where the satellite crosses the equator. The ascending node is the point on the earth's surface where the change is made from southern hemisphere to northern hemisphere and the descending node is when the satellite passes from northern hemisphere to southern hemisphere.

Azimuth and elevation
These are the means by which the position in space of a satellite are defined. The azimuth is the direction – 0°=north, 90°=east, 180°=south and 270°=west – and the elevation is the angle above the horizon. 0° is horizontal and 90° is straight up.

Eccentricity
This is a term used to describe an elliptical orbit; it is a measure of the amount the shape deviates from a circle; 0 is a circle, and 1 is a straight line. It is a measure of the ellipse's flatness.

The epoch
This is a term used to define the date for which the various parameters defining a satellite orbit are valid. This is stated in terms of a year, day and fraction of a day, and is required because the parameters of an orbit vary with time due to drag, changes in the satellite's orientation, etc.

EQX
EQX is short for equator crossing point, and is defined as the time (UTC) and longitude at which the ascending node of a satellite orbit crosses the equator. The EQX longitude is measured in degrees west. The time between two EQXs is the time taken for the satellite to orbit the earth, and is called the period.

The Keplerian elements
The Keplerian elements of a satellite are a set of parameters that are used to calculate the orbit of the space vehicle.

The mean anomaly
The mean anomaly of an elliptical orbit is the distance from perigee of a spacecraft in terms of an angular distance along the orbit. Rather than the usual 360° in a circle, the mean anomaly, occasionally known as the *phase*, has 256 steps numbered 0 to 255. Perigee is 0, and apogee is 127.

Mean motion
The mean motion of a satellite is the number of passes the satellite makes through perigee each day.

Right ascension of the ascending node
This is a means of defining the position of the satellite with reference to a fixed point, called the first point of Aries. We do not have to worry too much about this in our calculations as we just get it as part of the satellite data.

Listing 6.3 shows a simple circular orbit calculator. The program requires certain orbital parameters of the satellite to be tracked, and these are obtainable from organisations such as Amsat. They are also published occasionally in the various amateur radio magazines. The most up to date information regarding satellites, though, is available 'off air' from Amsat–UK on 3780 kHz, at 1015 hours local time on Sunday mornings.

```
10 REM Simple circular orbit predictor program
20 REM Joe Pritchard
30 :
40 CLS
50 PRINT "          Data entry for Reference Orbit"
60 PRINT "          -------------------------------"
70 PRINT : PRINT
80 INPUT "Reference number orbit        ",REFNUM
90 INPUT "Julian date of orbit          ",JULDATE
100 INPUT "Time of orbit (H,m,s)        ",HOURS,MINUTES, SECONDS
110 INPUT "Period of orbit (m,s)        ",PERIODMINS,PERIODSEC
120 INPUT "Longitude of Equator Crossing ",LONGEQX
130 INPUT "Longitude increment per orbit ",LONGINC
140 :
150 PRINT : PRINT
160 PRINT "          Orbits of interest"
170 PRINT "          ------------------"
180 PRINT : PRINT
190 :
200 INPUT "First orbit to be calculated ",ORBIT1
210 INPUT "Last orbit to be calculated  ",ORBIT2
220 :
230 REM put period into seconds as smallest time unit handled
240 :
250 PERIOD=PERIODMINS*60+PERIODSEC
260 :
270 REM Now loop around the orbits from refnum up to orbit2.
280 :
290 FOR I=REFNUM TO ORBIT2
300 :
310 REM Only print the data if the orbit number is after the first one wanted
320 :
330 IF I>=ORBIT1 THEN GOSUB 640
340 :
350 REM now calculate parameters for the next printing.  Start off by
360 REM calculating next Equator Crossing longitude in longeqx
370 :
380 LONGEQX=LONGEQX+LONGINC
390 IF LONGEQX>360 THEN LONGEQX=LONGEQX-360
400 :
410 REM Now calculate the Equator Crossing time by adding the period to the
420 REM start time of the orbits, and convert the resultant seconds into
430 REM hours, minutes and seconds
440 :
450 SECONDS=SECONDS+PERIOD
460 MINUTES=MINUTES+(SECONDS \60)
470 SECONDS=SECONDS MOD 60
480 HOURS=HOURS+(MINUTES \ 60)
490 MINUTES=MINUTES MOD 60
500 :
510 REM if needed add 1 to Julian Date
520 :
530 JULDATE=JULDATE+(HOURS \ 24)
540 HOURS=HOURS MOD 24
550 :
560 REM If more than a year, then subtract 365 to bring day number into
570 REM range for the year.  Note that this program does NOT accomodate
580 REM leap years
590 :
600 IF JULDATE > 365 THEN JULDATE=JULDATE-365 : REM not leap year
610 NEXT I
620 END
630 :
```

```
640 REM subroutine prints the data estimates times for which satellite will
650 REM be 'visible' for a station at about latitude 50' North
660 REM according to the 'rule of thumb' which indicates that a satellite
670 REM in a circular orbit will be 'visible' from about EQX time + 5 mins
680 REM to EQX + 50 minutes
690 :
700 :
710 REM print date as a day number - Julian Date - starting at Jan 1st as 1.
720 :
730 PRINT I;" ";JULDATE;" ";HOURS;":";MINUTES;":";SECONDS;
740 PRINT " at longitude ";LONGEQX;
750 :
760 REM calculate acquisition and loss times
770 :
780 AOSMINS=(MINUTES+5) MOD 60
790 AOSHOURS=(HOURS + (AOSMINS \ 60)) MOD 24
800 LOSMINS=(MINUTES+50) MOD 60
810 LOSHOURS=(HOURS + ((MINUTES+50) \ 60)) MOD 24
820 PRINT "  Visible: ";AOSHOURS;":";AOSMINS;" to ";LOSHOURS;":";LOSMINS
830 RETURN
```

Listing 6.3

Satellite telemetry

Several of the satellites transmit data down to earth about the functioning of the satellite itself and the environment around the satellite. This telemetry can be decoded using a computer, and the data processed to provide data such as satellite temperature, battery levels, etc. The details of the telemetry broadcast by different satellites differ, so in this section I shall just give some basic hints about what to expect.

Doppler shift

Because the signal is coming from a rapidly moving source, the radio signal will suffer from Doppler shift, the frequency changing as it approaches you and goes away from you. The signal will start slightly high of its listed frequency as it approaches you, pass through the listed frequency at the point of approach closest to you, then will apparently decrease in frequency as the satellite moves away from you. The faster the satellite, the more pronounced the Doppler shift will be. Generally, the speed of the satellite relative to the receiving station will depend upon the orbit of the satellite; the higher the orbit, the slower the relative speed. It is of practical significance because you may have to retune the receiver to keep the telemetry signal at a readable level. The

Doppler shift can also be used to estimate the period of the orbit, as follows. The satellite signal is tuned in, and the instant that the Doppler shift changes direction is recorded. Stay tuned to the channel, and listen for the next orbit, and again record the time that the shift changes. The difference in time is the period of the orbit.

Modes used

The commonest mode of telemetry transmission is CW, the telemetry information being transmitted as a series of numbers and letters. The exact information represented by a piece of telemetry information depends upon the satellite concerned, and I do not have the space to discuss this here. Other modes used include ASCII at 1200 baud, and even voice, using a speech synthesizer to read out the telemetry figures.

Receiving the data

Much of this material comes down on VHF frequencies in the 2 m and 70 cm amateur radio bands, and so suitable receiving equipment or converters will be required. In addition, it is often a good idea to record the satellite pass rather than attempting to decode it 'live' using a computer, mainly because of the interference that most computers generate at VHF frequencies! The tape can then be played back through suitable decoders, dependent upon the transmission mode used. At least one commercial data decoder has been produced that includes satellite telemetry frame decoding as one of its operational modes. Details of the receiving equipment required here are rather beyond the scope of this book, although it is very simple and any receiver designed for 2 m amateur band reception will allow reception of satellite transmissions.

Once decoded, the morse or ASCII will require some further work to convert the received information into actual details about the spacecraft. The received data is in the form of coded numbers, each number representing the particular type of information – say, battery voltage – and a value that is plugged into an equation to give the actual value of the parameter – in this case battery voltage. The actual equations used to process the downloaded telemetry depend upon the satellite concerned, and details are available from Amsat–UK.

SEVEN

Miscellaneous software

So far, we have examined a lot of different applications for computer software in the shack, much of it specially written or modified for use in our hobby. In this chapter, I should like to round up a few ideas about other programs you might like to consider using in the shack, and also look briefly at the problem of transferring data between different machines.

Commercial software in the shack

Many programs available for use in other fields can be put to good use in amateur radio. In this section I shall look at various categories of software and suggest some uses.

Word processors

The obvious use of a word processor in the shack is to create reports to other stations. An example 'blank form' is shown in Figure 7.1. This was created using WordPerfect 5 on the IBM PC, but similar results could be obtained using View on the BBC Micro or Tasword on the Amstrad computers. The forms can be printed off, duplicated and then filled in when you wish to get a QSL card out of a station. I prefer to fill in these forms using block capital handwriting, but there is nothing to stop you typing them out!

Any word processor with an ASCII text mode can also be used to prepare text off line for sending via RTTY, AMTOR or packet radio links (see later chapters). Most word processors use control codes in the text to provide formatting instructions, and an ASCII text option on your word processor will allow you to dispense with

Listener Report

To Radio Station: ....

From: ....
....
....
....

Date of reception | | | | at .... UTC
to .... UTC

SINPO | | | | | |

Comments on the Signal.

Comments on Program Material.

I hope that this report is useful to you, and I would welcome a QSL card or other confirmation if this report is found to be of value.

Thank you for your time.

Signed ....

Figure 7.1

the formatting codes. This is important as most digital radio systems cannot cope with these control codes. On the BBC Microcomputer, for example, such files can be used using the SPOOL option of Wordwise. On the popular Wordstar or New-Word wordprocessors, the non-document mode is the ASCII text mode. In addition, this mode can be used to process files of text read off air by RTTY, AMTOR or packet reception systems. For example, I often download data from packet bulletin boards into text files rather than printing it out. I can then read and edit the text at my leisure – it also has the advantage of not requiring half a rain forest to print out!

Spreadsheets

These programs, such as Viewsheet, SuperCalc or Calcmaster, are almost always thought of in terms of accountancy type problems. After all, they are designed for handling tabular or numeric information. However, many spreadsheet packages include a graphing option which might be of use if you are, for example, processing statistics for any purpose. For example, you could log the signal strength of a station over a period of hours or days, then plot it as a graph, as shown in Figure 7.2. It is this sort of work that might make your report stand out from everybody else's at the station from which you are trying to get a QSL card! More prosaic uses for spreadsheet programs could include totalling up your scores in amateur radio contests, carrying out repetitive calculations or even storing a log book – the data stored in most

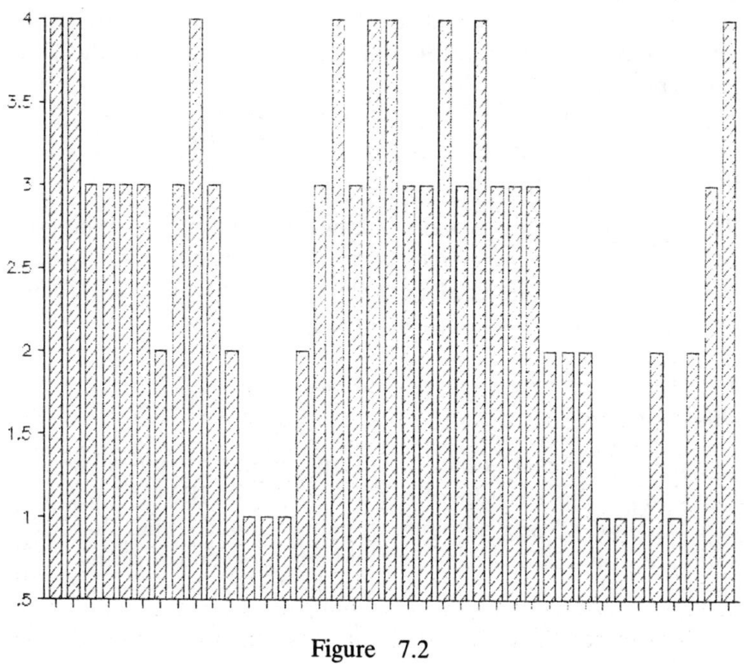

Figure 7.2

spreadsheet programs need not be purely numeric, and many spreadsheets, especially on the IBM PC clones, will allow you to sort on the various columns. Figure 7.3 shows an extract from a spreadsheet stored log book.

Date	Station	Freq	Time	SINPO/RS	Comments
01/02/89	Tehran Radio	15084	1500	44334	
01/02/89	Africa Number 1	4830	1930	33333	Usual music prog.

Figure 7.3

Database packages

We have already seen the obvious uses for databases in keeping the station log book. However, any data that requires storing and occasionally updating can be put in to a computer database. Some possible uses include storing details of useful magazine articles or addresses, 2m or 70 cm repeater details. The only point to remember is that if personal details of other individuals are stored on a computer system you may have to register under the Data Protection Act.

Graphics programs

Packages are available to help to draw diagrams or even to plot out circuit paths for printed circuit boards. In addition, packages such as GEM Draw on the IBM PC will allow you to create QSL cards or log book sheets, as we have already seen.

Other software

There are a variety of other types of program that you will be able to use in the shack. Users of Amstrad 6128 and IBM PC machines can tap into a vast amount of public domain and shareware software, some of it written by radio amateurs and covering topics similar to those described elsewhere in this book. Much software can be used for all types of purposes, provided that you use a little imagination.

Communicating between two machines

One of the problem areas that you may encounter is transferring data between two different computers. I experienced this when I downloaded some large text files on to my BBC Microcomputer from a packet radio bulletin board. I then wanted to edit these files and pass them to a friend who had an IBM machine. The problem was that the BBC computer will not read IBM discs, and vice versa, without some quite messy programming! I got around this problem, as I shall soon describe, and in this section I shall look in general at the problems of exchanging data between computers.

Use of the serial interface

The easiest way to carry out the data transfer described here is to make use of the RS232 interface of the computers, if they both have them. After all, that is what RS232 was invented for! The BBC B and most IBM PC clones have an RS232 compatible interface fitted as standard, and add on interfaces can be purchased for the Amstrad 6128 machines. The usual use that this interface is put to is to drive either a printer or a modem or, for us radio hobbyists, to communicate with a data decoder or terminal unit, as featured in Chapter 14. The main considerations to take into account when using this interface to communicate between two machines in this way are:

Hardware standards
No, not all 'standard' RS232 interfaces are the same! For example, the version used by the BBC Microcomputer has slightly different electrical characteristics to that used by the IBM PC. However, this does not usually cause too many problems.

Cabling
Most problems encountered when attempting to use the RS232 standard to communicate between computers are related to the cabling; a suitable cable will be described below.

Setting up
The RS232 standard does not define a set standard for the data transferred; you can thus vary the number of bits in each byte sent, the speed at which it is sent, and a variety of other features. The essential feature here, of course, is to set *both* machines up in the same way!

A suitable lead

Any lead used in this sort of link must have the following connections:

Computer 1	Computer 2
Data transmitted pin	Data received pin
Data received pin	Data transmitted pin
Ground	Ground

This type of connection, where the transmitted data from one computer is linked to the received data of the other computer, is called a *null modem* link. Now life starts to get a little more complicated, as most computer to computer links require *handshaking signals* to be connected in some way as well. These signals basically control when a computer sends and receives data; for example, one computer might indicate to another that it cannot receive any more data at that moment. Unfortunately for us, not all computers have the same quota of handshaking lines.

BBC handshaking lines

The BBC RS423 connection has two handshake lines, RTS and CTS. The *RTS*, or *ready to send*, line is asserted by the BBC Micro whenever the BBC can accept more characters from the other device. The *CTS*, or *clear to send* line is read by the BBC Microcomputer and the BBC will only send data to the other device if the other device asserts this line. If this line is not asserted by the other device, then no data will be sent by the BBC Microcomputer.

PC and 6128 handshake lines

The actual lines available on the Amstrad 6128 serial interface will clearly depend upon the manufacture, but in many cases will be equivalent to those offered by the IBM PC clone. The usual lines are:

DSR or *data set ready* which is turned on when the device at the other end of the cable from your computer (which in this case, could be another computer) is ready to roll.

DTR or *data terminal ready* is an output signal from the computer which, when on, indicates that the computer is ready to send or receive data.

In addition, a line called DCD is often available, and this is on when a carrier signal has been detected from the other device. The CTS and RTS lines are also present.

Making the connections

Linking two machines with full RS232 interfaces is rather simple. The connections that need to be made are as follows (consult your machine's manual for pin-out details of your RS232 connector).

Computer 1	Computer 2
Ground	Ground
Transmitted data	Received data
Received data	Transmitted data
RTS	CTS
CTS	RTS
DSR	DTR
DTR	DSR
DCD	DCD

A greater problem occurs when one of the machines does not have some of the required connections; in this case we can often fool one or both machines into playing along. For example, connecting a BBC to another BBC/Master/Electron computer is easy enough:

BBC Microcomputer 1	BBC Microcomputer 2
Ground	Ground
Transmitted data	Received data
Received data	Transmitted data
RTS	CTS
CTS	RTS

For linking the BBC to another computer, we have to ensure that the other machine has all of its control needs met by whatever connection we use. One possible approach is to use the connections as shown for BBC to BBC link *but* with the addition of extra connections at the non-BBC computer end. We would need to link

DTR, DCD and DSR together at the non-BBC end. An alternative connection method is:

BBC Microcomputer	**Other computer**
Ground	Ground
Transmitted data	Received data
Received data	Transmitted data
Connect RTS and CTS together	Connect RTS, CTS and DCD together
	Connect DSR and DRT together

Of course, you may end up trying to connect two machines together of a dubious nature; in this case the only advice to be given is that received data goes to transmitted data, transmitted data to received data, and ground to ground. The handshaking connections can then be worked out by trial and error using one of the commercially available breakout boxes.

Software for transfers

Once we have got a cable sorted out, we need some software to actually transfer the files. Fortunately, two of the machines mentioned have ready made transfer programs in their operating systems, and for the BBC Micro it is easy to write programs to do the work.

IBM PC clone software

The MODE command can be used to set up the baud rate, parity and word length as per your manual. The COPY command can then be used to transfer data from a file through the serial port of your computer or vice versa. The syntax is:

```
COPY COM1: fred.txt /b
```

in which case data is copied from COM1 to a text file called fred.txt, and:

```
COPY fred.txt COM1: /b
```

which copies a file called fred.txt to the device connected to COM1:. Some versions of DOS do not require the ':' after COM1, and a few versions of DOS are a little 'shirty' about handling these commands and so you may have difficulty in using them on some machines. Note that the '/b' option will ensure that the file will be copied in its entirety, and not just until a character 26 'end-of-file' marker.

On the Amstrad 6128, the easiest way to transfer files is to use the PIP command of CP/M. This will require you to boot up the computer under CP/M, and to have a serial interface connected that is recognised by CP/M as the AUX device. The syntax is:

PIP A:fred.txt=AUX:

to copy a file from the serial interface, and:

PIP AUX:=A:fred.txt

to copy a file to the serial interface. Note that PIP expects files to end with an end of file character, character 26. Fuller details of PIP can be found in CP/M manuals, such as the excellent *The Amstrad CP/M plus* by David Powys-Lybbe and Andrew Clarke, published by MML Systems Ltd.

As for the BBC Microcomputer, you do not get any software for transferring files, but you do get a good operating system through which input and output can be redirected through the serial port. For example, the following listing sends the contents of the file 'fred' to the serial interface.

```
10 REM BBC Micro file transmission
20 :
30 *FX3,5
40 *FX2,2
50 :
60 Y%=OPENIN("fred")
70 REPEAT
80   D%=BGET#Y%
90   VDU D%
100 UNTIL EOF#Y%
110 CLOSE #Y%
120 *FX3,0
130 *FX2,1
140 END
```

Listing 7.1

The reverse of this process can be carried out by the simple listing shown below, which transfers bytes from the serial interface to a file called 'fred'.

```
10 *FX2,1
20 *FX3,0
30 Y%=OPENOUT("FRED")
40 REPEAT
50   X%=INKEY(0)
60   BGETY%,X%
70 UNTIL X%=26   :   REM see text about this line
80 CLOSE #Y%
90 *FX3,0
100 *FX2,0
110 END
```

Listing 7.2

Note that for this program to work correctly, the stream of bytes from the serial interface representing the file must end with a CHR$(26), as detected by line 70. If the file needs to have CHR$(26) in it before the end of file, then you would need a different method of detecting the end of file.

File transfer problems

There are three main types of problem that you will encounter. These are that there is no transfer at all and the machines appear to hang, data transferred is corrupt and unusable or not all the data is transferred.

Machines hang up
This usually indicates that there is a serious mismatch in baud rates, word length, etc., or that the cable connecting the machines is not correctly wired up.

Corrupt data
This usually indicates that the baud rate may be slightly wrong, that the parity bits/word lengths are not the same or that the handshaking required between the machines is not correct.

Incomplete transfer
This usually indicates that character 26 is being treated as an end-of-file marker and that it occurs in the file before the actual end of file.

An additional point to watch is that if you are transferring program files, rather than ASCII text files, then a full 8 bit word length must be used, as otherwise the program instructions would be corrupted by the data transfer process.

EIGHT

Interfacing the radio to the microcomputer

So far in this book, we have looked at the use of the computer as number cruncher, data analyser and filing system. In none of the applications that we have looked at has the computer actually been directly linked to the radio set; the data in each case so far has been entered into the computer by hand. But perhaps the major use of computers in amateur radio is the use of the computer to decode certain types of radio transmission – such as AMTOR, RTTY or packet radio – or even to control parts of the radio station. In this chapter I shall give a brief introduction to the subject of interfacing the computer to the radio receiver so that the analogue signals representing incoming radio signals can be converted into data that is understandable to a computer. Figure 8.1 shows the principal components in a computer-radio receiver hook up. There are two main parts to the interface.

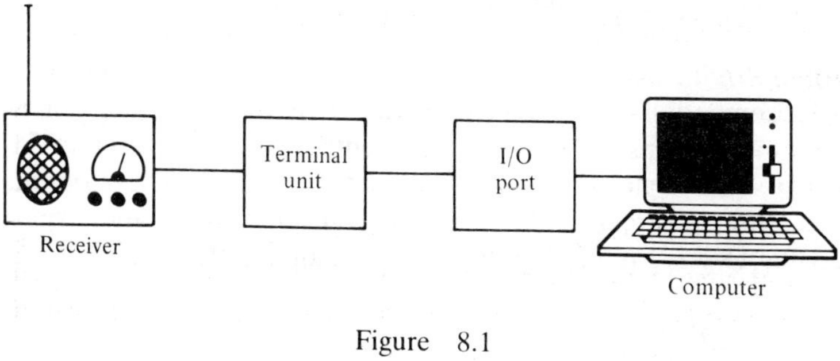

Figure 8.1

Terminal unit

The terminal unit takes audio signals from the radio receiver and converts them into a signal that is capable of being read by the computer interface (below). For example, the terminal unit may accept audio tones representing morse code signals as an input and output a 5V signal in the presence of an input tone and a 0V signal in the absence of a tone. For a series of incoming tones, therefore, the terminal unit would produce an output sequence of '1's and '0's for processing by the computer I/O interface. The terminal unit is a crucial part of any system that is used to decode radio signals, and we will look at these in greater detail later in this chapter.

The computer I/O interface

This part of the interface is responsible for taking the digital signal from the terminal unit and converting it into a form that is readable by the computer. We examined, in Chapter 2, a means of interfacing a morse key to a computer, and looked briefly at the concepts of address decoding and three state devices. The simplest I/O interface is just like this; a single input bit, addressed by the computer using a suitable logic array. Most computers, though, will have more complex I/O circuitry, usually allowing for at least eight input/output lines addressed as a single memory location in the computer memory map. We have already described the process of addressing and three state devices. These I/O circuits are often called user ports, and although the characteristics of user ports vary from computer to computer, the most common features are as follows:

TTL-level inputs and outputs
A user port data bit, when configured as an input, will recognise a voltage of 0V as a logic '0' and 5V as a logic '1'. This is known as TTL compatibility, and the inputs can be driven by the popular 74 series logic chips. When used as an output, the pin will go to 5V when set to logic '1' and 0V when set to logic '0'. These output bits, though, are not able to source much current, and so are unable to drive things like light bulbs, motors, etc.

Programmability

Some user ports are simple, having eight input lines and eight output lines which are usable only as inputs and outputs respectively. Other user ports, like the one on the BBC Microcomputer, have programmable pins, in which the 'direction' – whether the pin is used as an output or an input – is programmable. This allows the user, for example, to set 5 of the pins to act as outputs and 3 as inputs from BASIC or machine code programs.

These user ports are parallel devices; that is, the data flows in and out of the computer in 'chunks' of bits at a time, rather than the serial interfaces where data flows in and out of the computer one bit at a time. The data from the radio is a serial data stream, and can be transmitted from or read into the computer via just one input or output bit, if desired. For certain modes of transmission, such as RTTY, it might be useful to use some circuitry between the terminal unit and the user port to turn the serial bit stream of data from the terminal unit into a parallel byte to be read into the computer user port, effectively a character at a time. If we connect the bit stream from the TU directly to the user port, then software in the computer has to look after the task of assembling characters from the incoming serial bits. Such hardware serial to parallel converters can also do the reverse task – converting parallel bytes from the computer into a serial data stream for transmission to the radio for transmission of a RTTY signal. These devices are called *UARTs universal asynchronous receiver transmitters* – and we shall look at them briefly later in this chapter.

The easiest way to get an idea of the types of user ports available on computers is to look at some practical examples. Some computers do not have user ports at all; instead, the various address, data and control lines of the microprocessor are brought to the outside world on some form of socket or edge connector, and it is the responsibility of the user to provide the address decoding and three state buffering required for any user port. Such connections are often called *expansion buses* and an example is the bus on the back of the Amstrad 6128 computer, where the Z80 control lines are bought out to allow the addition of a user port, serial interface, and so on.

It would be impossible in a book of this size to go into great detail about the construction and use of user ports; there are many other books on sale which deal with this, and a perusal of computing magazines will often reveal articles of use. For this reason, I shall examine briefly user ports for the BBC Micro and Amstrad 6128. I have not considered the IBM PC, as this is a rather more complex machine to interface and somewhat beyond the scope of this book. In addition, the I/O addresses available depend to a great degree on what other cards are present in the machine, and how they are configured.

The BBC Microcomputer

The BBC Microcomputer is very well provided for as far as user ports go. The pin outs of the two ports of most use to us as SWLs are shown in Figure 8.2. The *user port* is a digital interface, using

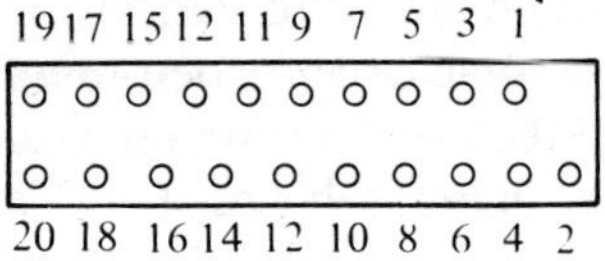

User port
(looking into socket)

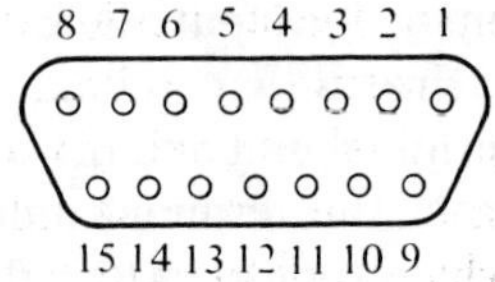

Analogue port
(looking into socket)

Pins 1, 3	+ 5 V
Pins 5, 7, 9, 11, 13, 15, 17, 19	0 V
Pin 2	CB1
Pin 4	CB2
Pin 6	PB0 (I/O bit 0)
Pin 8	PB1 (I/O bit 1)
Pin 10	PB2 (I/O bit 2)
Pin 12	PB3 (I/O bit 3)
Pin 14	PB4 (I/O bit 4)
Pin 16	PB5 (I/O bit 5)
Pin 18	PB6 (I/O bit 6)
Pin 20	PB7 (I/O bit 7)

Pin	Function
1	+5 V
3, 2	0 V
4	Channel 3 I/P
5	Analogue 0 V
6	0 V
7	Channel 1 I/P
8	Analogue 0 V
9	Light pen I/P
10	Digital input 1 (PB1)
11	Ref. voltage (VREF)
12	Channel 2 I/P
13	Digital input 0 (PB0)
14	Voltage ref. (VREF)
15	Channel 0 input

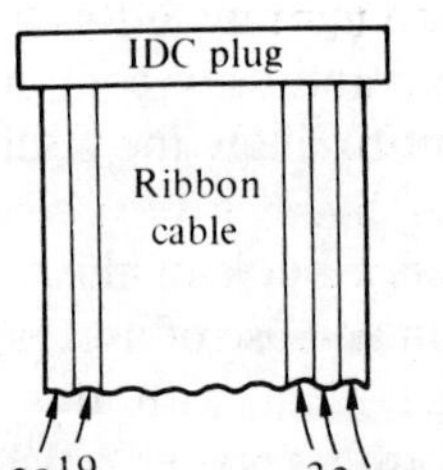

Figure 8.2

TTL level signals. It can be programmed to be either eight bits of input, or eight bits of output, or a mixture of the two. The *user port* is part of a complex chip inside the BBC called a 6522 *versatile interface adaptor (VIA)*, and this chip is also responsible for the Centronics printer interface on the computer. The chip also contains timers, and so is quite useful for providing accurate time delays and with suitable programming can measure frequency, generate square wave signals and a host of other functions which I cannot really go into in this book. There are places in the programming examples, though, where I have made use of some of the facilities offered.

Programming the user port to set up lines as input or output is quite simple, though. On a 'straight' BBC Micro, with no second processor attached, address &FE62 is the data direction register, which controls which bits in the user port, at address &FE60, are inputs and which are outputs. Placing a value of 255 in address &FE62 will set all the bits to outputs, and setting &FE62 to 0 will set all the lines to be inputs. A '1' in a bit position in &FE62 sets the corresponding bit in &FE60 to be output, and a '0' in a position will cause the corresponding bit to be an input. These bits are compatible with the low power TTL chips (LS TTL) and usually output bits are used to drive a single TTL input, and the output from this TTL gate used to drive other chips. This buffering, as well as giving the output from the user port more 'oomph', also offers protection against inadvertent short circuits, etc. A bit configured as an input can also be buffered, as shown in Figure 8.3. This diagram also includes examples of how other electronic circuits can safely interface with the user port. One point to note on the BBC user port is that accidentally short circuiting the 5V line to 0V will crash the computer at the very least, so care should be taken to prevent this from happening. The usual connection to the BBC user port is via a 20 way IDC female connector with a length of ribbon cable attached. I have found that it is often quite useful to build a terminal box, using 4 mm terminals or even 'choc-block' connectors, to make connection to the user port easier when you are running up circuits for quick experiments. (Figure 8.4)

The second interface of use on the BBC Microcomputer is the analogue interface, which allows the BBC to convert analogue voltages in the range 0 to 1.8V into a digital value in the range 0 to

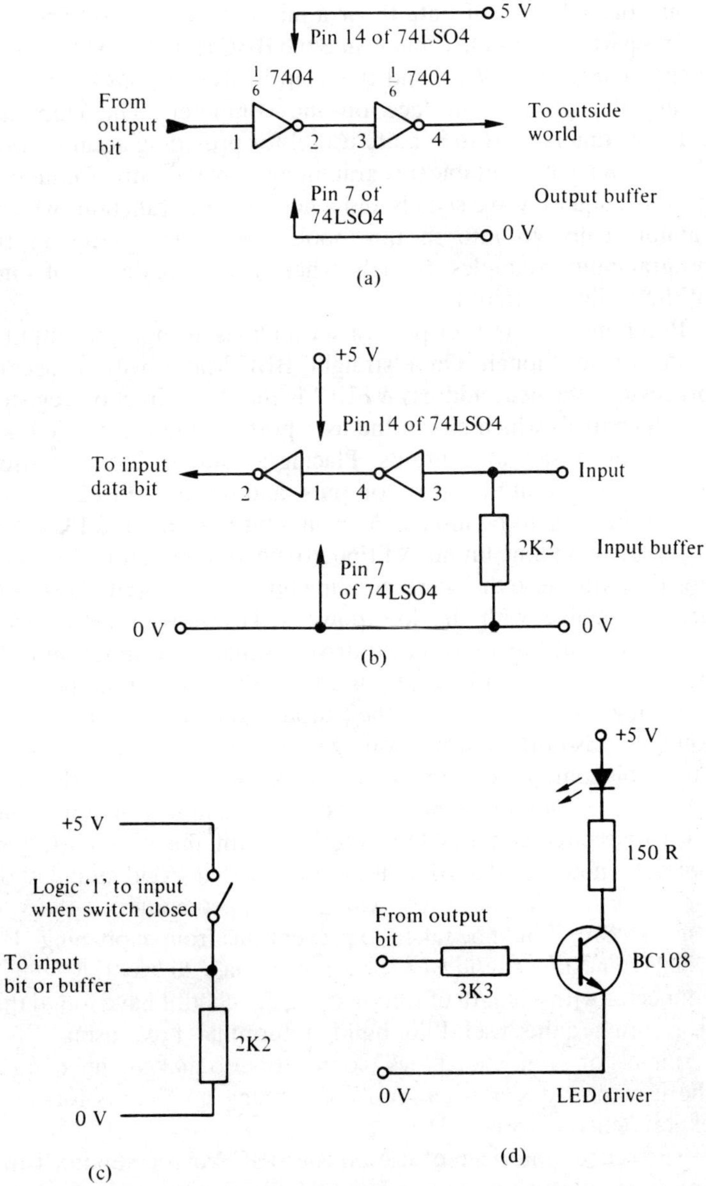
5 V
Pin 14 of 74LSO4
1/6 7404
1/6 7404
From output bit
To outside world
1
2
3
4
Pin 7 of 74LSO4
Output buffer
0 V
(a)
+5 V
Pin 14 of 74LSO4
To input data bit
2
1
4
3
Input
2K2
Input buffer
Pin 7 of 74LSO4
0 V
0 V
(b)
+5 V
+5 V
Logic '1' to input when switch closed
To input bit or buffer
2K2
0 V
(c)
150 R
From output bit
3K3
BC108
0 V
LED driver
(d)

Figure 8.3

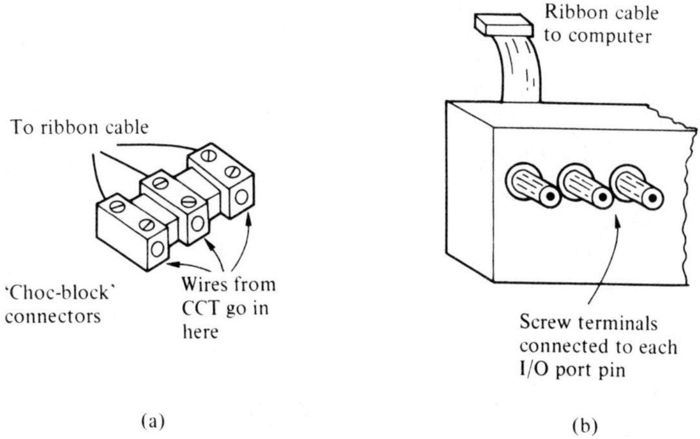

Figure 8.4

65535. This means that the BBC Microcomputer can actually measure electrical voltage and any parameter that can be converted into a voltage. The BBC ADC is read by the ADVAL() function, and is quite well documented in the *User Guide* and the *Advanced User Guide*. The only points to watch here are as follows:

1 any voltage applied to channels 1 to 4 of the ADC must be in the range 0 to 1.8V; any voltages outside this range could lead to destruction of the ADC chip in the BBC.
2 under normal circumstances, the four channels of the ADC are sampled in turn with a rate of one conversion every 10ms. This means that under normal circumstances a single channel is read every 40 ms. This can be speeded up to give a reading of one channel every 5 to 10ms by disabling three of the channels and reducing the accuracy of the conversion by using some of the BBC Micro's operating system commands, but this is still quite a slow rate, and the BBC ADC cannot be used for certain applications, such as SSTV or FAX.

Like the user port, it is quite useful to take the various connections out to a terminal box or a 'choc-block' connector for ease of connection to other circuits. Some examples of programming the BBC user port and ADC are to be found in Chapter 16.

The Amstrad 6128

This computer is without any user port; there is an expansion bus on the rear of the machine, but you will have to build or buy a user port to make proper use of it. A circuit diagram will be shown later in this chapter for a suitable user port. It is possible to use the printer port for an output port, and the joystick port as an input port, but it is better to build a separate user port. Figure 8.5 shows the various ports on the Amstrad 6128, and also shows how the printer port and joystick port can be used as output and input ports

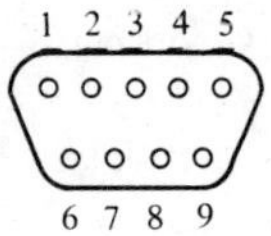

Pin 8, 8 Common #1 (Joystick 1)
Pin 9 Common #2 (Joystick 2)
Pin 1 Up Pin 2 Down
Pin 3 Left Pin 4 Right
Pin 6 Fire 2 Pin 7 Fire 1

Joystick

(a)

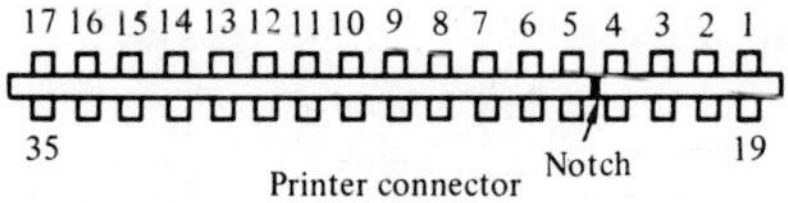

Printer connector

Pin 1 Strobe
Pin 2 D0
Pin 3 D1
Pin 4 D2
Pin 5 D3
Pin 6 D4
Pin 7 D5
Pin 8 D6
Pin 11 Busy
Pin 9, 14, 16, 19 – 28, 33 0 V

(b)

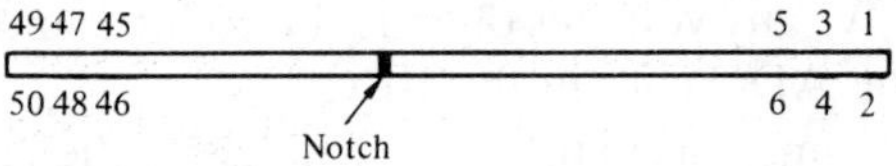

1 Sound O/P
2, 49 0 V
3–18 Address lines A15–A0
Pin 19–26 Data lines D7–D0
Pin 27 5 V
Pin 28 MREQ
Pin 29 M1
Pin 30 RFSH
Pin 31 IORQ
Pin 32 RD
Pin 33 WR
Pin 34 HALT
Pin 35 INT
Pin 36 NMI
Pin 37 BUSR2
Pin 38 BUSAK
Pin 39 READY
Pin 40 BUS RESET
Pin 41 RESET
Pin 42 ROMEN
Pin 43 ROMDIS
Pin 44 RAMRD
Pin 45 RAMDIS
Pin 46 CURSOR
Pin 47 LIGHT PEN
Pin 48 EXP
Pin 50 CLOCK

(c)

Figure 8.5

respectively. These ports can be accessed via the PRINT £8 and JOY() commands, but for accessing a user port you would need to use the INP and OUT commands of Locomotive BASIC.

The joystick input expects one or more of its pins to be grounded to 0V when an input is required. I have been able to read morse via the joystick interface by connecting a key between 0V and one of the input pins, but the speed is limited by the keyboard read rate of the Amstrad and so this interface is not of much practical use for interfacing to a receiver. A much better idea is to build a simple user port to plug into the expansion bus on the back of the computer. A simple circuit, containing eight bits of TTL input and eight bits of TTL output, is shown in Figure 8.6. This uses the I/O address bus of the Z80 microprocessor, so as not to conflict with the memory of the Amstrad. The BBC User Port is actually addressed as a location in memory, but on the Amstrad all the memory address space is taken up with memory. As it is configured, this user port is accessed by the instructions:

OUT (&FAE0),N

where N is the byte to be output, and:

N = INP(&FAE0)

where N is the byte read from the user port. The user port is very simple, providing 3 state input through the LS245 chip and a latched output (that is, we write a value to it, and the chip retains that value on the output lines until a new value is sent) via the LS373 chip. Note that this circuit has been built and tested for use with an Amstrad that has not got any other 'add ons' connected; they may also use address FAE0 because there are not too many I/O addresses in the Amstrad that users can use for their own peripherals.

There are several commercially available interfaces for the Amstrad 6128 and 464 computers and if you have never built any electronic circuitry before you might be well advised to start with a commercially built unit.

Hints for using user ports

Whatever type of port you have got, here are some basic tips for using it:

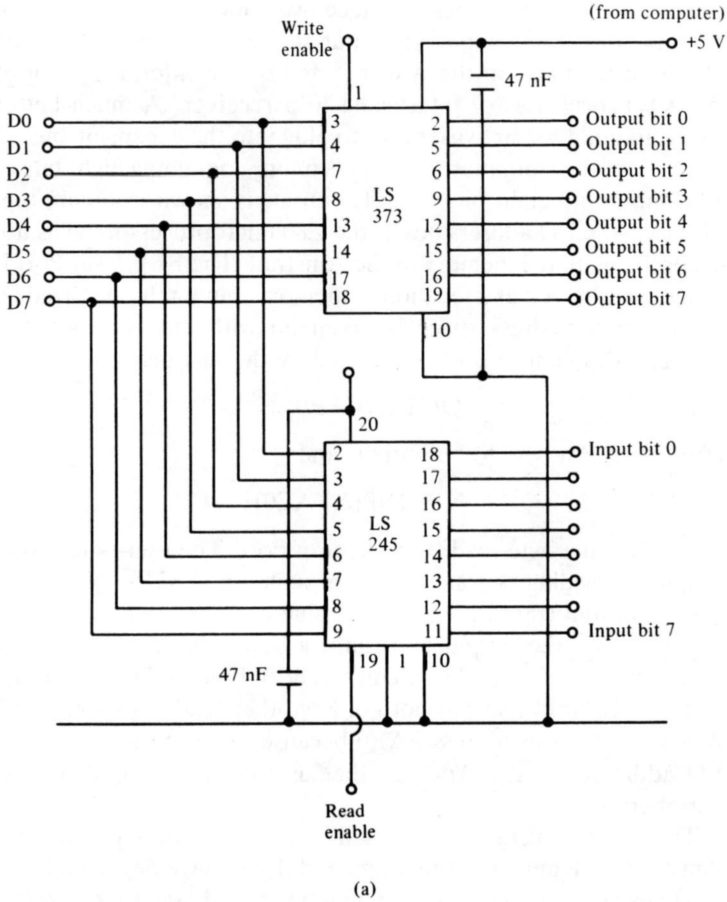
(from computer)
+5 V
Write
enable
47 nF
D0
D1
D2
D3
D4
D5
D6
D7
LS
373
Output bit 0
Output bit 1
Output bit 2
Output bit 3
Output bit 4
Output bit 5
Output bit 6
Output bit 7
LS
245
Input bit 0
Input bit 7
47 nF
Read
enable
(a)

Figure 8.6

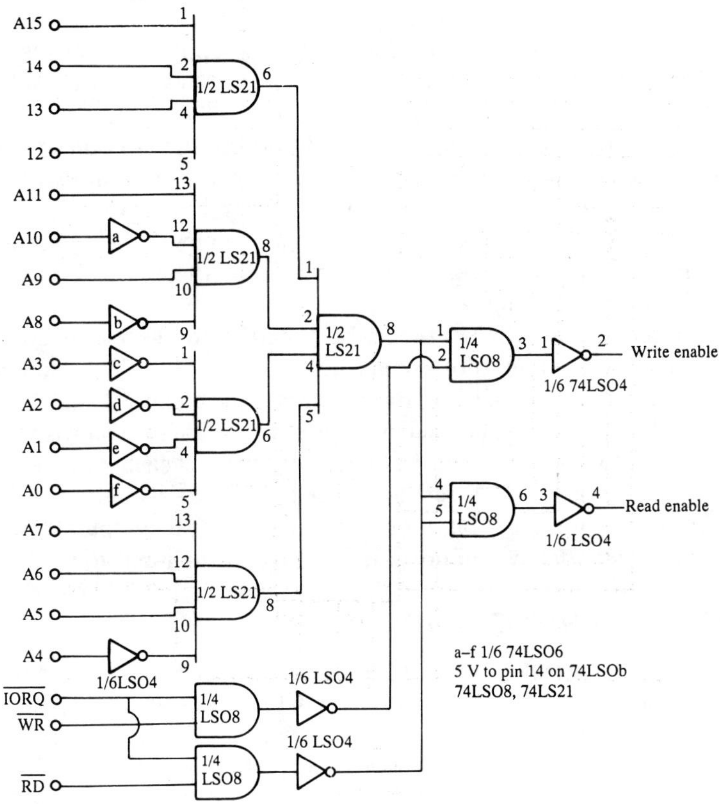
A15
14
13
12
A11
A10
A9
A8
A3
A2
A1
A0
A7
A6
A5
A4
IORQ
WR
RD
1/2 LS21
1/2 LS21
1/2 LS21
1/2 LS21
1/2 LS21
1/4 LSO8
1/4 LSO8
1/4 LSO8
1/4 LSO8
1/6LSO4
1/6 LSO4
1/6 LSO4
1/6 74LSO4
1/6 LSO4
Write enable
Read enable
a–f 1/6 74LSO6
5 V to pin 14 on 74LSOb
74LSO8, 74LS21

(b)

1 if it is an 'add on', *always* turn off the computer power before plugging in or unplugging the user port. Failure to do this will probably damage the computer.
2 on powering up with a user port connected, turn off immediately if there is anything unusual with the screen display, start up sequence, etc. This could indicate a faulty user port or that it is incorrectly plugged in.
3 do not connect any voltage outside the range 0 to 5V to digital user ports, and with analogue ports only apply voltages inside the limits specified by the manufacturer. *Never* even consider plugging mains voltages into a user port!
4 if you are adding circuits to the user port for input or output that require power, then it is often a good idea to use an external power supply if at all possible. This is because the power supplies of computers are usually built to power the computer and a couple of peripherals, not any old circuit that the users decide to add later!
5 in general, and unless otherwise stated in the user port documentation, inputs not connected to any TTL voltage source generally assume a logic '1' level, and so the common value read back from an unconnected 8 bit user port is 255. If you wish the inputs to assume a logic '0' value, then connect each input to 0V by a separate 2k2 resistor. Eight resistors would thus be required for an 8-bit user port, and are called 'pull down' resistors, as they pull down the voltage at the input to 0V.

General tips for 6502 and Z80 interfacing

The most common central processors on small, older home computers are the 8 bit Z80 and 6502 CPUs. Machines using these are often very suitable for interfacing because they are cheap and fairly straightforward to handle. Also, when you can pick up a second hand one for maybe £15 you are not too worried about eventually blowing it up!

Both these chips have 16 address lines, outputs from the CPU, and 8 data lines, which can be either inputs or outputs from the CPU depending upon what the CPU is doing. In addition, they both have a variety of control lines which the CPU sets to '1' or '0' depending upon what is happening in the computer.

The big difference as far as interfacing is concerned is that the Z80 has 65 536 locations in its address space for memory and a further 65 536 locations for I/O devices, accessed by combining the address lines with a line called IORQ, while the 6502 fits all its I/O requirements and memory requirements into the 65 536 location memory map. There is nothing to stop Z80 users doing this as well, but most computers have a full complement of memory and so finding a space for an I/O port in a Z80 memory map is often quite a challenge.

In general, therefore, use the I/O addresses on Z80 systems. This may require that a small machine code routine is needed to actually access the I/O addresses, as not all BASIC dialects have the required instructions to directly access I/O addresses. In memory mapped systems, the PEEK and POKE instructions from BASIC, or their equivalent, such as '?' on the BBC, can be used.

When adding an interface to the machine, check the memory and I/O maps for an apparently empty space and find out whether full or partial decoding is used by the computer designer. For example, on the Amstrad 6128 the I/O address map is only partially decoded, and if you attempt to use certain addresses in the I/O map you stand an excellent chance of burning out one of the chips in the computer!

Any chips directly connected to the computer buses should be LSTTL types (indicated by their 74LS numbers) or their CMOS counterparts, as these will draw only a little current from the computer buses and will not upset the workings of the computer too much. One point to note is that the leads from the computer bus to the interface board should not be too long; if they are, then some odd 'crashes' may occur due to the capacitance of the leads causing what are known as 'loading' problems for the CPU.

The terminal unit

The terminal unit is simply a piece of equipment that converts the audio signal from the receiver into an electrical signal that a computer user port can make use of. Typically, for the purposes of decoding modes like RTTY or CW, this means that the presence or absence of an audio tone at the TU input must give rise to, typically, a TTL level logic signal at the output. Whether a logic '1' output represents the presence of a tone depends upon the way in which the TU is designed, but I find it easier to think that '1' means that something is there!

Terminal units are, on the whole, frequency sensitive. For example, an input tone of 1 kHz may give a logic '1' output, but tones of 900 Hz or 1.1 kHz may give a logic '0' output. These circuits are often called FSK decoders, because they are used to decode FSK (frequency shift keyed) signals consisting of alternating tones of two different frequencies into a string of '1's and '0's. A simple FSK decoder circuit is shown in Figure 8.7. The two components Rf and Cf set the frequency to which the FSK decoder responds, and in use the receiver BFO would be tuned until the output indicator LED started indicating a string of '1's and '0's. This system will obviously only respond to one frequency, so if such a system were used for decoding RTTY, where we have alternating sequences of two frequencies, we would tune the receiver BFO to cause one of the two frequencies to give the '1' output and assume that '0' outputs from the decoder were due to the presence of the other frequency (or loss of signal).

In practice, this single tone approach can work and I have successfully decoded RTTY and CW on a TU like this using software listed later in this book. More complex terminal units, though, will have two decoders, one tuned to one of the frequencies being transmitted and the other tuned to the second frequency. The outputs from these two decoders could then be read in on different bits of a user port, or combined electronically before being presented to the user port. The advantage of this approach is that electrical noise and interference has less effect on the decoding process than for the single tone approach, but the setting up of the decoders has to be more accurate. In the single tone method, we can set up the decoder to respond to virtually any audio tone, then tune the receiver or its BFO until the incoming signal generates that tone at the input to the TU. We need not worry about the other frequency because of the assumption that we made that in the absence of one tone the other will be there. But if we are actually decoding both tones, then the spacing between the frequencies decoded by the tone decoders must be the same as the frequency spacing (the shift) between the two transmitted tones. This makes setting up of the 2-tone decoders more difficult, and also can make them less flexible because different RTTY stations, for example, use different shifts between their tones. (See Chapter 10 for more details.) We would thus have to re-align the decoders when changing shift to maintain 2-tone decoding, as if we did not

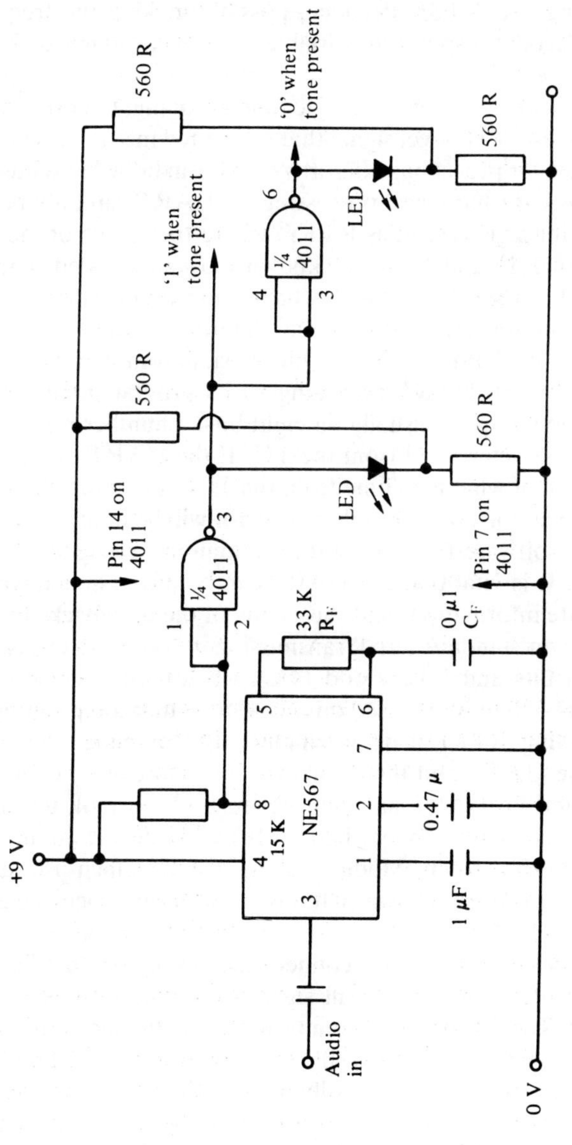
+9 V
560 R
560 R
'0' when tone present
'1' when tone present
¼ 4011
¼ 4011
LED
LED
560 R
560 R
Pin 14 on 4011
Pin 7 on 4011
33 K
R_F
0 µ1
C_F
15 K
NE567
0.47 µ
1 µF
Audio in
0 V

Figure 8.7

one decoder would be correctly tuned but the other would be spaced away from the first by the original shift, rather than the new one required. For experimenters, I would suggest building a simple single-tone FSK decoder, possibly making the frequency that the decoder responds to variable by using a variable resistor as Rf in Figure 8.7.

Whether we use 2-tone or single tone decoding, the usual output from a TU is a TTL level signal that can be fed into the user port of a computer for processing via software, or can be fed into the input of a UART for hardware processing. A UART can only be used for handling signals such as RTTY, where the timing of the tones representing '1's and '0's is well known and standardized. The TTL signal is fed into the UART, which must be programmed with details about the anticipated format in terms of data bits, start and stop bits, baud rate, etc. The bit stream from the TU is then analysed by the UART according to its programming, and the UART then outputs, usually on eight bits, a number representing the last 'character' read from the TU. If the UART cannot make head or tail of what has come from the TU – there may have been interference, for example – then an error will be indicated and it is up to the software running on the computer to recognise this and act on it. It is vital that the UART can be programmed with the appropiate information, and this is one of the drawbacks – RTTY is a very non-standard serial transmission in computer terms, using five data bits and a very odd (45.45) baud rate. However, the advantage of a system based on a UART is that the programming for receiving RTTY is very simple – the computer simply programs the UART and then waits for bytes to come in. Incoming bytes from the UART are then use to access a look up table of printable characters (see Chapter 10) and the incoming text is printed on the screen. Modes such as ASCII, which uses a more standard serial character format, are more easily processed using a UART.

If, however, you simply connect the output of the TU to an input bit of the user port, all signal decoding must be done by software. The computer program has to time the incoming signals, break the string of '1's and '0's into characters, and process the characters into text. This usually means machine code programming, whereas code for driving a UART is usually capable of being written in BASIC. However, direct interfacing of TU to user port in this way gives an incredible amount of flexibility, and I have to admit that I have never used a UART; I went straight from using direct interfacing of the TU to the user port to a commercial data decoder unit.

Using a terminal unit

Here are a couple of pointers for using a terminal unit, whether it is home made or commercially acquired. For the sake of argument, I have assumed that the TU gives a '1' output when a tone of the desired frequency is at the input.

Audio input to the TU
This is perhaps the most important part of using terminal units. Too much audio input, especially on the simple TUs like that shown above, can cause problems in that the TU will give a '1' output over a very wide range of frequencies, and will also be more prone to respond to noise signals with a '1' output. Indeed, in some cases the TU will even give a '1' output with *no* tone applied at the input! If the audio input is too low, the TU will not be able to lock onto the tone signal, and so no output will be obtained. There are two possible sources for audio on a receiver; a headphone socket, which usually provides a fairly high level signal into a low impedance of 8 to 16Ω. This signal is also usually controllable by the receiver volume control. An alternative source of audio on some receivers is a low level source that is intended for output to a tape recorder or some other such device. It is usually a high impedance source giving a few tens to a few hundreds of mV, which is often adequate for many decoders. The simple TU described above will take signals from either of these types of source. The easiest way to roughly set the input signal level to that needed is to tune in an AM signal with the BFO turned on, and then adjust the BFO until an output indication is obtained on the TU. Now decrease the level of audio signal from the receiver until no output is obtained from the TU. Now increase the receiver output level slightly until an output is obtained. Tuning the receiver through the carrier should now give a narrow frequency range over which the TU will achieve lock and output a signal. In use, of course, you may have to adjust the output level of the receiver to accommodate different levels of received signal, and if you do this then you should still adjust the receiver output level as

described above. If the receiver has an RF gain control, I often use this to vary the output to the TU because this will work on signals taken from the receiver at the low level tape recorder output sockets, as well as the headphone socket. One point to note is that, as with all short wave radio listening, receiver overload can give rise to a lot of whistles and noise in the loudspeaker which could cause spurious '1's to appear at the TU output. If you fear overloading, turn down the RF gain, shorten the aerial or insert some attenuation between the aerial and receiver. Details of solving overloading problems are given in *Newnes Short Wave Listening Handbook* by Joe Pritchard.

Tone frequency

The tone frequency to which the decoder is set can have implications for the receiver settings. For example, imagine we have a decoder set to 1kHz, and a receiver with an audio bandwidth for CW reception of 500Hz. The decoder is not going to get much 1 kHz audio from the receiver to decode, and so for best results the frequency at which the decoder operates should be within the audio bandwidth of the receiver mode selected.

Overloading and distortion at the TU

This is related to the problem with the audio input level. It is possible that if the receiver output is overdriven in any way – say by having the volume up too loud or applying too much RF gain – then sine wave audio signals are likely to be passed on to the TU in a distorted fashion. This can give rise to harmonics, which can again trick the TU into 'false locking'. For example, the presence of a distorted 500Hz tone could give rise to a 1kHz tone which might interfere with a 1kHz tone being decoded by the TU. Similarly, in extreme cases you may find that beat notes are generated – a 500Hz tone and a 1500Hz tone mixing together under certain conditions to give a 1kHz tone and a 2kHz tone. Again, the 1kHz tone could confuse the decoder. The solution here is to simply reduce the signal level reaching the TU or receiver.

Commercial data decoders

I shall be discussing this topic in greater detail in Chapter 14, and so all I shall mention here is that these units carry out the function of a TU and decoding software for many modes, passing data to a host computer usually via a serial interface. The data can then be directly displayed on a VDU screen, printed, saved to disc, etc. Much of what has been said about the problems with TUs also applies to commercial decoders.

Monitoring incoming signal strength

A further example of using the computer to monitor a parameter of the received signal is to use an ADC, such as that found in the BBC Microcomputer or one such as that shown in Chapter 12, to monitor the strength of the incoming radio signal. A block diagram to do this is shown in Figure 8.8. There are two ways in which we can provide an input signal to the circuit shown; the first is simply to take the audio output from the loudspeaker socket and feed it directly into the ADC. This has the advantage of simplicity, but the disadvantage that the reading sent to the computer will vary with the information being transmitted on the radio signal, rather than just varying with the signal strength. For example, a quiet piece of music would give a lower reading on the ADC than a loud piece of music. The second way is to use the something called the AGC voltage of the receiver; most superheterodyne receivers include a circuit called an AGC circuit – automatic gain control – to vary the amplification provided by the IF stages dependent upon the strength of the signal. A strong signal will need less IF gain, and vice versa. A voltage is fed back to the IF stages from the detector to control the gain, and this voltage is often metered in a receiver to provide a signal strength meter. A connection can be made across the meter, observing polarity, to use the voltage to drive the ADC. (Figure 8.9). The only point to watch is that the voltage is within the range of whatever ADC is used, and that you should only do this alteration if *you are sure of what you are doing*!

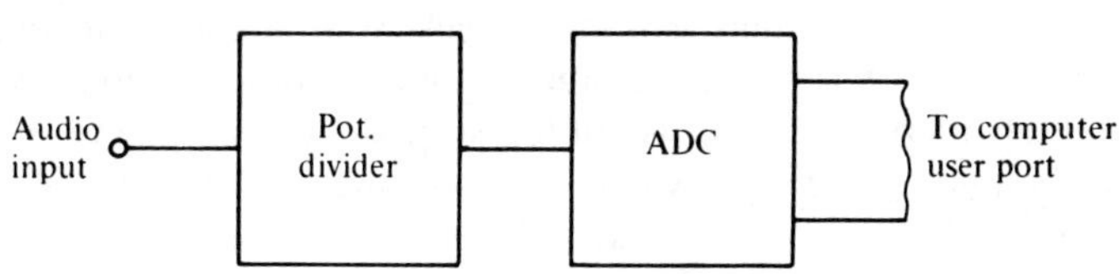

Figure 8.8

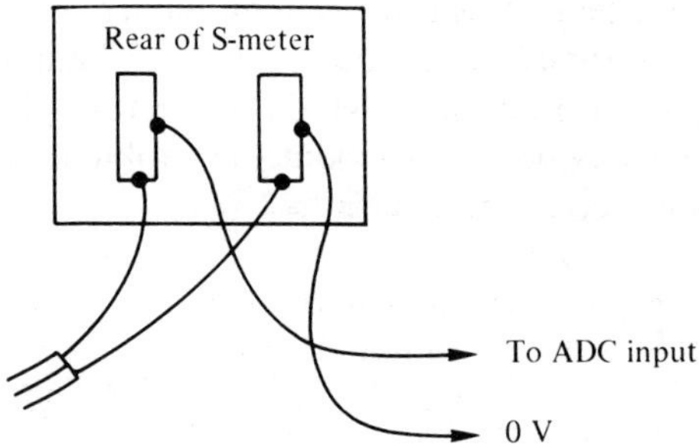

Figure 8.9

Control of the radio station

As well as using the computer to decode and generate radio signals in modes such as RTTY or SSTV, we can also use the computer actually to control certain aspects of the radio station. For example, we can use the computer, through a suitable interface, to control the tuning of many receivers, allowing us to tune the receiver automatically until a signal is located. Alternatively, the computer might be programmed to rotate aerials to point in a certain direction, or start a tape recorder at a particular time after first setting the receiver to a particular frequency. These applications all require the use of a user port, and I have detailed some of these ideas in Chapter 15.

Interference problems

Here is a simple experiment for you to try; turn on a radio receiver, and position it near to a computer running a program. Chances are, you will hear a phenomenal quantity of noise produced by the computer, especially if the receiver has a built in aerial of some sort. This is the major disadvantage to using the computer in the amateur radio shack; the amount of radio frequency interference generated by most home computers is absolutely incredible. This is not too surprising if we stop to think that computers work by switching electronic circuits from 0V to 5V and back again very quickly; this transition, which can occur millions of times each second, can be shown to generate radio waves over a wide range of frequencies and at considerable signal strength. For example, a computer may have a 1MHz oscillator providing clock signals to the microprocessor, and a 16 or 18MHz oscillator involved in driving the video circuitry. This will clearly give a 1MHz and 16 or 18MHz signal, as well as harmonics of these signals – 2, 3, 4, 32, 48MHz and so on. In addition, there may be other oscillator circuits in the computer, and various peripheral devices such as disc drives and printers may also generate noise signals. TVs and VDUs also generate large amounts of interference – for example, a TV uses a 15kHz oscillator to produce the picture, and this signal will generate interference over much of the low frequency RF spectrum.

Methods of RFI propagation

Radio frequency interference (RFI) generated by the computer has to get into the receiver to cause us problems. The earlier on in the receiver the interference enters, the louder the interference will be as compared to the desired signal. Thus, if the interference gets into the receiver circuits at the aerial input, it can easily be as loud as the signal that is being tuned in. RFI can enter the receiver in the following ways:

Radiation
Here, the signal is radiated as a radio wave by the computer or peripheral and is received in the receiver as if it were a 'normal' radio signal. The RFI may enter the receiver at the input stages, IF stages or even by direct breakthrough into the audio circuits of the receiver.

Direct injection
Here, the interference travels from the computer into the receiver as an electrical signal passing down a connection between some part of the computer system and some part of the radio receiver. The connection can be a direct link between the audio output of the receiver and an input to a computer user port, or might be an indirect connection via the mains leads of the computer equipment and the radio equipment.

Combination of the two
It is possible for the computer to inject RFI into the home's mains wiring down its mains lead, which then gets reradiated by the wiring of the house and picked up by the receiver as previously

described. The house wiring will act as an aerial in this situation, and so a computer in a totally different room can cause interference to a receiver.

Let us examine what aspects of a computer and radio receiving system affect the level of RFI generated by computers and received on the radio set.

Activity of the computer

Interference is often worse when the computer is performing some task, such as running a program or accessing peripherals such as discs or printers. Do not forget that the interference in these latter cases may be due to the peripheral device rather than the computer itself.

Proximity of receiver and computer

If the computer and receiver (or receiver aerial) are quite close together, then the interference is likely to be worse than if the two pieces of equipment are far apart. The proximity effect is also noticed between cables; if, for example, we ran the mains cable of the computer next to the aerial cable of the receiver, then any RFI on the mains cable would be introduced fairly easily into the receiver input by radiation. In general, any part of the computer system should be kept away from the receiver or any cabling associated with the receiver.

Is the computer screened?

Many computers have plastic cases; this is not too good from our point of view because any RFI generated by the computer will be radiated straight out through the case. Computers with a metal case, or with internal metal boxes around parts of the circuitry that may radiate, will produce less interference, due to the screening effect of the metal, which will reduce the amount of radiated RFI. The same thing applies to peripherals, as well, and interference is reduced in some cases if the case of the receiver is metal rather than plastic. In general, earthed metal cases for equipment will reduce interference, and later in this chapter I shall discuss screening as a cure to interference.

Type of computer technology

Certain computers will give less interference than others. Often, this is as much due to the chips used in the computer as to any screening methods used. Low power MOS chips are often quieter in RFI terms than TTL chips are. In addition, fast digital circuitry will tend to generate more interference than slower circuitry.

Type of aerial

In general, an external aerial feeding the receiver via coaxial cable is going to suffer less interference than a receiver whose aerial is in the same room as the computer, or is using the telescopic aerial of the receiver.

Is an ATU used?

An aerial tuning unit (ATU) will often give amazing improvements of signal to noise ratios with all sorts of interference, including computer noise. This device is used to match the impedance of the aerial to that of the receiver input at a given frequency, and will thus maximise signal transfer at that frequency. Due to the wide-band nature of computer noise, this will minimise noise getting into the front-end circuits of the receiver at frequencies other than that desired, which will reduce the overall effects of the computer interference. Over the past few years, some companies have marketed devices which allow you to specifically 'tune out' interference, and these devices will give good results with computer noise.

Frequency of reception

You will find that computer noise will exhibit itself in two ways. One will be a prominent rushing, whistling or buzzing noise synchronized with computer activity, often on specific frequencies, and the other type of interference is just a general increase in the background noise over a wide range of frequencies. This latter type of interference can be hard to spot until you turn off the computer or peripheral causing the problem; the silence can then be deafening! The level of noise will vary across the RF spectrum; certain computers will peak at different areas of the spectrum; for example, my PC seems to generate most noise in the low VHF regions, but the apparent level of noise at different frequencies may be due to the leads that are radiating the interference simply being of a resonant length at that frequency. However, most computers will generate certain 'spot' frequencies, no matter how well they are screened, and much work with screening and filtering is simply to reduce the numbers of the spot frequency interference problems and to reduce the general background noise to as low a level as possible.

Filtering

As well as screening the computer, filtering can be applied to leads into and out of the computer, and to mains cables. Whereas screening is involved in reducing radiated interference, filtering will take out signals of a particular frequency flowing through electrical circuits whilst leaving signals of desired frequency unaffected. I shall detail this later in the chapter, but filtering can have considerable effects on the levels of interference.

Method of connection between receiver and terminal unit

Figure 8.10 shows a typical receiving set up; one important point to note is that there is at least one direct connection between the receiver and the computer, through the terminal unit. The 0V line of all three pieces of equipment is common, and the ground of a computer will often have a considerable level of digital noise on it. This does not affect the computer, but will certainly be noticeable on the receiver. Let us just think about what electrical signals we need to transfer between the receiver and the terminal unit, and the TU and the computer. In general, we are interested in signals from the receiver in the range 0 to 3 – 4kHz. Anything above this

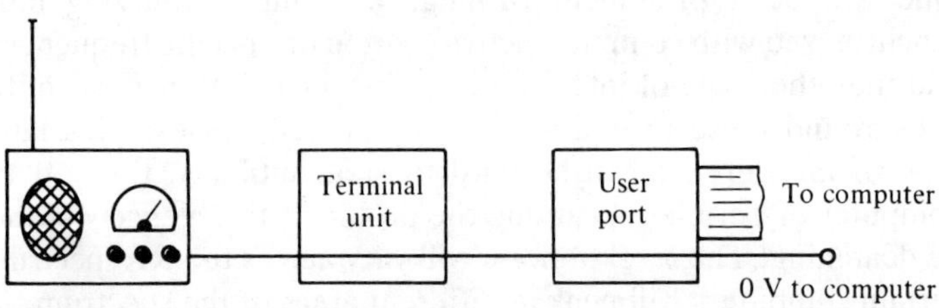

Figure 8.10

range can be discarded. From the TU to the computer, we are generally transferring either a serial bit stream at the rate of the signal received (e.g. for 100 baud ASCII we would be passing a 100 baud bit stream from the TU to the computer, a series of 8 bit bytes to be read in to the user port or an RS232 signal. We can thus adopt two methods of reducing interference via direct injection, by filtering the receiver audio input to the TU, and somehow breaking the direct connection between the computer ground and the TU. Figure 8.11 shows a simple filter, using chokes and capacitors, to insert between the receiver audio output and the TU input. Note that this type of filtering may have adverse effects on very rapid signals if too much of it is applied. You might also try connecting a filter like this between the computer and the terminal unit, but this would still have a direct 0V link between all three pieces of equipment. However, it is almost certainly going to reduce the interference somewhat. The best connection between the TU and computer though, if possible, is to break the direct electrical connection with an opto-isolator. This consists of a light source and a sensor in a single package, and accepts TTL signals from the TU as inputs and gives a TTL signal out to the computer. This is obviously best suited when only a single data bit is used, although there is nothing to stop you using one for each bit in a parallel data transfer system. In the simple form shown in Figure 8.12, it is not suitable for RS232 interfaces. One important thing to remember is that the power supplies for the computer, opto-isolator and terminal unit should be separated; there is no point in powering the TU from the computer, as this will effectively bypass the opto-isolator. It is quite alright, though, to power the output side of the opto-isolator from the computer and the input side from the TU power supply.

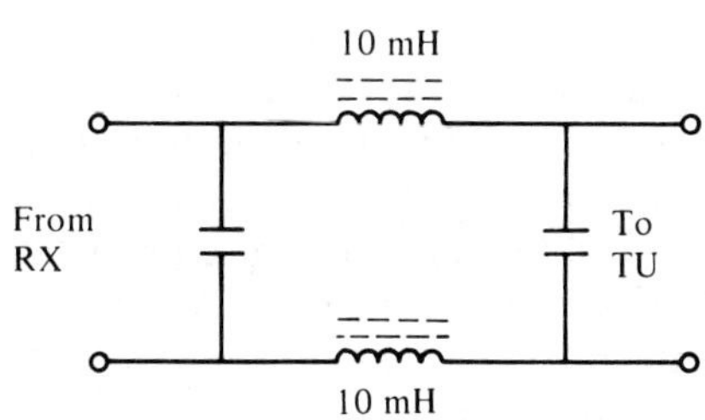

Figure 8.11

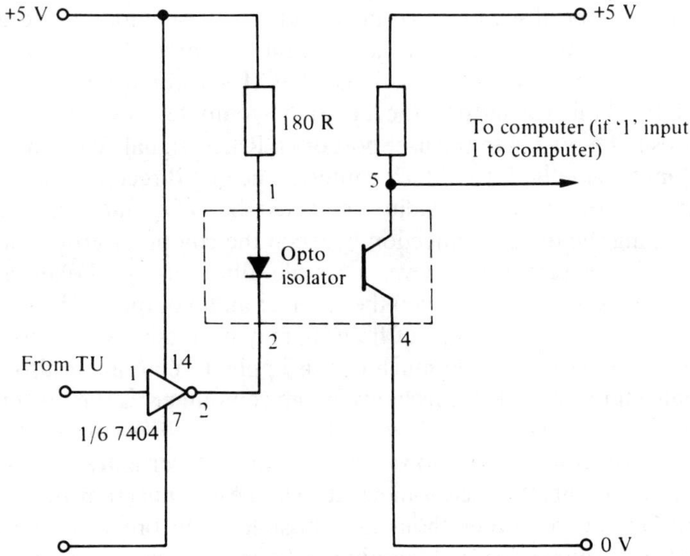

Figure 8.12

Filtering

We have just briefly mentioned filtering between the different parts of the receiving set up, and here I would like to elaborate on the subject.

Using ferrite rods and toroids

Ferrite is a brittle grey material made of finely divided iron oxide particles, which is used in radio for winding coils of considerable inductance with relatively few turns of wire. The simplest form of filtering we can adopt is to wrap leads and cables around a ferrite rod or through a ferrite toroid, as shown in Figure 8.13. This can be done with signal wires between the pieces of the equipment or with mains cables (using different ferrite rods, however!) and can reduce interference considerably, especially that travelling down the mains cables of different pieces of equipment. One point to note is that you may find that the number of turns of cable on the ferrite has an effect on the degree of interference suppression – more turns will not always give more suppression. When setting up this type of interference suppression it is a good idea to set a

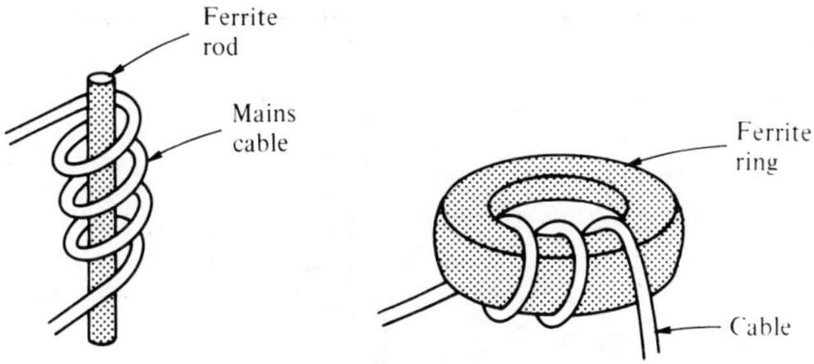

Figure 8.13

simple program running on the computer, and tune for 'maximum interference' on the receiver. You can then vary the turns on the ferrite until the interference is minimised; it is very unlikely that you will totally eradicate it. You might also try wrapping the leads between the computer and any peripherals around a ferrite rod, as well as the power leads of peripherals. When applying filters in this way, fit them as close to the equipment as possible, as this will reduce the amount of RFI getting in to the cable which can be radiated as interference.

Filter circuits

A further way of filtering the mains leads is to use some form of filter circuit inside the plug, or to use a plug or distribution board that includes an RFI filter inside the plug. Figure 8.14 shows a

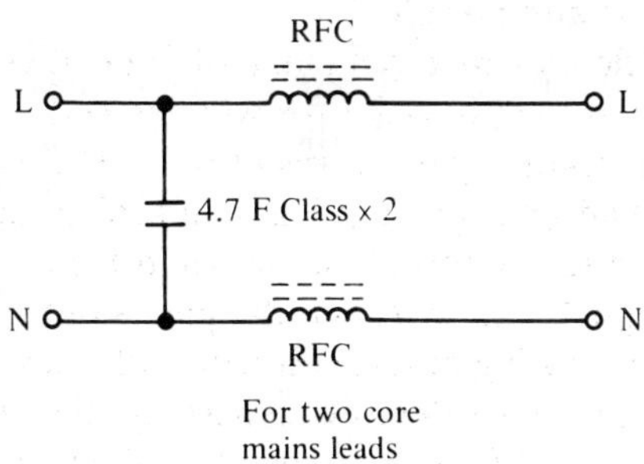

RFC – chokes rated for mains current drawn

Class x 2 – mains rated capacitor

Figure 8.14

simple filter which can be used to filter a mains lead. Only build and fit this, however, if you are *very sure* of what you are doing; if there is *any* doubt at all, get an expert involved, as mains voltages can kill. The commercially available RFI filters will remove interference in the range 100kHz to 30 or so MHz, and cost between £10 and £20 to purchase. If you can only afford one, fit it to the computer power lead, or, if your computer system is powered via a 4 way distribution board, to the power lead feeding the distribution board.

Screening

To reduce radiated RFI we need to screen the equipment that is radiating. There are two prime sources of radiated RFI; the equipment itself and unfiltered leads connected to the equipment.

With regard to leads, the simplest solution is to apply filtering and then, if radiated RFI continues, consider screened leads. This is possible for signal carrying leads, but is not feasible for mains leads. If you use a screened signal lead, do not forget to earth the screen to the chassis of the equipment.

When we come to look at the equipment, then the best approach is to purchase equipment with a metal case in the first place! However, this is not always possible, so there are two solutions. The first is to re-house the equipment in a metal case. Companies have made metal cases available for some computers, but the second option – adding screening – is a better bet. Basically, screening requires that all gaps through which radio waves could escape are covered in a metallic coating of some sort, whether that coating is foil, sheet metal or even electrically conductive paint. To detect whether the screening of the computer or peripheral is a little lacking, move your hand around the case of the computer; frequently poor screening exhibits itself as an increase in RFI when your hand approaches some parts of the case, due to your body acting as a radio aerial.

The screening that you can apply yourself drops into two categories:

Metal foil
The computer circuitry needs to be removed from the case and the case lined with aluminium foil, glued where appropriate. Care must be taken to ensure that any ventilation holes, socket holes and

screw holes are left clear of foil and that when the case is put back together a good electrical connection will be present between the different parts of the case. To ensure this you may need to make physical connections between different parts of the case using wire. The earth connection to the foil must be made by drilling the case and using a nut, bolt and washer to make connections to the aluminium foil as you cannot solder it. The main problems start when you come to actually put the circuitry back into the case; you must ensure that there is no possibility of inadvertent short circuits between the circuit board and the metal foil. I have found plastic card to be useful here; a sheet or two laid on top of the metal foil will form a rigid layer between the computer circuit boards and the foil and thus reduce the risk of short circuits.

Conductive paint

In recent years, electrically conductive paint has become available which can be sprayed on to the inside of plastic cases to provide a screening layer. When spraying a plastic case, try the paint out first on part of the case that is not too important, and allow the paint to dry thoroughly, just to make sure that the paint does not dissolve or distort the plastic! Before spraying the case, you must remove all the computer's electronics, including any built in hard or floppy disc drives and switches. After spraying, a nut, bolt and washer can be used to make electrical contact with the case screen. The rest of the points above for metal foil still hold true for conductive paint.

General points about interference

To conclude this chapter, here are a few points about RFI reduction to bear in mind:

1 keep aerial leads and receivers as far away as practicable from the computer and peripherals.
2 try to plug the computer into a different mains socket than the receiver.
3 use filtering and screening where necessary.
4 use opto-isolators to break the continuous 0V line from receiver to TU to computer.
5 check your peripherals; some configurations of your system may generate more interference than others. For example, the RGB

output of the BBC Microcomputer is well known for generating interference. Do not use an RGB monitor, but use the composite video or TV output instead. In fact, do not even have a lead connected to the RGB output!

6 some computers are noticeably better than others. For example, the Psion Pocket Organiser, with a serial interface, is surprisingly quiet on most frequencies, as is the Toshiba 1200 laptop PC. MSX computers, originally hailed as games machines, are also quite good due to the more stringent Japanese and US requirements for RFI suppression.

NINE

Morse code

It is an interesting irony that the oldest form of radio communication should be one of the hardest to decode using a computer, but that is precisely the situation with morse code, or CW as it is also known.

As we have already learned, the basic method of sending morse is to turn a carrier wave on and off to generate a sequence of short signals (*dots*, or *dits*) and long signals (*dashes*, or *dahs*). Each letter in the alphabet, and numbers and punctuation, can be sent as a sequence of dots and dashes using the morse code, as described below.

A	· –	S	· · ·
B	– · · ·	T	–
C	– · – ·	U	· · –
D	– · ·	V	· · · –
E	·	W	· – –
F	· · – ·	X	– · · –
G	– – ·	Y	– · – –
H	· · · ·	Z	– – · ·
I	· ·	1	· – – – –
J	· – – –	2	· · – – –
K	– · –	3	· · · – –
L	· – · ·	4	· · · · –
M	– –	5	· · · · ·
N	– ·	6	– · · · ·
O	– – –	7	– – · · ·
P	· – – ·	8	– – – · ·
Q	– – · –	9	– – – – ·
R	· – ·	0	– – – – –

ERROR SIGNAL	· · · · · · · ·
MESSAGE ENDS	· – · – ·
MESSAGE STARTS	– · – · –
?	· · – – · ·
.	· – · – · –
,	– – · · – –

A morse signal is defined by certain parameters. These are as follows:

Dit length
This is the length of the '·' part of the morse sequence, and it is the basic timing element of the morse signal. In computer terms, the 'dit' is the bit length for this means of serial communications.

Dah length
This is the length of time that the '–' element takes to send, and is formally defined as being three times the dit length.

Inter-element gap
This gap is the amount of time between consecutive dits and dahs that make up an individual morse code character. It is defined as a period of silence equal in length to a dit.

Inter-letter gap
This is the length of time separating the last element of one character in a word from the first element of the next character in the word. It is specified as being the length of a single dah.

Inter-word gap
This is the gap between the last element of the last character of one word and the first element of the first character of the next word. It is defined as a period of silence seven dits long.

There are some variations to this timing allowed; for example, a technique called *Farnsworth spacing* is often used when learning morse; here, the inter letter gap is made considerably longer than would be expected from the dit length.

Morse speed is described in terms of 'words per minute' a rather woolly phrase which basically indicates the number of average words that is transmitted in morse in one minute. A standard exists, using the word PARIS as the average word in terms of morse elements to be transmitted, and a speed of 12 words per minute would allow the word PARIS to be transmitted twelve times in that period. When people are tested for morse ability, as is required for the UK Class A Amateur Radio Licence, a text is supplied to be transmitted. A more scientific way of describing morse speed is in the length of time, in milliseconds, that a dit takes to send. A general rule is:

6 words per minute has a dit length of 200 ms
12 words per minute has a dit length of 100 ms
18 words per minute has a dit length of 65 ms

You might think that with all timings being related to the dit length, decoding morse by computer should be easy. Well, there are two problems. The first is that the dit length will vary from morse operator to morse operator, as they all have different sending speeds. This means that any morse code software used to decode morse automatically must estimate the dit length before it can start deciding whether a received signal is a dit or a dah. The more serious problem is that, humans being human, the dit length will vary during a transmission, and that no one is perfect in estimating dash and inter element lengths, thus leading to dashes that might be two or four times the dit length, with longer or shorter inter-element lengths. In addition, this may vary throughout the transmission. The software should therefore keep a running check on dit length and spacing as it decodes, and adjust its own timing to suit that of the incoming morse. This is a problem, and no morse software is perfect in decoding under all conditions, as the adaptation to changes in sending speed or style take a finite amount of time to be reflected in the decoder software, thus leading to the potential loss of one or more elements of the transmitted signal. In fact, it is a good rule of thumb that if your morse decoding software receives flawless morse from a station over a period of time, chances are that the transmitting station is actually using computer generated morse!

Simple decoding software

The raw material for decoding software is a sequence of binary '1's and '0's that can be detected by a computer user port as representing 'key down' times, when the transmitter is actually sending dots and dashes, and 'key up' times when there is no signal being received. The output from a single tone FSK decoder, as previously described, can be used, with the presence of a dot or a dash being represented by a '1' output from the FSK decoder and the presence of no signal being a '0' output. The lengths of the '1' signals will clearly indicate whether a dot or a dash is being received. The FSK decoder should have as narrow a bandwidth as possible, because short bursts of interference may easily cause momentary '1' outputs from the decoder to the computer, that could easily be misconstrued as dits by the computer. More details about tuning in morse signals, and the adjustments to make to your receiver, will be given later in the chapter.

Writing decoding software is not too difficult when the signals being decoded are fairly strong, well sent, and do not vary too much in sending speed. The main considerations in decoding are that the program should accommodate a variety of sending speeds and that the dots and dashes received should be processed to provide a unique character identifier to indicate which character is to be printed out.

```
10 REM Morse code decoding software for the BBC Microcomputer
20 REM
30 REM
40 ?&FE62=0 : REM set all lines to input
50 DIM letter$(66), power%(5)
60 FOR I%=1 TO 64: READ letter$(I%): NEXT
70 FOR I%=1 TO 5: READ power%(i%) : NEXT
80 :
90 dit%=55
100 gap%=dit%
110 letter%=3*dit%
120 :
130 REM start decoding here
140 :
150 REPEAT
160   UNTIL (?&FE60 AND 1) = 0 : REM wait for a space
170 :
180 C%=0 : REM character being built up in C%
190 P%=0 : REM pointer to a power of 2 table in power%()
200 :
210 IF P% < 5 THEN D%=power%(P%) : P%=P%+1 : REM pick up next power if
215 :                                        REM needed.
220 REPEAT
230   UNTIL (?&FE60 AND 1) = 1 : REM wait for a mark
240 :
250 T%=0: REM counter for mark time
260 REPEAT
270   T%=T%+1
280   UNTIL  (?&FE60 AND 1) = 0 : REM count up the mark time
290 :
300 REM now we analyse the mark time to see if it's a dot or a dash.  In
310 REM addition, we need to decide whether the dit and dah lengths need
320 REM to be altered to take account of any chnages in sending speed by
330 REM altering the value of dit%
340 :
```

```
350 IF T% > dit%*2 THEN C%=C%+D%*2 ELSE C%=C%+D%
360 :
370 REM if the mark length is longer than dit%*2 then treat as a dah.
380 REM add 2* the current power of 2 to C%.  If it's a dit, then simply
390 REM add the power of 2.  We can't just use the power of 2 because we
400 REM have a 3 state system - dit, dah and silence.  This will
410 REM eventually lead to a value between 0 and 63 in C%
420 :
430 REM now update the dit length by a weighted average.
440 :
450 IF T%<dit%*2 THEN dit%=(4*dit%+T%) / 5
452 letter% = 3*dit% : REM you might like to experiment with this line
453 gap%=dit%
460 :
470 REM now time the space to see if we can print the letter out yet
480 :
490 T%=0
500 IF T% > letter% THEN GOSUB 1000:GOSUB 1100:GOTO 130
510 T%=T%+1 : REM increment counter while still space
520 IF (?&FE60 AND 1) = 0 THEN GOTO 500
530 IF T%>gap% THEN GOSUB 1000: GOTO 180
540 GOTO 210
560 :
1000 REM subroutine to print out a single letter
1010 :
1020 IF C% < 65 THEN PRINT letter$(C%); ELSE PRINT "-";
1030 RETURN
1040 :
1050 DATA e,t,i,n,a,m,s,d,r,g,u,k,w,o,h,b,l,z,f,c.p,-,v,x,-
1060 DATA q,y,-,j,-,5,6,-,7,-,-,-,8,-,-,-,-,-,-,-,9,4,-,-,-,-,-,-,-
1070 DATA 3,-,-,-,2,-,1,0,-,-
1080 DATA 1,2,4,8,16
1090 :
1100 REM print a single space out
1110 PRINT " ";
1120 RETURN
```

Listing 9.1

Listing 9.1 shows a simple morse code decoding algorithm which will decode morse at a variety of speeds and will adapt itself to different sending speeds. It is written for the BBC Microcomputer, and uses bit 0 of that machine's user port at address &FE60 for input. The program can be modified to run on other machines by replacing the procedure calls with subroutine calls, changing variable names if your system will not take long names of integer variables, and changing the address of the input port used to suit your system.

How the system decodes letters

I decided to use the following system to convert a sequence of dots and dashes into a unique identifier. A dash is anything that is longer than twice the duration of a dot, and a simple power of two table is used to code incoming morse elements into a letter code:

1 initialize a pointer into a table of powers of two up to 2^5; most characters in morse only have five elements. Set the pointer to 1 and then wait for a key down on the input port. Initialize a character code to 0.
2 time the key-down period; if it is a dot then add the value 2^n, where n is the value of the pointer into the power of 2 table, to the character code. If it is a dash, then add twice the value of 2^n to the character code.
3 increment the pointer; if it is less than 6 then wait for the next key down and go to stage 2. If the space period exceeds a pre-set time then assume that the last element was the last dot or dash in the character. In this case, do not go to stage 2 again.
4 if we have already received five elements or we have decided that the end of a character has been reached, then use the code assembled to look up the character to be printed.
5 print the character and then go back to stage 1.

There are problems with this simple approach; for example, if any of the punctuation elements of morse are received with more than five elements, then an error will certainly occur.

How the system copes with speed changes

Accommodating changes in sending speed is slightly more involved, and I have used a technique called *weighted averaging* to get the system to respond to changes in sending speed. This system has been used in several published program listings, so I claim no originality for it. In this system, the duration of the last received dash, for example, is added to a multiple of the expected dash length, and an average is calculated which will be used for the new expected dash length. For example:

(Expected Dash Length * 4) + Current Dash Length / 5

is a typical weighted average, in that the new Expected Dash Length will be quite similar to the old Expected Dash Length unless a radical change has occurred in the Current Dash Length. This has the effect of filtering out transient changes in sending speed by weighting the new value in favour of the old value. For a change to have a long term effect, therefore, it must occur frequently.

The value of 4 used above as a weighting factor will give a system that will respond to changes in sending speed rather well, but it may be thrown out occasionally by one-off, quick changes in sending speed or signal fades. A larger value will be less responsive to transient changes but will take longer to respond to real changes in sending speed. As in much of life, you pays your money and you takes your choice.

In the program listing, lines 200 to 220 wait for a dot or dash to be received, and then lines 250 to 300 get the length of the incoming signal. If the key is released, and a '0' detected, before the incoming signal is greater than twice the dot length then it is treated as a dash. Lines 370 to 420 then look at the space time and if it is less than twice the dot length treat it as a gap in a single letter and go and get the next dot or dash. Any longer than this and we treat it as a gap between letters and so we can now go and print the letter whose code has been assembled in C%.. Finally, a further check is made on the duration of the space in lines 440 to 490 and if it is longer than a dot we assume a word break and print a space.

In use, the program is simply run and a morse code signal tuned in off air. After a few characters, text should start appearing on the screen. There are a variety of amendments that you can make to this program, and in Listing 9.2 I have provided a rather sophisticated system which also allows incoming morse to be recorded and played back for self testing purposes as well as allowing the morse to be printed on a printer if connected. Again, this listing is for the BBC Microcomputer, but it could be modified to suit any other computer using BASIC.

```
10 REM Morse code decoding software for the BBC Microcomputer
20 REM Includes printer control and playback of morse.  Jump to
22 REM playback routine by pressing ESCAPE key.  Routine plays back
23 REM first 1000 characters of morse received
24 :
25 ON ERROR GOTO 5000
30 ?&FE62=0 : REM set all lines to input
50 DIM letter$(66), power%(5), morse%(1000)
60 FOR I%=1 TO 64: READ letter$(I%): NEXT
70 FOR I%=1 TO 5: READ power%(i%) : NEXT
80 :
90 dit%=55
100 gap%=dit%
110 letter%=3*dit%
111 INPUT "Store morse received? ",store$
112 INPUT "Print Received Morse? ",pr$
113 :
114 REM pr$="Y" will turn printer on.
115 REM store$="Y" will stuff letter codes into morse%()
116 :
```

```
117 pointer%=1
118 IF pr$="Y" OR pr$="y" THEN VDU 2 : REM VDU 2 turns printer on
120 :
130 REM start decoding here
140 :
150 REPEAT
160   UNTIL (?&FE60 AND 1) = 0 : REM wait for a space
170 :
180 C%=0 : REM character being built up in C%
190 P%=0 : REM pointer to a power of 2 table in power%()
200 :
210 IF P% < 5 THEN D%=power%(P%) : P%=P%+1 : REM pick up next power if
215 :                                  REM needed.
220 REPEAT
230   UNTIL (?&FE60 AND 1) = 1 : REM wait for a mark
240 :
250 T%=0: REM counter for mark time
260 REPEAT
270   T%=T%+1
280   UNTIL (?&FE60 AND 1) = 0 : REM count up the mark time
290 :
300 REM now we analyse the mark time to see if it's a dot or a dash. In
310 REM addition, we need to decide whether the dit and dah lengths need
320 REM to be altered to take account of any chnages in sending speed by
330 REM altering the value of dit%
340 :
350 IF T% > dit%*2 THEN C%=C%+D%*2 ELSE C%=C%+D%
360 :
370 REM if the mark length is longer than dit%*2 then treat as a dah.
380 REM add 2* the current power of 2 to C%. If it's a dit, then simply
390 REM add the power of 2. We can't just use the power of 2 because we
400 REM have a 3 state system - dit, dah and silence. This will
410 REM eventually lead to a value between 0 and 63 in C%
420 :
430 REM now update the dit length by a weighted average.
440 :
450 IF T%<dit%*2 THEN dit%=(4*dit%+T%) / 5
452 letter% = 3*dit% : REM you might like to experiment with this line
453 gap%=dit%
460 :
470 REM now time the space to see if we can print the letter out yet
480 :
490 T%=0
500 IF T% > letter% THEN GOSUB 1000:GOSUB 1100:GOTO 130
510 T%=T%+1 : REM increment counter while still space
520 IF (?&FE60 AND 1) = 0 THEN GOTO 500
530 IF T%>gap% THEN GOSUB 1000: GOTO 180
540 GOTO 210
560 :
1000 REM subroutine to print out a single letter
1010 :
1020 IF C% < 65 THEN PRINT letter$(C%); ELSE PRINT "-";
1025 IF store$="N" OR store$="n" THEN GOTO 1030
1026 IF pointer% < 1001 THEN morse%(pointer%) = ASC(letter$(C%))-32
1030 RETURN
1040 :
1050 DATA e,t,i,n,a,m,s,d,r,g,u,k,w,o,h,b,l,z,f,c.p,-,v,x,-
1060 DATA q,y,-,j,-,5,6,-,7,-,-,-,8,-,-,-,-,-,-,-,9,4,-,-,-,-,-,-,-
1070 DATA 3,-,-,-,2,-,1,0,-,-
1080 DATA 1,2,4,8,16
1090 :
1100 REM print a single space out
1110 PRINT " ";
1120 RETURN
2000 :
5000 REM this is the playback routine. First thing is to turn the printer
5010 REM off. Then we play back the morse in the morse% array at a rate
```

```
5020 REM set by the user.
5030 :
5032 VDU 3 : REM turn off the printer
5035 INPUT "What is the dit length ",dit%
5040 INPUT "What is the letter spacing ",spacing%
5060 FOR P%=1 TO pointer% : REM go through the text string
5070 :
5080 K%=morse%(pointer%)-64
5090 RESTORE 5190
5093 FOR I%=1 TO K%:READ B$:NEXT I% : REM get the morse string
5095 :
5096 IF K% < 1 THEN SOUND 1,0,100,dit%*8 : REM generate a silence for
5097 :                                 REM spaces or punctuation
5098 :
5100 FOR J%=1 TO LEN(B$) : REM scan thru the morse characters
5101 :
5110 IF MID$(B$,J%,1)="." THEN SOUND 1,-12,100,dit%
5115 :
5120 IF MID$(B$,J%,1)="-" THEN SOUND 1,-12,100,dit%*3
5130 SOUND 1,0,100,dit% : REM this is a delay of a dit length
5140 NEXT J%
5150 :
5151 REM Next line is also a delay, of the inter-letter gap
5152 :
5155 FOR F%=1 TO spacing%: SOUND 1,0,100,dit%:NEXT F%
5160 :
5165 NEXT P% : REM go for next letter
5166 :
5167 REM Now print out the letters
5168 :
5169 FOR I%=1 TO pointer%
5170 PRINT CHR$(morse%(I%));
5172 NEXT I%
5173 END
5174 :
5180 DATA A,B,C,D,F,G,H,I,J,K,L,M,N,O,P,Q,R,S,T,U,V,W,X,Y,Z
5190 DATA .-,-...,-.-.,-..,.,..-.,--.,....,..,.---,-.-,.-..,--,-.,---,.--,
5200 DATA --.-,.-.,...,-,..-,...-,.--,-..-,-.--,--..
```

Listing 9.2

Testing your sending

A morse key can be connected to the input of such a program to allow you to test your own morse sending. The computer will show up failings in your morse that a human operator would not detect, but make sure that the computer program is working first before you try testing your morse! The key needs to be connected in such a way as to mimic the output from the FSK decoder. In the case of the programs described here, therefore, the key needs to give a '1' output when the key is down and a '0' output when the key is up. Figure 9.1 shows a simple circuit for connecting a morse key to a user port to give both outputs if required.

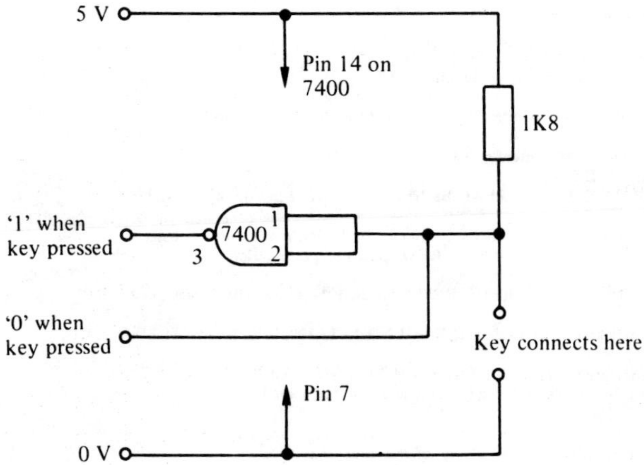

Figure 9.1

Tuning in morse

Morse transmissions can only be resolved with a CW or sideband setting on your receiver, and typically have a narrow bandwidth. When tuning in CW for reception by ear, it is simply a case of tuning the signal for maximum loudness and clarity, but when tuning in CW for machine reception, life is more complicated for the following reasons.

FSK decoder frequency

A simple FSK decoder will respond to one frequency. In some designs, this may be tunable but in most it is not variable and so you need to tune the receiver main tuning or BFO control to bring the tone generated by the incoming dots and dashes into the centre of the FSK decoder tuning range.

Receiver bandwidth

If the FSK decoder or terminal unit used requires an incoming tone of more than a few hundred Hz for CW reception, you may have difficulty using the CW setting of your receiver, especially if it has a very narrow bandwidth. If you cannot get a squeak out of your decoder when tuning the receiver in the CW setting, try setting the receiver for LSB or USB reception instead.

Receiver volume
The audio output for the FSK decoder can, as we have already described, be taken from a variety of places in the receiver. If the drive is insufficient the decoder or terminal unit will not lock on to the dots and dashes and you will get either nothing or an intermittent output from the decoder to the computer. If the audio input signal to the decoder or TU is too great, this will tend to overload the decoder or TU and lead to increased interference from neighbouring signals, resulting in poor results.

The first thing to do is to check which mode will give good results with your TU or decoder. I do this by tuning in an AM broadcast signal – say in the 49 metre band – in LSB, USB or CW receiver modes and then tune the receiver whilst monitoring the terminal unit or decoder lock indicator. Try different volume settings, and see which settings of volume and mode give the best lock indication. This will be when a small movement of the tuning control causes the lock indicator to signal a lock and then lose it again. Too much audio here will give a lock indication almost all the time that there is a tone of any frequency present – this is not a good idea, as interference will get through. Use the good-lock receiver settings for CW decoding, and when decoding CW signals use the minimum amount of audio input that is consistent with solid copy. Do not forget that interference spikes will easily be read as letter 'e's or 'h's by most software.

Morse code tutor programs

Generating morse is much easier than decoding it, and morse keyboards have been on the market for some years, allowing the user to type text in on a computer keyboard and send perfect morse code on their transmitter. Computers also have uses when it comes to teaching people the morse code. Traditionally, morse tuition was via records containing morse code messages or the slow morse transmissions sent by various amateur radio organisations, as well as amateurs sending morse code to one another on morse practice oscillators. The records had one big disadvantage, in that the morse on them was easily memorised, thus leading to a false sense of ability based on your sending and receiving speed with known material. A computer can easily be programmed to generate random morse letters and messages at any speed you please, as shown by the program in Listing 9.3. An additional feature of computer morse tutor programs is that the morse code generated, though random, can be configured to suit your own learning requirements. For example, you may have difficulty with numbers, so you could just get the program to generate numbers.

```
10 REM Random Morse Generator for BBC Microcomputer
20 REM Generates a set number of random letters and plays the
30 REM morse through the BBC Sound Channel
40 :
50 INPUT "Number of letters to be sent: ",number%
55 INPUT "Dit length in 20ths of a second: ",dit%
56 INPUT "Letter spacing in 20ths of a second: ",spacing%
57 S$=""
60 FOR L%=1 TO number%
70 :
71 REM Now select a random letter by getting a random number
72 REM between 1 and 26.  To include numbers, alter this next
73 REM statement and add a further data statement.
74 :
75 K%=RND(26) : REM this is for BBC Microcomputer
80 RESTORE 220: FOR I%=1 TO K%:READ A$:NEXT I%
90 RESTORE 230: FOR I%=1 TO K%:READ B$:NEXT I%
95 :
96 REM A$ now holds the letter, B$ the dit and dah pattern
97 :
100 FOR J%=1 TO LEN(B$) : REM scan thru the morse characters
101 :
102 REM For GWBASIC, use SOUND 400,dit%.  Here, the duration
will
103 REM be in 1/18th seconds (approx).  For the Amstrad
computers,
104 REM use the command SOUND 1,300,5*dit%
106 :
110 IF MID$(B$,J%,1)="." THEN SOUND 1,-12,100,dit%
111 :
112 REM For GWBASIC, use SOUND 400,dit%*3.  Here, the duration
will
113 REM be in 1/18th seconds (approx).  For the Amstrad
computers,
114 REM use the command SOUND 1,300,15*dit%
115 :
120 IF MID$(B$,J%,1)="-" THEN SOUND 1,-12,100,dit%*3
130 SOUND 1,0,100,dit% : REM this is a delay of a dit length
140 NEXT J%
150 :
151 REM Next line is also a delay, of the inter-letter gap
152 :
155 FOR F%=1 TO spacing%: SOUND 1,0,100,dit%:NEXT F%
156 :
160 S$=S$+A$
170 NEXT L%
175 :
176 INPUT "What letters were heard: ",A$
180 PRINT "You heard ",A$
200 PRINT "I sent    ",S$
210 GOTO 50
215 :
220 DATA A,B,C,D,F,G,H,I,J,K,L,M,N,O,P,Q,R,S,T,U,V,W,X,Y,Z
230 DATA

.-,-...,-.-.,-..,.,..-.,--.,....,..,.---,-.-,.-..,--,-.,---,.-
-.
240 DATA --.-,.-.,...,-,..-,...-,.--,-..-,-.--,--..
```

Listing 9.3

In addition, Listing 9.4 has the ability to accept text typed in at the keyboard and send it as morse through the computer sound system. This can be useful when practising morse at home, as it allows a member of the family who does not know morse to be co-opted into typing in test messages for you!

```
10 REM Morse code generator sending text strings rather than
20 REM random letters
30 :
35 INPUT "What is the dit length ",dit%
40 INPUT "What is the letter spacing ",spacing%
50 INPUT "What is the text string ",S$
60 FOR P%=1 TO LEN(S$) : REM go through the text string
70 :
80 K%=ASC(MID$(S$,P%,1))-64
90 RESTORE 190
93 FOR I%=1 TO K%:READ B$:NEXT I% : REM get the morse string
95 :
96 IF K% < 1 THEN SOUND 1,0,100,dit%*8 : REM generate a silence for
97 :                              REM spaces or punctuation
98 :
100 FOR J%=1 TO LEN(B$) : REM scan thru the morse characters
101 :
102 REM For GWBASIC, use SOUND 400,dit%. Here, the duration will
103 REM be in 1/18th seconds (approx). For the Amstrad computers,
104 REM use the command SOUND 1,300,5*dit%
106 :
110 IF MID$(B$,J%,1)="." THEN SOUND 1,-12,100,dit%
111 :
112 REM For GWBASIC, use SOUND 400,dit%*3. Here, the duration will
113 REM be in 1/18th seconds (approx). For the Amstrad computers,
114 REM use the command SOUND 1,300,15*dit%
115 :
120 IF MID$(B$,J%,1)="-" THEN SOUND 1,-12,100,dit%*3
130 SOUND 1,0,100,dit% : REM this is a delay of a dit length
140 NEXT J%
150 :
151 REM Next line is also a delay, of the inter-letter gap
152 :
155 FOR F%=1 TO spacing%: SOUND 1,0,100,dit%:NEXT F%
160 :
165 NEXT P% : REM go for next letter
170 GOTO 50
180 DATA A,B,C,D,F,G,H,I,J,K,L,M,N,O,P,Q,R,S,T,U,V,W,X,Y,Z
190 DATA .-,-...,-.-.,-..,.,..-.,--.,....,..,.---,-.-,.-..,--,-.,---,.--.
200 DATA --.-,.-.,...,-,..-,...-,.--,-..-,-.--,--..
```

Listing 9.4

Use with a morse oscillator

Some people may prefer to use the output from a computer morse tutor to drive a morse practice oscillator rather than the sound system of the computer. This is particularly so in teaching situations, where the computer sound system may not be loud enough to be heard all over a classroom. Figure 9.2 shows a simple circuit to allow a single bit of a computer user port to control a morse

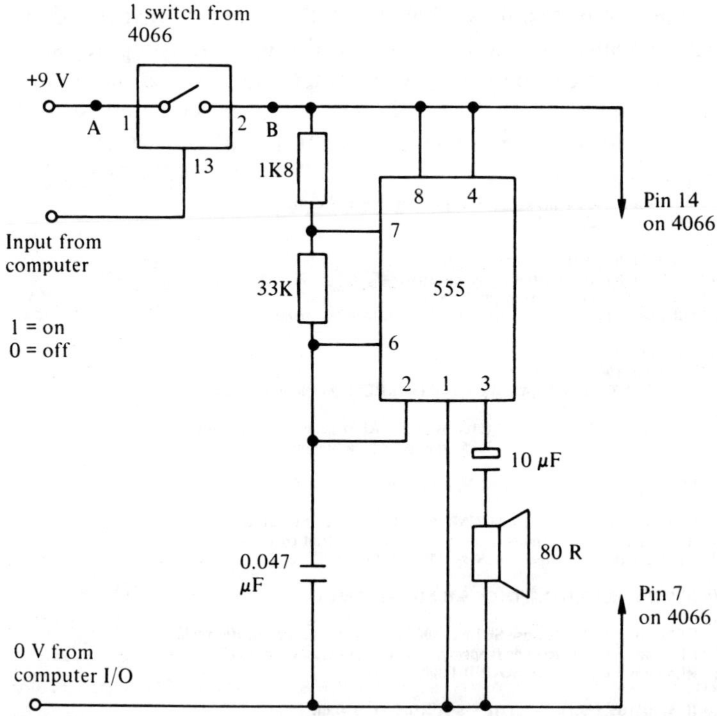

Figure 9.2

oscillator in place of the morse key. This is easier on the BBC and Amstrad 6128 computers where, provided that the current normally passing through the key contacts is low, the internal cassette relays can be used to switch an oscillator on and off – provided you can stand the clicking! (Figure 9.3)

Enhancements to the tutor program

The simplest enhancement is to include Farnsworth Spacing between letters, so that individual letters can be sent at a fast speed with a large inter letter gap. The gap can then be reduced as you get faster, while the letters are still sent at the same speed as before. You thus get used to the sound of letters when sent at speed.

One further enhancement that can be made is to use the other sound channels of your computer (BBC Microcomputer and

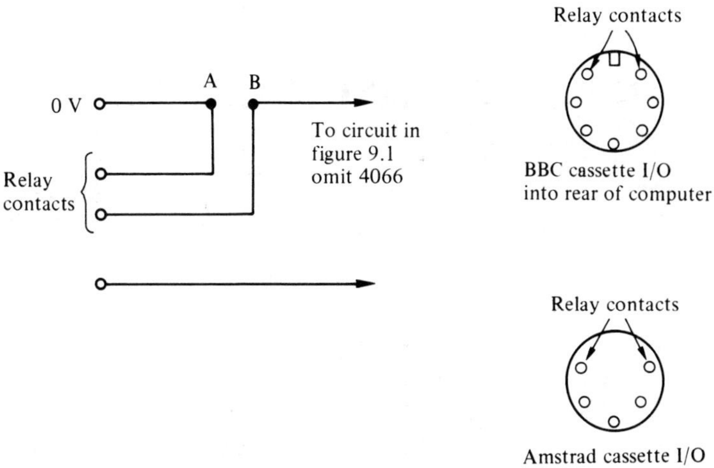

Figure 9.3

Amstrad 6128 users) to generate artificial interference whilst the program is generating morse code for practice. Alternatively, you might like to take the output from your computer or computer controlled morse oscillator and mix it with off-air signals recorded from a short wave radio. This allows the best of both worlds, with interference and noise from the radio with practice morse that you can control the speed and content of.

You could then tape record these combinations of morse and interference to create tapes which you can use whenever you want and re-create once you have become tired of them or have learned all the material.

Well, that is it for morse code. We shall now go on to look at the other transmission modes which cannot be read without the aid of computers or machinery – RTTY, AMTOR, FAX and packet radio.

TEN

RTTY and ASCII signals

RTTY is the oldest form of machine to machine communication used by amateurs. Like many other inventions, *Radio TeleType* had its origins in the Second World War, when the Germans used a form of it to transmit highly sensitive information. The wire based form of Teletype goes back much further – to the early part of this century in fact.

A RTTY signal is sent as a collection of characters represented by a serially transmitted sequence of five pulses. In addition to the pulses representing the character to be transmitted, each character is preceded by a *start* pulse and followed by a *stop* signal, as shown in Figure 10.1. Such a system is known as an *asynchronous* system – the stations at the two end of the link need not be synchronized, or in step, with each other all of the time; the start and stop signals are used to indicate to the receiving station when a character is about to be received.

A pulse sequence is sent as a series of 'on' and 'off' signals. In communications parlance, the 'on' or '1' signal is called a *mark*

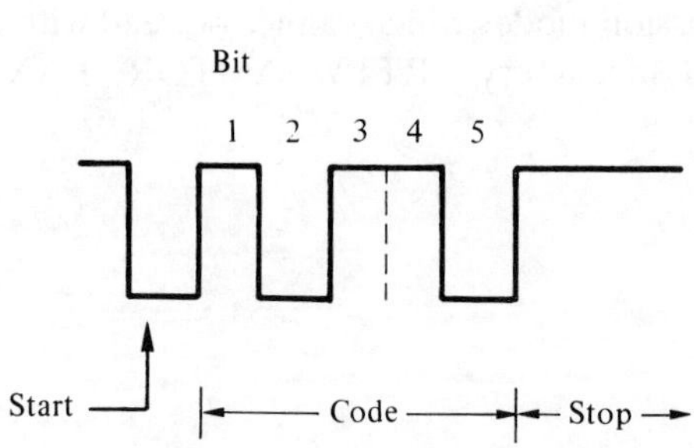

Figure 10.1

signal and the 'off' or '0' signal is called a *space* signal. When a RTTY signal is being transmitted, the usual status for the signal is mark unless anything is being sent. When a character is to be sent, the start pulse is sent as a space signal one bit length long. Then come the five data bits, each one bit length long. Finally, the stop pulse consists of a mark signal 1.5 bits long. The length of a bit depends upon the speed at which signals are transmitted; the faster the desired rate of data transfer, the shorter a bit time will be. Data transfer rate is expressed as something called the *baud rate*, which is the number of data bits per second assuming continuous data transmission. From the baud rate, you can calculate the length of an individual bit of data as follows:

bit length = 1 / baud rate (seconds)

Thus, for 50 baud the bit length would be 1/50 second, or 20 ms. Between characters, the RTTY signal always assumes a mark state.

The Baudot code

The code used for transmission in RTTY is a 5 bit code known as International Telecommunication Union Number 2 code, or ITU 2 or Baudot code. If a bit is to be sent as '1', then a mark tone is transmitted, and if a '0' is sent a space tone is transmitted. The five bits are sent with the least significant bit first. The 5 bit Baudot code allows us to code for 32 separate characters, which is not enough for a full set of letters and numbers. So, two of the codes are used as *shift* characters, called *figures shift* and *letters shift*. The full Baudot code is as follows:

Decimal value	Letters shift	Figures shift
3	A	-
25	B	?
14	C	:
9	D	$
1	E	3
13	F	!
26	G	&
20	H	
6	I	8
11	J	Beep

15	K	(
18	L	)
28	M	.
12	N	,
24	O	9
22	P	0
23	Q	1
10	R	4
5	S	·
16	T	5
7	U	7
30	V	=
19	W	2
29	X	/
21	Y	6
17	Z	+
8	Carriage return	
2	Line feed	
31	Letter shift LS	
27	Figure shift FS	
4	Space	
0	Blank	

The characters that are common to both figures and letters shift are obviously those that are commonly needed in both shifts. To see how the shift system works, imagine that we want to send the sequence 'FROM G1UQW':

LS F R O M G FS 1 LS U Q W

The figure shift character is sent before we send the digit '1', and the letter shift is used to go back to sending text.

ASCII code

A related code used by some amateurs is based on the standard ASCII character set used by computers. Whereas micros use an 8-bit ASCII code, ASCII coded RTTY (called ASCII from now on) uses a start bit, seven bits for encoding the character, a single bit to act as an error check and a single stop bit. The seven data bits allow us to code for 128 different characters. The first 32 are used for control functions, such as line feed, carriage return, bell, etc. The rest of the characters are printable and on your home computer you can print them out by something like:

```
10 FOR i=32 TO 127
20 PRINT i; "    ";CHR$(i)
30 NEXT i
```

The error check bit, called the *parity bit* provides a simple means of detecting whether the data has been corrupted in transmission or not. It is not perfect, but is better than nothing. It works in the following way, depending upon how the system has been set up.

Even parity requires that the total number of bits set to '1' out of the seven data bits and the parity bit be an even number. For example, if the seven data bits contained three '1's, the parity bit would be set to '1' giving an even number of '1's in the block. If there were, say, four '1's in the seven data bits the parity bit would be set to '0'.

Odd parity requires that the total number of bits set to '1' out of the seven data bits and one parity bit be an odd number.

The receiving station can thus detect whether an error has occurred by counting the bits and looking at the parity bit. There is no error correction involved, but it does allow us to at least detect an error when it has occurred.

RTTY modulation methods

On the short wave bands two frequencies are used to represent the mark and space states of the RTTY signal. An audio tone is used to represent the mark signal, and a slightly different tone is used to represent space. The radio transmitter sends a constant signal modulated with one or other of the tones, depending upon what is being transmitted. One way of doing this is to shift the frequency of the carrier being transmitted – this is called *frequency shift keying*, or FSK, and is effectively done by shifting the frequency of a single sideband transmitter depending upon whether a mark or space signal is to be sent. The SSB transmitter will be set to the mark frequency and the transmission of a space signal will cause the transmitter to operate on a slightly lower frequency. On the VHF frequencies, a modified method called *audio frequency shift keying* is used where the audio tones are used with NBFM modulation. It is also possible to feed audio frequency tones into an SSB transmitter and use AFSK with SSB rather than FSK. If done properly, there is no discernible difference.

The difference in frequency between the mark and space tone is called the *shift*, and most amateur stations use a shift of 170 Hz with the mark frequency higher than the space frequency. This is called *normal shift*, and in Europe tones of 1445 Hz for mark and 1275 Hz for space are commonly used, with the radio transmitter being adjusted such that the mark frequency is the quoted carrier frequency. In other parts of the world, the mark tone might be, for instance, 2125 Hz with a space of 2295 Hz, giving a 170 Hz shift but with space higher than mark; where the space is higher than the mark frequency we have *reverse shift*. The shift need not just be 170 Hz; other shifts that are common are 425 and 850 Hz, the latter being especially common with weather stations.

In general, the wider the shift the easier it is to decode the signal and the lower the error rates. However, a wide shift signal occupies considerably more space than a narrow shift signal. When we are decoding RTTY signals, we need to know the shift size and whether it is normal or reverse shift. Many RTTY terminals can switch shift size and the 'sense' of the shift – whether it is normal or reverse shift. We shall look at these aspects of thc RTTY signal later in this chapter. It is the shift of the signal that is important in decoding the signal, as we shall later see. The shift used also has an impact upon the susceptibility of the signal to interference. If a signal has a narrow shift, then fading or interference is likely to affect both mark and space signals because they are close together in frequency; a wider shift will reduce the chances of interference to both signals.

One method of transmitting which has historical interest is where the RTTY signal is sent with the mark being represented by the presence of a radio signal and the space by its absence. This is simple to generate, requiring only that the transmitter is turned on and off, but is more prone to interference from noise signals than FSK or AFSK signals.

Simple transmission techniques

Figure 10.2 shows a block diagram of a simple RTTY or ASCII transmitting arrangement. Text typed in to the computer terminal must be converted into a stream of start, data and stop bits as

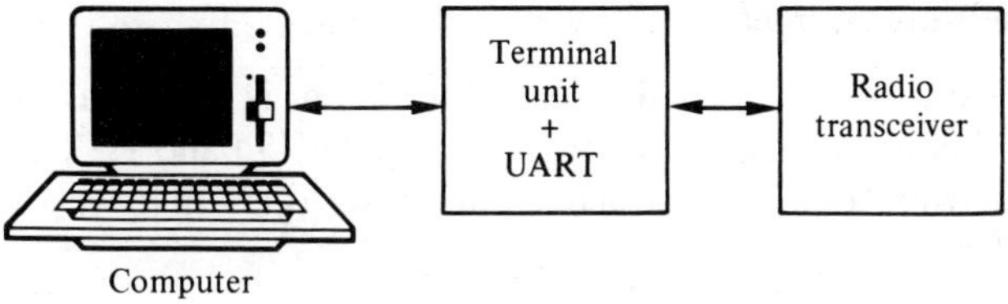

Figure 10.2

already described and then passed on to the terminal unit where these bits are used to modulate the radio transmitter. The first problem that we have to consider is one of converting the characters in the computer memory forming the text message into a serial output of bits for the terminal unit. There are two ways of doing this, one using hardware and one using software. The latter is cheaper and is quite common in RTTY transmitting set-ups, and the former is less intensive of computer power but requires more hardware.

The hardware solution

The hardware method of parallel to serial conversion uses a device called a *UART – universal asynchronous receiver/transmitter* – chip which accepts data bits in a parallel from and outputs the data bits as a serial bit stream of a format that is defined by the way in which the chip has been programmed. For example, for standard RTTY we need to be able to program the UART chip to give an output of 5 data bits and 1.5 stop bits. The UART also outputs the serial stream at the required baud rate, and the baud rate is also set by programming the UART. Not all UARTs have the ability to be programmed in this way, and so care needs to be taken when designing a UART based system to get the correct chip. The serial bit stream from the UART is then used to modulate the radio transmitter depending upon the modulation method used.

Software to control the UART is very simple, generally requiring simply a loop to poll the UART and detect when the UART is ready to receive a data byte to convert in to serial format, then a command to write the desired byte to the UART. This can generally be done using BASIC rather than machine code.

The software method

Software production of the serial bit stream is quite easy to do. Listed below is a simple algorithm to create 45 baud RTTY serial output from a single character. The basic rules that we have to consider are:

1 bit 0 of the Baudot code representation of the character is transmitted first, preceded by a start pulse, which is always a space.
2 the duration of each bit is given by 1/45 seconds – 22.2 ms. (Actually, the baud rate is 45.45 baud for standard amateur RTTY, but 45 is close enough.) Obviously, with different baud rates we simply change this value.
3 after the five data bits have been transmitted, we send a stop bit, a mark, for 1.5 bit lengths – in this case 33.3 ms.

```
        Get Character in.
        Convert Character to Baudot Code – call this
        Baudchar
        Set output port to '0'
        Wait 22.2 ms
        BitCount = 1
LOOP:   Store the bit of Baudchar pointed to by Bitcount to
        the output port.
        Wait 22.2 ms
        BitCount = BitCount + 1
        If BitCount < 6 then goto LOOP
STOP    Set output port to '1'
        Wait 33.3 ms
```

A series of characters can be sent in this way, with the signal reverting to a mark tone between characters. If the characters are being typed live at the keyboard, the overall baud rate is less than that expected, as much of the time available on the channel is not occupied. Sophisticated transmission software allows text to be prepared for transmission off-line and then squirted out in one long burst. This is much more efficient.

ASCII transmission is very similar to this, except that different numbers of bits are sent. In addition, if the software method is used we must also write a segment of program to calculate the parity bit to be sent.

However the serial bit stream is prepared, it is then used to switch the transmission frequency as already described. A simple circuit for doing this is shown in Figure 10.3.

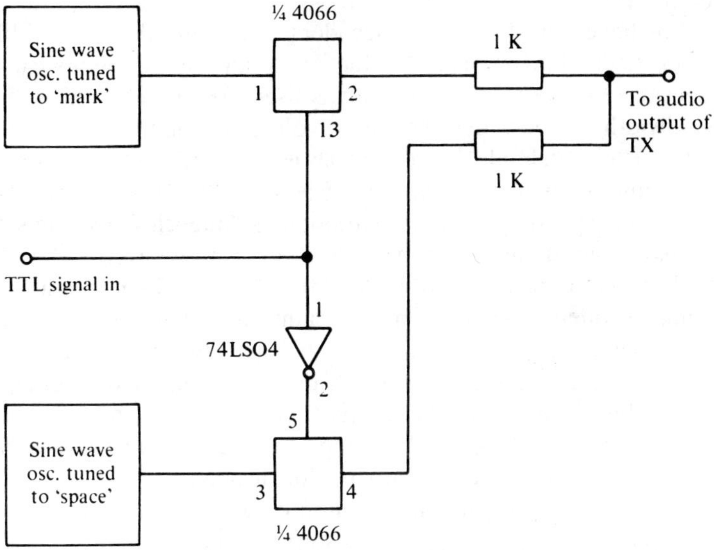

Figure 10.3

Receiving RTTY and ASCII

Receiving RTTY or ASCII is more difficult than transmitting it; this is the same with all modes of data transmission! The audio output from the receiver can be fed to a commercial decoder unit, as will be discussed later in this book, or you might like to consider writing your own decoding software and using some simple hardware such as the FSK decoder discussed in Chapter 8. The basic receiving approaches to consider are as follows:

FSK decoder options
A single tone decoder, where the circuit responds to either the mark or space tone, can be used to decode RTTY giving a logic '1' output, for example, at the mark frequency and a '0' output at the space frequency. This type of decoder, which was the same thing that was used for CW decoding, is more prone to interference than

the alternative form of FSK decoder, where the circuit responds only to the two tones used for mark and space signals and does not respond to interference signals. The circuits shown in Figure 10.4 are typical of these two types of decoder, using integrated circuits to cut down the component count.

Whichever of these tone decoders are used, the bandwidth needs to be fairly narrow at the mark and space frequencies, especially where the 170 Hz shift is used. With wider shifts the bandwidth can be wider. The input voltage to the filters from the radio receiver should be as low as is practicable to give good reception, as to large an input voltage will cause distortion of the signal and possibly lead to harmonic frequencies and thus a 'garbage' serial output string. The output from a typical FSK decoder will be a string of '1's and '0's when a RTTY message is being decoded, and in normal circumstances (see later for the exceptions) the output should be at a '1' level when no characters are being received, switching briefly down to a logical '0' whenever a space bit is received by the receiver. This bit stream must then be decoded into Baudot code characters, and these converted into the character set of the microcomputer for display.

The conversion of the bit stream into baudot characters can be done using a UART or purely by software means.

With a UART, the same criteria apply as for transmitting RTTY; the UART must support the bit pattern used by the Baudot or ASCII code. The TTL signal representing the RTTY signal is applied to the UART input, and the software on the host computer simply polls the UART and reads a valid byte back when a complete character has been decoded. The resultant byte is then used as a key to a look up table to convert the Baudot code into ASCII for standard RTTY, or is printed directly for ASCII. We shall look at this aspect in greater detail shortly.

For software, we can write programs to recognise any particular code we please, and all that is required is a means of providing accurate time delays, as the following algorithm for decoding 50 baud RTTY into Baudot shows:

```
CHARREAD   Store 0 to CHARACTER
           Wait until input=0
           Wait 30ms                  ; should now be half
                                      ; way into Bit 1
```

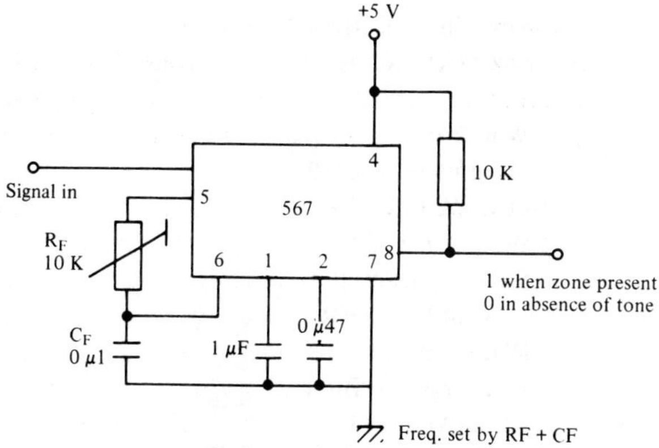

Single tone circuit

(a)

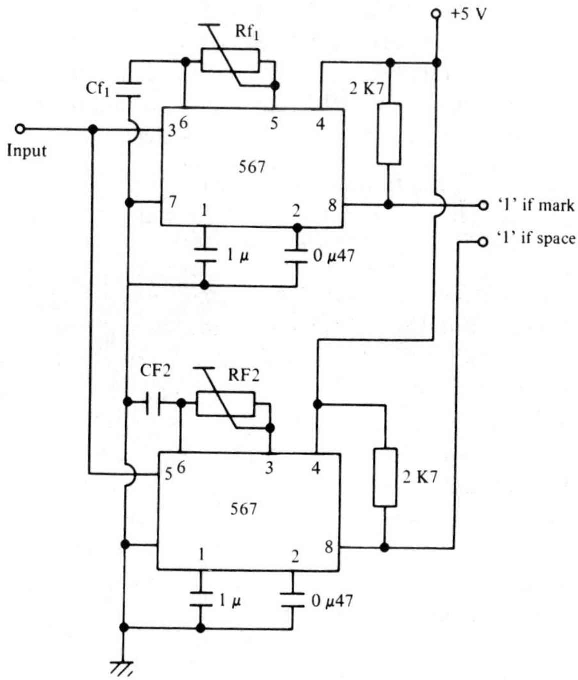

Dual tone

(b)

Figure 10.4

```
Store input to Bit 1
of CHARACTER              ; store into LSB of
                          ; CHARACTER variable
Wait 20ms
Store input to Bit 2
of CHARACTER
Wait  20ms
Store input to bit 3
of CHARACTER
Wait 20ms
Store input to Bit 4
of CHARACTER
Wait 20 ms
Store input to Bit 5
of CHARACTER
Go and Decode and
print CHARACTER
Wait 20ms                 ; now into stop bit
Goto CHARREAD             ; round for next
                          ; character
```

Obviously, for a different baud rate the time delays would have to be changed. In addition, the repeated 'wait, store bit' sequence can be replaced in the program by a loop which counts from 5 down to 0 (usually easier on computers than counting upwards) to read in bits. A similar algorithm can be used for decoding RTTY characters, though we would, of course, be reading in seven bits of data and would also have a different time delay, as ASCII RTTY is usually transmitted at 100 baud. In addition, the final delay would probably have to be 'tweaked' dependent upon the computer printout and decoding routines so as to be a little shorter than expected to allow for the time taken to decode and print the character.

Inverted shift is a method of transmission that may be encountered on the air where the 'resting' signal is the space condition and the start bit is a '1'. The Baudot codes sent are also inverted, '1's replacing '0's and vice versa. If you anticipate receiving signals of this type, then there are two solutions. The first is to modify the software to respond to the inverted bits, and the second is to tune the signal in on the other sideband to that on which the signal was transmitted.

Once a Baudot code character has been created in this way, we need to convert it into a character that can be printed by the computer to either a screen or the printer. This is done by means of a look up table, two areas of memory holding the ASCII codes corresponding to the Baudot codes. We need two tables to cope with the fact that we have got two Baudot character sets to deal with, one from letter shift and the other from figure shift. A full look up table can be seen in the RTTY decoder listing (Listing 10.1).

```
10 REM RTTY Decoding software for BBC Microcomputer
20 REM For use on other members of BBC Series, alter the
30 REM addresses used for the system VIA.
40 :
50 REM next line may not be needed for all printers
55 :
56 *FX6,0
60 :
70 PROCassemble_code_1 :        REM assemble decoder software
80 PROCassemble_code_2 :        REM assemble key handling software
90 CALL start
100 END
110 :
130 DEFPROCassemble_code_1
140 DIM machine_code 200 :      REM dimension space for machine code routine
150 ?&FE62 = 0 :                REM set all lines to input
180 time=&70 :                  REM page 0 location to hold half bit length, low byte
182            :                REM in &70, high byte in &71
190 character=&72 :             REM holds character as it is formed by program
200 char_lookup=&73 :           REM locations &73 and &74 store address of the
202                   :         REM look up table in use for getting a printable
204                   :         REM character.
210 key%=&75        :           REM used by function key routines
220 reverse=&77     :           REM indicates if reverse shift has been chosen or not
230 revtemp=&78     :           REM used to create a reverse shift character
235 :
236                             REM now start assembling the 6502 machine code
240 FOR pass = 0 TO 2 STEP 2
250 P%=machine_code
260 :
270 [OPT pass
280
290 .start
300 JSR letter_shift            \ set letter shift up as default
310
320 .wait_for_space
330 LDA #1
340 BIT &FE60
350 BNE wait_for_space          \ loop around until input line 0 goes low
355 :
```

```
360 JSR half_bit_delay        \ wait for half a bit
370 LDA #0                    \ initialise character code to 0
380 STA character
390
400 LDX #5
410 .get_next_bit
430 JSR full_bit_delay
440 LDA &FE60                 \ get next bit into Accumulator
445 CLC                       \ clear carry flag
450 ROR A                     \ rotate A right, thus putting bit 0 into C
460 LDA character
470 ROL A                     \ rotate A left, thus bringing C into bit 0 of A
475 STA character             \ store character back into memory
476 DEX
477 BNE get_next_bit          \ loop around until 5 bits have been obtained
480
490
500 LDY character             \ get character code into Y register
510 LDA reverse               \ first check to see if shift-reversal has been requested
520 CMP #0
530 BEQ no_reverse
540 STY revtemp               \ if we get here, we need to reverse the shift of the
550 LDA #31                   \ received character code by subtracting it from 31
560 CLC
561 SBC revtemp
570 TAY                       \ now copy new code back to Y register for look up
580 .no_reverse
590 CPY #31                   \ check to see if it's a letter shift character
600 BNE not_let_shift
604 JMP start                 \ if letter shift, jump to beginning
606 .not_let_shift
610 CPY #27                   \ now check for figures shift
620 BNE not_fig_shift
622 JSR figure_shift          \ force into figure shift mode
623 JMP wait_for_space
628 .not_figure_shift
630 LDA (char_lookup),Y       \ get ASCII code into A from index provided
631                           \ in Y and the current address stored in
632                           \ char_lookup and char_lookup+1
640 JSR &FFE3                 \ use OS routine to print it out
650
670 JSR full_bit_delay        \ wait until thru stop bit
680 JMP wait_for_space        \ get next character
690
700 .letter_shift
710 LDA #letters MOD 256      \ store address of letter table to char_lookup
720 STA char_lookup
730 LDA #letters DIV 256
740 STA char_lookup+1
750 RTS
760
770 .figure_shift
780 LDA #figures MOD 256      \ store address of figure table to char_lookup
790 STA char_lookup
800 LDA #figures DIV 256
```

```
810 STA char_lookup+1
820 RTS
822
830 .half_bit_delay
840 LDA time                              \ get low byte from time variable and store in
850 STA &FE68                             \ VIA time register
860 LDA time+1
870 STA &FE69                             \ set up high byte and start timing
880 LDA #32                               \ set up bit mask for interrupt detection
890 .wait_for_interrupt
900 BIT &FE6D                             \ check the interrupt flag for time out
910 BEQ wait_for_interrupt                \ and loop around till it happens
920 RTS
921
922 .full_bit_delay
923 JSR half_bit_delay
924 JSR half_bit_delay
925 RTS
930 ]
932                                       REM that ends the first block of assemble code. Now set up the
933                                       REM letter and figure tables
934
940 letters=P%
950 figures=letters+32
960 NEXT pass
965
970 DATA 0,84,0,79,32,72,78,77,13,76,82,71,73,80,67,86
990 DATA 69,90,68,66,83,89,70,88,65,87,74,0,85,81,75,0
1010 DATA 0,53,0,57,32,96,44,46,13,41,52,64,56,48,58,61
1030 DATA 51,43,0,63,33,54,37,47,45,50,0,0,55,49,40,0
1050 FOR I%=0 TO 31:READ A%: ?(letters+I%)=A%: NEXT I%
1060 FOR I%=0 TO 31:READ A%: ?(figures+I%)=A%: NEXT I%
1070 ?time=16
1080 ?(time+1)=39
1090 ENDPROC
1100
1110 DEFPROCassemble_code_2
1120 $&C30="*FX7,    ":$&C00="*SPOOL ":$&C07="TEXT":$&C20="*SPOOL"
1125 DIM code2 500 :                      REM dimension area of memory for second m/c
1130 FOR pass=0 TO 2 STEP 2
1135 P%=code2
1140 [ OPT pass
1150 .event                               \ start of event handling code, entered on key press
1160 PHP
1170 PHA
1180 TXA:PHA
1190 TYA:PHA                              \ save all registers on stack
1200 STY key%                             \ store key press in page 0
1210 LDA key%
1215
1216                                      \ now check identity of key pressed
1217
1220 CMP #13 : BEQ linefeed
1230 CMP #128 : BEQ printer_on            \ turn printer on if f0 pressed
1240 CMP #129 : BEQ printer_off           \ turn printer off if f1 pressed
1250 CMP #130 : BEQ open_file             \ open text file if f2 pressed
1260 CMP #131 : BEQ close_file            \ close file if f3 pressed
1270 CMP #132 : BEQ shift                 \ f4 - force letter shift
1280 CMP #133 : BEQ fifty                 \ f5 - 50 baud reception
1290 CMP #134 : BEQ seventy               \ f6 - 75 baud reception
1300 CMP #135 : BEQ oneten                \ f7 - 110 baud reception
```

```
1310 CMP #136 : BEQ fortyfive          \ f8 - 45 baud reception
1320 CMP #ASC("R") : BEQ shiftrev      \  reverse shift
1321 CMP #ASC("N") : BEQ noshift       \  normal shift
1330 .done
1340 PLA:TAY                           \ get Y register off stack
1350 PLA:TAX                           \ get X register off stack
1360 PLA                               \ recover A register from stack
1370 PLP                               \ recover flags from stack
1380 RTS
1390
1400 .linefeed                         \ generate a blank line to separate
                                       text
1410 JSR &FFE7
1420 JSR &FFE7                         \ call to linefeed code in operating
                                       system
1430 JMP done                          \ jump back, recover registers and
                                       finish interrupt
1440
1450 .printer_on                       \ turn printer output on
1460 LDA #2
1470 JSR &FFE3
1480 JMP done
1490
1500 .printer_off
1510 JSR &FFE7
1520 LDA #3
1530 JSR &FFE3
1540 JMP done
1550
1560 .open_file                        \ open a text file called text on disc
1570 LDX #&C00 MOD 256
1580 LDY #&C00 DIV 256
1590 JSR &FFF7
1600 JMP done
1610
1620 .close_file                       \ close text file
1630 LDX #&C20 MOD 256
1640 LDY #&C20 DIV 256
1650 JSR &FFF7
1660 JMP done
1670
1680 .shift                            \ force system into letters shift
1690 JSR letter_shift
1700 JMP done
1710
1750 .fifty                            \ set up 50 baud reception
1760 LDA #16: STA time
1770 LDA #39: STA time+1
1780 JMP done
1781
1790 .fortyfive                        \ force system into 45 baud reception
1800 LDA #103: STA time
1810 LDA #43: STA time+1
1820 JMP done
1822
1830 .seventy                          \ go into 75 baud RTTY
1840 LDA #10: STA time
1850 LDA #26: STA time+1
1860 JMP done
1870
1872 .oneten                           \ go into 110 baud reception mode
1880 LDA #136: STA time
1890 LDA #19: STA time+1
1900 JMP done
1901
1902 .shiftrev                         \ reverse shift of incoming text - set
                                        flag for decoder
```

```
1903 LDA #1
1904 STA reverse
1905 JMP done
1906
1907 .noshift                          \ reverse effects of shiftrev
1908 LDA #0
1909 STA reverse
1910 JMP done
1911
1915 ]
1916 NEXT pass :                       REM for second piece of machine
                                       code
1920 ?&220 = event MOD 256 :           REM set up address of event
                                       handler
1930 ?&221 = event DIV 256
1930
1940                                   REM now turn on the events, and
                                       set up base value for function keys
1950
1960 *FX14,2
1970 *FX225,128
1980
1990 ENDPROC :                         REM end of this procedure
```

Listing 10.1

It is organized in numerical order of Baudot code, so that entry 1 of the letters shift table will hold the ASCII code for ‘E’, entry 2 will hold the code for ‘Line feed’, usually character 10, entry 3 will be ‘A’ and so on. A similar arrangement is required for the figure shift table. The shift characters are not looked up in the table, though they have a dummy entry, and when these are detected we simply tell the program to look at the other look up table. Other features that we must take special care with when using character look-up tables are:

Line feed and *carriage return* are usually coded as characters 10 and 13 respectively, but some computers will generate a line feed when given just a carriage return character printing an extra line feed will thus give double spaced text!

Unshift on space is a method by which ‘garbles’ due to the receiving end misinterpreting a character as a figure shift code, with the result that subsequent characters are looked up in the figure shift table. This can obviously cause long runs of rubbish if listening to a station transmitting text! One solution is that after every space transmitted, the receiving program goes back to using the letters shift table automatically. This technique can cause problems when the received information is made up of a lot of numbers, like the output of weather stations (see below). In this instance, the figure blocks transmitted will be displayed as letters unless the transmitting station sends a figure shift character whenever a space is sent – not common!

```
CHARPRINT     If Character=2
                  Do Linefeed
              endif
              If Character=8
                  Do Linefeed
                  Do CarriageReturn
              endif
              If Character=31
                  Point to Letters Shift Table
              endif
              If Character=27
                  Point to Figures Shift Table
              endif
              If Character=11
                  Make Bell Sound
              endif
              If UnshiftOnSpace
                  If Character=4
                      Print A Space
                      Point to Letters Shift Table
                  endif
              endif
              Read Character from Look Up Table
              Print Character
```

RTTY and ASCII decoding software

Listing 10.1 shows a simple RTTY decoder program for the BBC Microcomputer. The comments in the listing detail how it works, and the listing should be easily transported onto other micros. In general terms, the following must be taken into account when writing RTTY or ASCII decoder software.

Speed is clearly essential, and BASIC is thus not really suitable for writing this type of software. Machine code or compiled languages such as C or Pascal are essential, and in Listing 10.1 I used 6502 Assembler to get the speed. On higher baud rates, it is essential to take into account in the time delays any overheads when printing characters, etc. A few comments on this listing are worth noting at this point, so here we go.

The RTTY program

This listing is a simple RTTY receiving terminal program for the BBC Microcomputer. It will also work with a little modification on the Master series. The basic principles, though, are applicable to any decoder software. The only feature of the software that will be difficult to transfer on to another computer would be the function keys, which use the BBC Events to allow the function keys to operate without the need for polling the keyboard throughout the decoding process.

Lines 150 to 230 initialise variables and memory locations; &FE60 and &FE62 are in the user VIA of the BBC Microcomputer, and &FE62 is the data direction register, which specifies which lines are to act as output and input, and &FE60 is the actual port address. The decoding software is in lines 290 to 680. Line 300 always ensures that we start in letter shift mode, and lines 330 to 350 wait for bit 0 of the user port to go to 0. Once this happens, the time delay subroutine is called to wait half a bit length into the start pulse before initializing the character to 0 and setting the X register up to count five input bits. Lines 420 to 480 then deal with getting five bits into the character storage location for decoding into a printable code. Before the character is printed, a check is made on the location 'reverse' to see if the user has requested a reverse shift by typing 'R'. If so, then the character code is subtracted from 31; otherwise it is just printed using the letters or figures look-up table.

The BBC VIA is also used to generate a time delay for the timing of input pulses. The system defaults to 50 baud, which is set in lines 1070 and 1080. The VIA requests a delay in μs, and I have made the basic unit of timing a 'half bit' to accommodate the 1.5 stop bits.

The code between lines 1110 and 1950 deal with the setting up of function keys to perform certain jobs while the program is running. The details of how this works are described in the BBC *Advanced User Guide*.

Using the program

The program starts off in 50 baud mode, and the function keys are used as follows:

Function key	Function
F0	printer turned ON
F1	printer turned OFF
F2	open a file to a disc or tape called TEXT
F3	closes the file TEXT
F4	letters shift forced
F5	select 50 baud
F6	select 75 baud
F7	select 110 baud
F8	select 45 baud
R	reverse shift
N	normal shift
RETURN	force line feed, carriage return

ASCII decoding

There is not much ASCII to be heard on the bands in comparison with other modes of transmission, but the program in Listing 10.1 could easily be altered to receive ASCII. The delays would need to be those used for 100 baud, and a different look up table would be required. The bit reading sequence would also have to be modified to read in seven bits of data.

General points

Time delays are required in these programs, as already indicated. There are two ways of generating these delays, either by hardware or by pure software. Listing 10.1 uses the 6522 VIA in the BBC Micro to generate a set time delay in microseconds. This method is very effective, provided that your computer has the facility available. the second method involves programming a loop in software that takes a known amount of time to execute. This is easy to implement in theory but can be 'fiddly' to get a precise delay. The other thing to watch with these delays is that if the machine uses interrupts to a significant degree, the delays may vary slightly as the software loop is interrupted by the machine to run various other routines. This is unlikely to cause serious problems but is worth bearing in mind, especially at high baud rates.

Tuning in RTTY signals

RTTY signals are easy to recognise on the air, and are often referred to as 'jingle bells' sounds. In the amateur bands, RTTY is concentrated in certain sub-bands, as follows:

80 metres	3580 to 3620kHz
40 metres	7035 to 7045kHz
20 metres	14 080 to 14 110kHz
15 metres	21 075 to 21 120kHz
10 metres	28 045 to 28 150kHz

These frequencies are very approximate, but tuning around these areas with the receiver in LSB mode will almost certainly reveal some RTTY signals. The usual baud rate is 45 baud, but with the advent of computers 50, 75 or 100 baud RTTY has become popular and so any listener must be prepared to try different baud rates if the signal cannot be read. The usual shift used for 45 baud is 170Hz, but some amateurs using higher baud rates also use wider shifts. The narrow shift makes recognition of amateur RTTY fairly simple, as the shift in tones of 170Hz is much less marked than commercial RTTY shifts. If you cannot find a RTTY signal and you want to know what one sounds like, the Bracknell meteorological station on 4489 kHz is on the air much of the time sending metreorological information by RTTY. If you just get a continuous tone, then the station will soon resume its traffic of either RTTY or FAX signals.

With experience, you can often estimate the baud rate and rough shift of a RTTY station, but as a beginner you will be well advised to concentrate on strong stations with little interference or fading. Unless your receiver has a special RTTY mode, set it to LSB mode and, if possible, disable the AGC. If this is not possible, set a fast AGC so that the receiver will respond quickly to changes in the signal strength. A narrow bandwidth will be useful in terms of reducing interference, as will a two-tone decoder as mentioned above. With amateur RTTY, accuracy in tuning is vital, and a general rule of thumb is that an accuracy of ± 25 per cent of the shift is needed to get reasonable results. For 170Hz shift, therefore, an accuracy of about ± 40Hz is needed. The fact that accurate tuning is required means that certain receivers are not suitable for RTTY reception. These are principally synthesized receivers with a tuning step size of 1 or 5 kHz – clearly, if the tuning rate available is in steps of this size RTTY signals will not be tunable unless some means of fine tuning is provided by the receiver. In addition, any receiver used should not drift in frequency.

As to actually deciding when correct tuning has been achieved, the easiest way is to probably tune for readable text on the screen. The decoder unit/software should be set for unshift on space, if available, and non inverted reception. If you cannot get any sensible text on the screen then try varying the baud rate, shift and sense of reception (whether it is inverted or non-inverted). The latter can also be done by simply switching over to USB if you are in LSB mode and re-tuning the receiver. It may be, of course, that the transmitter is *not* actually an amateur station or weather station!

Amateur RTTY operating techniques

Traditional RTTY operation required teleprinters and nonsynthesized receivers. This required that the operators be tuned 'spot on' to one another before messages were exchanged. To facilitate this, constant signals consisting of 'V's or the sequence 'RY' would be sent to allow the receiving station to tune in. 'RY's are still common on the bands, and after a while you will begin to learn what they sound like. After a run of 'RY's, the transmitting station will send a CQ call or call another station. Abbreviations are often used, similar to those used by morse code stations. A few useful rules of thumb for transmitting stations are:

1 if you are using a computer to send RTTY, do send a carriage return/line feed at the end of every line; other computers will have no problems if you do not, but some operators with mechanical RTTY machines will have difficulty! In the same vein, keep lines short; because you have an 80 column display does not mean that everybody has. Keep lines short until the nature of the other station – whether it is computer or teleprinter, what their line lengths are, etc. – has been established.
2 at the end of each line, if possible, send a letter shift signal to force a letters shift at the receiving end.
3 where signals are weak or are suffering interference, do not be afraid to repeat chunks of your message, for example:

G G G G [return]
1 1 1 1 [return]
U U U U [return]
Q Q Q Q [return]
W W W W [return]

4 now that many operators do use computer terminals, you may like to try sending a bell command to draw the operator's attention to the incoming message. Use with care!
5 Do not forget that when you are not sending text, you are still transmitting a signal; so, do not change frequency without turning off the transmitter!

Commercial RTTY systems

Many RTTY systems now exist, and they are much more sophisticated than the simple program described above. Advanced features in software include the following:

Auto baud rate allows the receiver to identify the baud rate and 'sense' of the incoming signal.

Split screen allows you to prepare a reply to a message in one half of the screen whilst reading the incoming message in the other half of the screen. This can be quite useful if you are a slow typist, as much of the reply can be composed before you start transmitting.

Definable function keys allow the user to pre-program certain keys with commonly used messages, such as the callsign of the station, CQ calls, RY sequences, etc.

RTTY bulletin boards

These are RTTY stations which are computer controlled and allow RTTY users to leave messages for other operators. Some of these also allow access to messages left on the board in other modes, such as AMTOR. RTTY Bulletin boards tend to be accessible at 45 or 75 baud, but if possible you should use the higher baud rate if your system will support it.

Weather RTTY stations

There are thousands of radio stations in the world transmitting RTTY broadcasts for the benefits of pilots, seamen and other people to whom up to date weather information is crucial. Amateur weathermen, sailors, etc. may use this data, and since 27 February 1989 the Department of Trade and Industry waived the requirement for a licence for the reception of weather information for non-commercial, private use. If you intend using the data for commercial purposes, copyright clearance would be required from the appropriate source of the data you are using. If you are in any doubt about the use you intend putting the information to, contact the Meteorological Office (in the UK) for advice. Copying information from any of the other RTTY stations, including Press stations, is still illegal in the UK unless you have got the appropriate permission from the DTI, so be warned!

Apart from weather information, meterological RTTY stations are quite useful for testing home-brew RTTY equipment and software, giving long periods of traffic with a wide shift.

Weather RTTY is usually transmitted at 50 baud with a shift of 850Hz. This makes them very easy to decode using the simplest types of terminal unit. The meteorological stations tend to be gathered in certain frequency bands, as follows:

3200 to 3350kHz
3750 to 3850kHz
4700 to 5000kHz
5200 to 5500kHz
7300 to 8200kHz

To see what they sound like, the easiest station for UK listeners to go for is Bracknell on 4489 kHz. This transmits information most of the day, and so you should have no difficulty decoding the signals from there, even using a simple home made terminal unit and the software in the listing above.

The information transmitted by these stations is in the form of groups of five digits, thus making meteorological stations very easy to identify. Actually converting these in to sensible weather information, though, is quite hard work, and the best source of help is *The Meteo Code Manual* published by Klingenfuss. Actually computerising the decoding of these 5-figure blocks is not an easy task, as the format of the message depends upon the type of weather data being sent. In general, a message will start off with a sequence such as:

ZCZC 871 55555

where ZCZC is the 'start of message' signal, 871 is a serial number incremented on each transmission and the 5 digit code is an identification sequence. The next line of code may be something like:

SMEU22 EGRR 291300

where the first block identifies the type of information following and the geographical area to which it refers – in this case 'Europe. The second block indicates the station that put the data together – in this case Bracknell – and the last block indicates the day of the month (29th) and the time (1300) when the data was originally compiled. The last part of the 'header' is a line such as:

AAXX 29124

where AAXX indicates that the following message contains reports from a land weather station (AAXX) taken at 1200 hours (12) on the 29th of the month (29).

The following data then consists of lincs of 5 digit blocks, each line ending with a 'break' symbol (=) and the whole message finishing with the sequence:

NNNN

The actual decoding of the 5 digit blocks is beyond the scope of this book. Other messages from these stations have different formats, and in total there are about 50 or 60 different types of message format that meteorological stations transmit, ranging from the sort of information described above to weather reports radioed in from aircraft on their normal flights.

Points to watch

When receiving weather stations, the main thing to watch for is *not* to select your unshift on space option if it is available, as otherwise you will get a load of 5-letter blocks! In fact, if you tune in half way through a weather broadcast, you may get 5-letter blocks until the next header sequence is sent. You might like to try modifying the program listed above to include a 'force figure shift' option if you have got an interest in weather information. In addition, some weather stations transmit in reverse shift so you may want to try both shift senses when tuning in a new station.

That is all I want to say about RTTY and ASCII; in the next chapter I shall go on to examine a mode that gets around one of RTTY's biggest drawbacks – it is proneness to interference.

ELEVEN

AMTOR

We have already seen that RTTY signals suffer from a couple of problems, in that the intelligence of a RTTY message is easily lost if the signal suffers fading or interference. For example, if we suffered a burst of interference we could lose one or more characters, or cause a character to be mis-read as a shift character, thus causing a garble to occur until the correct shift was re-asserted by the transmitting station or the receiving software un-shifted the received code. In addition, the start and stop bits do not carry any data; they are redundant in data but clearly vital to the receiving end of the link. What was required was a means of text transmission that minimised the effects of interference, and the SITOR system was developed for commercial use. *SITOR* is commonly used in ship to shore communications and between fixed land stations. It includes an error correction protocol and can transmit the same amount of text in the same time as a 50 baud RTTY signal. In the late 1970s, Peter Martinez, G3PLX, developed a version of this system for amateur radio, and called it *AMTOR* which stood for *A*mateur *M*icroprocessor *T*eleprinting *O*ver *R*adio.

The AMTOR protocol

SITOR is defined by a document called *CCIR Recommendation 476* and this document is also applicable to AMTOR. The definitive document as far as radio amateurs concerned is Peter Martinez's article 'AMTOR, an improved radioteleprinter system, using a microcomputer' in the August 1979 issue of *Radio Communications*. AMTOR uses a 7-bit character size, which you might expect to give 128 possible different characters. However, only 35 of these codes are actually used, those containing four bits set to '1' (mark) and three bits set to '0' (space). It is the fact that AMTOR only uses a subset of the codes available that allows AMTOR to detect errors and correct them. Only data bytes with four '1's and three '0's are correct AMTOR characters; anything else is an error and the system will be able to respond to correct this error before displaying the message, as we shall shortly see. A couple of moments thought will indicate that this error detection procedure will not be perfect; a garble could occur that could change the status to two or more bits in the data stream whilst leaving four bits at '1' and three bits at '0' – this would pass this error check but would print a rubbish character.

Master and slave stations

Each bit in an AMTOR transmission is 10 ms long, resulting in a transmission rate of 100 baud (Figure 11.1). Characters are transmitted over an AMTOR link with the least significant bit being transmitted first. There are no start or stop bits; the transmitting and receiving stations must therefore be synchronized to each other for correct operation, and the receiving station will synchronize itself to the transmitting end. An accurate clock at each end of the link ensures that the two stations remain synchronized through fades and interference. The station first initiating a transmission is called the *master station (MS)* and the other station is called the *slave station (SS)*, and the slave station always synchronizes itself to the master station. Details of the synchronization process will be given shortly. Irrespective of whether the station is the MS or SS, the station transmitting information at a moment in time is often called the *information sending station (ISS)* and that receiving data is called the *information receiving station (IRS)*. In broad terms, the ISS will send a block of characters to the IRS which will then error check and perform error correction if necessary. Once the ISS has finished, the IRS will take over the role of the ISS and vice versa. There are three modes of AMTOR operation, known as AMTOR Modes A, B and L and these will be discussed in some detail later.

Modulation methods used

On the short wave bands, AMTOR is transmitted using frequency shift keying with a 170 Hz shift between the mark and space

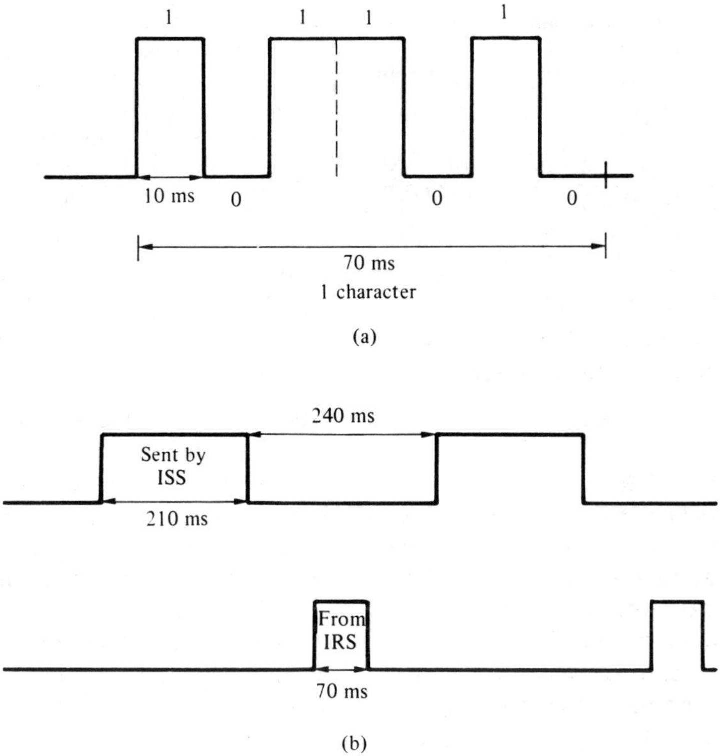

Figure 11.1

frequencies. The mark frequency is usually 1445 Hz and the space is 1275 Hz. The signal is usually generated as an SSB signal with the mark signal being the carrier frequency that will be listed in the log.

On VHF and UHF the technique of AFSK is used on FM with the mark and space frequencies as above. When using SSB on the short waves, AMTOR transmissions tend to be made using upper sideband.

AMTOR uses a fairly narrow bandwidth, and can be quite effective with low powers. Some writers have argued that in terms of getting information from point A to point B AMTOR can be as effective as CW. The narrow bandwidth used reduces the susceptibility of weak AMTOR signals to interference, especially if the receiving equipment is optimised to AMTOR.

The AMTOR character set

We have already noted that all AMTOR characters have four '1's and three '0's. The 35 characters covered are shown below – you will see that they are almost identical to the RTTY character set with the exception of the AMTOR control signals. The practical upshot of this is that AMTOR is not really a suitable medium for transferring computer programs and data over the air, despite its error correcting abilities, unless some means of coding for such common software characters as '>', '=' and '<' is used.

Amtor character set

AMTOR code	Letters case	Figures case
1000111	A	-
1110010	B	?
0011101	C	:
1010011	D	$
1010110	E	3
0011011	F	!
0110101	G	&
1101001	H	
1001101	I	8
0010111	J	Bell
0011110	K	(
1100101	L	)
0111001	M	.
1011001	N	,
1110001	O	9
0101101	P	0
0101110	Q	1
1010101	R	4
1001011	S	'
1110100	T	5
1001110	U	7
0111100	V	≃
0100111	W	2
0111010	X	/
0101011	Y	6
1100011	Z	+
1111000	Carriage return	

1101100	Line feed	
1011010	Letter shift	
0110110	Figure shift	
1011100	Space	
1101010	Blank	
1100101	Control 1 (CS1)	
1101010	Control 2 (CS2)	
1001101	Control 3 (CS3)	
0001111	Alpha (Idle character)	a
0110011	Beta (Idle character)	b
1100110	Repeat	RQ

AMTOR station requirements

Whereas RTTY can be generated mechanically, that is simply impossible for AMTOR. A microcomputer is required, along with a stable clock capable of producing a pulse every millisecond to provide the accurate timing signals that AMTOR requires. Microcomputer clocks are on the whole not stable enough, because the signal must not drift with time as otherwise the required synchronization will be difficult to achieve. This 1kHz clock needs an accuracy of better than 30 parts per million – that is, the frequency should vary by no more than 30 thousandths of a hertz. You can also get a full AMTOR decoder board which takes in signals off the air and decodes them 'on board', sending ASCII coded text to the serial port of the microcomputer.

If you do not wish to go to the expense of a separate AMTOR controller board, then several of the data modems that we shall discuss in Chapter 14 also include an AMTOR mode. Alternatively, the micro can decode AMTOR signals from a terminal unit. Software will be required that can decode the AMTOR characters, and in addition a terminal unit will be required to convert the audio tones into mark and space signals for input to the microcomputer. The receiver must be stable and drift free, and in addition the receiver and terminal unit combination must be capable of resolving the 170Hz shift used to transmit AMTOR signals. On the whole, a terminal unit/receiver set-up that can decode RTTY will probably work with AMTOR, although care needs to be taken if the terminal unit has been designed to be a 'RTTY only' unit, as the filtering may be too tight and cause distortion of the 100 baud AMTOR signals.

The transmitter used must be able to transmit on full duty cycle for considerable periods of time when Mode B (see below) is used, and if the transmitter does not have an FSK setting then the periods used for transmission must be carefully monitored to ensure that we do not blow up the transmitter! In addition, for using AMTOR Mode A the transmit/receive relay of the transceiver must be able to switch over in less than about 20ms. With older transmitters, this used to be quite an important consideration, but with most modern pieces of equipment the transmit/receive relay speed is perfectly adequate for AMTOR.

AMTOR operating modes

Before starting with the details of AMTOR operation, it will be useful to look at the three ways in which AMTOR can be used. These are called operational modes, and we shall look at them in greater detail later. The common feature between both the AMTOR transmission modes is that when no messages are being sent by the ISS the system fills in the gaps with Beta 'idle' characters to ensure that synchronization is maintained. A further point to note is that control codes received are not printed by the IRS.

Mode A is also called ARQ and is used between two stations in two way communication. Messages are sent in blocks of three characters by the ISS. Error correction is by means of control signals sent from the IRS to the ISS signalling whether a repeat of a block of the signal is required.

Mode B is also called FEC and is used when one station wishes to communicate with several others. Here, error correction is via the same text being sent twice by the ISS, five characters apart. The IRS does not have to send any signals to the ISS, which is just as well because there is going to be more than one IRS! A modification of Mode B is FEC SELCAL, where the text is sent twice but to a specified station.

Mode L is for listening to AMTOR Mode A traffic. The 'eavesdropping' station sends no control characters and so cannot make use of the error handling ability of the AMTOR system. However, it is useful for SWLs!

Bit synchronization

Before an AMTOR contact in any mode can be established, the IRS can has to synchronize itself to the ISS in two ways. First, it has to achieve *bit synchronization* where it effectively synchronizes its 1 kHz clock to that of the ISS, thus ensuring that the IRS will be reading the data signals from the ISS correctly. Once bit-sync has been established, the next thing to do is to achieve *character synchronisation* where the IRS 'frames' 7-bit chunks in the incoming data stream into characters. Let us look at bit sync first.

Because AMTOR is a synchronous system, the ISS will be sending something even when the operator is not typing any text in at the terminal. These 'idle' codes are the 'a' and 'b' code (Alpha and Beta) listed above.

The whole business of synchronization is effectively one of setting up a phase locked loop between the two clocks using software as well as the 1kHz clocks already mentioned. A simplified algorithm for maintaining synchronization is shown below; this does not actually achieve synchronization,but helps to keep synchronisation once attained.

```
Start:    WAIT 5ms                        ; wait until half way
                                          ; into first bit
          CHARBITS = 0                    ; set bit count
Inner:    PHASEDIFF = 251                 ; set phase error
                                          ; counter
          Store input bit into CHARBUFF   ; put bit into correct
                                          ; location in character
                                          ; input buffer
          If input bit <> last bit        ; check status of last
                                          ; bit against status of
                                          ; current bit – if not
                                          ; the same then . . .

        PHASERROR = PHASERROR + PHASEDIFF

          endif                           ; add up the phase
                                          error
          CHARBITS = CHARBITS+1
          If CHARBITS = 7                 ; got 7 bits
             CHECK-CHARACTER              ; character sync
             END                          ; and output routine
```

```
            else
                 WAIT 10 ms                  ; wait until into
                                             ; next character
            endif
            GOTO Inner

Interrupt:  PHASEDIFF = PHASEDIFF + 1
            CHARCLOCK = CHARCLOCK + 1
            If PHASERROR > MAXERROR
                 PHASERROR = -MAXERROR
                 CHARCLOCK = CHARCLOCK - 1
            endif
            If PHASERROR < - MAXERROR
                 PHASERROR = MAXERROR
                 CHARCLOCK = CHARCLOCK + 1
            endif
            END
```

Let us see how all this works. As you can see, there are two routines; the first one is executed as part of the main software loop, and deals with character decoding. It is fairly similar to the RTTY decode algorithm that we saw above, but with the difference that we refer to 'PHASEDIFF' and PHASERROR'. These two variables are at the heart of how we keep synchronization between the two clocks, and the main work of keeping sync is done in the interrupt routine, of which more in a moment. PHASEDIFF is initialized to −5 at the start of each bit decoding sequence, and is also incremented once per millisecond via the interrupt routine triggered by the 1kHz clock. So far, so good, but how do we start locking the clocks together? Well, each time the state of the input bit is different from the previous input bit, the count in PHASEDIFF is added to PHASERROR. To see how this will help us, let us do some simple arithmetic.

The system waits until it is half way through a pulse, then sets PHASEDIFF to −5. Immediately, the interrupt routine carries on incrementing PHASEDIFF and so by the time of the next possible transition, in about 5ms time, PHASEDIFF will have been incremented roughly five times, depending upon the phase and frequency error between the clocks at the ISS and IRS. We can say, therefore, that if the clocks are in perfect synchronization PHASEDIFF will be 0 at transition and so 0 will be added to the

PHASERROR variable. If the IRS clock were running a bit fast, then PHASEDIFF might get up to +2 by the transition time, so PHASERROR would now be PHASERROR + 2. If, on the other hand, it were running slow then we might only be at −3 or −2, so at transition PHASERRROR might equal, say, PHASERROR + −3. Aha, you say, what happens if we have, for example, two '1' bits following each other – there would be no transition. What happens then? The answer is nothing; as soon as the character decode routine has got the first bit in to the character decode buffer, it waits 10 ms and then resets PHASEDIFF to −5. There are enough transitions in AMTOR characters to ensure that PHASERROR will be updated on a frequent basis.

So, PHASERROR gets updated, and clearly if the clocks are significantly out of synchronization an error will build up in one direction or the other. So, the interrupt routine checks the value of PHASERROR against a limiting value, MAXERROR, and if it is outside the range of −MAXERROR to +MAXERROR takes action to synchronize the clocks by adjusting the value in CHARCLOCK by 1 to either speed it up slightly or slow it down. A large value for MAXERROR will make the system tolerant to losing lock once it has been acquired, but acquisition is slow; conversely a low value leads to quick acquisition and quick loss. Like many things in life, the selection of a value for MAXERROR is a matter of compromise. Martinez originally suggested a value of 512.

Although we have concentrated here on the errors in timing synchronization being due to the clocks at either end being out of sync, there is a further possibility. The ionosphere between the two stations is not stable, and so the time delay for signals reaching the IRS from the ISS will vary slightly with the ionospheric conditions. I shall have a little more to say about this in Chapter 15. Once bit-sync has been achieved, we can look at character synchronization. By the way, despite the fact that the system can accommodate some variations in timing, you still need the clock circuitry to be as precise as possible – a 999Hz clock is simply not good enough!

Character synchronization

There are two ways in which we can achieve character synchronization. The first is to monitor a number of incoming characters after bit synchronization has been achieved and check the numbers of '1's and '0's in these characters. We obviously need to 'frame' the data correctly – that is, determines a point in the incoming data stream as a start point that ensures that in each 7-bit chunk from there onwards we have a valid AMTOR character of four '1's and three '0's. Figure 11.2 shows the sort of problem we have. As can be seen frame 'a' is the correct frame, and although frame 'B' gives a valid AMTOR character for the first seven bits, subsequent characters are not valid. This indicates that we must examine a sequence of characters, the more the better, to be definite that we have a true AMTOR character lock. The easiest way to do this is to allow the receiver software to accumulate, say, 70 bits of data (10 possible characters) and check that this sequence is framed correctly. The following algorithm indicates one way in which we might do this for Mode B. The bit synchronization code has been omitted for clarity, and we enter this routine assuming that bit synchronization has been established.

```
                WAITTIME = 5 ms          ; get half way into
                                         ; first bit
BLOCKINPUT      CHARLOCKCOUNT = 0
                CHARBUFFER = BUFFERSTART
CHARINPUT       wait WAITTIME ms
                BITCOUNT = 0
BITINPUT        input bit from port
                store bit in bit BITCOUNT of CHARBUFFER
                BITCNT = BITCNT + 1
                if BITCNT <> 7
                    wait 10 ms
                    goto BITINPUT
                endif
                CHABUFFER = CHARBUFFER + 1
                CHARLOCKCOUNT = CHARLOCKCOUNT + 1
                if CHARLOCKCOUNT <> 70
                    goto CHARINPUT
                endif
CHECKDATA       for i = BUFFERSTART to BUFFERSTART + 70
                    ONESCOUNT = 0
                    ZEROCOUNT = 0
                    for j=0 to 6
                        if bit j of i is 1 then
                            ONESCOUNT = ONESCOUNT + 1
                        else
                            ZEROCOUNT = ZEROCOUNT + 1
                        endif
                    next j
```

```
        if ONESCOUNT = 4 AND ZEROCOUNT = 3
            LOCK = true
        else
            LOCK = false
        endif
    next i
    if LOCK = false
        WAITTIME = WAITTIME + 10
        goto BLOCKINPUT
    endif
```

This algorithm waits for 10 characters before running the CHECKDATA routine which checks that data that has been read in. If lock has been established, we can go in to a simpler decoding loop as indicated above, whereby we simply get a character in and check the bit count before printing it. We can then allow a certain number of 'bad' characters before deciding that character lock has been lost. Once we decide that we have lost lock, we need to repeat the above process to re-acquire character lock. If, after the CHECKDATA routine has run we have not acquired lock then we need to alter the frame being used on the incoming data and get another 10 characters in. The easiest way to change the frame is to add a character width on to the WAITTIME variable so that at the CHARINPUT stage we wait an extra bit before starting assembling a character in CHARBUFFER. Note that this algorithm expects that the delays taken to execute instructions are negligible compared to the time delays involved in decoding AMTOR; we are obviously going to need machine code or a compiled high level language here.

The longer the sequence of characters used to see if we have acquired lock, the lower the opportunity is for achieving a *false lock* where noise signals arrive in such a way that they simulate the legal AMTOR characters. However, the longer the sequence is,

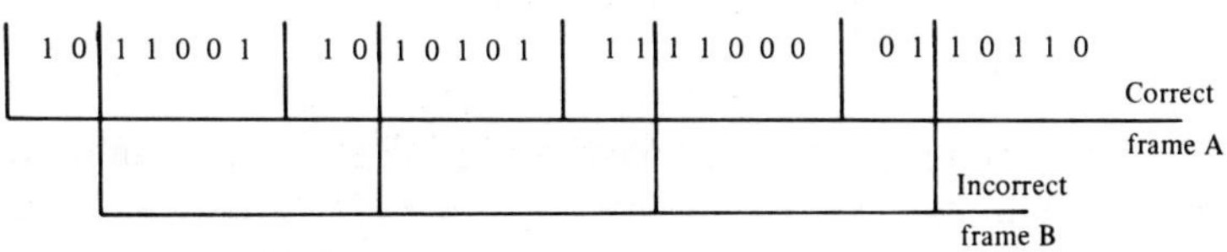

Figure 11.2

the longer it will take the system to acquire lock. A shorter sequence will speed up the lock acquisition process but will increase the chance of a false lock taking place.

This method of achieving lock can work on any sequence of characters being received from the ISS. An alternative method is for the IRS to wait for the a particular sequence of characters. This is the technique used in Mode A decoding, where we only have a block of three characters to work with. Here, we might adopt a technique along the following lines:

```
          SYNCBLOCK = 1
          NUMBERSYNCBLOCKS = 0
          NUMBERSYNCATTEMPTS = 0
LOOP      read in three characters
          if SYNCBLOCK = 1
              if three characters = x RQ z
                  SYNCBLOCK = 2
                  NUMBERSYNCATTEMPTS = NUMBERSYNCATTEMPTS -
              else
                  WAIT 10ms          ; move one
                                     ; bit along
                  NUMBERSYNCATTEMPTS = NUMBERSYNCATTEMPTS
                  NUMBERSYNCBLOCKS = 0
              endif
          else
              if three characters = x x RQ
                  SYNCBLOCK = 1
                  NUMBERSYNCBLOCKS = NUMBERSYNCBLOCKS + 1
              else
                  WAIT 10ms          ; move along one
                                     ; bit
                  NUMBERSYNCBLOCKS = 0
          NUMBERSYNCATTEMPTS = NUMBERSYNCATTEMPTS + 1
              endif
          endif
          IF NUMBERSYNCBLOCKS = 4
              return          ; all done
          endif
          IF NUMBERSYNCATTEMPTS < 40
              goto loop
          endif
```

In this system, NUMBERSYNCATTEMPTS is the number of failed attempts at synchronization, and NUMBERSYNCBLOCKS is the number of consecutive correct synchronization blocks received.

The process of achieving bit and character lock is essential to AMTOR in any of the modes. How AMTOR responds to errors after lock has been established is what differentiates the different AMTOR modes from each other. Having said that, let us examine each AMTOR mode in greater detail.

AMTOR Mode A

AMTOR Mode A is the mode of operation commonly used by two amateur stations wishing to communicate with each other. AMTOR Mode A is also called *ARQ*, which stands for the following mouthful: *automatic repeat request mode*.

Let us examine the sequence gone through by two stations in a Mode A contact. The contact is initiated by the master station which sends the 4-letter callsign of the station of interest in groups of three letters. AMTOR uses 4 letter callsigns derived from the callsign of the stations involved. For example, my callsign is G1UQW – in AMTOR QSOs the callsign is derived by removing the digit '1' and using GUQW as my AMTOR *selective callsign*, or SELCAL. If the master were to be interested in just one particular station, say G7ZZZ, a contact would be initiated by the master transmitting the following *synchronization blocks* repeatedly until an acknowledgement is received:

G RQ Z   Z Z RQ

The IRS with this callsign set up will attempt to synchronize on these blocks as described above; indeed, a quick means of synchronization would be to look for the RQ codes in the appropriate places in the sync blocks and providing it can synchronize and recognise its own callsign it will respond.

Block times

Before investigating the IRS, it might be a good idea at this point to look at the timing of these blocks; each one consists of three characters, and each character consists of seven bits of duration 10ms each. This gives a total block length of 210ms, and each block is separated from the following one by 240ms. During this time, the IRS can acknowledge the ISS. As we shall soon see, the acknowledgement signal from the IRS is just a single character, taking up 70ms. This gives us 170ms in the inter-block gap in which nothing vital happens; however, this time is crucial in the real world because of two very important facts – that radio waves travel at a finite speed and that the change over from transmit to receive in a radio transceiver takes a finite amount of time. The transmit/receive switch-over on the radio equipment must therefore be as rapid as possible for AMTOR Mode A use, and the use of Mode A also limits the range over which AMTOR can be used because the switch-over time at the ISS plus the time taken for the ISS signal to get to the IRS plus the time taken for the IRS to switch from receive to transmit plus the time taken for the IRS signal to get back to the ISS must be less that 170 ms. This makes certain contacts, such as long-path contacts between Europe and Australasia, very awkward, as the time taken for the transmissions to travel between ISS and IRS will vary depending upon the ionosphere. Clearly, the use of Mode A AMTOR to communicate via amateur radio 'moonbounce' or satellite is just not possible. Figure 11.1 shows these timings diagrammatically.

The IRS will use these blocks of callsign and RQs sent repeatedly by the ISS to achieve bit and character lock, and once this has been achieved we are, as they say, in business. As soon as lock is achieved, the IRS will acknowledge the ISS by sending a CS1 byte back to the ISS. Note that this does not make the IRS a sending station; it is only sending acknowledgement information. The ISS now receives this and sends a further block of three characters. If this is received correctly by the IRS – i.e. the character codes received contain four '1's and three '0's – then the IRS acknowledges again but this time sends a CS2 signal. The ISS then responds with the next block, and the IRS goes back to sending a CS1 signal. This process continues with the IRS acknowledging the ISS with alternating CS1 and CS2 signals until interference or fading causes an error at one end or the other. The actions that occur then are as follows.

IRS receives a bad block

If the IRS error check reveals an error, then providing that lock is still established the IRS will switch over to transmit and send the last CS code that it transmitted *again*, thus breaking the normal pattern. The ISS detects that it has received two identical CS codes in succession, and retransmits the erroneous block again. Figure 11.3 shows this in action. The ISS will repeat this procedure until a successful acknowledgement is returned by the IRS.

ISS loses acknowledgement

Of course, it is possible that in this time the IRS may lose lock and have to re-acquire it or the signal sent by the IRS may be obliterated by interference or lost in a fade. The ISS makes no assumptions here as to whether the IRS got the last block or not. Instead, it assumes the worst and rather then keeping plugging away with the message block stops sending messages and instead sends a block containing three RQ codes. It then waits for a reply from the IRS, which, on reception of a block of RQs in this way sends the lost control signal again. This process is repeated until the ISS receives a CS code to act on, and then the contact proceeds as mentioned above until the next error occurs or, hopefully, the ISS has finished what he or she wants to say and is ready to hear the IRS. What we need to do now is to swap the roles of ISS and IRS.

ISS/IRS switchover

There are two cases to consider here. The first is where the IRS wishes to 'butt in' on the ISS, and the second is where the ISS relinquishes transmission to the IRS – the AMTOR equivalent of an 'over to you'.

IRS interrupts ISS
The operator at the ISS instructs his or her AMTOR terminal that a change is required, and the AMTOR system then instructs the

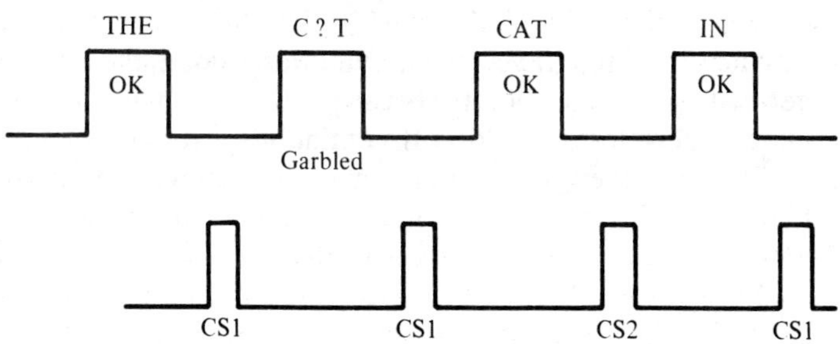

Figure 11.3

IRS to send the CS3 signal instead of the usual CS1 or CS2. On receiving this, the ISS transmits the sequence 'b a b'. On receipt of this block, the IRS changes to ISS and sends a block of three characters containing the following:

If the station that has just changed its status to transmit was the master station, then it sends back and RQ and two other characters as a block.

If the station that has just changed its status to transmit was the slave station it sends back a block of three RQ codes.

As soon as the original ISS detects the RQ code in these blocks, it changes over to be the IRS and acknowledges the new ISS with the CS1 code. The new ISS can now transmit data to the new IRS in the same ways as before.

ISS relinquishes transmission

If the operator of the ISS wishes to allow the IRS to 'speak', then the sequence '+?' is sent by the ISS. The IRS recognises this sequence, *and no other* as meaning that the ISS has initiated a request for the IRS to take over transmitting. It is no use typing in 'over' and expecting the other station to be able to talk to you, as both stations will still be locked in their original configurations. The IRS will now send a CS3 code back to the ISS, and the switch-over proceeds as for the first case.

Resynchronization in Mode A

If long bursts of interference or fading causes synchronization to be lost, AMTOR systems will allow up to 32 retries to get an acknowledgement from the ISR under normal operation. If this fails, then the ISS assumes lock has been lost and the master will start sending

G RQ Z   Z Z RQ

until resynchronization is achieved. Once this is done, the message transfer will go on as before because the two machines will remember where lock was lost. If continuous errors occur in 64 blocks of data, then the contact may be terminated by the AMTOR system. This is only likely if a very poor link is in existence.

End of transmission

Only the ISS may terminate a contact, and this is done by sending a block of three alphas. The command to do this varies from

AMTOR unit to AMTOR unit, but whatever it is it will always generate these three characters. If the IRS wants to finish the contact then it must become the ISS by the means described above.

AMTOR Mode B

AMTOR Mode B is also called FEC – *forward error correction* because of the way in which error handling is taken care of. In broad terms, Mode B requires less interaction between the ISS and ISR, and is particularly suitable for circumstances where one ISS wishes to communicate with, at least at first, several IRSs. A few seconds though will indicate *why* the ARQ system cannot be used with more than one recipient station; the ISS would only be able to accept return signals from one ISR. Mode B uses a totally different system therefore to reduce the risk of errors. There are two types of Mode B AMTOR; the first might be called a 'broadcast' mode, as the signal is aimed at all interested listeners. The second is a specific mode, aimed at a particular station, is not commonly used by amateurs and is more often found in use by the maritime services.

FEC is used for things like amateur news broadcasts and propagation forecasts, CQ calls and other general interest signals. In addition, it is often used for establishing contacts with stations, and once synchronization between stations has been achieved, both stations switch over to Mode A. In addition, it can be used for QSOs in conditions where Mode A is not suitable, such as over long propagation paths or in situations where the transmit/receive switch overs are too long to allow Mode A to work.

Forward error correction

FEC works on the very simple principle of sending the same data twice, separated by a few characters to reduce the risk of a particularly prolonged burst of interference or fading taking out both copies of the character.

The master station is the only transmitting station in this mode, the IRS stations being passive recipients of the data. The signal starts with the ISS sending an alternating sequence of 'RQ a' to allow the IRSs to synchronize. The message then starts, with a repeat message following, as shown in Figure 11.4. The 'a'

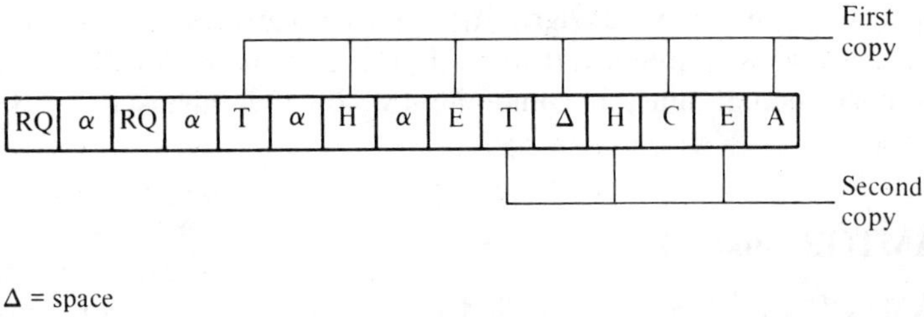

Figure 11.4

characters are also used, as can be seen, to separate the two copies of the message and ensure that they are 5 characters apart. Once the ISS finishes transmitting a particular message, the 'RQ a' pattern is sent repeatedly until the next message is sent, thus allowing receiving stations to keep synchronization with the ISS.

Error correction on FEC is very straightforward. The first copy of the character is examined and if it is a legal AMTOR character it is printed out as such. The second copy of the character will then be ignored. If the first copy is corrupt, the system checks the second copy of the character. One implication of this is that the receiving system must get both copies of a character into memory before it checks the first copy of the character. If the second copy is alright, it is printed. If not, a character will be printed to indicate a 'double fault' by the system. This can be a space, or something like a '*' or '–' depending upon the software used for decoding. The two copies of each character are 350 ms apart, which is quite a way in terms of interference bursts, and so the chances of getting at least one good copy of a letter are fair.

AMTOR Mode S

Mode S is the 'selective' version of Mode B. Although not used much on the amateur bands, it might easily become more popular offering a closed group of IRSs for a particular ISS to transmit to.

AMTOR equipment offers the user an opportunity to input a 4 character callsign, as indicated earlier in this chapter. In Mode S, the initial 'RQ a' sequence is sent to allow the receiving station to synchronize, followed by the 4-letter selective call of the intended IRS. If you wish a group of stations to be IRSs, then clearly they must have the same callsign programmed in to their AMTOR systems. After the callsign, the message information is sent inverted, with '1's changed to '0's and vice versa. The IRSs that have detected their callsign are expecting this and invert the incoming data before converting it to legible text for display. Again, the FEC method of error correction is employed.

AMTOR Mode L

Mode L is the listening mode, and is a means by which we can eavesdrop on Mode A conversations. In Mode L, no transmissions are initiated by the listening station, not even CS1 or CS2 acknowledgements and so it is not possible for the Mode L station to request repeat blocks from the ISS. The AMTOR software, however, still monitors each incoming character and if the character has become corrupt and no longer has the appropriate number of '1's and '0's then it will not be displayed. However, that is all that takes place; no attempt at error correction is possible but at least the printout or display does not fill up with absolute rubbish!

On the air with AMTOR

Well, that was the theory, so how does it all come together on the air? AMTOR QSOs are often to be heard in the amateur radio HF bands, particularly on 80 and 20 metres. The centres of activity are around 3588 kHz and 14 075 kHz. Activity can also be heard on VHF around 144.590 MHz. The first thing to do is to recognise what Modes A and B sound like; after all, we cannot decode signals if we do not know what they are!

Mode A signals are often described as CHIRUP CHIRUP CHIRUP whilst the station is attempting to establish contact with another station, then changing to CHIRUP CHIR CHIRUP CHIR once a Mode A QSO has been established, the 'CHIR' being the CS1 or CS2 character coming back from the ISR. Do not forget that in some cases you may only hear one end of the conversation, as in all amateur radio modes.

A Mode B transmission will be a longer burst of signal; these are less common under normal circumstances than Mode A transmissions. A Mode B transmission sounds a lot like 100 baud RTTY but with none of the inter-character mark tones common on RTTY transmissions being generated by 'hunt and peck' typists like me!

Receiving AMTOR

Once you find a transmission, it is time to try to tune it in. Set up the receiver in USB mode and if possible turn off the receiver AGC; rely on manual RF and AF gain controls. Instruct your AMTOR unit to enter the correct mode, and then tune the receiver around the signal until the tuning indicator on the AMTOR unit indicates that you are on frequency, or until the status lights of your AMTOR unit indicate that lock has been achieved and text starts appearing on your screen. Synchronization should occur within a few seconds of the signal being tuned in; if nothing happens after that time then you may have a problem. Later in this chapter there is a list of trouble shooting steps to follow.

If you are monitoring a Mode A transmission using Mode L, then you are almost certain to get some bad characters if the link between you and the two stations in QSO is poor, so do not think that corrupt characters indicate you have got a problem!

Transmitting AMTOR

AMTOR contacts between amateurs are usually initiated in Mode B if you are not sure of the SELCAL of the station you wish to communicate with. In addition, you need to instruct your AMTOR controller of your own SELCAL. In my AMTOR unit, the command is:

MYSELCAL GUQW

where GUQW is my own SELCAL. Do not forget that you will not be able to partake in Mode A contacts unless your SELCAL is set up. Now you can send a CQ call, but using Mode B rather than Mode A. Enter Mode B on your AMTOR system and type something along the lines of:

```
CQ  CQ  CQ  DE  GiUQW
SELCAL IS GUQW
CQ  CQ  CQ  DE  GiUQW  K
```

Once this is transmitted, you can simply sit in Mode B and wait for a call from another station who will now attempt to contact you using your SELCAL. As soon as your AMTOR system recognises the incoming SELCAL as being its own, it will switch automatically to Mode A and become the IRS. The station that has called you will be the ISS.

If you know the SELCAL of the station in question, then you can go into Mode A immediately and send out a 'connect' attempt to the other station. On my unit, the command to do this is:

ARQ xxxx

where xxxx is the SELCAL of the station I am attempting to contact. Your transmitter will now start sending the SELCAL – RQ sequence discussed above until a response is obtained from the other station. If the station responds, you will be the ISS and the other station the IRS.

Once contact is established, you may send your message by simply typing it in. During transmission, any status lights on your AMTOR system will be flashing away depending upon how good the link is. Once you have finished what you wanted to say, you must initiate a change over by the '+?'. Failure to do this will result in the IRS not being able to become the ISS unless the IRS sends a CS3 code. On my system, I can do this if I am the IRS by entering CTRL-C at the keyboard whilst receiving data, then typing in the CHANGE command.

Like all amateur radio modes, there are certain standards of operating which, if adhered to, make life easier for all concerned. The first is the usual 'listen before transmitting' maxim. The second is to move away from the AMTOR calling frequency once a contact has been made. The technique for this is to use the calling frequency to decide on a frequency on which to operate away from the calling frequency, then cease transmission and change frequency. It is a very anti-social activity to QSY whilst you are still transmitting AMTOR!

Like all data modes, make full use of any type-ahead facilities offered by your system; the ability to prepare a text for transmission whilst receiving data from the other station is valuable.

Trouble-shooting

Switch sideband

It is quite possible that the station is using the other sideband to you, so simply switch over to LSB if you are on USB and vice versa, then retune as required and wait for lock to occur.

Audio output level

Modern terminal units and data decoders are quite tolerant to a wide range of audio input levels, though too great an input signal could be overdriving the receiver output circuits or decoder input circuits, causing distortion and harmonics which will produce all sorts of problems in the locking process. Check your audio output level by using an oscilloscope and looking for any signs of 'flat-topping' from the receiver audio output stage. A suitable arrangement for this is shown in Figure 11.5. Also, check the specifications of your decoder, and make sure that the output from the receiver is not overdriving the input filters of the decoder. Of course, if the input signal is too low then you will also have problems.

Terminal unit bandwidth

A terminal unit capable of receiving 100 baud RTTY or ASCII should have no problems with AMTOR, but it is possible that some filters may be too heavily optimised for dedicated 45 or 50 baud RTTY operation, and the AMTOR signals can cause 'ringing' in the filters. In this case, there is no option but to change your filter. If, like me, you use a multi-mode data decoder you can suffer from the opposite problem, where the filters used in the decoder input are designed for several modes, including packet radio, rather than having dedicated filters for each mode. This may result in a fairly wide filter bandwidth being used for

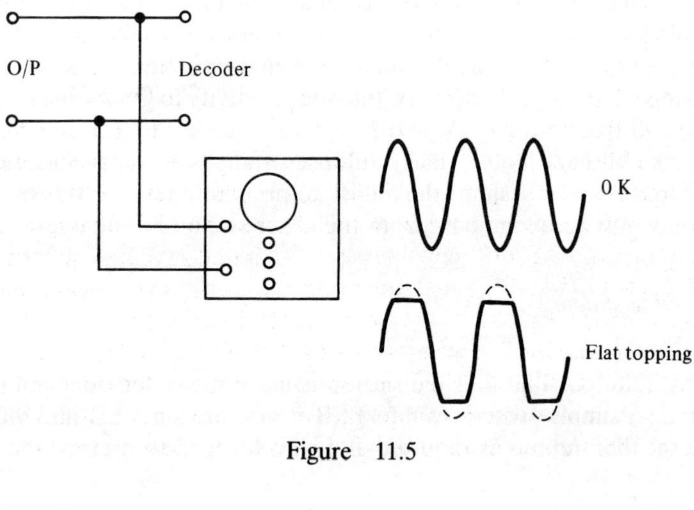

Figure 11.5

AMTOR, thus allowing more interference into the decoder and so degrading the systems small signal performance for AMTOR.

Terminal unit status lights

If you have a commercial multi-mode terminal unit or AMTOR decoder, the chances are that the system will bear at least two status lights to let you know what is happening. Not all systems will indicate the statuses listed below, but you should find at least a couple of them supported by your own system:

Repeat request
This indicates that your system is being requested to send a repeat block to the IRS.

Phasing error
This indicates that the system is currently trying to synchronize with the other machine. Continuous phasing errors might indicate a hardware problem or a very poor link.

Idle indicator
This signifies at the IRS that an AMTOR idle signal is being received. The link is established and synchronisation achieved but no data is being sent from the ISS.

Summing up AMTOR

The error detection and correction abilities of AMTOR have made it quite a popular mode and one that seems to be gaining in popularity as more equipment becomes available at a cheaper price. I have listed some suppliers of equipment in the Appendices. It has always been more popular in the UK and Europe than in the United States, where packet radio has become more popular. On short wave, AMTOR will probably get through when packet radio, RTTY or ASCII signals are lost, and although the baud rate of AMTOR may seem low compared to that of 300 baud HF packet radio, the actual rate of data transfer can be higher than experienced with packet over normal HF radio paths.

Current technical developments in AMTOR include the use of AMTOR 'mailboxes' where messages can be left for other radio amateurs not on the air at the time of transmission, and links into the packet radio network. Work is also being done to develop a protocol by which computer data and program files can be sent over AMTOR links. It is useful to compare AMTOR with packet radio (Chapter 13), but do not assume that the two modes of operation compete with each other; I have found that a lot of pleasure can be obtained from both, and that each has its strengths and weaknesses.

TWELVE

SSTV and FAX

So far, the communications modes that we have discussed have been textual modes; that is, only text can be sent easily, and graphical images or pictures cannot be sent at all. Some enterprising individuals have managed to send pictures over RTTY links by using characters to make up the outline of a picture, but on the whole this is quite difficult and the results are not always that good!

In this chapter I want to examine two methods of sending pictures over radio; *slow scan television (SSTV)* and *facsimile (FAX)*. The first of these has been used by amateur radio stations for some years, using cameras and special monitor screens, and the second has been used for many years commercially for sending press photographs, weather maps and other graphical information over radio. I shall give outline information on how these signals can be decoded using computer techniques, and how to get the best out of commercial SSTV and FAX decoding equipment.

Slow scan television

The first question to ask is 'What is SSTV?' Well, conventional television gives us very good picture quality at a rate of 50 frames per second, giving the illusion of movement. However, to do this a vast amount of data needs to be transmitted for each picture; so much, in fact, that a conventional television picture takes up several megahertz of frequency bandwidth. This has meant that broadcast television pictures have only been transmitted in the VHF and UHF regions of the radio spectrum where there are plenty of frequencies that can be used. A conventional TV picture has 625 horizontal lines, and a separate picture is sent every 1/50th second in the UK. One way in which the bandwidth occupied by a transmitted picture can be reduced is to reduce the number of horizontal lines transmitted in each frame and to reduce the rate of transmission, from 50 frames per second to, say, 1 frame every few seconds. This is precisely what is done with slow scan television; the picture information is encoded in signals which can easily fit in the 2.5 kHz bandwidth that is considered acceptable for single sideband transmissions, typically giving a picture with 120 lines that takes 7 or 8 seconds to transmit.

SSTV modulation methods

SSTV signals are sent as audio signals occupying a bandwidth of about 2.3 kHz, different frequencies within this range holding different pieces of picture information, as we shall see. We can thus use AFSK or FSK modulation to impose this data on a radio wave, and on the short wave bands you will find that USB is used. On the VHF bands, you will find a mixture of USB and FM used to transmit SSTV. This is similar to the situation with RTTY, and the signals can sound quite similar, but SSTV signals have more 'variation' in them, whereas RTTY signals simply consist of two tones.

SSTV standards

Because SSTV transmission and reception was originally done with purely analogue equipment, many of the time constants of the system were based on the mains frequency. This has given rise to two standards, which differ slightly, depending upon whether the system is being operated in a country with 50 Hz or 60 Hz mains electricity. Whichever standard is used, an SSTV picture has the characteristics shown in Figure 12.1.

Synchronization pulses

In TV terms, *synchronization*, or *sync* pulses, are used as 'markers' to indicate precisely what part of the picture is being transmitted at a given point. They allow the receiving equipment to re-synchronize to the transmitting equipment at the end of each line and each frame, or full picture. A sync pulse is indicated by a burst of 1.2 kHz audio of a specified length.

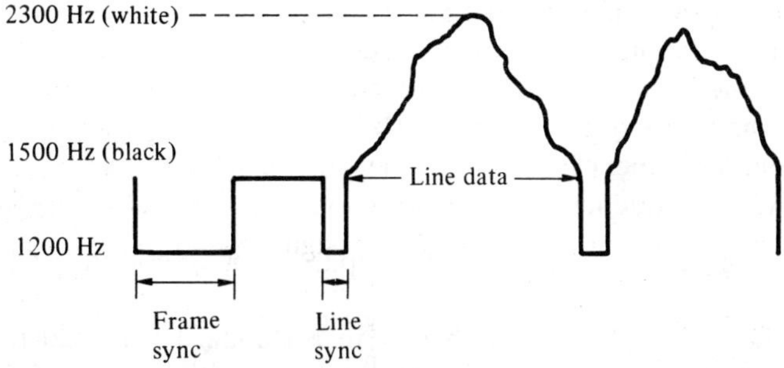

Figure 12.1

Line sync pulses indicate the start of a new line of picture information, and are sent at the start of each line.

Frame sync pulses indicate the end of a picture, and the start of the next picture. They are sent at the beginning of each frame.

Picture information

The actual black and white content of the picture is coded by audio tones of varying frequencies. White is represented by a tone of 2300 Hz and black by 1500 Hz. A continuous grey scale exists between these two frequencies, but in practice there are certain discrete levels of grey that are displayed. The tone at a particular moment in time thus indicates the brightness of a particular point on a given scan line of an SSTV picture.

50 Hz standard

number of lines	120
length of each line	60 ms
time per frame	7.2 seconds
line sync pulse	5 ms
frame sync pulse	30 ms
sync frequency	1.2 kHz
black frequency	1.5 kHz
white frequency	2.3 kHz

60 Hz standard
This standard has the following parameters:

number of lines	120
length of each line	66 ms

time per frame	8 seconds
line sync pulse	5 ms
frame sync pulse	30 ms
sync frequency	1.2 kHz
black frequency	1.5 kHz
white frequency	2.3 kHz

In both cases, the picture is built up from top to bottom, and left to right.

Although we have described here a standard with 120 lines, many pictures are seen now with 128 lines; initially these 8 extra lines did not hold picture information, and they gave a grey scale on the screen. However, they are used more commonly now to hold picture information. In addition, with the use of computers to generate and decode SSTV pictures, each horizontal line of the picture is often found to contain 64, 128 or 256 individual pixels.

SSTV decoding hardware

Decoding SSTV signals requires some additional hardware as well as the computer. The essence of SSTV decoding is to convert the incoming tones into a voltage, which would resemble that shown in Figure 12.1. This voltage can then be processed by a fast analogue to digital converter and inputted to the computer. The sync pulses can then be recognised, and the picture displayed. Let us start by looking at the first stage, converting the frequencies off air into a voltage. This can be done using a frequency to voltage converter, as shown in Figure 12.2. This circuit is typical of those used in these applications, and the output voltage given is proportional to the input frequency. There are several integrated circuits around now which can convert an input frequency into a voltage, but whatever circuit you use must be:

1 able to convert frequencies in the range 0 to 2500Hz into a voltage range for processing by an analogue to digital converter. This is typically 0 to 2.5V or so.

2 as linear in response as possible, giving a straight-line graph if the output voltage were to be plotted on a graph against the input frequency. Very few circuits are totally linear, but it makes subsequent processing of the SSTV signal easier if the F/V converter is fairly linear.

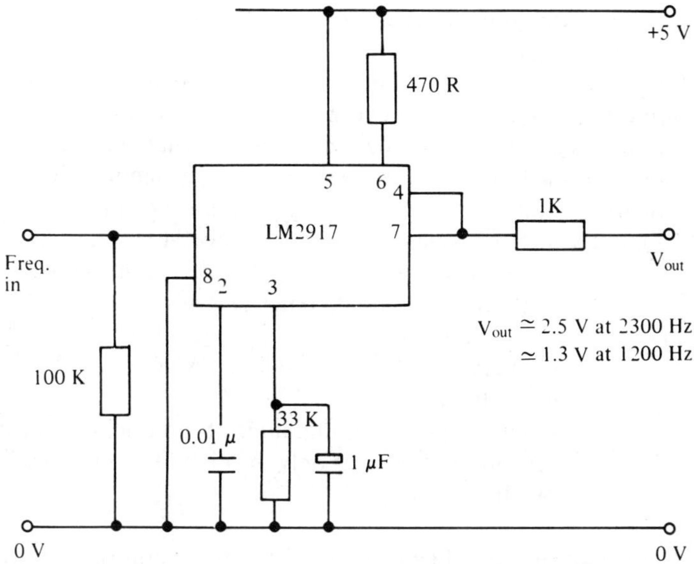

Figure 12.2

3 the response time of the circuit – the time it takes for the output voltage to reflect a change in the input frequency – should be quite fast, as otherwise the F/V conversion will not keep up with changes in the transmitted picture!

The circuit shown in Figure 12.2 uses the LM2917 chip, which was originally designed for use in tachometer circuits! It requires an input signal in excess of 250mV peak to peak to work correctly, and I have had best results from it fed from the loudspeaker socket of my receiver. Due to the way in which the circuit functions, the output voltage contains a degree of 'ripple', a slight variation on the output voltage even when the input frequency is constant. Although this can be solved by additional circuitry, it is easier to solve it after the analogue to digital conversion process, as we shall see later.

Once a voltage has been obtained, we need to convert this into digital signals that the computer can use. To do this an analogue to digital converter is used, which typically converts the input voltage into a byte that can be read in to the computer. The requirements of an AD converter for SSTV use are as follows:

1 that the input voltage range of the ADC should correspond to the output voltage range of the FV converter.
2 the ADC should be fast; that is, the time taken to convert an input signal into an output byte should be as short as possible. In SSTV, a few seconds thought will tell us what the maximum time for each conversion will be. If we ignore the 5ms synchronization pulse, and assume that we are going to aim for 128 points along each 66ms line, then we need to get a sample at least every 128/66ms. Call this 0.5ms for each conversion, and you can see that the ADC that comes as standard on the BBC Microcomputer will not be fast enough, as this has a conversion rate of one every 10ms. We need an ADC capable of a conversion every 10 or 20μs.
3 The ADC should require the minimum of interfacing with the host computer, preferably using only the eight data lines needed to transfer data to the user port.

The circuit shown in Figure 12.3 satisfies these criteria, and uses the Ferranti ZN448 ADC chip. This particular device is very easy to use, and I have an emotional attachment to it because the first ADC I ever built (that worked properly) was based around this chip! It is configured to run continuously, with the data lines changing constantly with incoming voltages. This may appear to be a problem, but we can get around it by the use of a further line of the user port to trigger the RD line of the ADC. In this case, the data at the output is enabled for reading only when the RD line is taken to a logic zero. The converter runs at about 900kHz, as determined by the chip's built in clock and the 150pF capacitor. If you have only eight I/O lines available, use seven bits for input and ignore the LSB of the ADC output and use bit 0 as the RD line.

SSTV decoding software

The software for resolving SSTV pictures can be split into two functional parts; data acquisition and picture resolution. In this section, I shall look at algorithms for these processes and indicate how they might be implemented.

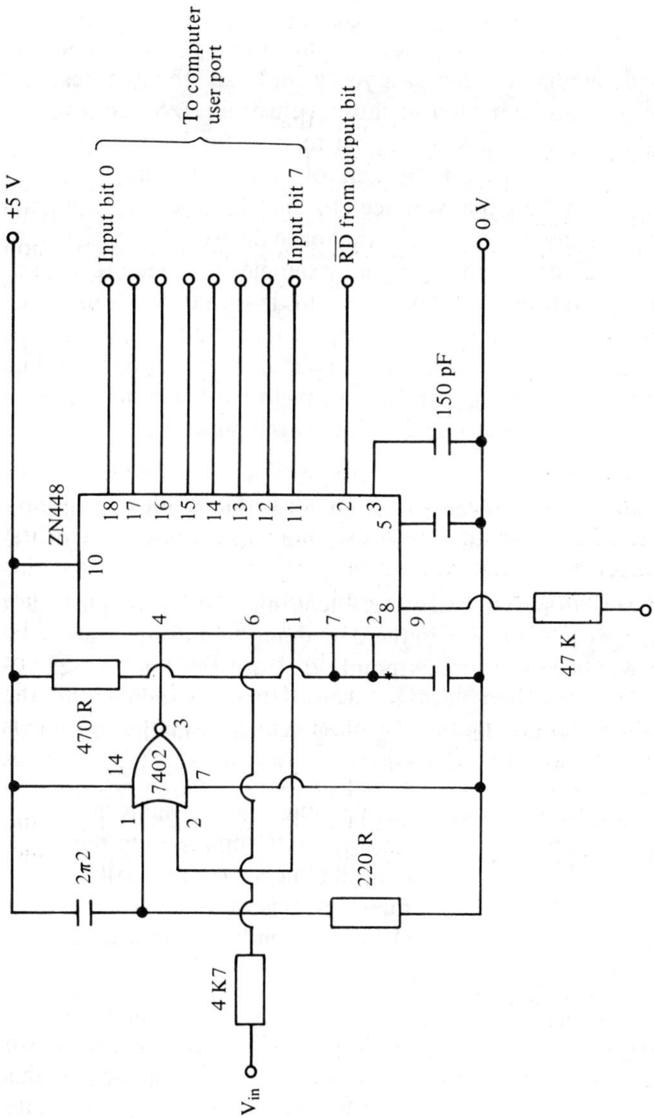

+5 V
Input bit 0
Input bit 7
To computer user port
RD from output bit
0 V
150 pF
ZN448
10
18
17
16
15
14
13
12
11
2
3
5
8
9
4
6
1
7
2
470 R
14
7402
3
7
1
2
2π2
220 R
47 K
−5 V
4 K7
V_{in}

Figure 12.3

Data acquisition

Getting the data off air into your computer is the tough part, requiring machine code for speed. Once the data is in the machine, you have the choice to process it in either machine code or BASIC, depending on how fast you want to see the pictures, and whether you are interested in subsequent frames. Some listeners record the SSTV signals off air on to tape for later processing, which allows them to get the best of all worlds – more on this later. The main thing that you need to consider when acquiring the data is how many pixels do you want each displayed picture line to have. This will determine how many samples you need to take of each line of the transmitted picture. This in turn depends upon the graphics ability of your computer, as discussed below. Let us assume that you want to display each picture with 64 pixels per line and that you are dealing with 128-line pictures. The other question you must ask is, when to deal with the sync pulses? There are two options:

1 store all the data received off air as a 'dump' into an area of computer memory, and then sort out the various parts of the signal later.
2 recognise the sync pulses at data acquisition and store particular bytes – say a '0' or '1' – in the data dump to indicate that a sync pulse was received at this point. Because the sync pulses are always 'blacker than black' in terms of the picture content of the signal there is no chance of getting sync information mixed up with the picture information.

In the following algorithm, I have adopted the second technique to store 128 lines of 64 pixel data, with a '0' representing the frame sync pulse and a '1' representing the line sync pulse. Although in the algorithm I have used frequencies, this would actually indicate the voltage read from the ADC corresponding to that frequency.

```
START:  NumberOfLines=128
        pointer=PictureDumpStart        ; PictureDumpStart
                                          is an area of
                                          memory reserved
                                          for dumping the
                                          data in.
```

```
SYNC     repeat until input = SYNC          ; loop until a
                                              SYNC frequency
                                              signal is detected.
         wait 10 ms
         if input <> SYNC goto SYNC         ; we are waiting for
                                              a frame sync
                                              signal which will
                                              be about 30 ms
                                              long. If we have
                                              got a line sync at
                                              this point then
                                              round again.
SYNC2:   repeat until input > 1400Hz        ; now wait for
                                              frame sync to end
                                              by going above
                                              1400 Hz.
         store FRAMESYNC to pointer         ; store a frame sync
                                              market into the
                                              picture buffer.
         pointer=pointer + 1
LINE:    repeat until input = SYNC          ; now we wait for
                                              the line sync to
                                              occur for the first
                                              line of the next
                                              frame.
LINE1:   repeat until input <> SYNC         ; assume that the
                                              sync signal just
                                              recorded is a line
                                              sync.
         store LINESYNC to pointer
         pointer=pointer + 1
         pixelNumber=0
PIXELS:  wait 1.03 ms                       ; this funny number
                                              is a pixel wide on
                                              the screen,
                                              assuming that we
                                              want to have 64
                                              pixels across the
                                              screen.
```

```
ADCCOUNT=0                        ; ADCCOUNT is a
                                    16 bit variable
                                    which is used to
                                    average out
                                    readings from the
                                    ADC to ensure
                                    that the 'ripple'
                                    from the F/V
                                    converter is
                                    smoothed out.
for counter=1 TO 8
ADCCOUNT=ADCCOUNT + input
next counter
ADCCOUNT=ADCCOUNT/8               ; 8 used because
                                    we can achieve
                                    the division by
                                    shifting bits,
                                    rather than by
                                    mathematics.
Store ADCCOUNT to pointer
pointer=pointer + 1
If PixelNumber<64 THEN GOTO pixel
If LineNumber<128 THEN GOTO line
END
```

Clearly, some fine tuning would be required to implement this algorithm on a computer, depending upon the speed of the processor and whether hardware timers were available. For example, the BBC User VIA could be employed to generate the various time delays required on that machine, but on IBM PCs we might have to resort to timing loops in software. In addition, a system specific look-up table would be required to hold the values of ADC output that corresponded to input frequenies. A good idea of this can be obtained from the equations given in Figure 12.2 for the F/V converter, but with suitable programming absolute accuracy is not required; we can 'fudge' things at the picture display stage. The main thing is that we can identify sync signals, and one way of doing this would be to choose a value, such as that corresponding to 1400Hz, and say that anything below this is a sync pulse and everything above this is picture information. This threshold approach is quite common. So, what do we do with a frame of picture information, acquired by the above algorithm?

Picture display

This is not quite as difficult, as we have actually assembled the picture into lines in the data acquisition stage. What we now do to display the picture is purely a matter of choice, limited only by the resolution of the computer display. Let us stick to the resolution of 64 horizontal pixels by 128 lines, as assembled above. The other parameters of the picture that we have to decide are:

1 grey scale content – or, the contrast of the final displayed picture. Do we want it in shades of grey or just black and white?
2 do we want to use 'false colour' rather than just grey scale shading?
3 how many 'physical' screen pixels correspond to an SSTV picture element. For example, a computer graphics screen with a horizontal resolution of 640 pixels and a vertical resolution of 320 lines would allow us to have a single SSTV picture element occupying a screen area of 10 pixels by 2 lines.

Let us start by looking at (3) and (1) first. This will depend on the way in which your computer display handles graphics, but you should be able to write a subroutine or procedure to create such an area on the screen. For example, you could specify a user defined graphic on the BBC or Amstrad 6128 eight pixels wide by two lines deep, along the lines shown in Figure 12.4. Using the graphics cursor, you could then scan the picture area of memory and select one of the UDCs in Figure 12.4 depending upon the shade of grey required by the image to be displayed. This would depend upon the value stored in the picture buffer, as described below. the display is thus built up of 'tiles', as shown in Figure 12.4. An

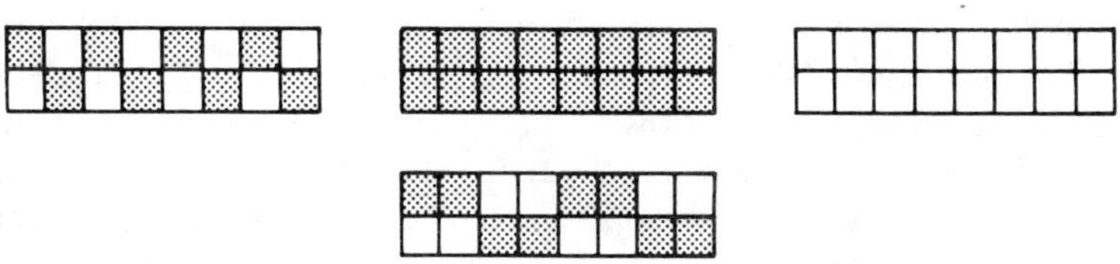

Figure 12.4

alternative would be to use the point plotting routines supported by your computer to simply plot pixels in this area, but this would take longer than using user defined characters.

Choosing a grey scale

The range of voltages between that representing 1500 Hz (black) and that representing 2300 Hz (white) clearly represent a range of shades between black and white. This is the grey scale of the transmitted image, and one decision we have to make is how many shades of grey we are going to try to represent on the screen of the computer. At one extreme, we could simply have two shades, black and white, with, say, everything above 1900 Hz being plotted as a white area on the screen and everything below 1900 Hz being plotted as a black area (assuming it is not a sync pulse). The number of shades of grey you can show depends upon the computer and the characteristics of the received signal; that may consist of just black and white, anyway! Figure 12.4 shows how grey scale characters might be defined as UDCs; the 'stippling' effect is a common method of using individual graphics pixels to give the appearance of shading.

False colour

One interesting approach is to plot solid areas of colour on the screen, each colour representing a certain range of input frequency, thus corresponding to the grey scale above. Clearly, how effective this approach is depends upon the number of colours available on your computer in the graphics mode and the actual content of the transmitted picture. The coloured image generated by this technique is not a true colour SSTV image; they are transmitted using slightly different techniques to those examined so far.

```
START:  pointer=PictureDumpStart-1
        NumberOfLines=128
        NumberOfPixels=64
        repeat
            pointer=pointer+1
        until DataAtPointer=FrameSync       ; scan dump area
                                              for the first frame
                                              sync byte
                                              recorded.
```

```
        ClearGraphicsScreen              ; clear screen for
                                           new picture.
        Xposition=0                      ; set X position
                                           to top left of
                                           graphics screen.
        Yposition=0                      ; set Y position to
                                           top left of screen.
        pointer=pointer+1                ; now we are
                                           looking at the
                                           first line sync
                                           signal.
        pointer=pointer + 1              ; jump to first data
                                           signal.
LOOP:   pixel = DataAtPointer            ; get stored output
                                           from ADC
        SelectGreyScaleCharacter         ; select an
                                           appropriate grey
                                           scale character to
                                           print out.
        MoveGraphicsCursor
        to Xposition,Yposition           ; move to
                                           appropriate place
                                           on screen
        PrintCharacter                   ; print grey scale
                                           UDC.
        Xposition=Xposition+1            ; increment X
                                           position to next X
                                           location for
                                           printing next
                                           character.
        pointer=pointer+1
        i DataAtPointer<>LineSync        ; check for end of
                                           line.
        Ypointer=Ypointer + 1
        pointer=pointer+1
        if Ypointer < 129 then GOTO LOOP
        END
            GOTO LOOP
```

The above algorithm could be implemented in any language that you please, but if you are interested in processing pictures in 'real time' then you clearly need to use machine code.

Colour SSTV

Colour images can be sent via slow scan television in a variety of ways. One technique is for the image to be sent three times, the first as the image appears through a red filter, the second a green filter and the third through a blue filter. This method takes three times as long to send an image as the monochrome method. A further method of sending colour SSTV is to send each line of the picture in red, green and blue after each other, as shown in Figure 12.5.

Figure 12.5

Viewing SSTV

Once you have got the equipment and software, whether home-brew or commercial, there remains the problem of actually tuning in the signals. SSTV signals can be found around the following HF frequencies:

3740 kHz
7040 kHz
14 170 kHz
14 230 kHz
21 340 kHz
28 700 kHz

When tuned in using USB mode, an SSTV signal sounds like a warbling noise with occasional 'beeps' as the frame sync signal is heard (typically once every seven or eight seconds). You may need to tune in signals in a trial and error way to see what settings you need on the receiver to get the best picture results – i.e. what a properly tuned SSTV picture 'sounds' like. Once you have done this, you can actually tape record off-air signals and play them back later for analysis. However, do remember that once you have recorded a signal you cannot actually alter the frequency of the recorded signal on playback! This might cause problems, for example, if you tuned in the signal incorrectly and ended up with the sync pulses outside the frequency range that your receiving equipment responds to as sync pulses. Of course, one way around this is to include in the software a means of varying the frequency threshold for sync pulses. You may also have problems with received pictures containing large amounts of black, as this may cause the sync pulses to be lost and so may cause distortion or 'tearing' of the image.

Facsimile reception

Facsimile (FAX) is a method of transmitting pictures by radio, encoding picture information as a series of audio tones. A document bearing the illustration can be scanned and the areas of light and dark on the picture are converted into audio tones for transmission by frequency modulation of the carrier wave. It is similar in this respect to SSTV, but offers higher resolution images and is principally used by weather stations for sending weather maps and other such graphical information over the air. Amateur FAX has only really become popular with the advent of software for home computers to generate and decode FAX, or the construction of FAX decoders to plug in to home micros. In this book, I am not going to explore the traditional fax machines in any detail; instead, I shall concentrate on using computers.

Differences between FAX and SSTV

Although audio tones are used to encode the images in both FAX and SSTV, there are some differences. The first is that a transmitted FAX image can be of much higher resolution than a transmitted SSTV picture. The practical upshot of this is that a FAX image takes longer to transmit than a typical SSTV image, often as long as 15 to 30 minutes! A single line of a FAX image – of which there may be up to a couple of hundred – takes about half a second to transmit, and there are no synchronization signals at the end of each FAX line like the line sync signals in SSTV. At the start of each FAX transmission there is a sequence of tones which indicates to the receiving equipment what type of FAX is on the way (see below) and acts as a 'frame sync' signal for the FAX receiver. The receiving end then gets into sync with the FAX transmitter, and receives no further resynchronization signals throughout the duration of the FAX transmission. Any drift in timing at the receiving end will thus cause problems, as outlined below.

How FAX is generated

A traditional FAX machine is shown in Figure 12.6, and in use a piece of paper containing the image to be transmitted is taped to the drum and the machine started. A light source and scanner mounted on the scanning head detect the image density at each point along the line being scanned as the drum rotates, and converts the density into a voltage which can be used to vary the frequency of an audio source or directly vary the frequency of a radio transmitter. After a full rotation of the drum, the scanning head moves along its track by a set amount, and the drum rotates again. This time, of course, the scanning head will be scanning a different line of the image, and so a full picture will eventually be transmitted. Correct reproduction of the image at the receiving end was originally by a similar piece of equipment but with a light source replacing the scanning head and the paper being light-sensitive, and thus responding to fluctuations in the light level (caused by changes in image density at the sending end) by forming dark or light areas on the paper. The rotation of the receiving drum and the movement of the light source must be synchronized accurately to the sending end, and this was done by having accurate timing at each end with synchronization being attained by mechanical means when transmission started.

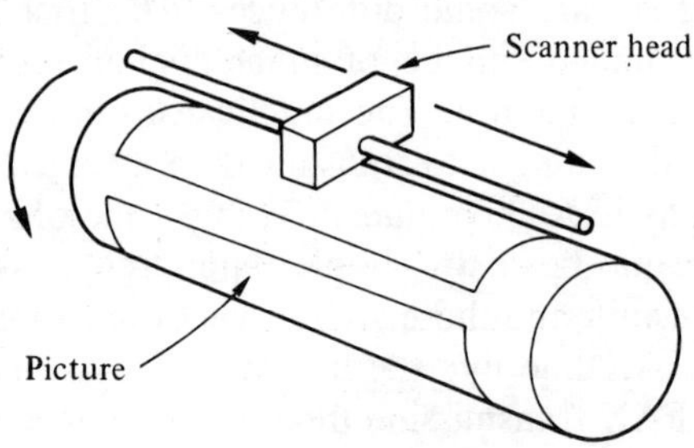

Figure 12.6

Modulation methods used

When used on radio, FAX is usually transmitted using frequency modulation on the short waves, and if Fc is the carrier frequency, white is represented by Fc+400Hz and black by Fc−400Hz. Grey scales are represented by intermediate levels. On low frequencies, the shift is ± 150Hz rather than the ± 400Hz on HF. Other techniques of modulation found include amplitude modulation, where the amplitude of a carrier signal is varied with the image density information, where a large amplitude indicates a white part of the image and a low level signal represents a black part of the image.

Although frequency modulation is used, FAX images can be tuned in and decoded as SSB signals, tuning the signal to give a tone that shifts between 1500Hz for black and 2300Hz for white – conveniently the same as for SSTV images.

Technical parameters of FAX

A FAX transmission consists of two main parts; the preamble, which contains details of the format of the FAX signal to follow and synchronization information, and the image. This is diagrammatically shown in Figure 12.7. *The IOC tone* is a tone burst which gives the IOC (see below) of the FAX being received. This is 300Hz for an IOC of 576 and 675Hz for an IOC of 288. FAX reception equipment or software can often recognise these tones and automatically set the IOC required.

The phasing signal is the most important part of the preamble, as it provides a synchronizing signal for the receiving equipment to lock on to. This consists of a series of alternating white and black 'tones', the start of the white signals indicating the start of the scan line. Any receiving equipment must detect this, and time the

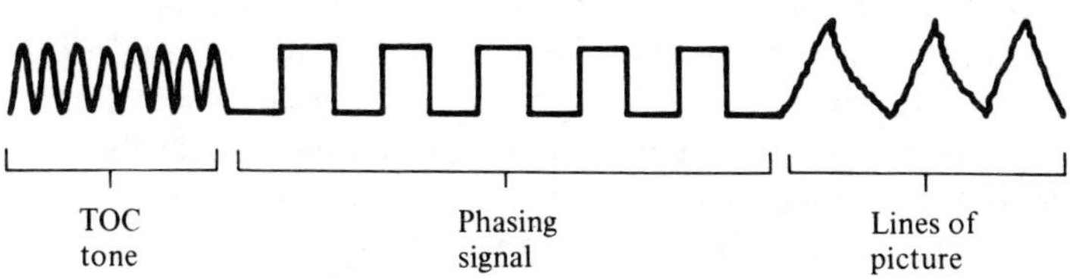

Figure 12.7

duration of each line, and then start a new line after each such line period has passed. More details of this are given below.

The actual image part of the FAX is defined by a variety of parameters. We have already seen how the signal is modulated with picture information. The other parameters are:

The index of cooperation, a quaint name for the aspect ratio of the image (the ratio of picture width to height) and is given by:

$$\text{IOC} = \text{transmitting drum diameter} \times \text{line density}$$

The standard IOCs in common use are 288 and 576, often based on a standard drum diameter of 152mm.

The line density is the number of scan lines per mm on the transmitted image. The usual values are 1.9 lines per mm or 3.8 lines per mm, and it is this parameter that gives the picture its 'vertical' resolution. The higher this value is, the more scan lines will appear in the image and so the more detailed the image will be.

The lines per minute parameter is the number of scan lines that are transmitted in a minute, and typical rates include 45, 60, 90, 120 or 240 lines per minute. Obviously, the higher this figure is, the faster an image of a given size can be transmitted. The most common scan speed is 120 lines per minute, corresponding to a single line transmission time of about 0.5 seconds.

The total transmission time of a FAX image thus depends upon the IOC, lines per minute and size of the picture. A FAX image is described in terms of the IOC and the lines per minute in the format:

$$\text{lpm/IOC}$$

and so 60/576 would indicate a FAX transmitted at 60 lines per minute with an IOC of 576.

Some FAX transmissions terminate with a *finish tone* of 450Hz to indicate that the image is now complete. More sophisticated software will look for this tone and stop processing a signal once it is received. A few moments' thought will indicate that this tone, and the IOC tone, are outside the tone range used to encode picture information when the signal is resolved on an SSB receiver.

Reception of FAX

If we ignore the traditional FAX machine, which is expensive and not widely available on the second-hand market, then we come to using the computer to decode FAX. It is beyond the scope of this book to give full details, but the following notes should prove useful. The basic equipment is similar to that used for SSTV; a fast ADC and a F/V converter. In addition, a crystal controlled clock is required to maintain the accurate timing needed for FAX reception.

An analogue FAX system will typically have a horizontal resolution in excess of 1000 pixels, each capable of being any shade of grey. This is clearly not feasible for most computer systems, and so the first thing to consider is the horizontal resolution you wish to achieve and whether you wish to show shades of grey or just black and white. In general, a simple black and white system will give the best horizontal resolution and will give reasonable results for experimenting and with weather maps. If we are dealing with a horizontal resolution of 320 pixels, then we can do some quick calculations to work out the number of samples we need to take on each line of the incoming image to plot 320 pixels.

If a line takes 0.5 seconds to send, and we want 320 samples, then we need to take a sample every 0.5/320 seconds – about one sample every 1.56ms. We already know the line period from checking the phasing signal as it is received, and this is where the crystal oscillator comes in useful; we time the line length in terms of this oscillator, rather than in terms of the computer's on-board clock, because the latter is likely to exhibit some drift. The crystal oscillator can be used to generate regular interrupts to the computer – say at a rate of one every 10 or 20μs – which can be used to decrement a counter to zero. If we load the counter with the line length as a multiple of the crystal oscillator period, then we have a simple clock which can be used to start a new line whenever the counter decrements to zero. In addition, by varying the value loaded into the counter we can account for any drift in the sending or receiving end of the FAX equipment.

It is fairly easy to get a point sampled every 1.5ms or so – indeed, most computers will support a horizontal resolution of 640 pixels, requiring a sampling rate of twice this – using machine code programming. The voltage read from the ADC will obviously represent the density of that point of the FAX image, and so can be used to plot a grey-scale point or, more likely, a black or white point, on the printer or screen of the computer.

One problem that might be encountered when displaying FAX images on a computer VDU screen is that the aspect ratio of the VDU screen is usually wrong for the FAX image. There are a couple of solutions here; the first is to display only half the image at once, storing the second half of the image in memory and allowing the software to flip between the two parts. The second is not to display all the received lines of the FAX, thus 'squashing' the FAX to fit on the screen. With a printer, we do not have this problem.

FAX off the air

The best source of FAX for the beginner is that transmitted by weather organisations for the benefit of seafarers and air travellers. This consists of weather maps, storm warnings, re-transmitted satellite pictures and so on, as described below. Apart from FAX decoding equipment, as outlined above, the main requirements for a receiving station are:

Good receiving aerial
This is almost essential for weaker stations, as it is vital that the signal at the input of the receiver is significantly stronger than any local interference from computer, printer or FAX decoder.

Stable receiver
Drift in a receiver will manifest itself by the picture going darker or paler in shade. The time taken to send a FAX image is in the region of 15 to 30 minutes, such that the immunity of the receiver to short and medium term drift is the more important; long term drift can be dealt with by retuning.

Sideband reception
A receiver capable of USB reception is required to resolve the audio tones making up the FAX picture. The receiver is then tuned so as to give an audio output of between 1500 and 2300 Hz when resolving FAX pictures.

Tuning resolution

If you are using a receiver with a frequency synthesizer, then the step size needs to be 10 Hz for the VLF transmissions due to the small shift, and no more than about 100 Hz for the HF transmissions. If your receiver, like mine, has an analogue fine tuning control, then this can be used to good effect to get spot on tuning.

When you are first setting up a FAX station, it is a good idea to concentrate on a strong station until you have got the knack of using your equipment. In the UK, a good station to start with is Bracknell, on 4782 kHz, although in some parts of the UK some problems caused by sky and groundwave signals arriving at your receiver out of phase may occur, causing distortion effects. This station transmits a variety of weather charts at 120 lines per minute with an IOC of 576. The station is not on continuously, but a carrier is usually to be found, and a perusal of the station's schedules will give all the data needed. Set up the receiver for USB reception, or whatever reception mode is recommended by the manufacturer of your FAX decoding equipment. This latter point is essential, for example, with the ICS FAX–1 decoder which does require LSB reception. Then listen for the 'tic tic tic' noise that is the synchronization signal. Each line of the image will then be heard, but there will be no sync pulses. However, it is likely that a 'rhythm' will be heard. Most FAX decoders will attain synchronization listening to the sync tones at the beginning of the transmission, but many will also allow you to 'force lock' and actually start printing an image half way through a picture. This may not, of course, be properly synchronized and so if possible wait for the system to synchronize itself to the start of a picture.

Weather FAX stations can also be found in the following frequency bands:

4200 to 4800 kHz
5100 to 5500 kHz
7500 to 8000 kHz
10 000 to 10 500 kHz
12 500 to 13 500 kHz

In general, many meteorological stations that send out RTTY information will also be found to transmit weather FAX images. A typical FAX, captured using an MFJ1278 terminal unit, Bearcat DX3000 receiver and an Epson printer is shown in Figure 12.8. On

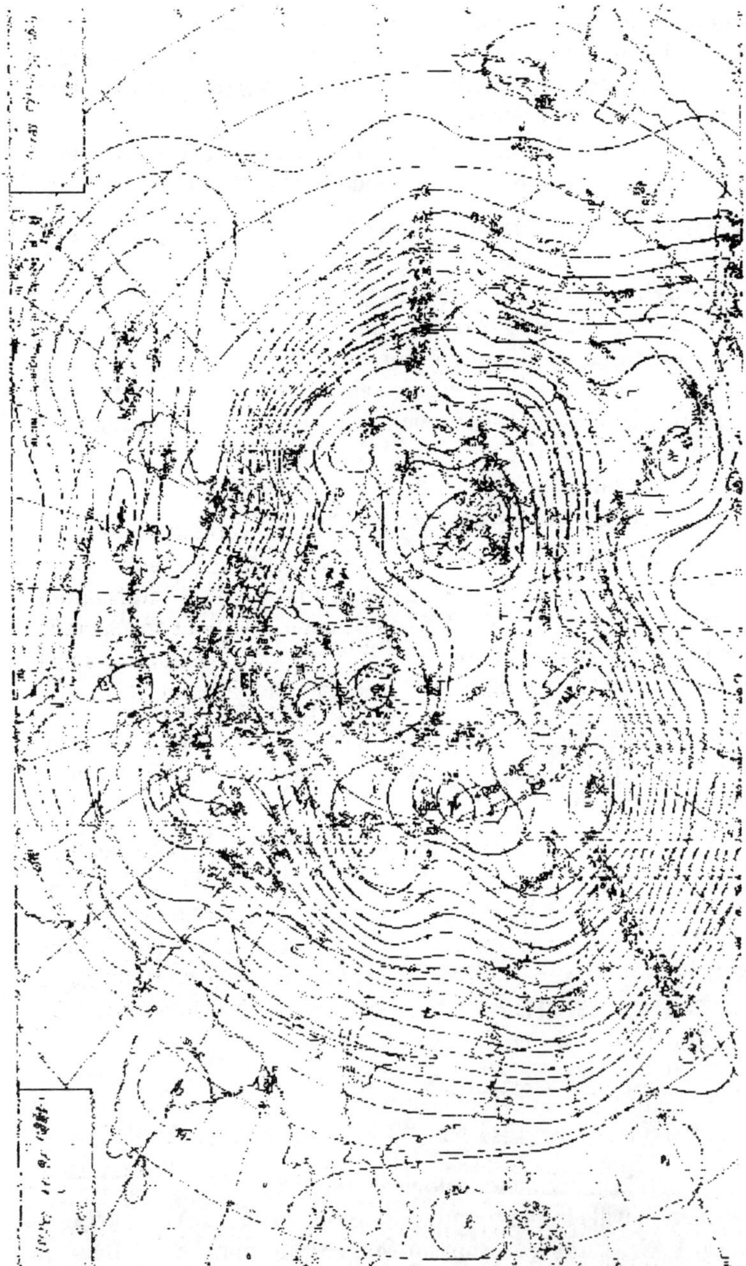

Figure 12.8

134kHz VLF, the German station at Offenbach can be resolved with a decent aerial system (or active aerial) and a suitable receiver. This station will often be found transmitting images first downloaded from satellites.

Amateur FAX is often to be found using the following frequencies:

3595 to 3605 kHz
7035 to 7045 kHz
14 100 to 14 110 kHz
14 240 to 14 250 kHz

using 120 lines per minute and an IOC of 288. Again, USB is usually used.

Weather FAX and the law

In the early part of 1989, the legislation on reception of weather station data was liberalised to remove the requirement for a specific licence in the UK. This means that weather information transmitted by RTTY and FAX can be copied without any specific permission being sought, but the information downloaded must *not* be used for commercial purposes, and is subject to the Copyright Act.

Other FAX signals

Other organisations transmit images by FAX, but, unlike weather FAX, the legislation covering these has not been changed and so UK listeners require permission from these organisations to copy FAX information transmitted. So, if you want live news pictures from the various news organisations, you will require permission from them as well as the appropriate dispensation from the DTI.

Computerised picture processing

If your decoder can store pictures to disc or tape, then you can clean up images using software. The general name for this is *digital signal processing*, and it can be applied to many types of signal. When dealing with graphics images, you might like to consider the following possibilities:

Noise removal
Spots of black or white on solid areas of tone on a FAX or SSTV picture can be removed by checking surrounding pixels and changing any single pixels to the colour of the background. Of course, there are circumstances when this cannot be done for fear of losing picture detail. However, you could write a routine that removes, say, single pixels whilst leaving clusters of three or more pixels as part of the image.

Edge enhancement
An edge, between two areas of different shade on an image, can often be 'hairy'. A similar technique to that of noise removal can be applied to sharpen up the edges in a picture. This is particularly useful if diagrams are being sent.

Printing images

Not surprisingly, a 'hard copy' of a FAX or SSTV image is often required. There are a variety of ways in which this can be obtained.

1 a print-out option may be contained within the software used to decode the image. This is frequently found on commercial software, and allows the picture to be dumped out to an Epson compatible dot-matrix printer. Some systems, like the MFJ 1278, that do not allow direct display of the image to a monitor without suitable terminal software, have a printer socket fitted to allow direct dumping of the picture to the printer as it is received.
2 an option in the program to store the image to disc for later processing by other software may be useful. For example, controlling software on the host computer may display the FAX or SSTV image on the screen and then offer the option to store the displayed image on disc as a file. The structure of the file will depend upon the software concerned, and may be a straightforward dump of the screen memory, as is the case in many pieces of software for the BBC Microcomputer, or may be in a specific file format suitable for reading by a particular piece of software. This image can then be printed outside of the FAX decoding software.
3 on most machines, an interrupt driven 'screen grabber' is usually available from software companies. This software can be

loaded into memory before you run the decoder software, and on pressing a particular key or combination of keys the displayed screen will be saved to file or printed. IBM PC clones will usually print the screen displayed when the ‘Print Screen’ function key is used. Note that the GRAPHICS.EXE program will need running to dump a graphics image to the printer properly on these machines. Alternatively, software such as FRIEZE (available with Microsoft Paintbrush) or CATCH (available with PAINT PLUS) allow some images to be captured for use in graphics packages.

THIRTEEN

Packet radio

When I first heard of packet radio I felt that this was probably getting a little close to home; after all, as a computer professional, did I really want to spend part of my hobby using an amateur radio mode that was rather similar to certain types of computer communication systems? Packet radio is a means of computer to computer communication via the amateur radio bands. There are, on the short waves at least, no commercial systems doing the same thing and the packet radio system was developed from a system called ALOHANET operated by the University of Hawaii in the 1970s. In this system, information was transferred between stations as bursts of data, called *packets*. The concept of the packet was not new; it had been used on several cable connected computer and telecommunications networks since the mid 1960s; what was new was doing it over radio links.

In a similar way to that in which Martinez developed AMTOR, Canadian amateurs took up the challenge and developed packet radio for amateur use in the late 1970s. A standard was developed by the Vancouver Amateur Digital Communications Group and was called the VADCG standard. Shortly afterwards, US amateurs adopted a standard called AX25 based upon the commercial computer communications system X25. In the mid 1980s British amateurs developed packet radio systems around the BBC Microcomputer using standards of their own design, but now more and more stations across the world are using the AX25 protocol as the basis of operations. In terms of take-up, packet radio has always been more popular in North America, and its use in Europe has only recently begun to increase. It is particularly common on VHF frequencies, though HF packet radio is quite popular.

Basic packet principles

Before looking at the details of packet radio, it will be useful to have a look at the basic elements of a packet radio system. In terms of equipment, the essentials are:

A suitable radio transceiver

Apart from covering the appropriate frequency bands of interest, any transceiver should be stable and have a quick transmit/receive switch-over. A slow switch-over will slow down the throughput of data by the system, but anything below 50 ms will be perfectly alright. This is similar to the requirement for AMTOR. In addition, the transceiver audio bandwidth should be wide enough to encompass the tone frequencies used for packet. A radio receiver can be used, of course, for monitoring packet transmissions. For VHF packet radio, virtually any rig capable of handling FM speech will work on packet, but on HF a radio is required that is stable to the degree of being able to resolve, say, 100 baud RTTY/ASCII as a rough guide. Serious packet radio work on HF requires good filtering at the IF stages of the receiver, and a filter of 400 – 600 Hz bandwidth in the IF stages of the receiver makes reception much easier.

A terminal node controller

The *terminal node controller*, or *TNC*, is at the very heart of packet radio operations. (Figure 13.1) It accepts data from a microcomputer and assembles it into a 'packet' for transmission. The TNC then sends the packet to the transceiver as a sequence of audio tones for transmission. The TNC also deals with receiving packets of data and disassembles these packets into a stream of text for the computer to display. In addition, the TNC deals with the error handling part of the packet protocol. To do all this, not surprisingly, the TNC is actually a small dedicated computer containing its own CPU and software as well as suitable filters and oscillators to resolve and produce the tones required for packet. Although the TNC is normally a self contained piece of equipment, software TNCs are occasionally used where, rather than a separate piece of equipment, a computer program running on a microcomputer can be employed to emulate a TNC.

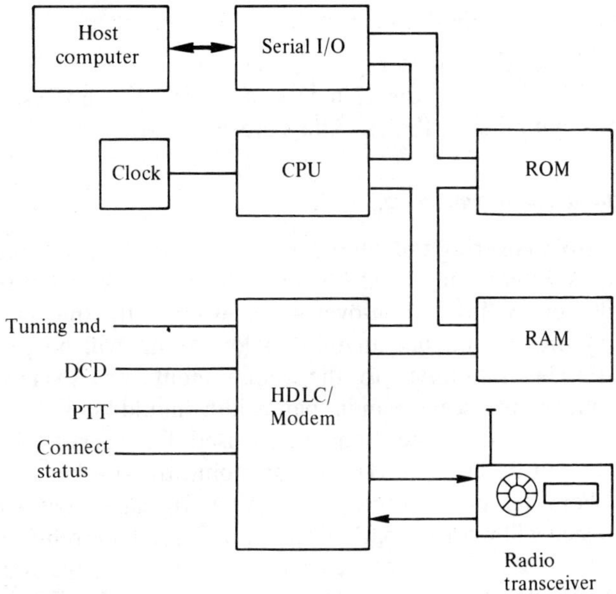

Start flag	Address	Control	PID	Data	FCS	End flag
1 byte	14–70 bytes	1 byte	1 byte	Up to 256 bytes	2 bytes	1 byte

Figure 13.1

I would recommend the purchase of a hardware TNC rather than the software approach, as many home computers may not have the power to run the software required, even if it were available. Many hardware TNCs also include facilities for decoding other modes, as described in Chapter 14. Clearly, the TNC should support the AX25 protocol, as it is likely that this will be the standard for some time to come. There are two versions at the moment; Version 1 and Version 2, and we shall look at the differences below. The most current version is AX25 L2 V2. The control of the TNC is effected by means of the computer sending commands to the TNC, and a standard for these commands has been established. It is called *TAPR* which stands for the *Tucson amateur packet radio* command standard. Some TNCs will deviate from this, however.

The hardware of the TNC has also become rather standard around the Z80 microprocessor chip. The TNC will also include ROM or EPROM software – if this is socketed, then upgrades of the programs from the manufacturers will be easier to install. This is particularly useful if the TNC doubles as a decoder for other data modes, as it means that in theory, at least, new modes can be added by simply modifying the TNC firmware. A TNC will also include an amount of random access memory to hold details of the set up of the TNC and to act as scratch pad memory for the TNC CPU during packet operations. This RAM, or a portion of it, is often battery backed, so that when power is removed from the TNC the set up details of the TNC, such as the baud rate at which it communicates with the computer, and so on are retained. The majority of the RAM, however, in many TNCs is used as a buffer, holding information for transmission or received data for viewing at the computer terminal.

The serial interface between the computer and the TNC is usually capable of running at any of the standard baud rates between 110 and 9600 baud, and is usually to the RS232/RS423 standard, although some TNCs also have a TTL compatible (5V for a '1', 0V for a '0') serial interface for communication for the computer.

The modem is responsible for converting the textual data from the user into audio tones that can be transmitted over the air in the form of a packet. As soon as a packet's worth of text has been entered by the user, data is directed to the *HDLC* – the *high level data link controller*. This device combines the text typed by the user with various control bytes into a packet. The HDLC then passes the resultant packet to the modem for transmission. The HDLC also sorts out incoming packets from the other station in the contact. The modem then modulates the radio signal according to a standard called *Bell 202* on VHF FM or *Bell 103* on the short wave bands. On VHF, data is transmitted at 1200 baud with a shift between mark and space frequencies of 1000Hz. On HF, the shift is only 200Hz and the data transmission rate is 300 baud. The modem also includes the necessary filters for decoding incoming tones into mark and space signals for the HDLC to work on. More details of the modulation methods used for amateur packet radio will be given below.

A TNC will also give the user some idea of what is happening via status lights. Most TNCs will support the following status indications:

Tuning indicator
This is an LED display that indicates to the operator when a signal is correctly tuned in.

DCD indicator
The DCD indicator – short for *data carrier detect* flashes on and off in sympathy with received packets.

PTT
This indicates when the TNC is actually transmitting data to the transceiver for transmission over the air to the other station in the link.

Connect status
The connect status indicator is lit when a connection has been established between two packet radio stations, and packets are being exchanged between the stations.

In many TNCs, the signals that drive these indicator lights are fairly easily accesible inside the TNC. This allows us to take certain signals, such as the DCD and connect status signal and allow them to signal in some other way that a connection has been made or a packet detected. For example, the connect status signal could be used to activate an audio oscillator momentarily when a connect is made; this would allow the user of the TNC to be busy doing other things yet still be aware of when a connect was established by another station.

One final feature about many TNCs is that the connections between the computer part of the TNC and the modem part are often made available on the circuit board so that a new modem board can be fitted if necessary. For example, higher baud rates would certainly require this, as would a change in the methods of modulation.

The microcomputer

The computer is used in two ways; with dedicated TNCs the computer simply controls the TNC via the RS232 serial interface or some other interface, and displays received packets. In addition, it is used by the operator to create text for transmission. If a software TNC is being employed then the computer must also emulate the TNC.

As to the actual operation of a packet radio link, the transmitting station sends a packet of data containing the callsign of the station with which contact is to be made. If the other station is in range and listening it will acknowledge receipt of the packet with one of its own. Packets can now be sent between the stations in a similar way to RTTY, with a packet being displayed when it is received. Should errors be detected, a repeat request can be generated to ask the station to send the packet again. The AX25 protocol specifies the structure of packets, ensures that both stations do not transmit packets at the same time and looks after error detection and correction. A packet radio link is a full duplex link – that is, transmission of packets can occur in both directions at once, the AX25 protocol ensuring that 'collisions' of packets do not occur. In addition, stations can act as repeaters for packets, the data being passed from station to station before it reaches its final destination.

The AX25 protocol

A packet radio system consists of at least two radio stations exchanging data packets. Described like that, it sounds rather simple, but for it all to work we need a set of rules. This set of rules is called a protocol, in this case, called AX25. To fully understand the way in which AX25 allows packet radio to work, we need to look at the slightly wider picture of computer to computer connections. A degree of standardization for communication between computer systems was developed in the late 1970s when the *Open Standards Interconnection Reference Model* was established, often known just as *OSI*. This is described in full in a document called CCITT X200.

The whole idea of the OSI model is that the process of data communication can be described in terms of seven layers of operations, ranging from the lowest layer, which deals with the actual nuts and bolts of moving a single data bit from point A to point B through to the top layer which actually deals with computer programs operating over the network. Each layer performs a particular part of the job of data communications, and communicates with the layer above and below it via a set of defined rules. In addition, two layers implemented on different systems must be able to communicate with each other if both systems are adhering to the OSI standard.

Layer 1 – The physical layer is responsible for transferring bits between one system and another. The specifications for Layer 1 include such things as baud rates, whether the link is duplex or simplex and the way in which data bits are encoded for transmission.

Layer 2 – The data link layer is responsible for accepting data from the higher layers and segmenting it into packets for transmission by Layer 1. This layer also includes error detection and correction systems and tells Layer 3 of errors. Layer 2 also deals with establishing the connection between two systems wishing to communicate data. The HDLC chip in a packet TNC deals with this part of the system.

Layer 3 – The network layer is responsible for passing error information from Layer 2 up to Layer 4, and also for sorting out the best way of routing data packets between the two stations in communication. This is necessary because it is possible that the stations may be in direct connection or they could be communicating through a series of 'packet switches' which act as relay stations. Data packets are given sequencing information so that individual packets making up a particular message between two systems can be directed via various routes to the desired destination. Not surprisingly, the packets may arrive at the destination out of the correct sequence.

Layer 4 – The transport layer arranges data packets in the correct order in case they arrive in the wrong order and is also involved in error detection and correction, establishment of connection and connection disconnection.

Layer 5 – The session layer oversees the activity of Layer 4, and initiates the establishment and disconnection of links.

Layer 6 – The presentation layer deals with managing the computer terminal for display.

Layer 7 – The application layer is the program being run over the communication link.

The AX25 protocol does not use all this structure; in fact, it simply uses the first three layers and part of the transport layer. However, the principles still apply, with each layer insulating a higher one from the low levels, giving a modular approach to the problem of data communications. Let us now look at the way in which the AX25 protocol implements the various layers of the OSI model; that way, we shall be able to see precisely how packet radio works.

The physical layer

We have already discussed the Bell standards used for data transfer. The modulation method used is called *non return to zero-space* usually abbreviated to NRZ-S. This is rather different to the other methods of modulation that we have seen, as here '0' simply causes a switch in output frequency and a '1' causes no change in output frequency. Thus we can no longer assign a particular frequency to a particular bit status. This is shown in Figure 13.2. Packet uses 8-bit words and the data link layer ensures that enough '1' to '0' and '0' to '1' transitions occur to allow both parts of the system to maintain synchronization. Where the data itself would not provide sufficient transitions, the hardware inserts an extra '0' after a run of five '1's to ensure a transition and the receiving software detects runs of five '1's and discards the trailing '0'; in the case of *flag bytes* (see below) this 'bit stuffing' does not take place.

The data link layer

The data link layer is where AX25 standardization first shows up. There are two versions of the AX25 standard, but both of them are based upon the HDLC standard defined in the X25 commercial data communications standard. The data link layer in amateur packet radio is an example of a *bit oriented protocol*, or *BOP*. This allows packet radio to send any type of digital information, as opposed to the text only modes of AMTOR and RTTY. Packet

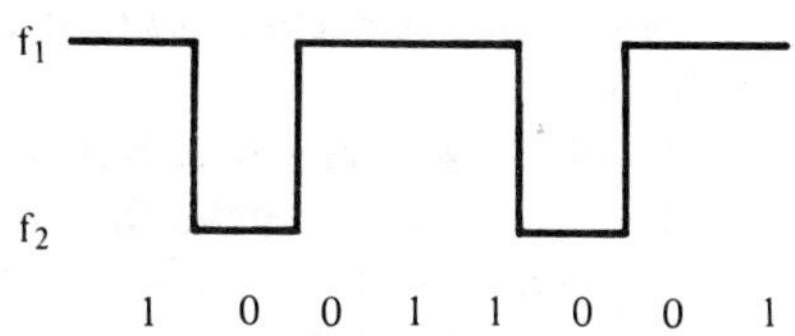

Figure 13.2

can thus send program files and graphics images as well as text. The HDLC deals with assembling and disassembling packets of data. In amateur packet radio there are two main classes of packet to consider. The first carries data between the stations, such as text, program files or graphics images. The second carries control information between the stations in the link. Figure 13.2 shows the construction of a typical data-bearing AX25 frame, or *information frame*.

The start flag has a unique bit pattern of 01111110. Note the run of '1's; the transmitting end does not bit stuff a start flag and so the sequence is protected; also, if the sequence were to occur anywhere else it would be stuffed, thus making the start byte sequence unique. This flag is responsible for setting the timing and synchronization for the rest of the sequence of bytes. The *end flag* has the same structure as the start flag and simply indicates the end of a frame.

The address field, not surprisingly, contains information about where the frame comes from and where it is going to. An address field will use a minimum of 14 bytes and a maximum of 70 bytes. This information is coded in the form of the callsigns of the stations concerned.

If the frame is an *unnumbered frame* (see below) as may be used when calling CQ, then only the sending stations callsign is included. Each callsign is encoded using a maximum of seven bytes. The first six bytes are used for the actual callsign, for example, G1UQW, and in the event of there being fewer than six characters in the callsign the remaining character spaces are filled with spaces (character 32). The seventh location is reserved for something called the *SSID* or *secondary station identifier*. The first and last bits of the SSID are reserved for special control functions, and four bits of this byte are used to actually store the SSID. This 4-bit number between 0 and 15 refers to the fact that a packet radio station may have up to 15 separate 'sessions' running at once, each session transferring packets of data. Each session may involve several different TNCs, or with sophisticated systems one TNC can support a couple of sessions. The SSID simply indicates which of these sessions, which will all have the same callsign, was responsible for sending the packet. In addition, if the SSID of a packet repeater station has its last bit set to '1' it indicates that this packet has already been sent by the repeater, thus preventing the packet being sent twice. The first group of seven bytes refers to the destination station, and the second group of seven bytes refers to the callsign of the ultimate destination of the data packet. The third group of seven characters holds the callsign of the first repeater, if any, the call is to be directed through, the fourth group the second repeater and so on. Clearly, if no repeaters are involved then these fields are left blank. A fuller discussion of *digipeating* is given below. The limitation of eight 7-byte groups for these digipeater callsigns limits the maximum number of repeaters that a packet can be passed through to eight, though for reasons discussed later this is not really a problem.

Control byte. This byte indicates the type of frame being sent. Packet radio uses a variety of different frame types to do particular tasks, such as initiating contacts, finishing contacts and so on. The actual order in which these frames are sent during a contact will be discussed below, but for now let us have a look at the different frame types, as indicated by the control field.

Information frames (I) carry information typed in by the user. The control code for an I frame is always going to be an even number; the data contained in the control byte is two 3-bit numbers, each bit containing the frame number and the number of the next frame expected from the other end of the link. Because there are only three bits per number, the sequence numbers are stored MOD 8. These frames can also acknowledge other I frames by sending one with an updated 'next frame number expected' number.

Unnumbered information frames (UI) are information carrying frames that are not error checked or acknowledged by the receiving station. They are thus used for 'one to many' transmissions. This frame type is an addition to the X25 protocol for amateur radio use, and allows the exchange of information without a connection with a specific station being made first.

Unnumbered acknowledge (UA) frames are sent as acknowledgement frames when a connect or disconnect frame is received. The connection is not made or broken by the sender until this acknowledgement is received.

Receive not ready (RNR) frames are sent by the receiver when it is no longer capable of receiving data frames from the sending end. This might be sent, for example, if the receiving station's TNC buffer was too full to accept any more frames. This is a supervisory frame.

Receive ready (RR) frames are sent to reverse the effect of the RNR frames and are used to indicate that the receiving station is able to receive data and also acknowledges receipt of an I frame. Again, it is a supervisory frame.

Reject (REJ) frames are used to request the retransmission of information frames that have been received out of sequence. Once the correct frames are received, the REJ frames are no longer sent. Another supervisory frame.

Set asynchronous balanced mode (SABM) is a long winded way of saying initiate a connection. This frame is transmitted when the sender wishes to initiate a contact. This is another unnumbered frame.

Disconnect (DISC) frames initiate a disconnection between two packet stations that are in contact. Again, DISC is an unnumbered frame.

Frame reject (FRMR) frames are sent in response to any frame received that does not make sense to the receiving station protocol.

Disconnected mode or DM frames are sent whenever a station receives a packet other than SABM when not connected to the sending station. A DM packet is also sent when the TNC is connected to another user, or when the link is terminated other than by a DISC frame.

Protocol identification data (PID) is a single byte which indicates whether any OSI Level 3 protocol is implemented on the system being used. It is the first byte of the data field.

The data field is where the actual message information is stored within the packet as 8-bit bytes, but is not necessarily present in all frames. Supervisory frames, for example, do not need any data and so do not have data fields.

The FCS field is the *frame check sequence* and is at the heart of the error checking procedures of packet radio. The HDLC calculates the FCS from the data in the frame between the start and end flags, and sends the 2-byte FCS with the packet. At the receiving end the HDLC recalculates the FCS and compares it with the received FCS. If there is a difference, the packet is deemed to be corrupt and a repeat is requested. This method of error checking is pretty good and the chances of a bad packet getting through are minimal.

The end flag is the same as the start flag and simply indicates the end of the packet.

The process of connection

Let us now examine the process that takes place when a packet radio connection is established on a totally clear frequency between two stations with no digipeating. This is a slightly simplified view of what happens, but more details will be added later. Say I wish to connect to G7ZZZ. I would start by typing in:

CONNECT G7ZZZ

The TNC will send an SABM packet containing my call and G7ZZZ in the address field and send the packet, provided that the channel is clear. (See below). If G7ZZZ is on the air and in range of my transmissions, a UA frame is returned to my TNC and a connection is thus established. If G7ZZZ were already in contact with another station, my TNC would receive a DM frame.

Now, I can type data in, and so can G7ZZZ, and the packets will be exchanged as information frames between the stations in a duplex fashion. Counts of received and transmitted frames are kept by both stations and this allows the correct sending of RR frames for correct reception of data and REJ frames for retries.

Once the QSO is completed, a disconnect signal can be issued by either station, a DISC frame transmitted and the two stations would then become free to initiate new connections.

CSMA

Of course, life is a little more complex than this. To start with, the chances are that there are likely to be other packet stations using the same frequency at the same time that you are. If we were to transmit a frame at the same time as another frame was 'in flight' on the frequency, then neither would be received due to mutual interference. This is called a packet *collision* and is clearly something to be avoided. We need to maximise use of the frequency whilst still ensuring that collisions do not take place. In technical terms, we wish to time-multiplex data on a particular frequency, and in packet radio a technique called CSMA is employed – *carrier sensed multiple access*.

A TNC will monitor a frequency when it is ready to send a packet, listening for an audio signal indicating that data packets are being sent on the channel. If the frequency is quiet then the TNC will wait for a short time set by a parameter called DWAIT, check again, then if clear transmit the packet. If it is busy then the TNC waits. Once the frame has been sent, the sending station will listen for a specified length of time (called FRACK) for an acknowledgement frame from the other station. If it does not receive such a frame, then clearly the frame transmitted has not been received properly by the other station and this is called a collision in packet terms. The system will now wait for a random period of time before re-transmitting the packet to minimise the chances of a second collision.

Nodes, digipeaters, gateways and other stories

Before going on to briefly examine some operating techniques for packet radio, we should look at some more terminology. In general, there are two ways in which packets can travel between stations; directly, or via a third packet radio station. In packet terms, a radio station is called a *node*.

A *digipeater* is a node that is capable of passing on packets from another station. Thus a digipeater can allow connects to take place between stations that are normally out of range of each other – a most useful feature! Any packet radio station can act as a digipeater, provided that you allow it to do so by using the appropriate commands. In the UK, certain stations on VHF have been licensed to act as dedicated digipeaters, which are unmanned stations which purely act as repeater stations. These are to be found on 144.650 MHz. These packet switch stations receive and transmit packets on the same frequency, and it is possible for stations to communicate via these repeaters to form a *local area network* of packet radio stations. In order to differentiate between nodes acting as digipeaters and digipeater stations, you will often hear (or should I say read?) amateurs referring to 'connecting via a node' when digipeating through a nondedicated digipeater.

The process of digipeating is fairly straightforward. Details for operating through a digipeater will be given below, but technically the following steps occur. If the TNC acting as a digipeater finds its callsign in a frame received it will transmit it on to the next digpeating station in the chain, or the final destination station, as if the packet had been originated at the station. The acknowledgement frames, however, are only sent from the ultimate destination station back down the digipeater chain to the originating station. The practical upshot of all this is that when a packet is lost when digipeating, it must be retransmitted from the start of the chain again. For this reason, the limit of eight stations for digipeating set by the protocol is very sensible, and so users should use digipeaters with great care!

A *gateway* is a facility offered by certain stations whereby two stations can connect to one another *even though both stations are transmitting on different frequencies*. The gateway station accepts input on one frequency and transmits the same packets out on another frequency, probably in another frequency band. For example, gateways exist with access to the HF bands from the VHF bands, or even to an amateur radio satellite! Gateways are usually part of mailbox stations (see below) and physically consist of two TNCs, each connected to a radio on the bands required.

Mailbox systems

A mailbox system is a means by which amateurs can leave messages for each other, post bulletins of useful information and access other facilities such as gateways.

To run a bulletin board, special software is required to control the TNC. The most popular software used is called the W0RLI system, after the radio amateur who wrote it. The person who controls the bulletin board (or *BBS*) is called the *SYSOP*, or system operator, and is responsible for the smooth running of the system. Various aspects of BBS running are dealt with by the UK Amateur Radio Licence, and certain types of message such as political or business messages are *not* allowed. In addition, if you wish to run the 'third party' BBS, where messages are left for amateurs other than the SYSOP, you require special permission.

The ultimate in bulletin boards is to put a suitable computer and TNC in an amateur radio satellite and thus allow the development of a 'store and forward' system, in which the data is sent up to the satellite and forwarded to an earth station when the satellite comes in to range of that station. Bulletin boards, digipeaters and gateways use the SSID to identify them; for example, I might run a bulletin board under the call G1UQW-2, and a digipeater as G1UQW-4.

The other layers of OSI

AX25 only specifies the lower layers of the 7-layer OSI model, and amateurs have been working hard on designing standards so that the higher levels of the protocols can be incorporated into packet radio as well. Networks of stations can be set up with software providing OSI Level 3 protocols which give much better results than the standard AX25 system alone.

A dedicated digipeater can be equipped with a computer program such as NET/ROM, which provides the normal functions expected from an AX25 digipeater but also provides more efficient means of transferring data.

The higher levels, such as the presentation layer, have also been considered and development of such things as protocols for transferring graphics images is being developed.

The KISS TNC

A recent development is the KISS protocol, which is supported by some TNCs, and might almost be seen as a backwards step until you think about it. All the KISS protocol does is the very low level operations of assembling and disassembling the packets of data and the transmission and reception of these packets. All the higher level activities can now be done by software on PCs. KISS TNCs can thus be used to handle the hard part of packet radio, the business of assembling and disassembling packets of data, while the higher levels of protocols can be tweaked to provide new or more efficient facilities.

An introduction to packet operating

There are slightly different approaches to take to operating packet radio on HF and VHF. To finish this chapter I shall explore the basics of using packet radio on these bands, and the sorts of things you will encounter as you get started in this mode.

As in all other types of amateur radio activity, the rule is *listen first*. My first packet QSO on VHF took place after quite a bit of listening, and even then I wished I had listened a bit more first! Monitoring QSOs is also easier on VHF because the requirements for packet on HF are more stringent and interference, etc., causes more problems.

Initial setting up

I deal with the interfacing between TNCs and computers in the next chapter, so here I shall assume that the TNC and computer are talking to one another.

Certain parameters will have to be set up for packet radio use. The TAPR command set is quite large, and there is no space here to cover the instructions completely so I shall just investigate the main commands to get you going. The standard TNC prompt when it is expecting a command is 'CMD:', and when this is displayed on the screen of your computer you are said to be in command mode. In most TNC systems, you can return to command mode at any time by typing a Control-C at the keyboard. It is important to remember that anything typed in when *not* in command mode is treated as data to be put in a frame and transmitted, so to ensure that a command typed in is treated as a command and executed, issue a CTRL-C to get back to command mode if you are at all unsure as to what status your TNC is in!

The first thing to do is to set up the callsign of the station using MYCALL. Obviously, if you are not transmitting you need not do this.

MYCALL G1UQW

The other parameters involved in the basics of establishing a packet QSO, such as FRACK, can usually be left at the default settings when you start. However, here are a few commands and what they do:

FRACK nnn nnn is a time, in seconds, for which the TNC will wait before repeating an unacknowledged packet of data. A setting of 4 or 5 is quite adequate on VHF, and the TNC will usually take care of increasing the time between retransmissions if digipeaters are specified in the packet.

PACLEN nnn is a number between 0 and 255 which refers to the number of characters in the information packet that can be entered before the frame of data is sent by the TNC. The default is 128 and this is fine for local VHF work but you might need to reduce it for DX work on VHF. On HF, PACLEN can be reduced to 40 or 50 characters.

RETRY nnn n is a number between 0 and 15 and specifies the number of times that the TNC will attempt to get packet through. A default of around 10 seems to be quite popular. Setting RETRY to 0 will prevent a disconnection, even if conditions are really poor. Again, on HF the setting should anticipate poorer links and so a value of 15 or 0 is a good idea.

TXDELAY nnn This command tells the TNC how long to wait after activating the transmitter before sending data. This is particularly useful if the switch over from receive to transmit is rather slow. The units vary from TNC to TNC, but typically nnn is in 40 ms steps.

MAXFRAME n where n is a number between 1 and 7 sets the number of packets that can be unacknowledged at any one time. If conditions are good 4 is a good default, but for poor link conditions on VHF or HF packet it is usual to set this to 1.

MONITOR ON The MONITOR command allows your TNC to decode any frame that it receives, whether or not it is addressed to your TNC. This allows you to see other packet activity that is present on the channel. Monitored traffic is displayed in the following manner:

G1ZZZ > G9ZZZ – 1: Hello Fred

where G1ZZZ is the source station and G9ZZZ the destination station. MONITOR OFF will disable this function so that the only packets displayed are those for your TNC.

RESPTIME nnn is a period of time that the TNC waits before sending an acknowledge packet. This is useful in cases where the transmit to receive switch-over of your QSO partner may be longer than you anticipate. Clearly, this needs to be as low as possible.

DIGIPEAT ON will allow your station to digipeat for other stations. This can be quite interesting when, during lulls in you own QSO, your station is used by someone else! For your first QSOs, it might be a good idea to set DIGIPEAT OFF to prevent any confusion. On HF, it is a very good idea to turn DIGIPEAT OFF as conditions on short wave are rarely good enough for digipeating to be effective.

Monitoring the channel

With the CMD: prompt displayed, you may simply wait for packets to be decoded and displayed by your TNC. This will give you some idea of the activity on your chosen channel and will indicate the stations around that you can call. In areas of reasonable activity, you will almost certainly see some *beacon frames* which are unnumbered information frames broadcast for all to read. A beacon frame can be sent automatically every few minutes by the TNC should you desire, but if the channel is fairly busy then sending lots of beacon frames is rather anti-social. A typical beacon frame might display as:

G1UQW > G1UQW *** JOE *** SHEFFIELD *** IO93FJ

If you wish to initiate a beacon of your own, the relevant commands will be in your TNC manual, but if you just want to send the packet equivalent of a CQ call, follow the steps below. The other consideration to make with automatic beacon transmissions is that there is no point sending them if you are not going to be around to actually receive any signals sent back to you!

A packet CQ call

Assuming you want to initiate activity, the steps are similar on both short wave and VHF, although fewer frames need be sent on busier channels as if you send a lot of frames you will just be causing interference!

Enter the command CONVERSE at the CMD: prompt, then hit the RETURN key a couple of times. On standard TAPR TNCs this will send a couple of packets out as unnumbered frames like:

G1UQW > CQ:
G1UQW > CQ:

which will be received by any active TNCs within range. Now wait for any acknowledgements from other stations who might try to connect to you. If there are no replies, try again. If someone does try to connect to you, you will be told of the Callsign of the calling station by the TNC and you will then be able to converse with the other station by typing in packets which will now be addressed to the station to which you are connected.

If you find a station to which you wish to connect, simply type in the command:

CONNECT G9ZZZ

at the CMD: prompt. If successful, the TNC will tell you of the fact and a connection is then established. If the other station is busy, or if it does not respond, the TNC will let you know.

Once you have finished a QSO, simply type in CTRL-C to return to command mode and enter the command:

DISCONNECT

to break the connection.

Using a digipeater is not much more difficult. When you are monitoring a channel, you may see a couple of callsigns in frames, rather than just one. For example,

G1UQW > G7ZZZ,G9ZZZ

would indicate that the packet is being transmitted from G1UQW to G9ZZZ using G7ZZZ as a repeater station. To establish this link, G1UQW would enter:

CONNECT G9ZZZ VIA G7ZZZ

at the CMD: prompt. If a connection is established, the QSO will proceed as above but the more repeaters there are in the chain, the longer the delay is likely to be. You can even connect to yourself through a nearby digipeater – a good way of testing out your system!

One of the requirements in the UK Amateur Radio Licence for those transmitting packet is that at intervals of no greater than 30 minutes an identification of the station, by either morse code or voice, has to be sent on the channel that you have been operating on. Not surprisingly, due to the fact that many TNCs either include a CW mode or can be persuaded to send CW by software in the host computer, the *CWID* is the preferred method by most amateurs. The CWID is usually sent as modulated CW on VHF FM – the PTT line is asserted and audio tones are sent over the air.

Frequencies and operating

On VHF, the principle UK packet frequencies are 144.650 and 145.675 MHz. On the short wave bands, the 'buuurp' noise of 300 baud packet will be found around the RTTY segments of the bands. The popular 20 metre band supports packet activity around 14 103 kHz, but other frequencies to consider are 3600 kHz, 10 147 kHz, 21 107 kHz or 7035 kHz. Packet operation on short wave is lower sideband, and if you are transmitting on HF be very careful not to clobber any other band users, such as the propagation beacons on 14 100 kHz. Tuning is rather critical on HF due to the small shift between mark and space frequencies. Most TNCs help matters here by having tuning indicators which tell you when you are actually tuned correctly to a packet signal.

When setting up the receiver, you need the fastest AGC (automatic gain control) setting that you can have; a slow AGC will make the receiver sluggish in responding to packets and so may cause problems in receiving data. If you cannot have a fast AGC, then either turn it off or disable the AGC by turning the RF gain down and the AF gain up. The same effect can be had by inserting an attenuator in the receiver input.

When a connect has been made on a busy channel, it is only good manners to move to a different frequency if at all possible.

Packet is a rapidly evolving amateur radio medium, and seems to polarize amateurs into two camps of lovers or haters of packet. In the Appendices, you will find some suggested further reading on the subject, as I have only been able to scratch the surface of packet here. Recent developments include the establishment, on microwave and UHF frequencies, of 9600 baud modems to communicate between different mailbox stations, to speed up the throughput of data to other mailboxes. Another recent development on the packet scene has been the regular operation on 2 m packet radio by Soviet Cosmonauts on the *Mir* space station. These signals are often audible and can be recorded on cassette tape for later playback. Happy packeting!

FOURTEEN

Commercial decoding equipment

In previous chapters I have examined the different amateur radio modes and in Chapter 8 examined the construction of simple terminal units for CW and RTTY decoding. Over the past few years several commercial units have become available which combine the terminal unit with a CPU and appropriate software to actually decode these modes and pass the textual information on to a home computer, or even display the information on a TV, printer or liquid crystal display screen.

A typical commercial data decoder will usually incorporate RTTY and CW decoding and probably a packet radio TNC. In addition, the more sophisticated units will include modes like AMTOR, ASCII and SSTV and FAX. Figure 14.1 shows a block diagram of a commercial data decoder. Let us look at the separate sections.

Switchable filters

The various data modes have different requirements in terms of optimum filter bandwidths, mark/space frequencies and so it is common for decoders to include a set of filters which are switched in either by manual switches or under software control.

Modem

The modem deals with converting received tones into mark/space signals for the software to decode and a modulator to convert '1's and '0's into tones for transmission by the radio transmitter. Again, different modes require slightly different things from the modem, and so the parameters of the modem circuit are similarly under switch or manual control.

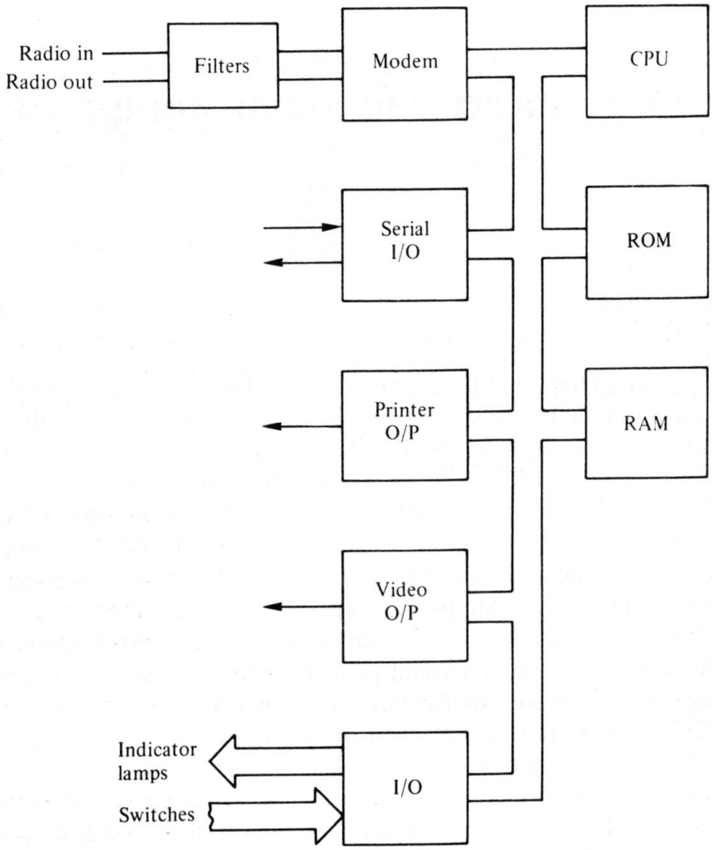

Figure 14.1

Serial interface

This interface, common to most decoders, allows the unit to be controlled by any computer with a serial interface. The usual standard employed is RS232 or RS432, but TTL level serial interfaces are occasionally found on data decoders. We shall look at this interface in greater detail below.

Printer interface

Some decoders incorporate a Centronics compatible printer output so that the decoder can dump output to a printer directly.

Video output

Some decoders incorporate manual switching of filters and reception modes, or even a keyboard, and so do not need a controlling computer. The output is directed to a video output compatible either with a standard TV receiver or with a composite video monitor, as used with some home computers.

LCD display

Some units, particularly smaller single mode decoders such as those dedicated to RTTY or CW decoding have a small LCD display, similar to that found on pocket calculators or digital watches, which displays the received text as it comes in off air.

CPU and decoding software

The decoder will incorporate a dedicated microcomputer which uses software in a ROM or EPROM (a form of ROM that can be erased) to decode the various modes that the decoder supports. The decoded text is then output to the controlling computer or any of the output devices listed above. The more expensive decoders allow the software to be upgraded when new modes become available. The software will also decode instructions from the RS232 input, and will deal with decoding in accordance with the selected mode, whether selected by switches or commands from the serial interface. In addition, it is responsible for switching the correct filters in to the circuit, and in the more sophisticated decoders will actually try to identify the mode being received!

Most decoders have a set of baud rates that they will receive for each mode – for example, 45, 50, 75 and 100 baud RTTY will be supported on most decoders, but not 65 or 80 baud RTTY if such signals existed. This is a feature of the way in which the decoding software is written, and the more sophisticated software will cope with all baud rates from, say, 50 to 150 in 1 baud steps.

Decoders also have the ability to implement features like unshift on space and invert sense. (See Chapter 10)

Calibration system

A decoder will often include a means of ensuring that the filters and the modem are set correctly for the tones and the tone separation that can be expected when the various modes are received over the air.

Radio ports

A radio port is simply the connection between the radio transceiver and the decoder. Typically, it is a 5-pin DIN plug which carries the received audio from the receiver, transmitted audio, ground and PTT control to turn the transmitter part of the radio on and off.

Status signals

The decoder will often include LEDs on its front panel to let you know what is happening. These include such things as tuning indicator LEDs to let you know roughly when a signal is tuned in, and mode-specific signals such as those on a TNC, indicators to let you know when AMTOR idle characters are being received, and so on. Some of these lights will have more than one function: the TNC DCD indicator is often used in other modes, for example, to show when an audio signal is present that has frequencies that fall within the pass band of the filter and modem.

The decoder will obviously require powering; this normally comes from a 9–12V mains adaptor which plugs into a suitable socket on the decoder. The current taken by a decoder is usually in the range of a few hundred milliamps and so this makes battery operation unacceptable in most cases, although a decoder could be run off of a car battery for mobile operations, providing care was taken to get a suitable stabilized supply from the car battery.

Interfacing the decoder and radio

The specific details of attaching a particular TNC to a radio will be given in the manual of the decoder. Here, I shall attempt to give some general pointers to solving problems. A typical decoder that incorporates transmission capabilities will usually accept the following connections from the radio:

Audio received line

This is the signal from the receiver. Most decoders do not care too much about the level of sound, and any value from a few hundred millivolts to several volts will usually give results. I have had good results from connecting the input of the decoder to the loudspeaker output of the receiver or the headphones socket. The main consideration to make is that the output from the receiver should not distort at all when feeding the decoder. In fact, it is a good idea to allow yourself to monitor the audio output to the decoder by connecting an extension speaker or amplifier across the input to the decoder. A further point to remember with regard to receiver audio output is that any tuning indicator on your decoder will require a fair signal from the receiver to work effectively, so do not turn the volume control of the receiver down too far! If you are using the decoder with a transmitter, it is also important to use screened cable for *all* the connections between receiver and decoder to reduce the possibility of RF feedback. Again, monitoring the receiver output to the decoder will tell you of the onset of this effect, as you will hear the feedback when you key the transmitter.

Transmitted audio line

This line carries the signal from the decoder transmit section to the transmitter. There are two possible inputs on the transmitter for this signal. The most commonly available is the microphone input line, and the other is an auxiliary audio input line which is meant for input such as packet or AMTOR transmissions. Whichever of these inputs you use, it is *crucial* that your decoder output does not overload the input to the transmitter. The effects of this may include the following:

Poor quality transmissions will result and this may be so bad that other stations cannot resolve your transmissions.

Excessive bandwidth may be the result of too much drive applied to the input. Apart from annoying nearby amateurs, this might also bring you to the attention of the licensing authorities.

Damage to the transmitter can result if the input which is used feeds some active circuitry which expects low level signals, as might be expected from a typical microphone. This could lead to overheating or even destruction of components.

The best way to prevent this is to monitor the quality of transmitted signals by using a receiver and feeding the transmitter output, at low power, into a dummy load. You should be able to hear any overloading as distortion of the signal. It is always possible to adjust the level of drive inside the transmitter, but I prefer to change the drive level at the decoder, as this does not affect the behaviour of the transmitter when used with a microphone. Many decoders will include a preset resistor in the transmitter section for adjusting the drive, or you can use a circuit such as that shown in Figure 14.2 to limit the drive. The level of drive is best selected by the following procedure.

1 set the transmitter to a very low power and connect its output to a dummy load.
2 your decoder will almost certainly have a means of sending a continuous tone to the transmitter for test and calibration purposes; if it does not, then set the decoder to transmit continuously in a mode that will give you lots of a single tone, such as RTTY.
3 tune the signal in on a receiver, and adjust the decoder output (or the circuit in Figure 14.2) until no further increase is heard in the received signal or until the signal just begins to sound harsh and 'fuzzy'. An oscilloscope can be used to examine the receiver output at this point if necessary. Now reduce the drive from the decoder until the output drops slightly or until the harshness disappears from the transmitted tone.
4 when listening to the tone, listen for hum or any sounds of instability; this could indicate feedback problems or mains breakthrough on the transmitter input.

The PTT line

This is used to signal the transmitter to switch on.

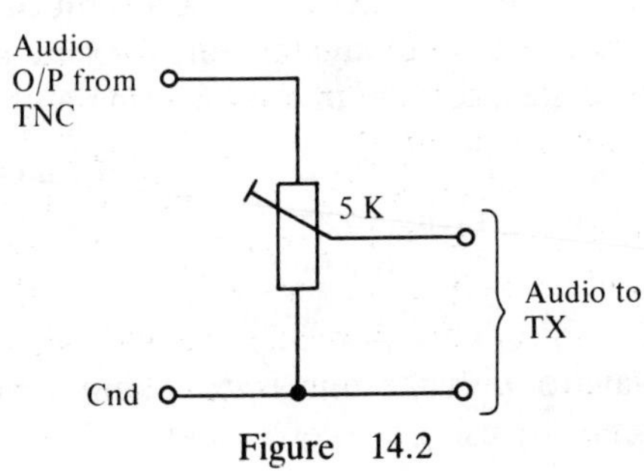

Figure 14.2

The ground line

This is the common earth line for all these signals, and can occasionally be a source of unexpected problems. If you use screened cable, the metal screen should be earthed. A bad joint here can often cause RFI problems if you are running a lot of power.

Whilst on the topic of RFI, do not forget that the decoder, being a digital device, can quite easily cause RFI by itself. For this reason, ensure that all fixing screws on the decoder case are fully tightened to ensure that the various parts of the decoder case, if metal, make good contact with each other. Some decoders, like the MFJ 1287 unit that I use, have the means of slightly adjusting the CPU clock oscillator so that you can move harmonic interference outside the frequencies of interest by adjusting a small trimmer capacitor.

Interfacing the decoder and computer

It is at this point that most people have problems. The typical decoder can be controlled by virtually any computer with a suitable interface. Here, I shall simply look at the RS232/RS432 serial interface, as this is the commonest communications medium. The RS232 standard deals with communications between two very tightly specified types of equipment; the DCE and the DTE.

A *DTE*, or *data terminal equipment*, is a computer and the *DCE*, *data communications equipment*, is a device such as a modem, TNC or data decoder. The interconnection specified by the RS232 standard is very sophisticated, but we can usually get by with a greatly simplified connection between the two pieces of equipment and still get perfect results. We should not really be too surprised by this; after all, the RS232 protocol was designed to allow easy DCE to DTE connection! Before we start, one important fact to remember is that *the direction of data transfer is always seen from the point of view of the DTE*. Thus, when we refer to a pin on a socket carrying transmitted data, this refers to data transmitted from the DTE; this means that the identical pin on the DCE will actually be *receiving* data from the DTE.

The exact details for your particular decoder will be found in the manual that comes with the equipment; here I shall give some general pointers.

RS232 pins

The standard RS232 connector found on most decoders is a 25-pin 'D' socket of which we shall use only a few of the available pins. Indeed, it is unlikely that all the pins in the socket are connected to the decoder circuitry, anyway. Some decoders have an alternative socket which gives TTL-level output signals to allow connection to computers which do not support RS232 but do have a user port that can be programmed to transmit and receive serial data. The usual connections offered by the decoder are:

Receive data the DTE receives data on pin 3 and the DCE receives data on pin 2 of a standard 25-way connector.

Transmit data the DTE transmits data on pin 2 and the DCE transmits data on pin 3 of a standard 25-way connector.

DCD this stands for data carrier detected and is set to '1' when the decoder detects an audio tone that might indicate data being received. This is pin 8 on the standard connector.

RTS stands for ready to send and is used in conjunction with CTS to establish a 'handshaking' between the decoder and computer. If used, the computer asserts RTS when it is ready to send some data, and then waits for the decoder to assert CTS before it starts sending data or commands to the decoder. This is pin 4 on the standard connector.

CTS is another handshake line, asserted by the decoder on receipt of RTS from the computer if the decoder is in a position to receive data. Pin 5.

Ground is quite simply the 0V line for both data and DC signals. There are two grounds in an RS232 connector, pin 1 and pin 7. Pin 1 is the chassis ground and pin 7 the data ground. Decoders often tie these pins together inside the case, but to make certain it is a good idea to connect pins 1 and 7 together inside your plug as well.

Specific decoders may offer more connections than this, but these are all you need to establish two way connection between decoder and computer. The exact connections we use depend upon two main points; first, what we are doing with the decoder – i.e. is there likely to be a lot of data transferred at once and secondly the speed of data transmission – the baud rate of the RS232 connection. Most computers and decoders can handle rates in the range 110 to 9600 baud.

The minimal RS232 link

The simplest connection simply needs wires between the following pins on the serial interfaces of computer and decoder:

Computer		Decoder
pin 2, transmit data	*to*	pin 2, receive data
pin 3, receive data	*to*	pin 3, transmit data
pin 7, ground	*to*	pin 7, ground

There is no hardware handshaking involved here; data is exchanged between the decoder and computer and for smooth operation relies on the data being processed before the transmit and receive buffers of the RS232 interfaces at the decoder and computer get full up! This is obviously a little hit and miss when high baud rates are in use, but for low baud rates and machines with large buffers it can be a quick method of getting things going! There are also ways of providing software handshaking, as described below.

RS232 with handshaking

Armed with the RTS and CTS lines, we can use the hardware handshaking abilities of the computer and the decoder to ensure that we do not lose data at any speed of transfer. In this cable, we need to connect the following pins together:

Computer		Decoder
pin 1,7	*to*	pin 1,7
pin 2	*to*	pin 2
pin 3	*to*	pin 3
pin 4	*to*	pin 4
pin 5	*to*	pin 5
pin 8	*to*	pin 8

There are some problems with hardware handshaking, mainly due to the fact that it is not a part of the RS232 standard; in the standard, handshaking was to be handled by software and the RTS/CTS had other applications. Not all decoder and computer combinations will allow hardware handshaking but most will.

Other parameters in the serial link

The baud rate and the data word structure must be identical on both decoder and computer for the system to work. In general, when setting up a link for the first time I tend to go for a low baud rate and set the word length of the computer serial interface to that required by the decoder. Again, this, and details of the parity, start and stop bits required, will be mentioned in the data decoder manual. Some decoders are smart enough to recognise the baud rate of the incoming serial data stream and so configure their own baud rate to match that of the computer. Once the software is set up on the computer (see below), you can turn on the decoder and try communicating with it by typing a few RETURNs on the computer keyboard. Something should come back from the decoder, and a 'log on' message will often be generated by the decoder once contact has been established between the decoder and computer.

At this point, problems will become apparent in two ways:

Nothing at all happens
This usually indicates that the cable has been incorrectly wired or there is some gross incompatibility between the serial output of the computer and that required by the decoder.

Garbage appears
This indicates that the cable is probably OK but that the parameters of the serial link are not the same at both ends. Check the baud rate, parity and start and stop bits.

It is possible that your computer may require additional information before it will start communicating with the decoder. For example, some computers will not allow data transmission to take place unless it has been told by the decoder that the decoder actually exists and is turned on! A signal may be generated on the decoder serial interface called *data set ready (DSR)* to indicate that this is so, but not all decoders have this signal. The easiest way around this problem is to connect pin 20 of your computer serial interface, a pin called *data terminal ready (DTR)*, directly to pin 6 of the computer interface, the DSR pin. DTR is always set to '1' when the computer is ready to communicate, so connecting DSR to this pin will always set DSR and DTR to the same value. Similarly, some computer terminals require that DCD be set to '1' at the computer end before data flow takes place. Again, we can connect this to pin 20 to make sure that this occurs.

If we use RTS and CTS, then in many cases we may need to permanently set DSR and DCD to '1' as just described. If no hardware handshaking is involved then the CTS and RTS pins can be ignored. If you do suspect problems due to RTS and CTS, it is worth asserting RTS at the decoder by connecting the pin to the '1' voltage that will be present on one of the pins of the RS232 interface. This is well worth trying if you cannot get any joy from a simple three connection cable, but check your manual first for details.

One rather esoteric problem that may occur is that the voltage levels used in either your decoder or your computer may not necessarily be totally compatible with the RS232 standard, which expects +12V for a logic '0' and −12V for a logic '1'. Actually, voltages between +5 and +25V will be treated as logic '0's and −5 to −25 as logic '1's, but if the voltage levels are close to the limits of the specification you may be a little unlucky. Another problem related to the electrical characteristics of the interface may arise if you try running the system over a long cable run between decoder and computer. By long, we are talking over 50 feet, which is unlikely in most amateur radio set ups.

Flow control

The correct way to establish handshaking between devices linked by the RS232 standard is to use a software protocol such as XON/XOFF. In this protocol, the decoder will send a particular code, usually CTRL-S, to the computer when it can no longer accept more input from the computer. For example, the buffer might be full and any more input from the computer would be lost. As soon as the buffer has space again, the decoder will send a CTRL-Q to the computer to indicate that the computer may start sending data again. The CTRL-S is called XOFF and the CTRL-Q is called XON. This protocol assumes that the computer and software controlling the decoder computers will accept and respond to these control codes.

Use of XON/XOFF flow control can occasionally cause problems; for example, you may find yourself monitoring a busy channel on a data mode but nothing appears on the screen; just hit

CTRL-Q on the keyboard a couple of times and you may find a large amount of data waiting for you. This will have been buffered by the decoder while the computer has been 'unavailable'.

Possible problems with decoders

Assuming that you have actually got the serial interface working and a suitable piece of software driving the decoder from the computer, you may still experience occasional problems.

Decoder prints garbage

The decoder may have somehow lost its set-up and is no longer using the same baud rate, etc., as the computer. This can happen if these parameters are set under computer control and the computer crashes, sending garbage to the decoder. The cure is to turn off the computer and decoder, leave them off for thirty or so seconds, then power them up again.

Decoder will not reset

If the decoder has battery backed RAM on board to hold the system defaults, such as baud rate, etc., then it is possible that this RAM may end up with some odd settings in it after a computer crash. Turning the decoder on and off will not clear this problem, and you will have to disconnect the internal battery backup for a minute or so to clear the RAM.

RFI

It is an unfortunate fact of life that you are as likely to get RFI from your decoder as you are from any other digital equipment, but the levels are likely to be lower. Steps to solve RFI problems have already been discussed, but a couple of extra steps are:

Adjust the clock
If you are interested in one particular frequency band, it is often possible to adjust the CPU clock of the decoder to move interference. *Only do this in accordance with the manufacturer's instructions.*

Decoder case
Most decoders have a metal case; ensure that all the screws are tightly fastened and that ground connections are made properly.

Cabling
RFI can easily sneak out of the decoder along cables. I put small value chokes and ferrite beads on the input cables from the radio set, and wrap the power lead from the decoder around a ferrite rod, quite close to the decoder. If a facility such as a printer connection is not used, do not connect a lead to it and leave that lead dangling. This can easily act as an aerial and broadcast RFI into your receiver.

Decoder control software

There is a vast amount of software around now to control decoders of various types. Commercial software for the BBC Microcomputer and IBM PC is quite common, which as well as handling the text modes also deals with accepting bytes from the decoder that represent FAX or SSTV images. In addition, the software will often allow preparation of data for transmission. The software is available on either ROM or EPROM chip or floppy disc, and details of suppliers are given in the Appendices. The Amstrad 6128 machines require the addition of a serial interface before they can be used to control a decoder, unless your decoder allows control via other means, when a user port might suffice. On the whole, any RS232 interface that allows the Amstrad to communicate with a modem will work with a decoder or TNC. Software is, however, a little more difficult to come by for these machines.

For the text modes, such as CW, RTTY, AMTOR or packet a wide variety of non-dedicated software can be used. The popular 'comms' programs that allow computer users to log in to computer systems via modems are quite adequate, and using an IBM PC I have had good results from such systems as Crosstalk or Datatalk. However, very simple BASIC programs can be used, and can be instructive to write. Writing your own driver software can also be very useful, as it allows you to do a variety of tasks such as automatically monitoring callsigns on a channel, QSO durations, etc., with suitable software. I shall give some hints for this in Chapter 15. However, for the moment, Listing 14.1 shows a simple BBC BASIC program for communicating with a data decoder which I have used with CW, RTTY, packet and AMTOR on my MFJ−1278. The program may need a little tweaking to work with other data decoders. The parameters for the baud rate commands can be found in the manual, but to save a lot of sweating over the parameter for the *FX156 command which sets the parity and word length of the BBC Micro's RS232 interface, I have included a list of values for the first parameter in the program listing.

```
10 REM Simple Terminal Program
20 REM BBC Microcomputer
30 :
40 REM Uses Default BBC Baud Rates - change them to whatever
50 REM your data decoder or TNC requires
60 :
70 *FX156,8,227
80 :
90 REM the 8 parameter sets the serial interface for 7 data
100 REM bits, even parity and 1 stop bit, as required by the
110 REM MFJ-1278 decoder that I use.  Other parameters are:
120 REM 0 - 7 bits, even, 2 stop
130 REM 4 - 7 bits, odd, 2 stop
140 REM 8 - 7 bits, even, 1 stop
150 REM 12 - 7 bits, odd, 1 stop
160 REM 16 - 8 bits, none, 2 stops
170 REM 20 - 8 bits, none, 1 stop
180 REM 24 - 8 bits, Even, 1 stop
190 REM 28 - 8 bits, odd, 1 stop
200 :
210 MODE 3
220 *FX2,2
225 G%=INKEY(1):IF G%=-1 THEN GOTO 300
230 *FX3,5
240 VDU G%
250 *FX3,0
260 GOTO 220
300 *FX2,1
310 *FX3,0
320 G%=INKEY(1) : IF G%<0 THEN GOTO 220
330 IF G%>31 OR G%=10 OR G%=13 THEN VDU G%
340 GOTO 220
```

Listing 14.1 Simple terminal program

On running the program with the correct parameters for the serial interface, you should see letters from your decoder appearing on the screen once the decoder has signed on. You will now be able to control the decoder through this program. If your decoder has a Centronics interface you will probably be able to print out FAX and SSTV pictures using even a simple text program like this. For the IBM PC machine, a similar program can be written in GW or Microsoft BASIC.

Advanced decoder facilities

We have already seen the basic facilities offered by decoders, and here I should just like to explore a couple of the more advanced features that the top-of-the-range models can offer. The first of these is the ability to analyse incoming data and actually tell you the characteristics of the signal in terms of baud rate, whether it is synchronous or asynchronous, whether the sense is inverted and so on. The second feature is based on this ability and is called *SIAM – signal identification and acquisition mode* in which the decoder recognises the mode in use and switches itself into a configuration to decode it when the signal is tuned in. This is most useful if you have never heard the modes, but practice on the amateur bands soon makes perfect. Although a nice feature, I have yet to be convinced that SIAM is worth paying the extra money for.

Once SIAM has identified a mode, there are two options, depending upon the decoder. The most advanced units will actually start decoding then and there, so that if SIAM decides that something is 108-baud RTTY – very unlikely on the amateur band – it will start decoding the text. The less sophisticated units will detect the baud rate as 108 but will only have the means to decode on certain set baud rates, say 100 and 110 if we are lucky. In this case, the SIAM system will switch in the nearest baud rate and probably print garbage.

Getting the most from your decoder

In previous chapters we have discussed the techniques used for tuning and decoding individual modes of transmission. Here, I should like to concentrate on a couple of points with respect to using data decoders.

Apart from mode setting switches, the only controls on most decoders are an on/off switch and a knob called the *threshold control* which simply determines the amount of input signal getting to the filters and demodulator part of the decoder modem. Turn the decoder on after turning on the computer.

In use, the threshold control should be set as follows. Tune in the desired signal with the threshold control set at about 50 per cent and the correct decoder mode selected. This should give the decoder's tuning indicator, if fitted, enough signal to achieve lock to give a true indication of how to tune. The DCD indicator on the decoder, if fitted, should start flashing in synchrony with the incoming signal, and text should start appearing on the screen. Now, back off the threshold control until the flashing just stops, then advance it slightly again. You may have to adjust the control occasionally to cope with bad fades, etc., but setting it in this way makes the decoder less sensitive to any noise on the channel.

Most decoder tuning indicators require you to centre a single LED on a string of LEDs or centre up a needle on a meter. Generally, tuning of synchronous signals like AMTOR or packet is more sensitive to errors in frequency setting than morse or RTTY, and the higher the baud rate and the narrower the shift the more critical the setting of the tuning. The tuning indicators require a certain strength to function correctly, and this is best determined by experiment. It is unlikely that you will get the tuning indicator 'bang on', because few modulated signals stay constant in frequency for any length of time and so the LED or needle will tend to dance around the centre point slightly. This is particularly so with low-baud-rate RTTY and CW.

Some users tape-record data signals off air and then feed the tape recorded signals into their decoders. This helps reduce the problems of RFI, but is not suitable for higher baud rates or synchronous modes like packet or AMTOR due to the inevitable wow and flutter on the tapes. I have had good results using this technique with a good cassette recorder with CW and RTTY up to about 75 baud.

FIFTEEN

Control of radio equipment by computer

One of the more interesting uses of the computer in the amateur radio shack is that of controlling the receiver and associated equipment. This can be something as simple as a timed recording of particular broadcasts, or as complex as automatically selecting the strongest signal out of a selection of frequencies carrying the same station and then retuning the receiver to that frequency. In this chapter I shall briefly examine some ideas in this area, and give some practical pointers.

Timed recording of broadcasts

One of the easiest things to set up on any computer is to use it to control a tape recorder, turning the recorder on and off at certain times. Many modern receivers have this capability built in, but if your set cannot do this, it is a useful facility to add. Apart from a tape recorder with a means of remotely stopping or starting the tape, a single output bit from the computer is required, unless your computer includes a tape control relay, like the BBC Micro or the Amstrad 6128 computer. Let us see what to do for these two computers first. A lead will be required, connecting the relay control pins of the computer tape interface socket to a jack plug suitable for your tape recorder. The pin-outs for these sockets are to be found in Figure 9.3, where we used the tape relay to control a morse oscillator. Figure 15.1 shows a simple relay driver for any output bit from a computer output port. As to software, the simplest program must:

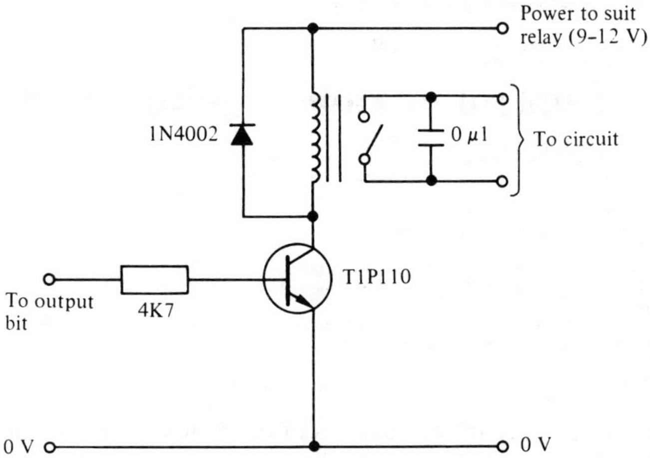

Figure 15.1

1 allow the current time and the times at which recording is to start and stop to be entered.
2 keep time to a reasonable accuracy; this is not always easy, especially if the computer concerned does not have a 'real time' clock and is reliant on purely software means to keep time.
3 close and open the cassette control relay at the appropriate time so as to activate the tape recorder.

Listing 15.1 shows a simple program for the BBC Microcomputer to do this. The program uses the TIME pseudo variable, which is incremented 100 times per second by the machine operating system. The value of this is converted into hours and minutes, and these values are compared with the hours and minutes figures entered by the user as the start and stop times for the recording. The *MOTOR 1 command is an operating system command to turn the cassette relay on, and *MOTOR 0 turns it off. Due to the fact that the TIME pseudo variable is only four bytes long, it cannot be used to keep time indefinitely, even if you were to leave the computer turned on all the time, and there is nothing built in to this program to take care of days, so really you are limited to entering start and stop times within the same day that do not run over into the following day. You might like to work out a way of overcoming this limitation.

```
10 REM Time switch program for BBC Microcomputer
10 :
20 INPUT "Current time (hh:mm) ",ct$
25 ch$=left$(ct$,2) : cm$=right$(ct$,2)
30 :
40 REM Now get a reference time from the TIME variable in seconds
50 :
60 reftime = INT(TIME/100)
70 :
80 ctimsecs = val(ch$)*60*60 + val(cm$)*60
90 :
100 input "On time (hh:mm)  ",ton$
110 input "Off time (hh:mm) ",toff$
120 :
125 ontsecs = val(left$(ton$,2))*60*60 + val(right$(ton$,2))*60
130 offtsecs = val(left$(toff$,2))*60*60 + val(right$(toff$,2))*60
140 :
150 REM now set ctimsecs to take reftime into account
160 REM and also other times as well
170 ctimsecs = ctimsecs + reftime
180 ontsecs = ontsecs + reftime
190 offtsecs = offtsecs + reftime
200 :
210 REM Now we loop around and check the time on and off
220 :
230 ctimsecs = ctimsecs + int(time/100)
240 if ctimsecs >= ontsecs and ctimsecs < offtsecs then gosub 1000
250 if ctimsecs >= offtsecs then gosub 2000
260 goto 230
270 :
280 REM The way in which timing is carried out here will mean that the
290 REM on off cycle is a one-shot event - the switch on will occur, then
300 REM the switch off. The following day, the system will not turn on
310 REM again, but you could modify the program to do that.
320 :
1000 REM Turn something on subroutine - in this case, the cassette relay
1010 :
1020 print "Turning on"
1030 *MOTOR 1
1040 :
1050 REM above call turns motor on
1060 RETURN
1070 :
2000 REM routine for turning something off
2010 :
2020 print "Turning off"
2030 *MOTOR 0
2040 :
2050 RETURN
```

Listing 15.1

For users of the Amstrad 6128, Listing 15.2 can be used. The TIME pseudo variable here is incremented 300 times per second, and rather than *MOTOR commands we have to make direct calls to the machine operating system; the CALL &BC6E instruction turns the cassette relay on, and CALL &BC71 turns the relay off.

```
10 REM Time switch program for Amstrad 6128 computer
10 :
20 INPUT "Current time (hh:mm) ",ct$
25 ch$=left$(ct$,2) : cm$=right$(ct$,2)
30 :
40 REM Now get a reference time from the TIME variable in seconds
50 :
60 reftime = INT(TIME/300)
70 :
80 ctimsecs = val(ch$)*60*60 + val(cm$)*60
90 :
100 input "On time (hh:mm)  ",ton$
110 input "Off time (hh:mm) ",toff$
120 :
125 ontsecs = val(left$(ton$,2))*60*60 + val(right$(ton$,2))*60
130 offtsecs = val(left$(toff$,2))*60*60 + val(right$(toff$,2))*60
140 :
150 REM now set ctimsecs to take reftime into account
160 REM and also other times as well
170 ctimsecs = ctimsecs + reftime
180 ontsecs = ontsecs + reftime
190 offtsecs = offtsecs + reftime
200 :
210 REM Now we loop around and check the time on and off
220 :
230 ctimsecs = ctimsecs + int(time/300)
240 if ctimsecs >= ontsecs and ctimsecs < offtsecs then gosub 1000
250 if ctimsecs >= offtsecs then gosub 2000
260 goto 230
270 :
280 REM The way in which timing is carried out here will mean that the
290 REM on off cycle is a one-shot event - the switch on will occur, then
300 REM the switch off. The following day, the system will not turn on
310 REM again, but you could modify the program to do that.
320 :
1000 REM Turn something on subroutine - in this case, the cassette relay
1010 :
1020 print "Turning on"
1030 CALL #BC6E
1040 :
1050 REM above call turns motor on
1060 RETURN
1070 :
2000 REM routine for turning something off
2010 :
2020 print "Turning off"
2030 CALL #BC71
2040 :
2050 RETURN
```

Listing 15.2

Listing 15.3 shows the equivalent program for the IBM PC, using GW BASIC. The subroutines at line 9000 onwards for actual motor control are specific to whatever user port, etc., you use to control the tape recorder, so I shall not detail them here; sufficient information has been given in Chapter 8 to write these routines.

```
10 REM Time switch for IBM PC machines
20 :
30 PRINT "Current Time is: ";TIME$
35 INPUT "Is this correct (Y/N) ",A$
40 IF A$="N" OR A$="n" THEN PRINT "Returning to DOS for you to set
time":SYSTEM
50 :
60 REM TIME$ picks time up from DOS time and date function
70 :
80 INPUT "Please enter ON time as hh:mm ",TON$
90 INPUT "Please enter OFF time as hh:mm ",TOFF$
100 :
110 REM now we have the turn on and off times in these two strings; now
120 REM just loop around until it's time to do something!
130 :
140 OMIN$=RIGHT$(TON$,2) : OHR$=LEFT$(TON$,2)
150 :
160 REM omin$ and ohr$ now hold the minutes and hours for the on time
170 REM now put of time equivalents in ofmin$ and ofhr$
180 :
190 OFMIN$=RIGHT$(TOFF$,2) : OFHR$=LEFT$(TOFF$,2)
200 :
210 IF OHR$=LEFT$(TIME$,2) THEN GOSUB 1000
220 IF OFHR$=LEFT$(TIME$,2) THEN GOSUB 2000
230 GOTO 210
240 :
1000 REM routine to check on time minutes and turn something on
1010 REM precise details of turning on must be left to the user as
1020 REM the code used will be dependant upon the interface used.
1030 :
1040 IF OMIN$<>MID$(TIME$,4,2) THEN RETURN
1050 :
1060 REM replace next line with code to turn ON your interface
1070 PRINT "Turning on at ";TIME$
1080 RETURN
1090 :
2000 REM routine to check off time minutes and turn something off
2010 REM precise details will depend upon the users interface
2020 :
2030 IF OFMIN$<>MID$(TIME$,4,2) THEN RETURN
2040 :
2050 REM replace next line with something more useful!
2060 PRINT "Turning off at ";TIME$
2070 RETURN
```

Listing 15.3

Other enhancements you might like to add are the ability to store several times in arrays and so have a whole sequence of recordings on one tape. This is a good way to compress a lot of regular monitoring – for example, for propagation monitoring – into a short space of time. If you are *really* smart, then with the Amstrad and BBC Microcomputers you could prefix each section of recorded audio on the tape with an electronic 'label' consisting of the frequency and time of day in the form of an ASCII file. For example, the following segment of code would do this for the BBC Microcomputer.

```
1000  *FX138,0,13
1010  Y%=OPENOUT('FILE1')
1020  PRINT #Y%, '4872 kHz, Bracknell Meteo'
1030  ti=hour$+':'+ min$
1040  PRINT £Y%,ti$
1050  CLOSE £Y%
```

Line 1000 inserts a RETURN key press into the keyboard buffer of the BBC Microcomputer, because line 1010 requires the RETURN key to be pressed before recording starts. After the file has been written, the CLOSE #Y% line will turn off the cassette motor, so you will need a *MOTOR 1 command to start things off again. The hour$ and min$ strings are assumed to have been set up elsewhere in the program. On a practical level, using this idea requires that the tape output from the computer and receiver be 'mixed' in some way before going to the tape recorder. Figure 15.2 shows one way of doing this. Another point is that the receiver output should, if possible, be muted when the file is being written to tape, as otherwise the file may not be readable. However, I have found that a low level receiver signal does not cause too many problems even if it is present at the same time as the computer. Alternatively, you could use a stereo recorder with the receiver sound on one track and the computer audio on the other track.

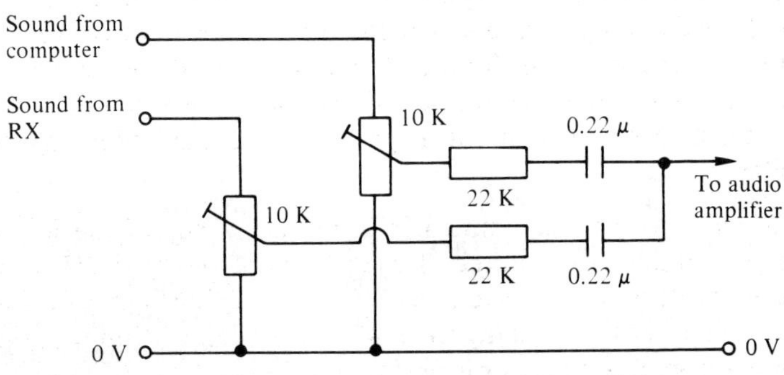

Figure 15.2

Control of receiver tuning

One of the interesting possibilities offered by modern synthesized receivers is the ability to control the tuning of receivers by computer. This subject is vast, and can get quite involved, so here I should simply like to look briefly at a few ideas of controlling both synthesized and non-synthesized receivers from the computer. First of all, let us briefly examine the two main methods of achieving receiver tuning. *Analogue tuning* is where the selection of the frequency of operation of a receiver is based around the property of resonance possessed by combinations of coils and capacitors, as mentioned in Chapters 1 and 3. Variation of tuning in these receivers is carried out by altering the capacitance or inductance in these tuned circuits, usually the capacitance, and this usually involves a variable capacitor whose capacitance is varied by rotating a control shaft. In turn, this varies the frequency of operation of the circuit continuously as the shaft is rotated. Modern electronics has come up with the varicap diode, a component whose capacitance varies with applied voltage, and this is used in some receivers to provide a tuning capacitance rather than a variable capacitor. Some receivers have a form of analogue tuning where set frequencies are available for selecting as required. These often use crystals to set the tuned frequency, but may offer only, say, 10 preset frequencies. *Synthesized tuning* involves no variable capacitors, but uses microprocessor technology to create a tuning system where tuning proceed in 'steps' – possibly as low as a few Hz – rather than continuously. A simple synthesizer is shown in Figure 15.3, and in use would supply the local oscillator signal in a superheterodyne receiver or converter. In such a receiver, the 'front end' tuning before the mixer would be fixed, and care is taken to avoid overloading before the mixer.

The main components of a synthesized tuning system are as follows:

The reference oscillator operates at the frequency of the lowest 'step' in frequency required. This is often 100 Hz or 1 kHz, and many synthesized receivers have a fine tuning control using variable capacitance tuning to allow finer tuning, if required. The output from this oscillator is fed into one input of a circuit called a *phase comparator*. The other input to this circuit comes from a frequency divider circuit, fed in turn by a *voltage controlled oscillator (VCO)* capable of operating at the frequency needed for the local oscillator. Part of the VCO output is taken for use as the local oscillator drive, as shown. The programmable *frequency divider* is all-important. The user enters the frequency of interest

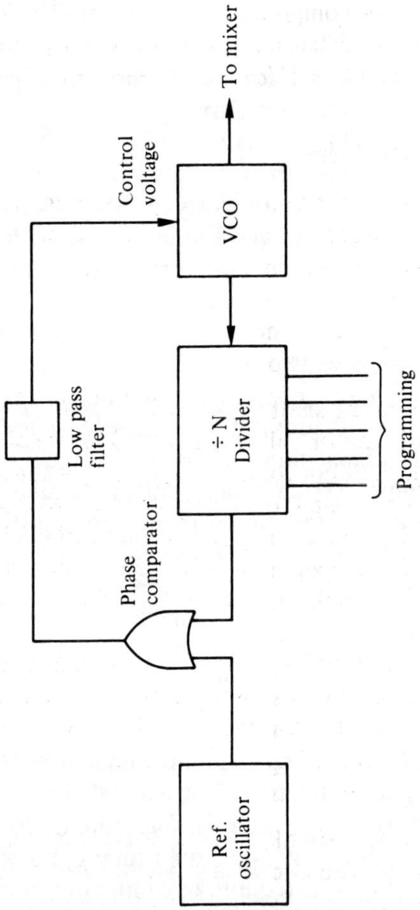

To mixer
Control voltage
VCO
÷ N Divider
Programming inputs
Low pass filter
Phase comparator
Ref. oscillator

Figure 15.3

on the keyboard, which sets the divider, via the *microprocessor control circuit*, to divide the VCO frequency by an amount that will give a signal at the reference frequency. The phase comparator then generates an error signal dependant upon how far apart the divided VCO signal and the reference frequencies are, and this error signal is filtered and used to correct the VCO until the two input frequencies to the comparator are the same. The VCO signal now going to the local oscillator is said to be locked, and the whole system is called a *phase locked loop synthesizer* (PLL Synthesizer).

Non-synthesized receivers

Computer control of non-synthesized equipment is quite difficult to achieve with any degree of accuracy and long term reliability. However, it is quite interesting from an experimental point of view, so here we go.

Tuning a receiver under computer control using a conventional variable capacitor requires two things:

1 a means of rotating the shaft of the tuning capacitor accurately. A type of electric motor called a *stepper motor* could be used here. This motor does not rotate continuously when a voltage is applied, but rotates in steps of, say, as little as 1 or 2 degrees at a time when a voltage pulse is applied. The direction of rotation is also controllable. Stepper motors are quite powerful and are capable of driving a tuning capacitor via a slow motion drive to make tuning even smoother.
2 a means of the computer knowing where the tuning control is, in terms of its rotation. If we use stepper motors, then provided we know where the tuning control started off we can work out where it is now by recording the pulses sent to the motor, and the direction of the motor travel.

Figure 15.4 shows a simple system for controlling a tuning capacitor in this way. The circuit uses a dedicated stepper motor driver chip, because this is the simplest way to control these things! The SAA1027 chip needs an input voltage of greater than 7.5V with a 12V supply to act as a logic '1' and a voltage of less than 4.5V to act as a logic '0'. To achieve this, a level shift is required on both the C and M inputs to allow us to drive the circuit from 5V logic levels. The C input can rest at a logic '1' and when pulsed

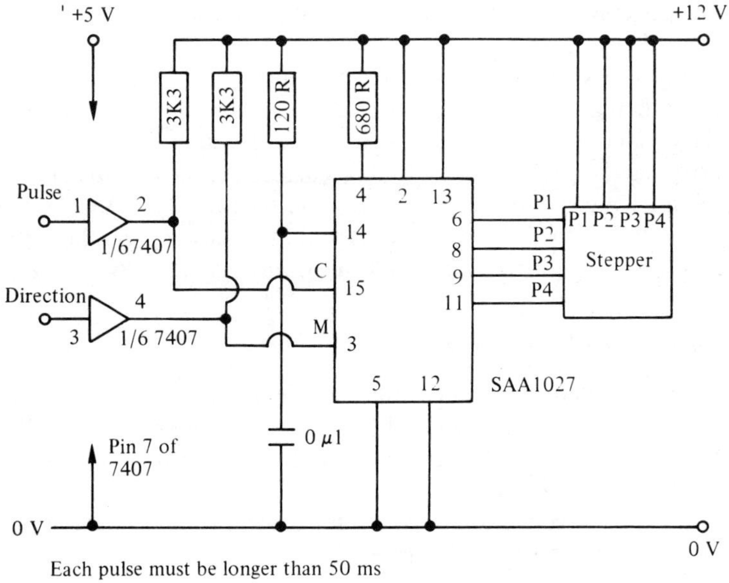

Figure 15.4

with five low to high transitions, followed by a return to the logic high resting state, will be enough to rotate the stepper motor one 'step'. The direction that the motor travels in is set by the state of pin 3 of the chip – the mode pin. When high, the motor steps anticlockwise and when low the motor steps clockwise (as seen from the shaft of the motor).

The program can be quite simple to write, and the basic algorithm is shown below. LOOKUP is a table of frequencies and the corresponding absolute rotation of the stepper in terms of degrees from the 'start point' of the variable capacitor, which is taken as 0. No slow motion drive is allowed for, so any frequency selected will be selected by a rotation of between 0° and 180° from this start point. In this example, I have assumed that the circuit tunes from 5 to 7 MHz, and that the start position is with the plates of the variable capacitor fully meshed – i.e. tuning 5 MHz. Anticlockwise rotation of the tuning control will increase the tuned frequency, and clockwise rotation will reduce the frequency. The problem with this approach is that you need to set up the table with frequencies to start with. Because there is a non-linear relationship between rotation and tuned frequency, and the motor can step at set step sizes only, it is almost impossible to interpolate to frequencies between those in the LOOKUP table. StepSize is the angle through which a single step of the motor turns.

```
START:        CurrentPosition = 0
              CurrentFrequency = 5000
              LowFrequency = 5000
              HighFrequency = 7000
GETFREQ:      Get DesiredFrequency from user
              if DesiredFrequency< LowFrequency GOTO GETFREQ
              if DesiredFrequency > HighFrequency GOTO
GETFREQ
              Search for DesiredFrequency in LOOKUP
              if DesiredFrequency not found GOTO GETFREQ
              store absolute rotation to NewPosition
              if NewPosition = CurrentPosition GOTO GETFREQ
              if NewPosition > CurrentPosition
                  Set Stepper Direction to Anticlockwise
                  Repeat
                      Pulse Motor 5 times
                      CurrentPosition = CurrentPosition +
                    StepSize
                  until CurrentPosition > = NewPosition
              else
                  set stepper direction to clockwise
                  repeat
                      pulse motor 5 times
                      CurrentPosition = CurrentPosition–
                  StepSize
                  until CurrentPosition < = NewPosition
              endif
              GOTO GETFREQ
```

As an aside, the same sort of technique can be used, with more powerful motors, to rotate aerials. I have used a similar arrangement to rotate an indoor mounted VHF beam aerial.

If the tuning is carried out using switched tuned circuits or crystals, relays can be used to switch in the appropriate tuned circuit when needed, and the circuit shown in Figure 15.1 can be used to switch the relay. Alternatively, diodes can be used to switch tuning when crystals are used, as shown in Figure 15.5.

With varicap diode tuning, a digital to analogue converter can be used to vary the tuning by varying the voltage across the diode. This has the effect of varying the capacitance of the diode, thus altering the frequency to which the tuned circuit is tuned. A practical example of an oscillator controlled in this way is found later in this chapter, when we examine a simple converter whose tuning is controlled like this.

Synthesized tuning

I shall now describe some simple techniques to allow computer control of simple commercially available receivers that use frequency synthesis; it is beyond the scope of this book to detail individual frequency synthesis chips.

Most commercial frequency synthesizers use a single chip at the heart of their circuitry, incorporating all the circuitry shown in Figure 15.3. The divide inputs are either taken out as inputs to the divider part of the chip, with one pin on the package for each

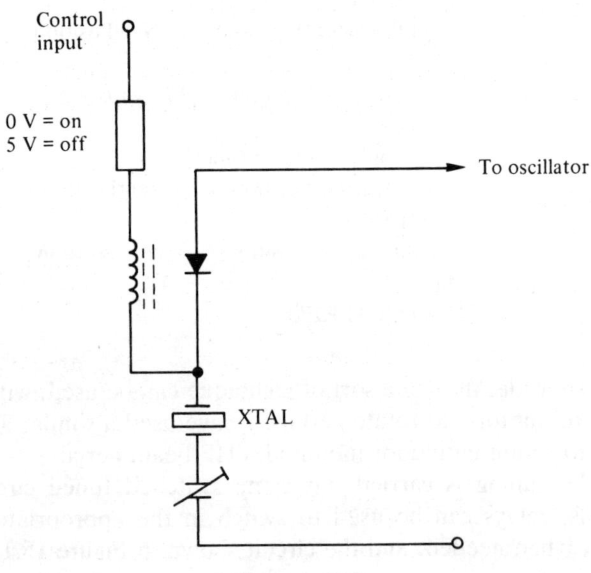

Figure 15.5

divide input needed, or are interfaced to the outside world via a serial interface on the chip which allows the division factor data to be fed to the chip serially down a single pin. This can make life more complicated for designers, but certainly makes the chip smaller!

The fact is, most commercial synthesized receivers have a microprocessor built in to control the frequency synthesizer, display the tuned frequency, provide memory and scanning facilities and so on, and this makes it very difficult to directly access the synthesizer chip. Anyway, why bother? Many of these receivers have a computer interface built in or available as an add-on extra, and those that do not can be made to talk to a computer without directly using the synthesizer, as I shall demonstrate later in this chapter.

The microprocessor handling the synthesizer in a receiver has the following jobs to perform:

1 accept inputs of frequency from a keyboard, and convert this frequency into a divider factor to be placed in the divider stages of the frequency synthesizer system of the receiver.
2 on some receivers, allow input from a 'tuning knob' to increment or decrement the received frequency by the step size of the synthesizer as the knob is rotated, by incrementing or decrementing the value placed in the divide stages of the synthesizer.
3 allow for 'scanning' of frequencies, where the user presses a key and the receiver jumps from frequency to frequency by predefined step sizes, often anything between 1 and 1000 kHz, which are selected by the user. Scanning can be up or down in frequency, and stops either when the user presses another key or when the receiver detects a signal, or when the user stops pressing the scan key.
4 provide memory for storage of frequencies, reception modes, etc., of interest to the user, which can be recalled later and used to provide input to the synthesizer.
5 provide a digital read-out of frequency and, in some cases, read-out of time and allow for timed recordings of received signals.

Control of mode selection

Control of the receiver mode selected is usually quite simple when compared to the complexities of controlling the tuning of receivers. This is because selection of mode is often by pressing a single switch, and this is easily simulated using relays or solid state switches like the CMOS 4066 analogue gates, described below. Of course, there can be some problems; I have a receiver that has just SSB mode, in which selection of USB or LSB is made by adjusting a small tuning control attached to the receiver's beat frequency oscillator. How far to go with computerising the operation of receivers that are not really designed to be computer controlled is up to you, but this particular problem was one I left alone!

Practical examples

Control of a converter

Let us see how we might put together a non-synthesized, computer-controlled converter using techniques mentioned above. We simply use a voltage controlled oscillator, where the tuning is controlled by a variable capacitance diode and a digital to analogue converter. Figure 15.6 shows such an oscillator, capable of tuning a range of frequencies, and how it can be connected to a mixer to produce an output signal capable of being received in the medium wave broadcast band at a position determined by the setting of the output tuned circuit, VCo and Lo. The system was designed to scan a band of frequencies and the output of the broadcast band receiver was monitored on a computer to give an analysis of band use throughout the day. In use, a voltage from the DAC will cause the oscillator to generate a signal which is mixed with the RF signals coming from the aerial. The difference signal is then fed to the broadcast receiver via Lo, which is positioned as close to the aerial in the receiver as possible. The receiver is tuned to a quiet frequency – preferably around the 1600 kHz end of the band – and then VCo is adjusted for maximum noise or signal from the receiver. Varying the tuning voltage by feeding different bytes to the DAC will change the frequency tuned and will allow stations to be received within the range of the coil, L1, the number of turns of which will set the tuning range of the converter. The tuning diode used has a capacitance that varies between about 550 pF at 0.5 V from the DAC to about 250 pF at 2.5 V, and in the prototype, with a 3 μH coil, this gave an oscillator coverage of 3.9 to 5.8 MHz, giving a converter coverage of 2.3 to 4.2 MHz, assuming a feed to the receiver of 1.6 MHz. This was covered in

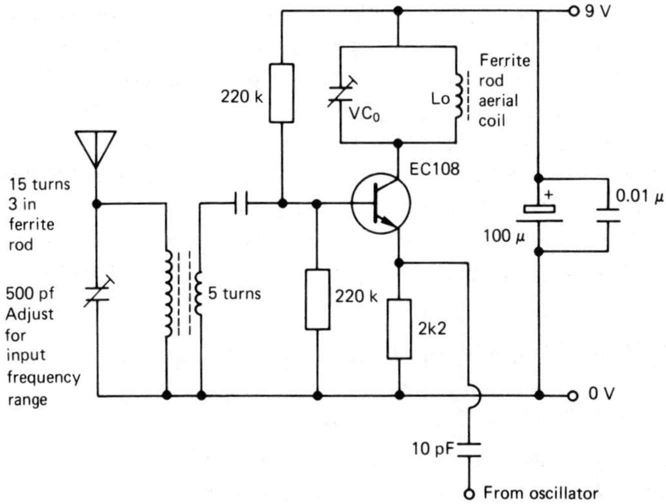

(a)

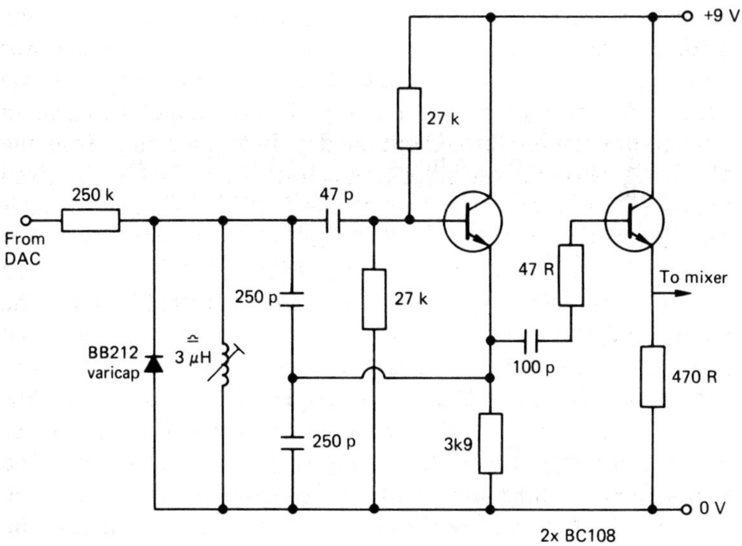

(b) Oscillator

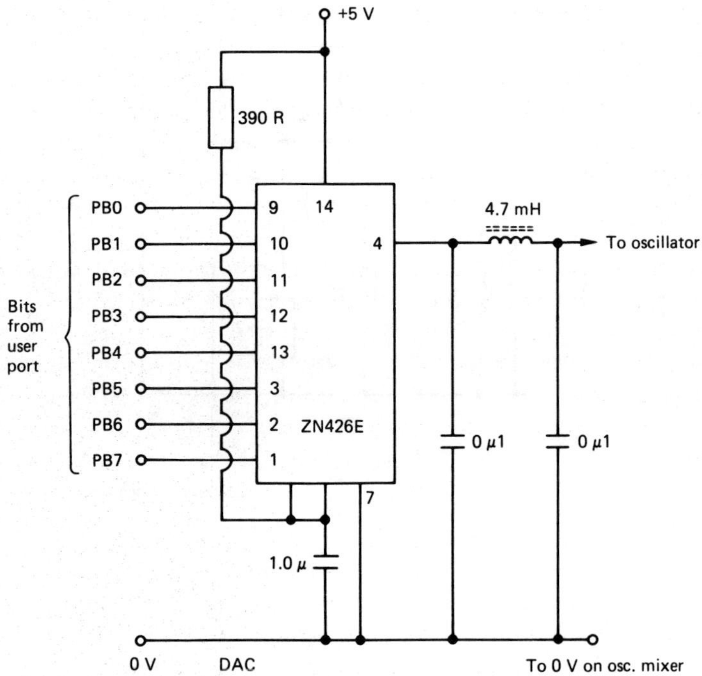

(c)

Figure 15.6

roughly 200 steps by the DAC, which was fine for my purposes, as I was not interested in actually listening to stations, just monitoring the presence or absence of signals throughout the band at different parts of the day. For accurately tuning in signals, you would need a means of finely adjusting the tuning – possibly by adding a small value tuning capacitor across the varicap diode, or even using another DAC and a varicap diode with a smaller change of capacitance with applied voltage. A suggested application for this circuit is given below.

Control of a synthesized receiver

Controlling a synthesized receiver is in many cases much easier, because most synthesized receivers have a keyboard through which frequencies can be entered. This keyboard can usually be placed under computer control, thus offering the possibility of remote control of the receiver to a high degree of speed and accuracy. One point to note is that *any changes to the insides of a commercial receiver will invalidate the guarantee and probably lower the future resale value* – you have been warned. In addition, you need to be sure of your abilities with a soldering iron, so if in doubt get help! I have done this work on my Bearcat DX1000 receiver, but I *do not* guarantee that it will work on other receivers and you must take great care whilst carrying out these changes.

The simplest way to hijack control of a receiver is to use CMOS switch ICs connected across the contacts of the normal keyboard switches, and then control these electronic switches from the computer user port. This involves no alterations to the normal working of the set, as the keyboard will still function after the changes have been made. In addition, the alterations are such that you can add extra switch functions as and when required if you do not want to do the whole thing at once. Let us start with a few tips for working on these receivers:

1 if at all possible, unplug the receiver keyboard from the main circuit board of the receiver, remembering which wires went where. This may not be possible in all cases but certainly makes life easier; however, in some cases the keyboard is soldered in or is an integral part of the main receiver circuit board.
2 when soldering, use a low power iron and take care not to splash solder all over the place. If you are working on a keyboard still connected to the receiver, unplug the soldering iron from the mains before making connections to reduce the risk of damage to the receiver from static electricity.
3 in all cases work with the receiver turned *off* and unplug it from the mains.
4 before touching any part of the receiver, touch an earthed object, such as a metal water pipe, metal draining board, etc., to discharge any static electricity that you may have accumulated. Do this frequently during your work.
4 keep all leads between the CMOS switches and the keyboard connections on the receiver as short as possible.
5 *do not* connect any leads carrying power to *any* of the switch connections on the receiver keyboard.
6 ensure that there is no risk of any of your work short-circuiting against other parts of the receiver.

In general, the keyboard will be on a printed circuit board, and you should be able to see the soldered joints for each switch as a pair of soldered connections. Inspection of the 'switch' side of the board should allow you to pair up soldered connections to switch functions – take care with this part of the proceedings, as it is important to get it right. If you *can* remove the keyboard from the receiver, then an ohmmeter can be used to determine which connections are made when a particular key is pressed on the keyboard. Once you have identified the connections corresponding to the switches that you wish to control from the computer, the circuit shown in Figure 15.7 can be built and connected up. After checking for shorts, etc., the receiver is powered up and testing is then carried out by applying a logic '1' signal to the switch control input; the receiver should then react as if the keyboard switch concerned had just been pressed. The process can then be repeated for other functions, testing each time. Note that the circuit board carrying the CMOS switches should be as near to the main keyboard as possible, and that any wiring should be kept clear of electrically noisy parts of the receiver, such as frequency readouts, etc.

If you have got only a few switches controlled in this way, then a single bit from the user port of your computer can be used to switch the CMOS switches off and on – note that the control signal needs to be held on for as long as you wish the CMOS switch to be turned on – but if you have got several switches then some form of encoder might be useful. Figure 15.8 shows a possible circuit, allowing control of several switches by a relatively small number of control lines from the computer.

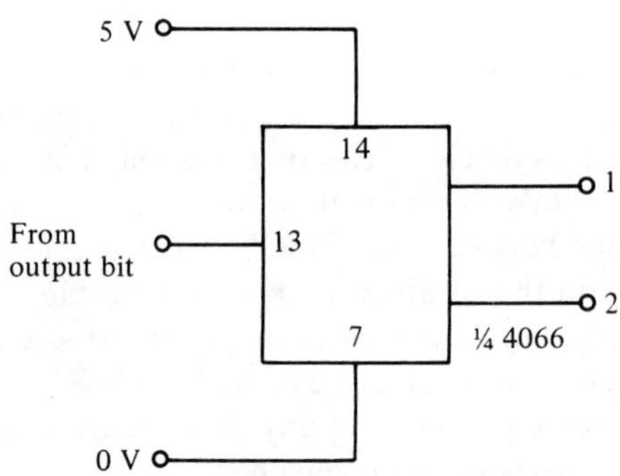

Figure 15.7

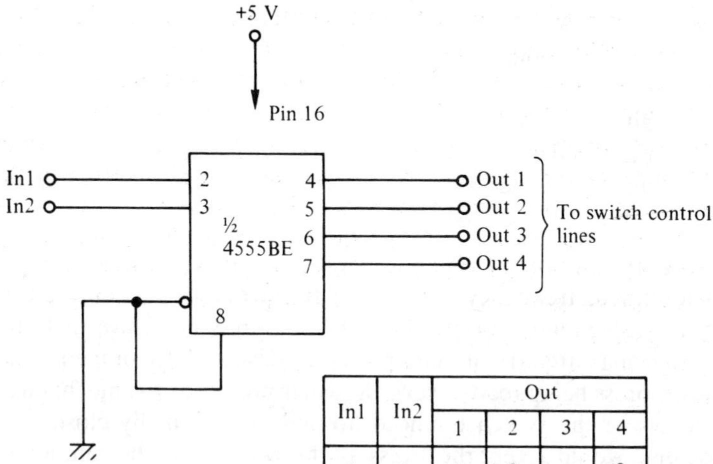

In1	In2	Out			
		1	2	3	4
0	0	1	0	0	0
0	1	0	1	0	0
1	0	0	0	1	0
1	1	0	0	0	1

Figure 15.8

To actually control the receiver, the I/O lines of the computer are turned on and off in the sequence needed to control the receiver manually. For example, to enter the frequency 12 000 kHz on my Bearcat, I execute the following sequence:

Turn '1' ON
Wait 0.1 second
Turn '1' OFF
Wait 0.1 second
Turn '2' ON
Wait 0.1 second
Turn '2' OFF
Wait 0.1 second
Turn '0' ON
Wait 0.1 second
Turn '0' OFF
Wait 0.1 second
Turn '0' ON
Wait 0.1 second

Turn '0' OFF
Wait 0.1 second
Turn '0' ON
Wait 0.1 second
Turn '0' OFF
Wait 0.1 second
Turn 'E' ON

The 'E' key is the ENTER key on that receiver, and is pressed to terminate frequency entry. The frequency is thus entered in about one second; I inserted the delays purely to ensure that any debouncing circuitry in the receiver, designed to prevent one switch-press being read as several switch-presses as the mechanical contacts of the switch bounced around before finally closing or opening, would accept the 'press' of the switch from the computer. You may need to experiment with this sort of parameter on other receivers. The first two switches I wired up in this way on my Bearcat were the up and down scanning switches – I was thus able to do the bandscanning work described below using the Bearcat rather than the converter described above. Of course, not all functions of the receiver can be controlled by this simple approach, but it does allow us to create a receiver whose tuning is computer controlled. On some receivers, though, computer control of virtually everything is possible by a built in computer interface.

Commercial control systems

Some of the more advanced amateur radio equipment and receivers have computer control interfaces built in as standard or as an easily fitted extra. In this section, I should like briefly to examine these systems. On the whole, they use the RS232 protocol and so will allow control by any computer fitted with a suitable interface. The Yaesu CAT (Computer Aided Transceiver) is a typical example of this sort of interface, and uses the RS232 protocol at 4800 baud, one start bit, eight data bits and two stop bits with no parity. The only point to watch is that a standard RS232 level signal cannot be plugged straight in to the back of a Yaesu receiver using this system, as the interface at the Yaesu end is designed to take a signal from an opto-isolator, rather than directly from a serial interface. The CAT system is supported by the FRG-8800 and FRG-9600 receivers, and allows control of parameters like IF bandwidth as well as tuning and mode – truly full computer control!

Icom use a similar computer control system in some of their equipment, for example, the IC-R7000 VHF/UHF scanning receiver which has a serial communications port built into it. Again, though, the voltage levels accepted by this system are not directly compatible with standard RS232 voltages, and so a further unit, called a level-shifter, is required to convert the voltage levels from RS232 to those required by the Icom interface.

Once a suitable interface has been arranged, commands are sent to the receiver as ASCII text. Details of these commands are to be found in the manufacturer's guides to the equipment. Because of the simple nature of the data sent, simple 'dumb terminal' programs, like we use with data decoders, can be used to send commands to the receiver. Alternatively, specific programs can be written to perform certain types of operation, as outlined below.

Some ideas for applications

In this section I should like to try to give you some ideas for the uses to which a computer controlled receiver can be put.

Scanning receiver

The receiver can be programmed to examine a range of frequencies, and monitor the signal strength on each channel. The latter facility may be available on the receiver as standard, or you may adopt the techniques mentioned in Chapter 8. The receiver can then stop scanning on a channel having a signal strength greater than a preset level. Alternatively, the computer could store the frequency and signal strength into memory, thus providing you with a *band usage monitor*, indicating the level of use of different parts of the radio spectrum at different parts of the day.

Frequency diversity reception

Many broadcasting stations transmit the same signal on a variety of frequencies to avoid interference. Why not program the computer with a list of these frequencies and have the computer switch frequency if the signal strength on a particular channel gets below a certain level?

Beacon monitoring

If you are interested in propagation, you can record signal strength levels from beacons into computer memory, along with the time of reception. The beacon frequencies can be stored in memory and then polled at specified times, thus providing you with a record of beacon activity over a whole day compressed into a fairly small amount of computer memory. The stored data can then be logged in a database or graphed using spreadsheet software, etc. Similarly, you might like to consider the idea of the computer triggering an alarm of some sort if the signal strength of a beacon exceeds a certain level, thus indicating the possibility of improved listening conditions on the band.

Programming a data decoder

Data decoders of the type discussed in Chapter 14 can be controlled via a serial interface, as we have already seen. In Chapter 14 we examined a couple of simple terminal programs to allow us to control data decoders. An interesting extension to this is actually to store and process the incoming text or bytes in a variety of ways. The simplest thing to do, of course, is to store the incoming text to a tape or disc file or just print it, but with a little imagination you can do other things as well. Just to start you off, here are a couple of ideas.

Packet radio channel usage

You could program the micro to record the time when packet data is being received from the TNC. This could then be used to work out the percentage of the time that a packet channel is actually carrying data. Most TNCs allow the full contents of a packet to be transmitted to the host microcomputer, not just the data part, and if this is the case you could extend the idea by recording the time at which stations are received, thus allowing automatic logging of stations!

Text recognition

Again, on a commonly used channel for CW or RTTY you could program the computer to recognise the text sequence CQ . . . and record the next couple of hundred characters. This will allow you to record CQ calls on the channel. Similar things could be done by looking out for the letters 'DE' which often precede a callsign.

There are, of course, hundreds of other applications that you can try out, limited only to your imagination. So, go and experiment!

SIXTEEN

Computer assisted circuit development

To finish off, in this chapter I should like to examine briefly the uses to which we can put the computer when developing electronic circuits. In Chapter 3 we have already examined the way in which the computer can be used as a pocket calculator to help solve some of the more knotty mathematical problems. Here, I shall describe how the computer can replace certain pieces of electronic test equipment and be used when we finally come to build and test circuits.

Computer requirements

Any computer to be used like this *must* have a user port for interfacing other pieces of equipment, and preferably should have an analogue to digital converter built in. This makes the BBC Microcomputer very suitable for this type of work, but other computers can be used and ADCs and user ports built as 'add ons'. In this chapter I shall base all listings around the BBC Microcomputer, but make suggestions as to other machines where appropriate. If you do not have an ADC available, the one shown in chapter 9 will be suitable for all the functions in this chapter; indeed, as it is quite fast it is better than the built-in BBC ADC for some applications!

Use of computer as a voltmeter

The easiest piece of test gear to simulate with a micro is probably the voltmeter. All that we need to do is apply a voltage to the input of the ADC (taking *great care* to ensure that the voltage is within the safe input range of the ADC) and read the digital value back from the ADC output. There are a few things to look out for:

1 take care not to exceed any of the ratings of the ADC, as this could lead to destruction of the ADC or, in extreme cases, destruction of part of the computer. Extension of the voltage range of the ADC can be done with potential dividers or operational amplifier circuits. Do not forget to take the input impedance of the ADC into account when using potential dividers. (Figure 16.1).

2 for accurate work you will need to calibrate the ADC, so that you can have a look-up table relating values from the ADC to actual voltages read in. Most ADCs are linear, so that if you know the ADC value read in for a particular applied voltage, you can interpolate for other voltages in the range of the ADC. There are two ways of calibrating an ADC. The first, the direct

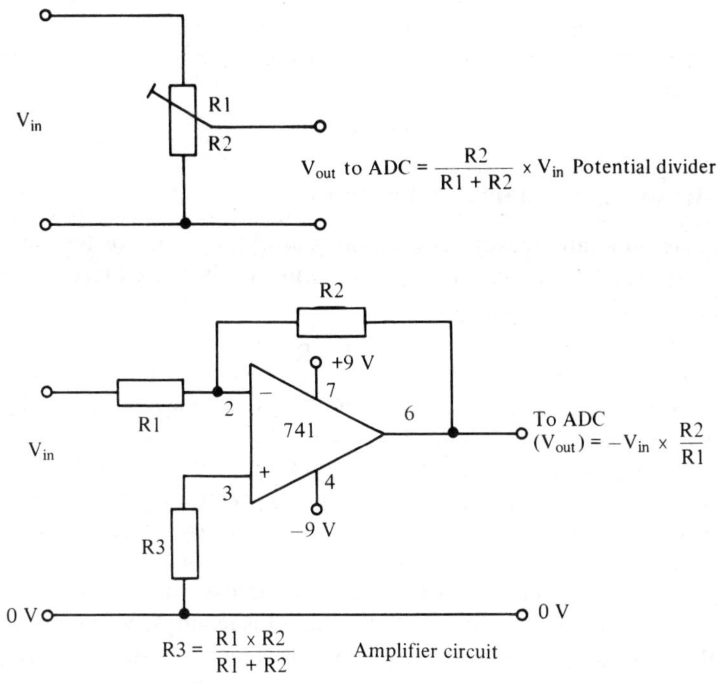

Figure 16.1

method, is to use a calibrated voltmeter to measure a few voltages then measure the same voltages using the ADC. The second calibration method uses a voltage reference of some sort; the simplest, though not the most accurate, is to use a silicon diode in the configuration shown in Figure 16.2. The voltage read at will be about 0.6V. The BBC Microcomputer uses three diodes to provide its own voltage reference of 1.8V, and this signal is available on the analogue port of the BBC Microcomputer, as described in Chapter 8. Note that this voltage reference is slightly susceptible to temperature changes.

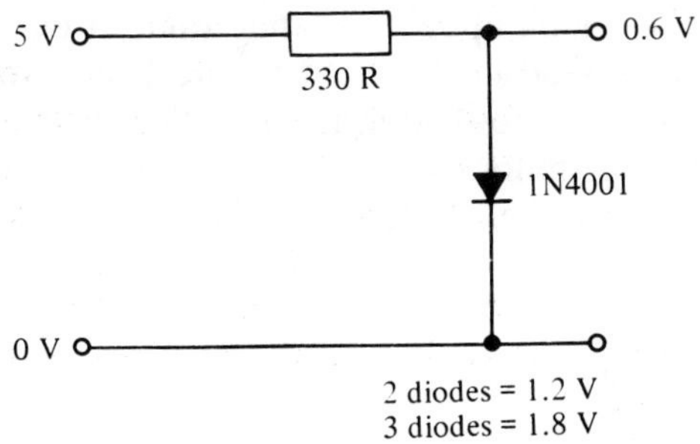

Figure 16.2

Measuring resistance and current

Once you can measure voltage with an ADC, it is not too much extra effort to measure resistance or current, because these factors are all related via Ohm's law:

$$V = I * R$$

thus knowing two of these parameters we can calculate the third. To measure resistance or current, we need to change that parameter into a voltage. This can be done using operational amplifier circuits for best results in terms of accuracy, but rough and ready measurements can be made as follows. Measuring current is fairly easy; simply pass the current through a resistor of known value, and measure the voltage developed across the resistor. The current is then given by I = V/R, where I is in amps, V in volts and R in ohms. There are two ways in which resistance can be measured; the first is to pass a known current through the resistor, and measure the generated voltage. This is not, however, the simplest way of doing things. It is much easier to use a potential divider circuit, as shown in Figure 16.3, and measure the voltage at the junction of the two resistors. From Chapter 3 we know that:

Vout = R2 / (R1 + R2) * Vin

so a quick rearrangement will give us:

R1 = (Vin / Vout * R2) − R2

Do not forget, though, in measuring current and resistance, that the input resistance of the ADC must be taken into account in these calculations as soon as the value of any resistance connected across the ADC input is more than a tenth or so of the input resistance of the ADC. For example, the value of R2 in the potential divider must not be too large, as otherwise the input resistance of the ADC would act in parallel with it to reduce the overall value of R2. As an example, the input resistance of the ZN448 ADC chip used in this book is about 100k, and so care needs to be taken to introduce this value into calculations is the value of R2 exceeds about 10 to 20k. The input resistance is just treated as follows:

R1 = (Vin / Vout * RT) − RT

where RT is given by:

1/RT = 1/R2 + 1/Rinp

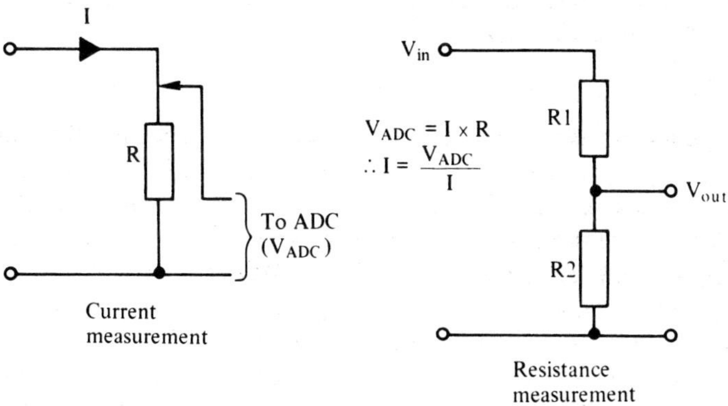

Figure 16.3

where Rinp is the input resistance of the ADC. These considerations place limitations on the values of resistance that can be measured by this technique. In addition, a rough value for R1 must be known before we start as the value obtained for R1 will be more accurate if R1 is roughly equal to R2.

Using the computer as an oscilloscope

With a fast ADC, most home computers can be pressed into service as a low frequency oscilloscope. Even the BBC's own built-in ADC can offer us some idea of how the output of a circuit changes with time. Indeed, because the image on a computer screen does not fade with time, the computer and ADC can make a very cheap storage oscilloscope for low frequency signals, or for capturing single events, such as the bounce of switch or relay contacts. Listing 16.1 shows a simple program for the BBC Microcomputer which plots the input to channel 0 of the ADC on a graphics screen. It is a fairly easy job to introduce time delays into the loop, and users of other computers should not have too much difficulty converting the listing. The *FX calls used are all operating system commands that control certain aspects of the BBC's ADC, and the ADVAL function simply returns a value from the ADC.

```
10 REM Simple data logger for BBC Microcomputer
20 REM plots the input voltage from Channel 0 of ADC on
30 REM a Mode 0 graphics screen
40 :
50 REM First of all, turn off all channels except Channel 0
60 :
70 *FX16,1
80 :
90 INPUT "Delay between samples (Seconds) ",F%
100 :
110 REM If a 0 delay is entered, the system will run 'flat out'
120 REM Now convert delay into 1/100ths of second used by the system
130 REM Time variable.
140 :
150 F%=F%*100
160 :
170 REM Now set up screen mode for plotting
180 :
190 MODE 0
200 X%=0
210 :
220 REM X% is the position along the X axis
230 :
240 REM initialise first plotting position to be at left edge and half
250 REM way up the screen
260 :
```

```
270 MOVE X%,512
580 :
590 REM Now start plotting...
600 :
610 REPEAT
620   IF F%=0 THEN \GOTO 700
630 :
640 REM only do this part if a delay is actually requested
650 :
660   TIME=0
670   REPEAT UNTIL TIME>=F%
680 :
690 REM The TIME variable is incremented 100 times a second.  Setting it
695 REM to 0 and looping like this will create a delay
696 :
700 REM Now force a start for the conversion on Channel 0
710 :
720   *FX17,1
730 :
740 REM now wait for that conversion to be completed by the system
750 :
760   REPEAT UNTIL (ADVAL(0) DIV 256) = 1
770 :
780 REM now we have a value to read back, so get it and scale it
790 REM to fit on screen.
800 :
810   Y%=(ADVAL(1) DIV 128) + 512
820 :
830 REM Now draw a line from the last point to the current place
840 :
850   DRAW X%,Y%
860   X%=X%+4
870 :
880 REM Now if the X% variable has exceeded 1200, prompt user to press
890 REM a key to carry on.
900 :
910 UNTIL X% > 1200
920 PRINTTAB(1,1)"Press a key to display another screen."
930 G=GET
940 GOTO 190
```

Listing 16.1

Using the computer as a frequency meter or counter

As well as measuring voltage, current and resistance, a computer with a user port can also be used to measure frequency, to measure the time between two events or just to count pulses. Again, there are limitations to the frequencies that can be measured using software alone, but the computer can still be a useful tool. In this section, I shall examine simple counting and frequency measuring software, as well as the bare minimum of hardware needed for good results. The essential point to note is that any electrical signal to be counted by a computer, via the user port, must have electrical characteristics that correspond to the ‘1’ and ‘0’ states expected by the user port – in most cases 5 V and 0 V respectively.

The first thing to look at then is the electronic circuitry needed to condition input signals of varying types for input to the user port.

Input conditioning

The main requirement for reliable counting and frequency measurement is that the signal reaching the user port should be in the form of a train of alternate logic '1's and '0's, irrespective of the nature of the signal being measured. Input conditioning circuits ensure that this is so, and a couple are shown in Figure 16.4. Figure 16.4a shows ą circuit that can handle small signals, and give a TTL level output. Figure 16.4b shows a simple circuit designed to condition larger level signals to suitable pulses. At the heart of each circuit is a Schmitt trigger, which basically cleans up ragged electrical signals to provide a clean signal capable of being counted.

Pulse counting

Pulse counting is fairly simple; we simply count full transitions of the input signal from '0' to '1' to '0' again; you can just count '0' to '1' or '1' to '0' transitions, but if you do this then do make sure you only count *either* '0' to '1' *or* '1' to '0' changes; counting both will result in double counting of the incoming pulses. The maximum rate of counting will obviously depend upon the speed of the program. If your computer has suitable on-board hardware, like the BBC Microcomputer, then the counting job can be made much simpler by making use of this hardware. Listing 16.2 shows a counting program in BASIC for the BBC Microcomputer, with details for conversion to other dialects of BASIC.

```
10 REM Simple BASIC pulse counter for BBC Microcomputer
20 REM Could be converted to other BASICs if the computer has
30 REM an appropiate user port for input.
40 :
50 CLS
60 INPUT "0 to 1 or 1 to 0 transitions (Enter 01 or 10) ",a$
70 IF a$="01" THEN PROCcount01
80 IF a$="10" THEN PROCcount10
90 GOTO 50
100 :
110 REM Now we have the details of what pulse is going to be counted,
120 REM we can call the correct procedure.  In other dialects of BASIC
130 REM you could call a subroutine instead of PROCcount01 and PROCcount10
140 :
150 DEF PROCcount01
160 :
170 REM first of all, initialist Bit 0 of user port for input
```

```
180 :
190 ?&FE62 = 254
200 :
210 P%=0
220 :
230 REM P% will hold pulse count; using upper case integer variables is faster
240 REM than using other variables on BBC Micro
250 :
260 INPUT "Count for how many seconds? ",T%
270 :
280 TIME=0
290 REPEAT
300 :
310 REM the REPEAT...UNTIL loop could be replaced by an IF...GOTO loop
320 REM and you will need to change the timing to suit your computer's
330 REM real time clock - TIME increments on the BBC 100 times a second
340 :
350 REPEAT UNTIL (?&FE60 AND 1)=0
360 :
370 REM wait for a 0 input
380 :
390 REPEAT UNTIL (?&FE60 AND 1) = 1
400 :
410 REM wait for 1 '1'; we now have a 0 to 1 transition, so count it!
420 :
430 P%=P%+1
440 :
450 UNTIL TIME>=T%
460 :
470 REM we get here when we've exceeded the time set
480 PRINT T%;" 0 to 1 pulses were recorded"
490 INPUT "Press ENTER to continue",a$
500 ENDPROC
510 :
550 DEF PROCcount10
560 :
570 REM first of all, initialist Bit 0 of user port for input
580 :
590 ?&FE62 = 254
600 :
610 P%=0
620 :
630 REM P% will hold pulse count; using upper case integer variables is faster
640 REM than using other variables on BBC Micro
650 :
660 INPUT "Count for how many seconds? ",T%
670 :
680 TIME=0
690 REPEAT
700 :
710 REM the REPEAT...UNTIL loop could be replaced by an IF...GOTO loop
720 REM and you will need to change the timing to suit your computer's
730 REM real time clock - TIME increments on the BBC 100 times a second
740 :
750 REPEAT UNTIL (?&FE60 AND 1)=1
760 :
770 REM wait for a 1 input
780 :
790 REPEAT UNTIL (?&FE60 AND 1) = 0
800 :
810 REM wait for 1 '0'; we now have a 1 to 0 transition, so count it!
820 :
830 P%=P%+1
840 :
850 UNTIL TIME>=T%
860 :
870 REM we get here when we've exceeded the time set
```

```
880 PRINT T%;" 1 to 0 pulses were recorded"
890 INPUT "Press ENTER to continue",a$
900 ENDPROC
```

Listing 16.2

Timing events

It is occasionally useful to be able to record the time taken between two events occurring. For example, we might wish to record the duration of a single pulse present at a user port input. Again, there are two approaches to the problem. If the computer has an on-board timer, such as the user VIA of the BBC Microcomputer, then it is possible to record very short times accurately – down to a few microseconds, in fact. If, on the other hand, you are reliant on software based timing, such as that offered by the TIME or TIME$ variables in BASIC or the event timer on the Amstrad 6128, then you are usually limited to measuring time in milliseconds. In BASIC, a timing function can be as straightforward as:

```
1000
1010 REPEAT
1020 UNTIL (?&FE60 AND 1) = 1
1030 TIME=0 : REM zero the BBC Micro's timer
1040 REPEAT
1050 UNTIL (?&FE60 AND 1) = 0
1060 PRINT TIME
```

In this example we are timing the duration of an input pulse on bit 0 of the user port. Lines 1010–1020 wait for the input line to go from '0' to '1'. The BBC TIME variable is then set to '0', and a loop is entered until the pulse ends, indicated by the input bit going back to '0'. The TIME variable is then printed, giving an approximate pulse duration in hundredths of a second. This will work on any micro with a real-time clock, and only the lines checking the user port have to be altered.

For more accurate timing on the BBC Microcomputer, the user VIA can be used. The following listing utilises the user VIA to allow measurement of time delays down to a millisecond.

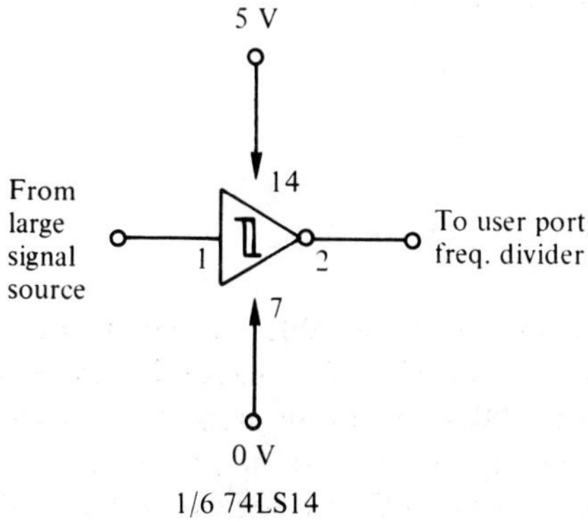

(a)

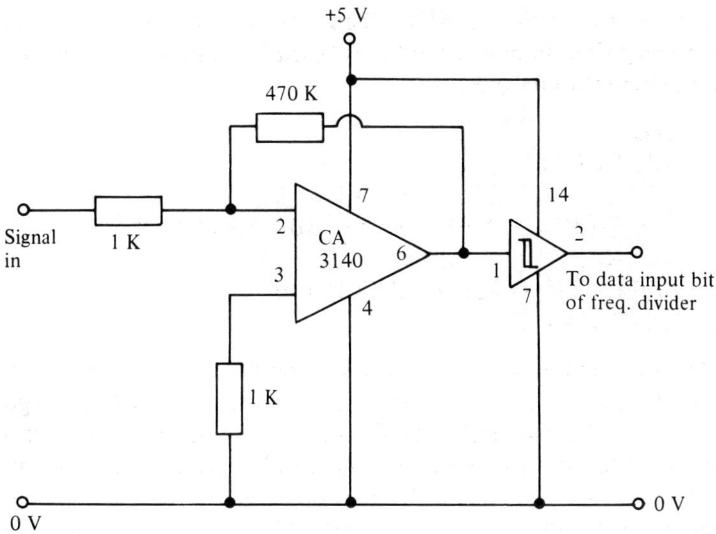

(b)

Figure 16.4

```
10 DIM CODE% 100
1000 T1CL = &FE64
1010 T1CH = &FE65
1020 INTREG = &FE6D
1030 ACR = &FE6B
1040 :
1050 FOR I%=0 TO 2 STEP 2
1060 P%=CODE%
1070 [ OPT I%
1071 .START
1072 LDA &FE60
1073 AND #1
1074 BNE START\ wait for a logic low
1075 .START2
1076 LDA &FE60
1077 AND #1
1078 BEQ START2\ wait for signal to go high again
1084 LDA #0 : STA &70
1085 .HIGH
1086 JSR DELAY
1090 LDA &FE60
1100 AND #1
1110 BEQ HIGH
1120 RTS
1130 :
1140 .DELAY
1150 LDA ACR
1160 AND #&3F
1170 STA ACR
1180 LDA #1000 MOD 256
1190 STA T1CL
1200 LDA #1000 DIV 256
1210 STA T1CH
1220 .LOOP
1230 LDA INTREG
1240 AND #&40
1250 BEQ LOOP
1260 LDA T1CL
1262 LDA #&70
```

```
1263 CLC
1264 ADC £1
1265 STA &70
1270 RTS
1280 ]
1290 NEXT
1300 :
1310 CALL START
1320 PRINT ?&70
1330 END
```

This program measures delays in 1 ms steps, as set by the DELAY subroutine in which a count of 1000 is loaded into a pair of VIA registers which are then decremented by the system clock at a rate of 1MHz. The memory location at &70 is incremented for each 1 ms period that the input line is high. The routine waits for the input to go from low to high before starting counting. Because only one byte is used to record the millisecond count, the longest delay that can be recorded by this program is 255ms. This could be easily changed.

Frequency measurement

Frequency measurement is fairly straightforward as a concept, and there are two ways of doing the job:

1 the first is to simply count the number of input pulses that occur within a given time period, and then scale that count to give a frequency in Hz. Thus if we were to record 1000 pulses in 0.5 seconds, we would have a frequency of 2kHz. So, we require an accurate means of measuring a time interval, and a means of counting pulses.

2 an alternative way to do the job is to remember that the frequency of a signal is simply the reciprocal of the period of the signal – that is, the length of time needed for the signal to make one full cycle. This is often easier to implement on a microcomputer, and the Listing 16.3 for the BBC Microcomputer uses this technique. Details of how the program works are given in the listing.

```
10 REM Simple frequency meter software using the VIA timer of
20 REM the BBC Microcomputer to get the period of an input signal,
30 REM from which the frequency is obtained. Input signal MUST be
35 REM on Bit 6 of the input port.
40 :
50 REM set up space for machine code
55 :
60 DIM mc% 500
65 :
66 REM Now set up variables holding VIA register addresses
70 :
90 ACR = &FE6B
100 Timer2Low = &FE68
110 Timer2High = &FE69
120 InputPort = &FE60
130 :
140 REM Now assemble the machine code into the area of memory mc%
150 :
160 FOR pass%=0 TO 2 STEP 2
165 P%=mc%
170 [OPT pass%
180 :
190 .measure_period
200 \ first of all, prepare for the use of interrupts
210 \ this involves setting and clearing flags. If this isn't done,
220 \ the BBC can get a little screwed up!
270 :
280 CLD
290 SEI
300 :
310 \ initialise Y register for loading into Timer 2 for count down
320 :
325 LDY #255
326 LDA #0
330 :
340 \ Although we're using Bit 6 of the Input Port for the data input,
350 \ we don't need to set bit 6 up in the A register for use with the
352 \ BIT command used in this program. This is because the status of
353 \ bit 6 is automatically transferred to the overflow flag when the BIT
354 \ command is executed. A is loaded with 0 for future use when we need
355 \ to initialise the ACR register.
360
370 .still_high
380 \ loop around here until bit 6 is set to 0
390 BIT InputPort
400 BVS still_high
410
420 .still_low
430 \ loop around here until bit 6 is set to 1
440 BIT InputPort
450 BVC still_low
460
470 \ if we get here, we now know we're at the start of a full cycle of
480 \ the input signal. We now count the number of microseconds in the
490 \ next high and low cycle of the input signal. This is the period.
500
510 STA ACR
520
530 \ ACR of VIA now ready to count down.
540 \ now initialise counter. As soon as high register set up it will
541 \ start counting down.
560
570 STY Timer2Low
580 STY Timer2High
590
600 \ now wait for input period to finish by waiting for bit 6 to go
605 \ low then high again
```

```
610
620 .pulse_high
630 BIT InputPort
640 BVS pulse_high
650
660 \ now bit 6 is at 0, wait until it goes high again – that is the end
662 \ of a full cycle
680
690 .pulse_low
700 BIT InputPort
710 BVC pulse_low
720
730 \ we've now got a vfull cycle, so store the counter contents in page 0
750
760 LDX Timer2Low
770 LDY Timer2High
780 STX &70
790 STY &71
800
810 \ all done, so back to BASIC
820 RTS
830 ]
840 NEXT pass%
850 :
860 CLS
865 REPEAT
870   period = 65535 – (?&70+256*?&71)
880   PRINTTAB(10,10)"Frequency is ";INT(1E6/period);" Hz      "
890 UNTIL FALSE
```

Listing 16.3

To measure the frequencies of signals beyond the range of the software discussed here, you can divide the incoming pulse train by 10 using TTL logic chips, as shown in Figure 16.5. This will, of course, reduce the resolution of the frequency counting software by a factor of 10, so if we were measuring in Hz in the first instance, we shall get a reading in tens of Hz after using a divide-by-ten circuit.

Using the computer as a signal source

As well as being able to monitor signals generated by other equipment, we can use the computer to generate signals. In its simplest form, we can take the output from the sound circuit of the computer and use this as a test signal. Do not forget that the output from most computer sound chips is a square wave. However, if the computer has a user port, there are other options available to us. The only point to remember is that, on the whole, computer user ports are not designed to provide very much current, and so it is a good idea to buffer the output in some way.

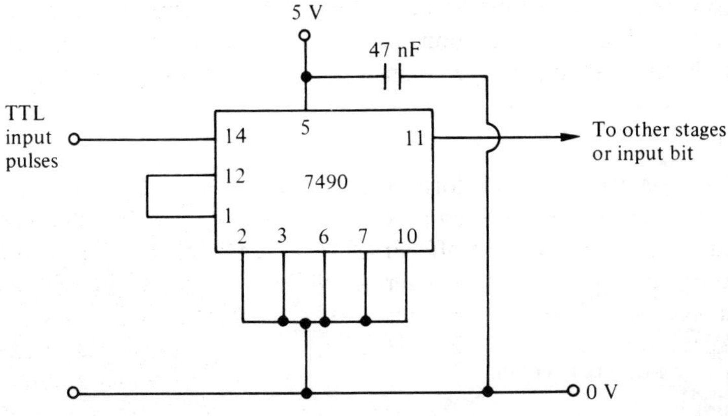

Figure 16.5

A suitable buffer circuit is shown in Figure 16.6, and as well as allowing the output to provide more current drive it will offer some protection to the user port in the event of problems arising in the circuit. Again, take *great care* in applying signals from the computer to any circuits where high voltages are likely to be present – they can cause you and your computer considerable harm!

Pulse generator

The computer can easily be programmed to generate a series of pulses of defined width by simply turning a bit of the user port on, waiting a while, then turning it off again. A time delay can be generated either in BASIC or machine code, and the advantage of

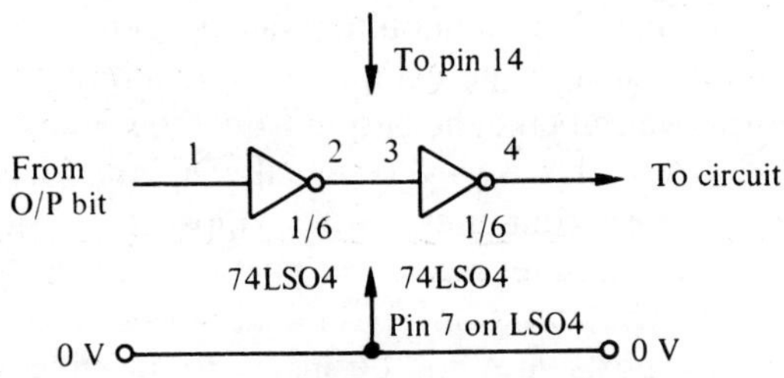

Figure 16.6

using the computer in this way is that fairly complex sequences of pulses of varying durations can be output using very simple programs – much cheaper than a commercial pulse generator.

Tone generator

Tone generation in the form of a square wave tone can be quite easily achieved by turning an output bit on and off rapidly. The duration of the on and off periods will set the frequency of the tone, and it is possible to generate 'white' noise by varying the on and off times using the random number function of the computer. Again, the user VIA of the BBC Microcomputer is quite useful, as it can be programmed to generate a square wave signal automatically, allowing the microprocessor to get on with more useful tasks.

Waveform generation

A user port equipped with a DAC can easily be used to create waveforms other than the simple pulses and square waves seen so far. A suitable DAC and amplifier are shown in Figure 16.7, and

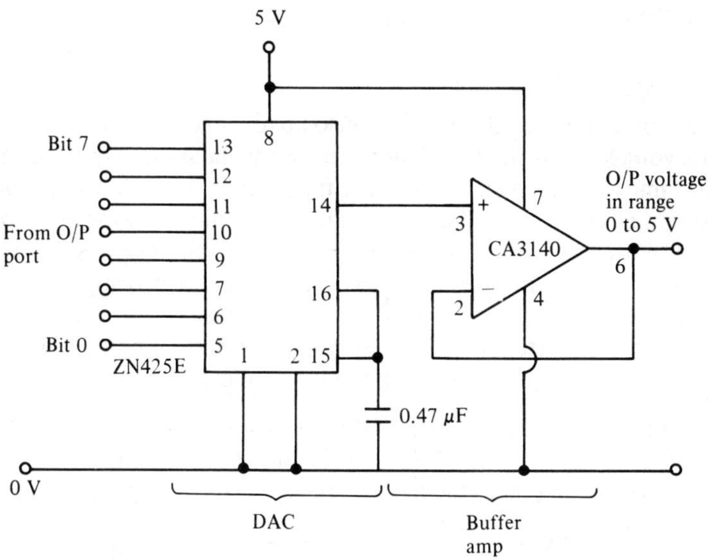

Figure 16.7

in use a sequence of bytes are sent out of the user port. For example:

```
1000 FOR I%=1 TO 255
1010 ?&FE60 = I%          : REM to BBC user port
1020 NEXT I%
1030 GOTO 1000
```

will cause a 'ramp' voltage to appear at the output of the DAC amplifier, increasing as the bytes sent increase from 1 to 255 then suddenly dropping back to 1 again. The frequency of this signal depends upon the speed at which the bytes are sent, and so there is a limit placed on waveform generation by this technique even if we use machine code. However, any waveform you like can be generated using this method by simply setting up a table of bytes representing the waveform to be generated in memory and then writing a computer program to send the contents of the table repeatedly to the DAC. A sine wave table, for example, could be produced by using the computer SIN() function and scaling the figures obtained to get a value between 0 and 255. Random noise could be obtained by placing random numbers in the table, and introducing a random delay between the sending of each byte to the DAC.

Using the computer with a VCO/DAC

A DAC, as described above, can also be used to control the output of a voltage controlled oscillator, as already mentioned in Chapter 15. Figure 16.8 shows how we might set up a system to test filters using a DAC, a VCO and an ADC. The output from the ADC is then plotted as a graph against frequency, and the response of the filter output to frequency changes can thus be investigated. A similar arrangement could be used to measure the output of amplifiers for different input frequencies. In setting up this sort of thing in practice, the following points should be observed.

1 after setting a frequency on the VCO, the reading from the ADC should be allowed to settle down to a constant value before moving on to the next frequency. This set-up is not really suitable for observing transient changes in circuit output.
2 the detector used may have a non-linear response with frequency. To see if this is the case, replace the filter under test with a

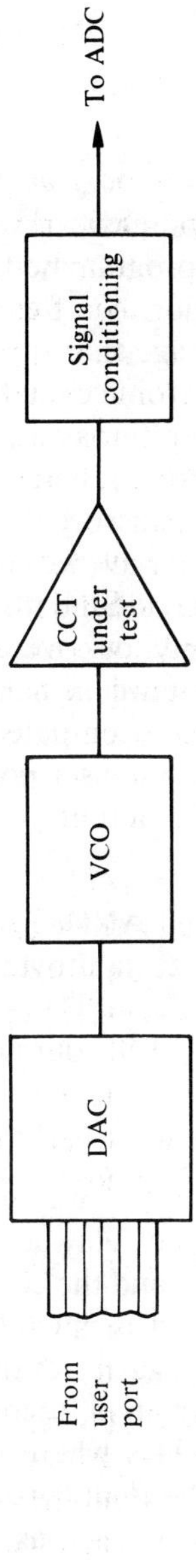
To ADC
Signal
conditioning
CCT
under
test
VCO
DAC
From
user
port

Figure 16.8

resistor network as shown in Figure 16.3. Then run the test and observe the output graph obtained – in a perfect world it should be a straight, horizontal line.

Digital electronics

Logic gate simulation

One interesting use for a computer fitted with an input/output port is that the computer can be programmed to act as a single logic gate or an array of gates, prior to a final logic circuit being put together. This has the advantage that re-programming a micro is easier than rebuilding an electronic circuit! For example, imagine we need a logical system which turns an output on whenever two out of three input bits are set to '1'. Before we sit down and build a circuit, we can set this up on a microcomputer to see if our design will work using these rules; after all, we could have made an error with the specification of the circuit and it would be annoying if we built the circuit and suddenly discovered that, although it is working, it is not doing what we actually want! The following subroutine for the BBC Microcomputer will do this. I have assumed that bits 0,1 and 2 of the user port are configured as the input bits, and that bit 3 is the output.

```
1000 REPEAT
1010 inputbyte = ?&FE60 AND 7
1020 IF inputbyte = 3 OR inputbyte = 5 OR inputbyte
= 6
     THEN output = 8 ELSE output = 0
1030 ?&FE60 = output
1040 UNTIL FALSE
```

Using the microcomputer in this way has some disadvantages, the main one being that the time delay between an input condition being applied to the input port and the corresponding output state being set up on the output port is much longer than it would be when using purely electronic gates, even when the software is written in machine code. Of course, there is nothing to stop you making use of these time delays where time delays have to be inserted into the circuit. In the final version, these delays will be provided by time delay circuits, such as monostables, but when developing the circuit you can use the computer to get a delay of just the right length by trial and error, especially if the computer has hardware timers on board to make things easy!

Logic gate testing

A simple piece of test equipment can be fabricated to check logic gates out to see if they work correctly. The inputs of gates can be driven by output bits from the computer user port, and the status of the logic gate output can be monitored to see if the expected truth table for the logic gate is obtained. If it is, then the gate is working; otherwise, it is not. More complex logic functions can also be tested in this way.

Simple logic analyser

To complete the picture, you can also use the computer as a low speed logic analyser, by monitoring the logic states on input lines of the user port and using either graphics or simple sequences of '1's and '0's on the screen to indicate logic states. By monitoring two or three points in a circuit, you can see how a change in logic state at one point in the circuit affects other points in the circuit.

Digital signal processing

Armed with a fast ADC and DAC, you can actually process analogue signals in the computer rather than by using analogue circuits. For example, you could read in a signal from the ADC, multiply each byte by two, then output it to the DAC – a simple example of digital signal processing in which the input signal is actually amplified. A more realistic application, though, is that of using digital filters to change a signal.

Digital filtering

The role of a digital filter is precisely the same as that of analogue filters; to modify signals dependant upon their frequency. However, there are two major advantages of digital filters over analogue filters. The first is that digital filters can have response curves that are absolutely impossible to create accurately with analogue filters. The second is that the response of the filter is easily changed simply by altering the program running on the computer. Not surprisingly, this program must be written in machine code or a compiled language for the speed required, especially if real-time filtering is required. A digital filtering system requires three things; a fast ADC to sample the signal under examination, a computer to store and process the samples, and a DAC to convert the processed samples into a voltage again.

The algorithm for digital filtering is very simple:

$$Vt = (a*INt) + (b*INt-1) + (c*INt-2) \ldots$$

and so on, where V is the output voltage at time t, INt is the input value at time t, INt-1 is the previous input value, INt-2 the input before that and so on. The multipliers a,b and c are simply constants which define how much of each of the samples is used to affect the value of the current output. If you are interested in experimenting, then two terms are enough – a and b – and to make the program as fast as possible, values for a and b should be chosen such that the calculations needed can be carried out by simple bit shifting – i.e. 0.25, 0.5 and 0.75 are good start points as these are all binary fractions, thus allowing the use of bit shifting rather than multiplication or division. If you are using two terms, then you need to store the current sample and the last sample taken in memory for real time work.

Of course, there is no reason why the job should be done in real time – you could store a large number of samples in memory, filter them by running the program over all the samples, then output it when required to the DAC. Indeed, there is no reason why the filtered output should go to a DAC either; a filtered set of samples can be processed in any other way that you please. One application for digital filtering that I have experimented with is the processing of SSTV and FAX images to reduce some of the noise, and commercially the process is used to process satellite images or synthesized speech.

Fourier analysis

The final application of computers in signal processing that I want to look at is the process of Fourier analysis. It can be shown (by people with much better mathematics than myself!) that any signal can be made up from sine waves of different amplitudes and frequencies. What is often required is to examine a signal and analyse it in terms of the frequencies of the sine waves, and their relative amplitudes, which make up the signal. This information then allows us to look at the frequency spectrum of a signal, and so if you have a fast ADC sampling output from a circuit under test we can examine differences between the frequency spectrum of the input and output signals and determine the frequency response of the circuit. Programs to do this are called Fourier Transforms, and the method I shall describe here is called a Fast Fourier Transform, because, compared to other methods of doing the job, this method is relatively fast. I do not intend to go into the theory of the Fast Fourier Transform (FFT) here, but instead give a usable listing (Listing 16.4) in GW BASIC for the IBM PC and give details of how to use it.

```
10 REM FFT Program.  Algorithm based on published sources
20 :
30 GOSUB 1000 : REM get number of points and set up arrays
40 GOSUB 2000 : REM generate some test data
50 GOSUB 3000 : REM Reverse bits
60 GOSUB 4000 : REM do the FFT
70 GOSUB 5000 : REM print out the results
80 END
90 :
1000 REM get input power of 2.  This will specify the number of data points
1010 REM that the system can handle
1020 :
1030 INPUT "Number of data points ",NUMDATPOINTS
1031 :
1032 REM Now evaluate power of 2 closest to the number of data points, and
1033 REM recalculate the number of data points if necessary
1034 :
1036 POWEROF2=0
1037 IF 2^POWEROF2  >= NUMDATPOINTS THEN GOTO 1050
1038 POWEROF2=POWEROF2+1
1039 GOTO 1037
1050 NUMDATPOINTS=2^POWEROF2-1
1055 NUMITERATS=POWEROF2-1
1060 :
1061 REM Now dimension the arrays
1062 :
1070 DIM TESTDATA(NUMDATPOINTS),REAL(NUMDATPOINTS),
       IMAGINARY(NUMDATPOINTS),CO(NUMDATPOINTS),SI(NUMDATPOINTS)
1080 :
1090 CONSTANT=6.28/(NUMDATPOINTS+1)
1100 FOR I=0 TO NUMDATPOINTS
1101 :
1102 REM Generate arrays of sines and cosines to save time later.  Generate
1103 REM enough to give a sine and cosine at each array element that will
1104 REM hold data later.
1108 :
1110 CO(I)=COS(CONSTANT*I)
1120 SI(I)=SIN(CONSTANT*I)
1121 :
```

```
1122 REM zeroise the arrays for the real and imaginary parts of the result
1123 :
1130 REAL(I)=0
1140 IMAGINARY(I)=0
1150 NEXT I
1160 :
1170 RETURN
1180 :
2000 REM Generate some test data, and place in the t array.  For your own
2005 REM applications, you may like to put your own data acquisition
2006 REM routines in here.  As an extension to this program, try adding
2007 REM some 'noise' by using the RND() funcion to add a term to line 2030
2010 :
2020 FOR I=0 TO NUMDATPOINTS
2030 TESTDATA(I)=COS(CONSTANT*I*(12))
2040 NEXT I
2050 :
2060 RETURN
2070 :
3000 REM Bit Reversal routine 'reflects' the data in the test data array
3002 REM into the Real array for processing by the FFT
3004 :
3010 FOR I=0 TO NUMDATPOINTS
3020 REVBITS=0
3021 J=POWEROF2-1
3045 FOR K=0 TO POWEROF2-1
3053 REVBITS=REVBITS+((SGN(I AND (2^K)))*(2^J))
3054 J=J-1
3070 NEXT K
3080 REAL(REVBITS)=TESTDATA(I)
3090 NEXT I
3095 :
3096 REM end of bit reversal subroutine
3097 :
3100 RETURN
3200 :
4000 REM Actually do the FFT
4010 FOR CURRENTINTERAT=0 TO NUMITERATS
4020   TEMP2POWER=2^CURRENTINTERAT
4030   DIFFERENCE=2^(NUMITERATS-CURRENTINTERAT)
4040   FOR K=0 TO (TEMP2POWER-1)*DIFFERENCE STEP DIFFERENCE
4060     FOR I=0 TO 2*(DIFFERENCE-1) STEP 2
4062 :
4063 REM Pointer I1 points to the first element in the arrays to be operated
4064 REM on by the FFT procedure.
4065 :
4070       I1=I*TEMP2POWER+(K/DIFFERENCE)
4075 :
4076 REM Pointer I2 is incremented  each time by 2^current  iteration number
4077 REM and so points to an element 2,4,8,16, etc. higher in the arrays than
4078 REM the element pointed to by I1
4079 :
4080       I2=I1+TEMP2POWER
4082 :
4083 REM next stage essential because we'll be modifying the contents of
4084 REM real and imaginary array elements that we need to use as raw data
4085 REM so just store copies for use in calculations
4086 :
4090       TEMPREAL1=REAL(I1)
4091       TEMPREAL2=REAL(I2)
4092       TEMPIMAGINARY1=IMAGINARY(I1)
4093       TEMPIMAGINARY2=IMAGINARY(I2)
4100 :
```

```
4110 REM Now do the calculations on the real and imaginary array elements
4120 REM pointed to by I1 and I2. Because these two pointers are related
4124 REM by a power of 2 when processing the arrays, the arrays must always
4125 REM hold a number of points that is a power of 2.
4126 :
4150         REAL(I1)=TEMPREAL1+(CO(K)*TEMPREAL2)-(SI(K)*TEMPIMAGINAI
4160         IMAGINARY(I1)=TEMPIMAGINARY1+(SI(K)*TEMPREAL2)
        +(CO(K)*TEMPIMAGINARY2)
4170         REAL(I2)=TEMPREAL1-(CO(K)*TEMPREAL2)+(SI(K)*TEMPIMAGINAI
4180         IMAGINARY(I2)=TEMPIMAGINARY1-(SI(K)*TEMPREAL2)
        -(CO(K)*TEMPIMAGINARY2)
4181 :
4182 REM This calculation is often known as the 'Butterfly' because if the
4183 REM arrays involved are drawn on paper with lines linking the elements
4184 REM being operated on, the whole effect is supposed to look a little like
4185 REM a butterfly's wings.
4189 :
4190       NEXT I
4200    NEXT K
4210 NEXT CURRENTINTERAT
4220 RETURN
4230 :
5000 REM Print out the results of the FFT. Only print out half the array
5002 REM as the two halves of the arrays mirror each other for this program
5003 REM The other 'half' of the data can be used in other, more advanced
5004 REM applications. You might modify this routine to graph the results
5010 :
5020 FOR I=0 TO NUMDATPOINTS/2
5030 :
5040 REM calculate the output by summing the real and imaginary parts of the
5050 REM data for each point, then display the answer. This summing operation
5051 REM is the same sort of thing that was used in the circuit analysis
5052 REM program described in Chapter 3
5060 :
5070 OUTPUT=INT(SQR(REAL(I)*REAL(I)+IMAGINARY(I)*IMAGINARY(I)))
5080 :
5100 PRINT OUTPUT
5110 :
5120 NEXT I
5130 RETURN
```

Listing 16.4

The FFT program

FFT programs process a table of numbers representing data from the real world collected from an ADC or a table of values generated by a mathematical function or even figures representing populations, etc., as the program can be used to look for periodicity in data sets. The number of entries in the table that need analysing will be limited by the size of the computer memory, but must be a power of 2 – i.e. 64, 128, 256, 512, 1024 and so on. The more pieces of data there are in the table, the more accurate the resultant FFT will be. In addition, if you are sampling a waveform you need a minimum of two table entries for each cycle of the input signal. In practice, you should aim to have more points than this per cycle of input signal, but failure to do so will result in erroneous results from the program. The algorithm used for the FFT is a fairly standard one that you will come across in many different text books. I have inserted comments where appropriate so you can try altering parts of the code. The main areas you are likely to want to change are the input and output segments; a graphical output can be provided which is easier to read than the table of figures printed here.

APPENDIX 1

The BASIC language

BASIC (beginners all purpose symbolic instruction code) was designed at Dartmouth College in the US in the early 1960s. It was intended for use as a training language but reached high levels of popularity as it was implemented in many different versions on small home computers. All small computers now have at least one version of BASIC available on them, and in many computers, like the BBC Microcomputer or the Amstrad 6128, BASIC is the language into which the machine 'boots' when it is turned on.

In this section the main features of BASIC are briefly discussed for those readers who have not used the language at all.

A BASIC program

A program in BASIC consists of, in most versions of the language, a series of numbered *statements*, each statement being an instruction to the computer. Unless directed otherwise by the program, the statements are executed in the order of their line numbers and if there is more than one statement on a line the statements are executed from left to right. Most BASICs allow multi-statement lines, with statements separated by ':'s. Lines are entered into a program by typing in a line number, the statements required, then pressing the RETURN or ENTER key on the keyboard. To insert a line between two existing lines, a line number is selected that lies between the two existing line numbers. For this reason, it is traditional for BASIC line numbers to go up in 10s. To delete a line, the line number is typed in by itself, and the RETURN key pressed. Typing in an existing line number, followed by some statements, will replace the existing line with the new statements.

Most BASIC languages also allow a more sophisticated means of editing BASIC programs. BASIC programs are started off by typing in the command RUN without a line number; this starts executing the instructions in the program from the first line of the program – that is, the lowest numbered line.

Commands

A command in BASIC, strictly speaking, is an instruction that is typed in to the BASIC system *without a line number*. These commands are acted upon immediately by the BASIC interpreter, and typical commands are:

RUN	Runs the program currently in memory.
LIST	Allows the current program to be listed out to the screen or printer.
NEW	Gets rid of the current program.
OLD	Recovers a NEWed program in some circumstances.
SAVE	Stores the current program to tape or disc with a given file name.
LOAD	Loads a new program into memory. This replaces any program already in memory.
RENUMBER	Renumbers the line numbers of a BASIC program.

Not all BASICs recognize all these commands, but they are fairly typical. Some of these commands can also be used within programs.

Numbers, strings and variables

The BASIC language allows us to use integers, real numbers (e.g. 1.2345) and exponential notation (e.g. 1E6) to represent numbers. In addition, BASIC can handle characters and strings of letters which can represent words or any other text.

Numeric or string *constants* are set by the programmer and are 'hard coded' into the program – that is, they cannot be altered without changing the program line. A *variable* is the means by which BASIC allows us to store numbers and strings in such a way that they can be altered as and when required by the program.

Think of a variable as a named 'pigeon hole' into which certain types of information can be stored. There are two main types of variable: *string variables* hold characters and text; and *numeric variables* hold numbers. *Array variables* can be either numeric or string variables, and can be viewed as subdivisions within the pigeon hole, each subdivision being capable of holding a number or string.

Variables are named, and most BASICs allow you to have names of any length, provided that they start with a letter and do not contain spaces and certain punctuation symbols. Thus, FRED is a legal variable name in most BASICs, but 1234 is not. If a variable is a string variable, it always has a $ symbol as the last character. Therefore, FRED is a numeric variable, but FRED$ is a string variable.

For arrays, we indicate the subdivision in use by a *suffix*. For example, FRED(4) is the fourth *element* of array variable FRED.

Arithmetic, relational and logical operators

BASIC supports the usual arithmetic operations −, −, / and *, as well as the ability to raise numbers to the power of another number, and a variety of mathematical *functions* (see below). Operations are carried out as if operations with equal priority are carried out from left to right. The priorities of the operations are as follows:

1 Expressions in brackets.
2 Exponentiation.
3 Multiplication and division.
4 Addition and subtraction.

The relational operators are used to make decisions based on the relative values of numeric or string expressions. They are written as:

Expression   Operator   Expression

and the operators supported by BASIC are equals (=), not equal (<>), greater than (>), less than (<), greater than or equal to (>=), less than or equal to (<=). In addition, AND, OR and NOT are also supported by most BASICs. A relational expression, created by combining two expressions with a relational operator, will return TRUE or FALSE (1 or −1, or 0, depending upon the BASIC used). For example:

$$2 > 4 \text{ is FALSE}$$
$$1 < 456 \text{ is TRUE}$$

Functions

BASIC also supports functions, which act on a numeric or string expression to return a value. A typical expression is SIN(), which will return the sine of the angle passed to the function. Thus to get the sine of 43', you would use SIN(43). There are a host of functions in BASIC, from simple trigonometry and arithmetic functions to functions that allow us to chop up strings to extract particular characters, or functions that allow us to search strings for the occurrence of particular letters.

BASIC statements

The instructions that go on lines with line numbers are known as *statements* in BASIC. Some of these, such as PRINT, can be used without a line number if you wish to carry out, for example, quick calculations.

Program flow control

END and STOP Both of these statements indicate to the BASIC interpreter that it is to cease running the program. In many dialects of BASIC, there is no real difference between the two statements, but originally END was compulsory and always had to be the very last statement in the program. STOP could be used anywhere where it was needed.

GOTO GOTO is a statement which passes control of the program to a new line number, rather than the line number immediately following the GOTO line. GOTO 300 will cause program execution to jump directly to line 300.

GOSUB

GOSUB also causes program control to jump to another line in the program. However, as soon as a *RETURN* statement is encountered control automatically passes back to the statement immediately following the GOSUB statement. The block of code ending in the RETURN statement is called a *subroutine* and the advantage of using GOSUB and RETURN is that one piece of code can be used to do similar jobs all throughout a program without the need for duplication. Thus:

```
1000 GOSUB 2000 : PRINT "Hello" :
STOP
2000 PRINT "Goodbye": RETURN
```

would result in the words "Goodbye" and "Hello" being printed to the screen (although not in the usual order!).

ON n GOTO

This allows a GOTO statement to select which line number to jump to based upon the value of 'n'. For example:

```
ON fred GOTO 100,200,300
```

will jump to line 100 if fred=1, 200 if fred=2 and 300 if fred=3. There is a similar command *ON n GOSUB* available in most dialects of BASIC.

IF...THEN

This allows BASIC programs to make decisions based upon the results of relational expressions. For example:

```
IF fred>34 THEN PRINT "Big"
```

will only print "Big" if the value in variable 'fred' is greater than 34. Although PRINT is used here, any statement can follow the THEN. In some BASICs, the THEN part of the statement is not always needed:

```
IF fred>34 PRINT "Big"
```

would work in these systems. Other versions of BASIC support the *ELSE* clause, which tells BASIC what to do if the relational expression is not true. For example:

```
IF fred>34 THEN PRINT "Big" ELSE
PRINT "Small"
```

would print "Small" if fred was less than 34.

FOR...NEXT This allows BASIC to carry out a set of statements a predetermined number of times. Although this could be done with IF . . . THEN and GOTO, this method is much nicer! For example:

```
1000 FOR I=1 TO 10
1010 PRINT I
1020 NEXT I
```

will print the numbers 1 to 10 on the screen. The value I is used as a counter by BASIC here, though any variable could be used. '1' here is the initial value of the loop, and is the first value that I will assume. '10' is the final value, and is the last one that I will assume. You can terminate a loop like this earlier than the final value by setting I to a value greater than the final value. An extension, *STEP* allows you to increment the counter in steps other than 1 or, by using negative steps, decrement the counter from a high initial value to a low final value.

Variable and data handling statements

LET This statement allows us to assign a value to a variable. For example, the line:

```
1000 LET fred=23
```

will assign the value 23 to the variable fred. Most BASICs do not force you to use LET; the line:

```
1000 fred=23
```

will do the job just as well in most cases.

INPUT

This statement also assigns a value to a variable, but is used when the user is expected to provide the data. For example, if we needed to ask the name of the user of the program, there is no way we could store the names of the earth's billions (born and yet to come) in a series of LET statements! Instead, we can use INPUT:

```
1000 INPUT "What's your name",n$
```

This statement would print the question "What is your name" on the screen and then accept whatever the user typed in, followed by a press of the RETURN key, into the variable n$. Most BASICs will allow you to INPUT to several variables at once:

```
1000 INPUT a,b,c
```

will wait for three numbers, separated by commas, to be typed in.

DIM

This statement is used to tell BASIC to set up space for array variables. The statement:

```
10 DIM fred(1000)
```

would set up an array variable 'fred' with space for 1000 numbers.

DATA

This statement allows us to store data that will be constant in a particular program in a compact form, rather than as a series of LET statements. The line:

```
1000 DATA 12,34,56,78,"fred"
```

stores 4 numeric constants and a string constant ("fred") in such a way so that another BASIC statement, *READ*, can assign these values to variables. So, the first READ would take '12', the second '34', and so on. A line to do this might be:

```
2000 READ a,b,c,d,a$
```

and after this a would hold 12, b=34, c=56, d=78 and a$ would hold “fred”.

If a program has more than one line of DATA in it, then we need to tell READ where to get the DATA from. A statement *RESTORE n* allows us to do this, where ‘n’ is the line number of the DATA statement we arre interested in. Thus

```
1990 RESTORE 1000
```

would tell READ to get the DATA from line 1000.

Printing information

The BASIC printing command is called *PRINT* and it simply outputs items to the screen in a format that depends upon the additional features of the PRINT statement that the programmer has employed.

The simplest use of PRINT is in the line:

```
1000 PRINT "Hello World"
```

which will simply print the text Hello World on the screen of the computer, the screen line immediately below the last item printed, hard up against the left edge of the screen. We may like the next item printed to follow immediately on after a piece of text; for example, we might like to accept a name from the keyboard, then print a ‘Hello’ message using the name. The lines:

```
1000 INPUT "Your name, please",n$
1010 PRINT "Hello "
1020 PRINT n$
```

would result in:

```
Hello
Fred
```

being printed on the screen, assuming that the name typed in was ‘Fred’. A simple change, though, of:

```
1010 PRINT "Hello ";
```

will result in:

```
Hello Fred
```

being printed; much better. This is one of the big advantages of BASICs PRINT; it is very versatile. All BASICs will also offer the ability to position where a piece of text or a number appears on a line by using a function called *TAB()*.

The line:

```
1000 PRINT TAB(20);"Hello"
```

will print the word 'Hello' 20 characters in from the left. Some BASICs allow two parameters to be passed to the TAB statement, allowing the vertical position on the screen to be specified as well.

The exact capabilities of PRINT depend upon the BASIC in use, but all BASICs will support the simple printing displayed here.

Other features

A very useful statement is *REM* which allows us to put comments in a BASIC program. For example:

```
10 REM This is ignored by BASIC.
```

The three BASICs used in this book all have graphics capabilities, as well as the simple statements listed here. In addition, they feature other statements for enhanced program control or access to the memory of the computer. In addition, they allow access to machine code programs from within BASIC, and allow you to define your own functions in addition to the ones that come with BASIC as standard. They also feature sound commands. The best way to get to know your BASIC is to play with it, using the manual you get with the computer. Once you have got the listings in this book working, try altering them to take into account extra facilities offered by your particular computer.

APPENDIX 2

Further reading

Newnes Short Wave Listening Handbook, Joe Pritchard, Heineman Newnes 1989.

Radio Communications Handbook, 5th Edition, Radio Society of Great Britain, 1982

VHF UHF Manual, 4th edition, G. R. Jessop (editor), Radio Society of Great Britain, 1983.

ARRL Handbook for the Radio Amateur, 65th Edition, ARRL, 1987.

Klingenfuss Guide to Utility Stations, 5th Edition, Jeorg Klingenfuss Publications, 1986.

Klingenfuss Air and Meteo Code Manual, Klingenfuss Publications, 1988.

Packet Radio Handbook, Jonathan L. Mayo, Tab Books, 1987.

Software for Amateur Radio, Joe Kasser, Tab Books, 1984.

Microprocessors and Interfacing, Douglas V. Hall, McGraw Hill, 1990.

Understanding and Expanding your Amstrad 464/664/6128, Alan Trevennor, Sigma Press, 1989.

Amateur Radio Software, John Morris, Radio Society of Great Britain, 1985.

Newnes Radio Amateur and Listener's Pocket Book, Steve Money, Heinemann, 1988.

AX25 Amateur Packet Radio Protocol, American Radio Relay League, 1989.

Tandon GW BASIC Users' Guide

BBC Micro Users' Guide

Amstrad CPC6128 Users' Guide

APPENDIX 3

Suppliers and useful addresses

Suppliers

Department of Trade and Industry,
Waterloo Bridge House,
Waterloo Road,
London SE1 8UA

Radio Society of Great Britain,
Lambda House,
Cranborne Road,
Potters Bar,
Hertfordshire,
EN6 3JE

Meteorological Office,
London Road,
Bracknell,
Hertfordshire,
RG12 2SZ

Siskin Electronics Ltd (TNC equipment)
2 South Street,
Hythe,
Southampton,
SO4 6EB

Technical Software (Decoder Software)
Fron,
Upper Llandwrog,
Caernarfon,
LL54 7RF

ERA Ltd, (morse/RTTY decoder)
26 Clarendon Court,
Winwick Quay,
Warrington,
WA2 8QP

Dewsbury Electronics (decoder equipment)
176 Lower High Street,
Stourbridge,
West Midlands,
DY8 1TG

J & P Electronics Ltd, (decoding equipment)
Unit 45,
Meadowhill Estate,
Kidderminster,
DY10 1HH

AMDAT (packet radio, decoder equipment)
Crofters,
Harry Stoke Road,
Stoke Gifford,
Bristol,
BS12 6QH

ICS Electronics Ltd., (image transmission/reception)
Unit V,
Rudford Industrial Estate,
Ford,
Arundel,
West Sussex.
BN18 OBD

G3WHO Software (BBC Micro software)
10 Appleby Close,
Great Alne,
Warks.
B49 6HJ

Interbooks (radio related books)
Lynton Industrial estate, Stanley,
Perth,
Scotland
PH1 4QQ

Magazines

There are two magazines well worth looking out for in the newsagents, as both have frequent items on computers in radio listening. They are: *Practical Wireless* and *Short Wave Magazine. In addition, Ham Radio Today* has occasional articles on such topics as packet radio.

Societies

The RSGB is worth joining for *Radio Communications* magazine and the QSL Bureau. Also, it is a good idea to support our national society, as they do a lot of work negotiating with the powers that be about frequency allocations, terms and conditions of the licence, etc.

In addition, the BARTG (British Amateur Teledata Group) deals with all aspects of amateur data communications. They can be contacted c/o Mr John and Mrs Pat Beedie, Ffynnonlas, Salem, Llandelo, Dyfed.

Index